The J. H. Bavinck Reader

The J. H. Bavinck Reader

Edited by

John Bolt

James D. Bratt and Paul J. Visser

Translated by

James A. De Jong

WILLIAM B. EERDMANS PUBLISHING COMPANY
GRAND RAPIDS, MICHIGAN / CAMBRIDGE, U.K.

Published 2013 by
Wm. B. Eerdmans Publishing Co.
2140 Oak Industrial Drive N.E., Grand Rapids, Michigan 49505 /
P.O. Box 163, Cambridge CB3 9PU U.K.

Library of Congress Cataloging-in-Publication Data

Bavinck, J. H. (Johan Herman), 1895-1964.
  [Works. Selections. English]
  The J. H. Bavinck reader / Edited by John Bolt, James D. Bratt and Paul J. Visser.
      pages   cm
  Includes bibliographical references and index.
  ISBN 978-0-8028-6592-2 (pbk.: alk. paper)
  1. Missions — Theory. 2. Theology. I. Bolt, John, 1947-
  II. Bratt, James D., 1949-   III. Visser, P. J. (Paul Jan), 1959-   IV. Title.

  BV2063.B3813   2013
  266 — dc23

                                                           2012047127

www.eerdmans.com

Contents

III. Christic and Asian Mysticism

Editors' Preface

The idea for this volume came from conversations between the editors in the spring of 2009, spurred on by the encouragement of Dr. Rimmer De Vries, generous benefactor of scholarly efforts in the Dutch neo-Calvinist tradition such as the Kuyper Center at Princeton Theological Seminary. The work of Herman Bavinck (1854-1921) had recently become better known in the English-speaking world thanks to the just-completed translation of the four-volume *Reformed Dogmatics* into English.[1] Yet, from the large body of missiological work of his nephew Johan Herman Bavinck (1895-1964), only a small portion had been translated into English, and of that, very little remains available. Bavinck's *Introduction to the Science of Missions* is still in print.[2] The posthumous *The Church Between Temple and Mosque*[3] is available in the used book trade, and an earlier work in missiology, *The Impact of Christianity on the Non-Christian World*,[4] consisting "chiefly of lectures . . . delivered at Calvin Theological Seminary and before various other academic and popular audiences . . . in the autumn of 1947," is hard to find. Finally, the

---

1. Herman Bavinck, *Reformed Dogmatics,* 4 vols., ed. John Bolt, trans. John Vriend (Grand Rapids: Baker, 2003-2008).

2. J. H. Bavinck, *An Introduction to the Science of Missions,* trans. David Hugh Freeman (Philadelphia: Presbyterian & Reformed, 1960). A new edition, published by Presbyterian and Reformed Publishing in 1992, is still available on Amazon.com.

3. J. H. Bavinck, *The Church Between Temple and Mosque: A Study of the Relationship Between the Christian Faith and Other Religions* (Grand Rapids: Eerdmans, 1966).

4. J. H. Bavinck, *The Impact of Christianity on the Non-Christian World* (Grand Rapids: Eerdmans, 1948).

two collections of what could be called "devotional writings," *The Riddle of Life*,[5] and *Faith and Its Difficulties*,[6] are also no longer in print.

In the meantime, the Reformed community in the Netherlands was rediscovering J. H. Bavinck and acknowledging his significance. An expanded edition of Bavinck's 1949 classic in religious psychology, *Religious Consciousness and Christian Faith*,[7] was reissued in 1989 by VU professor of philosophy, Dr. René van Woudenberg.[8] Dr. Van Woudenberg also compiled a collection of Bavinck essays and wrote an introduction to a volume on J. H. Bavinck in the Famous Theologians series published by Kok.[9] And ever since his death in 1964, Bavinck's missiology has received significant and growing scholarly attention in articles/essays,[10] another collection of essays,[11] and a doctoral dissertation.[12] The list of essayists in the collection reads like a

---

5. J. H. Bavinck, *The Riddle of Life*, trans. J. J. Lamberts (Grand Rapids: Eerdmans, 1958).

6. J. H. Bavinck, *Faith and Its Difficulties*, trans. Wm. B. Eerdmans Sr. (Grand Rapids: Eerdmans, 1959); this volume was written to accompany profession of faith occasions in the Reformed churches.

7. J. H. Bavinck, *Religieus Besef en Christelijk Geloof* (Kampen: J. H. Kok, 1949); the addition was a Dutch translation of Bavinck's essay "General Revelation and the Non Christian Religions," *Free University Quarterly* 4 (1955): 43-55. The latter essay appears in this volume as chapter 1; the former appears as chapters 3-5.

8. J. H. Bavinck, *Religieus Besef en Christelijk Geloof, Uitgebreid met "Algemene openbaring en de niet-christelijke religies"* (Kampen: J. H. Kok, 1989).

9. *J. H. Bavinck (1895-1964): Een Keuze uit zijn Werk* (Selections from His Writings), Serie Befaamde Theologen, ingeleid door René van Woudenberg (Kampen: J. H. Kok, 1991).

10. A partial list, in chronological order: Johannes Van den Berg, "The Legacy of Johan Herman Bavinck," *International Bulletin of Missionary Research* 7, no. 4 (1983): 171-75; Jannie Du Preez, "Johan Herman Bavinck on the Relation Between Divine Revelation and the Religions," *Missionalia* 13, no. 3 (1985): 111-20; Johannes Van den Berg, "Johan Herman Bavinck 1895-1964: Understanding Religion in Light of God's Revelation," in *Mission Legacies: Biographical Studies of Leaders of the Modern Missionary Movement*, ed. Gerald H. Anderson, Robert T. Cooke, Norman A. Horner, and James M. Phillips (Maryknoll, NY: Orbis, 1994), pp. 428-34; René van Woudenberg, "Christelijk Exclusivisme en Religieus Pluralisme," *Nederlands Theologisch Tijdschrift* 48, no. 4 (1994): 275-90; Paul J. Visser, "Religion in Biblical and Reformed Perspective," *Calvin Theological Journal* 44, no. 1 (2009): 9-36; Pieter C. Tuit, "The Gospel in Word and Deed: Johan Herman Bavinck's Missiology and Its Application for Today," *Calvin Theological Journal* 44, no. 1 (2009): 74-93; Paul J. Visser, "Religion, Mission and Kingdom: A Comparison of Herman and J. H. Bavinck," *Calvin Theological Journal* 45, no. 1 (2010): 117-32.

11. A. Pos et al., *Christusprediking in de Wereld: Studien op het Terrein van de Zendingswetenschap gewijd — van Johan Herman Bavinck* (Kampen: J. H. Kok, 1965).

12. Paul J. Visser, *Heart for the Gospel, Heart for the World: The Life and Thought of a Reformed Pioneer Missiologist Johan Herman Bavinck, 1895-1964* (Eugene, OR: Wipf & Stock, 2003).

who's who of late-twentieth-century Reformed missiology: A. Pos, Johannes van den Berg, R. Pierce Beaver, H. Bergema, Johannes Blauw, Harry R. Boer, J. J. F. Durand, E. Jansen Schoonhoven, G. C. Oosthuizen, R. Soedarmo, Johannes Verkuyl, and Anton Wessels. The scope of topics listed in bibliographic catalogs is wide-ranging and impressive: Christianity and other religions; Consciousness; Cosmology; Eliade, Mircea, 1907-1986; Experience (Religion); Missions — Theory; Reality; Revelation. In addition, Bavinck's influence on students pursuing the field of missions and missiology is impressive.[13] All this is to say that we judged ourselves to be on solid ground when we proposed a *J. H. Bavinck Reader* that would make some of the Dutch missiologist's seminal works in revelation and religion, religious consciousness, and the engagement of the Christian gospel with other religious traditions available in convenient form for an English audience.[14]

The initial selection of essays was made by John Bolt, with input from James Bratt and Paul Visser. Paul Visser also provided the introductory biographical sketch of Bavinck, the most thorough available in English up to this date. For foundational material on revelation and religion we chose an essay that originally appeared in English translation, "General Revelation and the Non Christian Religions," and Bavinck's inaugural address as professor of missiology at the Kampen Theological University and the Free University of Amsterdam in 1939, "Proclaiming Christ to the Nations." These chapters introduce the reader to key themes such as general revelation, the universality of religion, the engagement of Christian apologists with philosophy, and the missiological imperative of understanding key anthropological constants for gospel communication. Bavinck's most original and significant contribution may be his thorough examination of religious consciousness in relation to the Christian faith. Chapters 3-6 are a translation of a complete book on the subject, and Bavinck explores the topic from three perspectives: developmentally as an anthropological/psychological phenomenon; historically; and finally — to get to his real concern — missiologically. To demonstrate that Bavinck was not simply a theoretician of religion and religious consciousness, the final five chapters, taken from Bavinck's careful observations and reflections on his stay in Indonesia, are

13. Cf. Appendix II in Paul J. Visser, *Bemoeienis en Getuigenis. Het Leven en de Missionaire Theologie van J. H. Bavinck* (Th.M. thesis, University of Utrecht, 1987), p. 325. The list includes international students who came from North America, South Africa, and China.

14. The parallel we had in mind was the volume prepared by one of the editors, *Abraham Kuyper: A Centennial Reader,* ed. James D. Bratt (Grand Rapids: Eerdmans, 1998).

filled with concrete material from a variety of Javanese religious traditions and practices.

Our editorial practice was to employ modern Indonesian transliterations of the Javanese/Indonesian words Bavinck employs and to make use of English translations whenever possible, even if Bavinck cited his sources in Dutch or German. Bibliographic references in the footnotes have been brought up to contemporary scholarly standards; in a few instances, where we were unable to obtain full information, the reference is marked with an asterisk (*). Editorial notes were added to clarify the text or to provide information about references that might not be familiar to most readers. Our goal has been to keep in mind the general, interested reader as well as professional scholars. We do want to highlight one crucial translation decision at the outset. Knowledgeable readers will notice immediately that we have given the third major section of this volume, a translation of *Christus en de Mystiek van het Oosten,* the title "Christ and Asian Mysticism" rather than "Christ and the Mysticism of the East." To speak of "the East" in global terms *in distinction from the West* is misleading to contemporary readers for a number of reasons. First, its generality suggests a single monolithic worldview while the reality is remarkably diverse and complex. Second, it fails to clarify the importance of geographically oriented streams of religious faiths such as those of South and Southeast Asia (India, Sri Lanka, Thailand, Indonesia, Malaysia) in distinction from East Asia (China, Korea, Japan). Third, these changes are in keeping with Bavinck's own sensitivities. As the reader will discern, Bavinck is very aware of this diversity, and his treatment of the religious world of Indonesia in chapters 7-11 fully honors the diversity as well as the generalization. We would also alert the reader to Bavinck's repeated insistence upon the necessity of translating the gospel into the language and conceptual framework of different peoples. He also insists on the need to develop an indigenous Indonesian (Eastern) theology.

Consequently, we have tried to honor contemporary practice that prefers to accent geographical rather than ideological differences, though it is of course true that we would be misrepresenting Bavinck's thought if we ignored the contrast between Christianity and the religions of Asia as *in part* a contrast between East and West. At key points, especially in chapter 2, and chapters 7-11, we will be introducing further distinctions between, for example, the religious traditions of South and Southeast Asia and East Asia.[15] In keeping with this editorial practice, we have also substituted "Asian" for Bavinck's use of "oriental."

15. See Chapter 2, note 18, below.

As editors, we are convinced that the missiological writings of Johan Herman Bavinck remain relevant for evangelical, particularly Reformed, students and practitioners today. In a context where many evangelical students find it difficult to navigate the treacherous shoals that are bounded on one side by an absolutism that is isolated from the concrete religious experience of people and on the other by relativistic religious pluralism, Bavinck provides a sure guide and offers a constructive way forward. Reformed missiology begins with a conviction that God is present to all people, that no one can escape God's revelation in creation, conscience, and history. The world's religious traditions are a response to God! While there are analogies between the gospel of Christ and the religious traditions of the world, there is also a fundamental divide. Jesus is the Way, the Truth, and the Life. In affirming both the particularity of salvation in Christ and the universality of the Christian hope, Bavinck provides a sure guide to all of us as we navigate that demanding current with its numerous shoals. We are aware that we may have started something with the publication of this volume that will have consequences for the mission of Christ's church in ways we cannot even begin to imagine. At least, that is our prayer.

JOHN BOLT
JAMES D. BRATT
PAUL J. VISSER

Acknowledgments

The editors gratefully acknowledge the encouragement received from Dr. Rimmer De Vries and the financial support we received from the Heritage Fund of Calvin Theological Seminary, the Calvin [College] Center for Christian Scholarship, and the Dutch Reformed Translation Society. Calvin Theological Seminary students Brandon Jones, Gayle Doornbos, and Amos Oei provided research and copyediting/proofreading assistance, and, in Amos's case, firsthand experiential help in clarifying and confirming many of Bavinck's observations about Indonesia. Amos's assistance was essential in providing modern transliterations of Indonesian words used by Bavinck.

The editors especially want to thank Professor Diane Obenchain of the Calvin College Religion and Theology Department for helping us with her expertise in the world's religious traditions, her knowledge of their history and terminology, and her understanding of and sensitivity to the language of contemporary scholarship. She read through the complete translated manuscript, and far too many of the editors' notes include her touch to be able to single out all of them. In particular, our use of "Asian" instead of "Eastern" and taking note of the subtleties of the diverse Asian traditions owes everything to her wisdom. In addition, her infectious enthusiasm for her own introduction to J. H. Bavinck's work and for this project has been a source of inspiration. The quality of this manuscript and its usefulness to students and scholars of the world's religious traditions would not be what it is without her loving and generous guidance. Diane, thank you.

Introduction: The Life and Thought of
Johan Herman Bavinck (1895-1964)

1. Background and Early Years

Johan Herman Bavinck was the premier twentieth-century missiologist in the Dutch neo-Calvinist tradition. He extended the characteristic strengths of that tradition into new territories and a new era and did so compellingly enough that his thought reverberated in other schools of theology, and in nontheological disciplines as well. His work was marked by both broad range and deep personal faith, by profound learning and a winsome sympathy to people of other convictions, intermixed with a resolute loyalty to historic Christianity as understood on a self-consciously Reformed slant.

These qualities, indeed Bavinck's entire life-course, can only be understood in light of his being an heir to one of the leading families in the church founded by the 1834 Secession *(Afscheiding)* from the national Dutch Reformed Church *(Nederlands Hervormde Kerk = NHK)*. Johan was steeped from the cradle in the Seceders' biblical devotion and experiential piety. At the same time, he shared the Bavinck family's discomfort with the introversion of Seceder church life. His eminent uncle, Herman Bavinck, was a leading promoter from the Seceder side of a merger with the churches that stemmed from another separation from the *NHK*, the *Doleantie* led by Abraham Kuyper. Johan was born in 1895, just three years after this merger was effected in the formation of a new body, the Reformed Churches in the Netherlands *(Gereformeerde Kerken in Nederland = GKN)*, and he grew up saturated in the close theological reflection and ecclesiological care that marked the *GKN's* early years. His destiny, it turned out, was to apply these same qualities to the next circle of outreach, the *GKN*'s missions initiative. Personally, he brought to these efforts the Bavinck family's combination of cheerful disposition and practical bent of mind. His native modesty could make him tentative in decision-making, but, coupled with his intelligence, tended to yield deliberate and well-tested judgments.

Family Heritage

The Bavincks came from the county of Bentheim,[1] an area in Germany immediately to the east of the Dutch provinces of Drenthe and Overijssel. It was there that Jan Bavinck, the grandfather of Johan Herman, was born on 5 February 1826. During his youth, Jan underwent a spiritual development that would prove to be decisive for his own life and for his posterity. Under the leadership of Jan B. Sundag, a dissenting church came into being in Bentheim in close affiliation with the 1834 Seceder churches in the Netherlands. At sixteen, Jan became personally involved with this Alt-Reformierte Kirche. He wrote: "Under the guidance of my uncle, the Lord caused me to become ever more aware, on the one hand, of my own deep depravity, and on the other hand, of the salvation to be found in Christ Jesus. Through God's grace I surrendered myself to the Savior and made a conscious decision to follow, cling to, and serve Him."[2]

Before long, Jan had a deep, burning desire to become a minister; with the aid of Sundag, who sought promising young men for the ministry, this desire became a reality. Jan wrote: "I saw God's hand in it, the answer to my many prayers and an initial fulfillment of my heart's fervent desire." He undertook theological education at a school of the Christian Separated Reformed Church in the Netherlands *(Christelijk Afgescheiden Gereformeerde Kerk in Nederland = CGKN)*, where he attracted attention as a bright, hardworking student and was even asked to teach. In 1848, at twenty-two years of age, Jan was ordained to ministry in the *Alt-Reformierte Kirche* in Beneden-Graafschap (Ülsen and Wilsum). Subsequently, he became pastor of the church in Hoogeveen (1853) in the Netherlands where he continued his theological training. A year later, when the General Synod of the *CGKN*

---

1. Genealogical records compiled by members of the family reveal that the name Bavinck appears in Bentheim as early as 1594.

2. Jan Bavinck, *Een Korte Schets van Mijn Leven* (unpublished, handwritten autobiography).

meeting in Zwolle decided to establish a theological seminary at Kampen,[3] he was appointed to the faculty at just twenty-eight years of age. His reaction was typical of his character: "No! . . . This appointment seemed to me to carry such great weight that I considered turning it down right there on the spot at the meeting. How could I take my place and work alongside men who had had the benefit of an academic education?"[4]

Doubts about his own abilities jostled with his peers' affirmation. Jan finally wrote two letters, one accepting and one declining the appointment. He had a student pick out and mail one of them — it was the letter of declination. He soon regretted his decision and tried to reverse it, but the seminary Board of Trustees said no. Twenty-eight years later, when his son Herman received the same appointment, Jan wrote: "As for me, I saw the hand of the Lord in this, and I thanked Him for allowing my son . . . to occupy the position I did not dare to accept for lack of faith."[5]

Though Jan remained a parish pastor the rest of his life,[6] he also contributed to the continuing development of Reformed theology. Among other things, he wrote a two-volume interpretive commentary on the Heidelberg Catechism (1903) marked by careful research and mature theological learning. This model of a pastor-theologian grounded in a generous and unassuming character, a keen mind, great diligence, and ardent faith would carry through in two generations of Bavincks to come.

Jan Bavinck's eldest son, Herman,[7] ensconced the family name permanently in Dutch theological history. After graduating from *gymnasium,* Herman yearned to study at the state university in Leiden so as to acquire a firsthand knowledge of modern theology and a thoroughly academic training. After first taking a year at Kampen Seminary at the urging of his parents, Herman enrolled at Leiden in 1874 and achieved real distinction: he passed all of his examinations with honors and was awarded a Ph.D. degree *cum laude* (1880) for a dissertation dealing with the ethical thought of Ulrich Zwingli.[8]

---

3. For details about this decision, cf. Jan Bosch, *Figuren en Aspecten uit de Eeuw der Afscheiding* (Goes: Oosterbaan & Le Cointre, 1952), pp. 154-56, and Hendrik Algra, *Het Wonder van de egentiende Eeuw: Van Vrije Kerken en Kleine Luyden* (Franeker: T. Wever, 1979), pp. 152-56.

4. J. Bavinck, *Mijn Leven,* pp. 48-49.

5. J. Bavinck, *Mijn Leven,* p. 51.

6. He was pastor in Bunschoten (1857), Almkerk (1862), and Kampen (1873).

7. Detailed biographical information on Herman Bavinck can be found in R. H. Bremmer, *Herman Bavinck en Zijn Tijdgenoten* (Kampen: J. H. Kok, 1966), and in Valentijn Hepp, *Dr. Herman Bavinck* (Amsterdam: Ten Have, 1921).

8. H. Bavinck, *De Ethiek van Ulrich Zwingli* (Kampen: Zalsman, 1880).

After completing his graduate studies, Herman returned to serve his native church. In 1881, he was ordained in the *CGKN* at Franeker. For all his erudition, he was well liked there and could relate to even the humblest people. Within a year, however, Herman accepted an appointment as professor at Kampen Seminary, where he was assigned extensive teaching responsibilities in the Department of Theology (dogmatics, polemics, ethics, and encyclopedia of theology) and in the Department of Letters (antiquities, mythology, philosophy, and Greek). On 9 January 1883, he gave his inaugural address, *De wetenschap der heilige godgeleerdheid (The Science of Sacred Theology)*, and set out upon his *magnum opus,* the four-volume *Gereformeerde Dogmatiek (Reformed Dogmatics)*.

Although the *Afscheiding* and the *Doleantie* merged into the Reformed Churches in the Netherlands in 1892 *(Gereformeerde Kerken in Nederland = GKN)*, their respective theological institutions, Kampen Seminary and the Theological Faculty of the Free University in Amsterdam, remained separate. Institutional self-interest as well as theoretical differences kept the two apart, much to the dismay of Bavinck who devoted himself intensively to the consolidation of the schools. When that effort failed, he decided to leave Kampen to succeed Kuyper as professor of dogmatics at the Free University. His 1902 inaugural address, *Godsdienst en Godgeleerdheid (Religion and Theology)*, hinted of a turn in his own scholarship from the systematic theology of *Gereformeerde Dogmatiek* to broad interests in ethics, religion, and culture. These became evident when he published his *Beginselen der psychologie (Principles of Psychology)* in 1897.

As a theologian, Herman brought classical Reformed theology to face the problems of modernity; as a philosopher, he opposed the positivistic materialism of the nineteenth century; as a confessing Christian, he did not allow himself to be swept along by the winds of secularization. Rather, he tried to make the thought of Augustine, Aquinas, and Calvin accessible to modern people; in particular, to lead Reformed separatists into the broader space of the catholic (universal) church and into the interface between church and world.[9]

Herman also remained an unfailingly sensitive pastor. According to his students, he was a finely tuned, compelling orator, and his sermons were both profound and psychologically perceptive.[10] One of his students wrote

---

9. Cf. Bremmer, *Herman Bavinck,* p. 252.

10. Gerard Wisse, *Memoires: Onvergetelijke Bladzijden uit Mijn Levensboek; van Middelburg tot Middelburg* (Utrecht: Den Hertog, 1953), p. 29.

that "during Bavinck's lectures, sometimes he himself became so overwhelmed by the splendor of God that he forgot us and spoke staring out of the window into the endless distance, perfectly attuned to God's infinite glory; and we sat listening speechlessly while being introduced — for life — to the mystery of the salvation of the Eternal and Almighty One, who in Jesus Christ is our merciful Father."[11]

In short, Herman Bavinck, like his father, combined a degree of hesitancy with a high degree of intelligence. This made him, as G. Brillenburg Wurth wrote, not only "the unmistakably greatest Dutch dogmatician of the early twentieth century" but also a modest, "sometimes almost self-effacing" person who was very aware of his own limitations and his lack of leadership ability.[12] On the other hand, like his mother he was enterprising and practical and did not shrink from taking on large-scale projects. Last, but not least, in his confrontation with modern theology, the piety of his childhood was not lost but grew to even deeper dimensions. Growing up in the shadow of this uncle, Johan Herman Bavinck would exhibit many similarities with this great personality.

Johan Herman's father, Coenraad Bernardus Bavinck (1866-1941), followed more exactly in the footsteps of his father Jan. He completed his theological studies in Kampen in 1890 and was ordained as minister of the Christian Reformed Church in Hazerswoude. That same year he married Grietje Bouwes, a cheerful, practical woman, and in 1894 accepted a call to Rotterdam, where he served as minister until his retirement in 1930. Coenraad and Grietje had eight children, among whom Johan Herman was the fourth, born on 22 November 1895. The life of this family, too, was permeated by unaffected piety.

As a theologian, Coenraad lived in the shadow of his older brother, Herman, publishing only a few works. In 1921 he put out a brochure that dealt with the causes of the divisions in the Reformed churches in the Netherlands.[13] Typically, the brochure was remarkably charitable toward other communions and did not fail to criticize the denomination to which the Bavincks belonged. Coenraad also collaborated in the production of the 1926 document, *Ons aller moeder (Mother of Us All)*, in which he and four colleagues outlined what they considered to be a balanced solution to the

---

11. Johannes J. Buskes, *Hoera Voor het Leven* (Amsterdam: De Brug-Djambatan, 1960), p. 33.

12. Gerrit Brillenburg Wurth, "Herman Bavinck en Onze Tijd," *Trouw* (18 Feb. 1961).

13. C. B. Bavinck, *Welke zijn de oorzaken van het kerkelijk-gescheiden leven der gereformeerden in Nederland?* (Aalten: De Graafschap, 1921).

"Geelkerken question" which was threatening to split the *GKN* anew.[14] The piece took a moderate position, trying to do justice both to the persons involved and to the truth of the Bible. For all his modest publication record, Coenraad did have a studious bent of mind. He was interested in the early church, especially in the life and work of St. Augustine;[15] it is conceivable that son Johan Herman later made use of his father's knowledge in his own book on *Christus en de Mystiek van het Oosten (Christ and the Mysticism of the East)*. All in all, upon his death in 1941 Coenraad was described as a "real Bavinck": "His judgment in matters both great and small was thoroughly informed by his keen insight and great wisdom."[16]

The Young Psychologist, 1912-1919

Johan Herman Bavinck's career can be divided into discrete periods, but these built into a single cumulative process. Initially, his psychological interests led him to focus on the psychology of religion. Later, his ordination as a missionary to Java (1929) activated a dormant interest in missiology. His growing fascination with Asian mysticism and his experience as an instructor at the Theological School in Jogjakarta (1934-1938) drew his attention to issues of a theological nature. After his return to the Netherlands as professor of missions at Kampen Theological Seminary and the Free University of Amsterdam (1939) and as professor of Practical Theology at the latter institution (1954), all these themes came together as the object of systematic reflection. From one stage to the next, however, Bavinck's "transparent Chris-

14. In 1926 disciplinary measures were taken by the *GKN* against Rev. J. G. Geelkerken for his interpretation of certain aspects of the biblical account of creation. The synod of Assen had required Geelkerken, who was serving a congregation in Amsterdam, to accept its pronouncement that details reported in Genesis 3, such as the speech of the snake, were to be taken literally and understood as realities perceptible to the senses. Geelkerken refused to do so and was subsequently removed from office. This occasioned the formation of yet another Reformed denomination in the Netherlands, the *Gereformeerde Kerken in Hersteld Verband* (Reestablished Reformed Churches). Cf. Jan Nicolaas Bakhuizen van den Brink and William F. Dankbaar, *Handboek der Kerkgeschiedenis*, vol. 4 (Den Haag: B. Bakker/Daamen, 1965), p. 233.

15. Abraham Pos, "Leven en werk van dr. Johan Herman Bavinck," in Johannes van den Berg et al., *Christusprediking in de Wereld: Studieën op het Terrein van de Zendingswetenschap Gewijd aan de Nagedachtenis van de Professor Dr. Johan Herman Bavinck* (Kampen: J. H. Kok, 1965), p. 8.

16. "In Memoriam ds. C. B. Bavinck," *Het Zendingsblad* 39 (1941): 143.

tian devotion," commitment to the cause of the gospel, and "deep sensitivity toward the needs of his fellow human beings"[17] remained the same.

Prophetically, Johan Herman was named after his grandfather Jan and his uncle Herman, for he would show their same combination of profound piety and great erudition. Already in his youth Johan often spoke of his desire to become a missionary and loved to peruse the philosophical works in his father's library. After attending the Marnix Gymnasium in Rotterdam, Johan began studying theology at the Free University in Amsterdam in 1912. As is demonstrated by his preserved notebooks, Johan was a diligent, painstaking student with broad interests.[18]

Johan also displayed a family tradition in being attracted to the Reformed Young People's Movement during his student years. This movement, in a positive but critical way, was seeking to reorient Reformed life from a dogmatic, antithetical stance toward a more vitally existential, open form of religious experience. Johan also joined the interdenominational Dutch Student Christian Movement (SCM),[19] chaired at that time by Hendrik Kraemer,[20] which aimed at rethinking how to witness to Jesus Christ among the contemporary intelligentsia. These movements were criticized by leaders in the *GKN* because they had no specific ecclesiastical or confessional ties. By contrast, Johan saw their potential for enriching and deepening faith.[21]

Bavinck's growing interest in the psychology of religion likely reflected the general interest in psychology and mysticism at the time; in addition, mysticism appealed to him personally as a mode of religious experience.[22]

17. Johannes Verkuyl, *Contemporary Missiology: An Introduction* (Grand Rapids: Eerdmans, 1978), pp. 35-36.

18. These notebooks are housed in the Center for the Historical Documentation of Dutch Protestantism: 1800-Present/Free University of Amsterdam. Included are notes that Bavinck made on the theology of the Old Testament, Reformed dogmatics, the life of the apostle Paul, exegesis and interpretation, and the history of philosophy.

19. Like its equivalents elsewhere in the world, the Dutch SCM was a national embodiment of the World Student Christian Federation (WSCF), which was founded by John R. Mott and others in 1895; cf. Stephen Neill, Gerald H. Anderson, and John Goodwin, *Concise Dictionary of the Christian World Mission* (Nashville: Abingdon, 1971), pp. 569, 662.

20. Cf. Arend Theodoor van Leeuwen, *Hendrik Kraemer, Dienaar der Wereldkerk* (Amsterdam: Ten Have, 1959), pp. 11ff. At this time the first contact was established between Bavinck and Kraemer, a connection that would prove to be of great importance later on.

21. Jan Veenhof, "Geschiedenis van Theologie en Spiritualiteit in de Gereformeerde Kerken," in M. E. Brinkman, *100 Jaar Theologie, Aspecten van een eeuw Theologie in de GKN, 1892-1992* (Kampen: J. H. Kok 1992), pp. 33-35.

22. Johannes van den Berg, "De Wetenschappelijke Arbeid van Professor Dr. J. H. Bavinck," in van den Berg et al., *Christusprediking in de Wereld*, p. 28.

Thus, after completing his undergraduate studies, he went to Germany for graduate work, first at Giessen and then at Erlangen.[23] His doctoral thesis dealt with the degree to which the affective, sensory dimension of human life influences the processes of cognition and association, and chose the religious life of the medieval mystic, Heinrich von Suso, as a case study. On the basis of his research, Bavinck demonstrated that the processes of thinking and learning, far from occurring autonomously, are closely tied to an intuitive apprehension of given reality. It is precisely the operation of this feeling in the process of human reasoning that points to the influence of the human self.[24] His thesis being approved, Bavinck received his doctorate from Friedrich Alexander University on 11 July 1919, at age twenty-three.

Bavinck's dissertation reveals both his admiration for and wariness of the mystical life. This must be understood against the backdrop of his warm, vibrant piety, which created a bond between him and the mystics.[25] He once said: "I was born, as it were, with a strong penchant for monastic mystical experience; that's why I can speak of it: I have to fight against it every day."[26] Bavinck never left any doubt, however, that mysticism and the piety of biblical faith ultimately define two different worlds.[27] He would be a theologian of epiphany and worship, question and answer, revelation and response.[28] At the same time Bavinck's graduate research laid the foundation for his later missionary work, with its deep involvement in Asian mysticism and the questions of religious consciousness. As Abraham Pos said about Bavinck's graduate studies: "He made his own decisions, but at the same time, it was God's providential guidance which selected from a variety of career and work possibilities so that he would be able to

23. Bavinck was forced to find a university elsewhere because there was no professor available at the Free University at that time to supervise doctoral studies in his theological discipline of choice. It is not known why he opted for Erlangen. One of the reasons could have been that the university he attended there was an orthodox Lutheran institution, at which other Dutch theologians had also taken their graduate degrees.

24. Cf. Johan Herman Bavinck, *Der Einfluss des Gefühls auf das Assoziationsleben bei Heinrich von Suso* (Erlangen: Univ.-Buchdruckerei von E. Th. Jacob, 1919), pp. 25-26.

25. J. van den Berg, "De Wetenschappelijke Arbeid," p. 29.

26. Johannes Verkuyl, "Woord Vooraf," in *Religieus Besef en Christelijk Geloof*, enlarged with *Algemene Openbaring en de Niet-Christelijke Religies* (Kampen: J. H. Kok, 1975), p. xviii.

27. This is already clearly indicated in his 1928 book *Persoonlijkheid en Wereldbeschouwing* (Kampen: J. H. Kok, 1928), p. 50.

28. Cf. R. van Woudenberg, "Dr. Johan Herman Bavinck (1895-1964), Theoloog van Woord en Antwoord," in van den Berg et al., *Christusprediking in de Wereld*, p. 25.

best serve the cause of Jesus Christ. The first clear lines of this life's journey were plotted here."[29]

The Pastor, 1920-1929

After receiving his doctorate, Bavinck returned to the Netherlands without knowing what path he would follow next. At the conclusion of the First World War, the *GKN* began to intensify its work among Dutch people who had moved to Indonesia. This labor, pioneered on the west coast of Sumatra by W. G. Harrenstein, pastor of the *GKN* congregation in Medan, expanded so rapidly that help was urgently needed. The young Bavinck was appointed to the position of assistant pastor in Medan,[30] where he commenced his work in January 1920. In Harrenstein he found a fatherly friend who supported him in an unforgettable way during this initial period of practical work. Shortly, the talented assistant pastor received a call to become the regular minister of the *GKN* congregation in Bandung, "a city whose educational institutions attracted many young people."[31] His ordination occurred there on 3 July 1921, and on March 21 of the following year he married Trientje (Tine) Robers,[32] with whom he had three children.

During his tenure in Bandung, Bavinck continued to hone his pastoral and preaching talents. According to reports, he was an attentive pastor, who, after listening calmly and patiently to his parishioners, was able to offer modest and wise advice. This sowed great trust between parishioners and pastor. Bavinck's sermons were models of simplicity, clarity, and spiritual depth. He had a "great gift for making the gospel understandable for both young and old, intellectuals and the unschooled, Europeans and Javanese."[33] Moreover, Bavinck had been given a voice that enthralled everyone who heard him speak.[34] He was also very involved in youth work. Not surprisingly, the membership of his congregation doubled in a few years.

Yet Bavinck's concern extended far beyond the members of his parish.

29. Pos, "Leven en Werk," p. 12.
30. Cf. A. Algra, *De Gereformeerde Kerken in Nederlands-Indië* (Franeker: T. Wever, 1967), p. 181.
31. Verkuyl, *Contemporary Missiology*, p. 36.
32. Born 13 February 1900; died 12 January 1953.
33. Algra, *De Gereformeerde Kerken*, p. 117.
34. Verkuyl, in a letter to the author, dated 2 February 1990, wrote: "The anti-colonial leader and later president of Indonesia, Sukarno, who met J. H. Bavinck in Bandung prison, once told me [Verkuyl]: 'I will never forget that mellifluous voice of his.'"

In 1922 he wrote: "All spiritual work in Indonesia bears a more or less evangelistic character in that it aspires to bring the many who have turned away from the faith back into the fold."[35] With a view to reaching the many secularized Europeans in the area, the congregation in Magelang launched an evangelistic magazine, *De Zaaier (The Sower)*, to which Bavinck contributed on a regular basis. They also started publishing a series of short brochures. The first one was written by Bavinck and was titled *Levensvragen (Questions of Life)*. In addition to working with unchurched Dutch people, Bavinck directed his evangelistic activities to the indigenous population. The missionary interest he manifested as a boy now began to blossom, with the result that many Indonesians joined his congregation.

In 1926, Bavinck went back to the Netherlands on leave, not knowing if he would return to Indonesia. His uncertainty was closely tied to his wish to delve further into his established interest in religious psychology. During his stay in Bandung he had continued reading in this area and had published his reflections in a book titled *Zielkundige Opstellen* (*Psychological Essays*, 1925). This work was followed by a basic textbook, *Inleiding in de Zielkunde* (*Introduction to Psychology*, 1926). In its foreword he stated: "My chief aim was to try, insofar as possible, to classify and catalogue the phenomena of heart, soul and mind, and to provide insight into the structure of the human inner life." The opening page added: "The Bible teaches us about God, but in no lesser degree, it reveals the human heart to us. It consists of both theology and psychology, knowledge of both God and man."

Bavinck's research in psychology was so highly appreciated that he was offered an opportunity to take a few years off to pursue further studies.[36] Before accepting this offer, however, he hoped for help to discern if this really was "a call from God."[37] It is no longer possible to determine exactly what happened at this time, but Bavinck's path took another direction. For one, his *Inleiding in de Zielkunde* was not received favorably by the Dutch Reformed. It treated religion as part of the emotional life and defined it, at bottom, as a longing for communion with God. His critics countered that, because the confessional understanding of religion must presuppose divine revelation, the act of knowing must take logical precedence over feeling and emotion in religion.[38] This reception was probably discouraging to the un-

35. Johan Herman Bavinck, *De Heraut*, 30 April 1922.
36. Cf. Johan Herman Bavinck, *De Heraut*, 27 June 1926.
37. Johan Herman Bavinck, *Kerkblad Heemstede*, 13 October 1928.
38. Cf. Tjeerde Hoekstra, "Het Centrale in de Religie," *Gereformeerd Theologisch Tijd-*

assuming Johan Herman and might be the main reason why he did not continue in this direction.

To make things more complicated, the *GKN* congregation in the Dutch town of Heemstede extended a call to him in August 1926. Initially, he declined it because he was not sure if he would return to Bandung. Once he had decided to stay in the Netherlands, however, he accepted their second call: "I thank God that He took away the misgivings . . . that had made me decide to decline the first time, and that I now know with full conviction that this is His way. It is my fervent desire and prayer that He may allow me to work long and fruitfully in your midst."[39]

Bavinck was installed in Heemstede by his father on 9 January 1927. He quickly turned his attention to the dissension in his congregation caused by the Geelkerken controversy. True to his irenic nature, he set out to restore unity by means of honest and open discussion between the consistory and those who opposed the Synod's deposition of Geelkerken. Bavinck asserted, on the one hand, that Synod had the right to discern the appropriateness of a method of scriptural interpretation, but on the other, that Synod was wrong to judge matters of the heart and to drag people's personal faith into the matter.[40] As a result of these meetings as well as his appealing preaching and trust-inspiring counsel, Bavinck became a respected pastor.

Bavinck's publications from this period reveal his continued immersion in psychology and philosophy. The most extensive work he produced at Heemstede was *Persoonlijkheid en wereldbeschouwing* (*Personality and Worldview*, 1928). In this book, Bavinck closely linked philosophy with psychology, but reversed the usual neo-Calvinist approach by emphasizing the hidden personality behind every worldview. By so conditioning philosophy, he relativized it as an approach to truth. The real fault-line in philosophy, he insisted, is defined not by rational cogency but by the presence or absence of inner conviction regarding the truth of the gospel of Jesus Christ. It is solely personal submission to the truth of God that secures a worldview offering objectivity in the highest degree, a worldview conceived not by a person but by God.[41] In his philosophical reflections, Bavinck wanted to be a servant of

---

schrift 28 (1927): 236ff.; and Jan Waterink, "Iets over de Psychologie der Religie," *Gereformeerd Theologisch Tijdschrift* 28 (1927): 515ff.

39. Cited from Bavinck's letter of acceptance, dated 10 December 1926.

40. The discussions at these meetings are recorded in a separate notebook titled *Notulen van bespekingen met bezwaarden in 1927*, which can be found in the archives of the RCN congregation in Heemstede.

41. J. H. Bavinck, *Persoonlijkheid*, pp. 19-24.

Jesus Christ — not to champion ideas but, rather, to uphold realities about the truth of which he himself was existentially persuaded. This desire, to set people in the light of Jesus Christ as the Truth, is most important for understanding Bavinck's eventual shift from psychology to missiology.

In April 1928 H. A. van Andel, a pioneer missionary in Solo in central Java, came to the Netherlands to confer with his commissioning church at Delft about the possibility of sponsoring another missionary pastor. As they considered suitable candidates for this position, Bavinck was suggested as an excellent possibility. His psychological-philosophical insights and his mystical instincts equipped him perfectly for this missionary task among the educated, Dutch-speaking Javanese young people. The post seemed to draw the various lines of his life together in a wonderful way.

Bavinck found it difficult to make a decision, however, and eventually declined the call because it had two components: one from the consistory of Delft for work among Javanese young people, the other from the consistory of Solo for work among local Chinese immigrants. In his opinion, these mandates were too dissimilar and too extensive for one person to handle simultaneously in an acceptable way. A few months later, however, when the consistory of Solo dropped their part of the call, he decided to accept. This process reveals a great deal about Bavinck's personality: he was modest and hesitant, but, if the way became clear, also decisive. What Bavinck wrote to his congregation in Heemstede further illustrates his piety and sobriety. "Brothers and sisters, during the months in which we had to make our decision, we prayed much for God's light. When we began to realize the first time around that the composition of the work to which we were called made it impossible for us to accept that call, we saw that as God's guiding light and gave thanks for it. And when the obstacles standing in the way were totally removed, we saw God's light just as certainly in that. God spoke to us clearly in all of these things."[42] On 6 January 1929, Bavinck preached his farewell sermon at Heemstede on John 4:42: "They said to the woman: We no longer believe just because of what you said; now we have heard for ourselves, and we know that this man really is the Savior of the world." It was in this light that Bavinck viewed both his past and his future ministry.

---

42. Johan Herman Bavinck, *Kerkblad Heemstede*, 13 October 1928.

2. Missionary and Professor

"Leave your country, your people and your father's household and go to the land I will show you" (Gen. 12:1). Bavinck preached on this text at Delft on 10 January 1929 in his inaugural sermon as a missionary. He successfully sustained his missionary examination before classis and spent a year of study of Javanese language and culture at Leiden University, finally leaving for Indonesia the second time on 8 January 1930. As everyday life on Java still bore the heavy imprint of traditional culture, the place where Bavinck located was deemed by the *GKN* to be a God-given mission field of strategic importance for the whole of Java.[43] Bavinck wrote: "The beautiful and populous island of Java was not freely chosen by Holland as an area of missionary work. God had to constrain us to take up this work there. Thus, in a most direct sense, the mission in Java is the fruit of God's dealings with this great people."[44] Bavinck worked there as missionary pastor from February 1930 to July 1933.

Bavinck's Missionary Mind

Bavinck's work was marked by four characteristic features. First of all, he showed real capacity for entering into the Javanese mind. His first priority was to immerse himself in the native culture as the initial stage of cross-cultural evangelism: "A person who carries the gospel to them will have to lean over toward them as far as possible in order to bring them into as close a contact as possible with the crux of the gospel."[45] Javanese culture had been shaped by Hinduism and Buddhism, lending it a distinctly mystical character; later it had been influenced by Islam as well. In this context, Bavinck's mystical bent and skill at unraveling psychological processes were of inestimable value. With his desire to listen and with the respectful stance he assumed toward those holding differing opinions and convictions, he was able to establish good contacts with Javanese mystics and Muslim scholars.[46] He regularly conversed with them long into the night, passionate to understand

43. Cf. Dirk Pol, *Midden-Java ten Zuiden* (Hoenderloo: Stichting Hoenderloo, 1939), pp. 11-12.
44. Johan Herman Bavinck, *Zending in een Wereld in Nood* (Wageningen: Zomer & Keuning, 1946), p. 141.
45. Johan Herman Bavinck, "Christendom en Cultuuruitingen," *De Macedoniër* 36 (1932): 44.
46. Cf. Verkuyl, *Contemporary Missiology,* p. 38.

their secrets and mysteries. Bavinck became engrossed in the Javanese *wa-yang* puppet shadow-plays, coming to grasp the religious charge these plays carried as dramatic representations of mythological events.[47] In 1931, a Cultural-Philosophical Study Group was set up in Solo to help the Javanese, Dutch, and Chinese to get to know each other. Bavinck counted participation in this group among the most wonderful experiences of his life. For him, the best moments came when "our conversation rose above all earthly things and turned to the divine world beyond us. Then we no longer thought of ourselves as Chinese, Javanese or Dutch; then, in a certain sense, we all became children standing in the presence of the ineffable greatness of the Eternal One. It was apparent that there were boundary lines. And yet, during these night-time discourses, we realized, deeply and intensely, how fruitful and wonderful it was that we could speak with one another about these things in such an atmosphere."[48]

During these years Bavinck had regular contact with Hendrik Kraemer, of the *NHK*, who was serving as linguist with the Dutch Bible Society in Solo; as a specialist in Javanese culture and mysticism, Kraemer too was a member of the Cultural-Philosophical Study Group. Years later Bavinck wrote of him: "He was my teacher, the one who initiated me into the secrets of Javanese literature and in particular Javanese mysticism."[49] Likewise Kraemer said of Bavinck: "I have never had a student who came to understand Javanese mysticism more quickly or more thoroughly than Bavinck."[50] This openness was grounded in an unshakable faith in the truth of the gospel.

Second, Bavinck showed a passion for explicating the gospel message better. That is, his attempts to get inside the Javanese mind served his endeavor to find ways to communicate the gospel more effectively. This is first illustrated in his Javanese-language booklet, *Suksma Supana*,[51] which ex-

---

47. Johan Herman Bavinck, *Christus en de Mystiek van het Oosten* (Kampen: J. H. Kok, 1934), p. 100; Bavinck provides a succinct, clear explanation of these plays. Ed. note: In what follows, wherever there is a reference to one of the translated works in the present volume (referred to as *JHBR*), we will provide the reference after the Dutch work is cited (e.g., ET: *JHBR*, p. 110). The reference in this note, however, is to part of *Christus en de Mystiek van het Oosten* not translated and included in this volume.

48. Johan Herman Bavinck, "De Cultuur-Wijsgerige Studiekring," in *Het Triwindoe-Gedenkboek Mangkoe Nagoro*, part 7 (Surakarta, 1939): 9-11.

49. René van Woudenberg, "Dr. Johan Herman Bavinck (1895-1964), Theoloog van Woord en Antwoord," in Johan Herman Bavinck, *J. H. Bavinck: Een Keuze uit Zijn Werk* (Kampen: J. H. Kok, 1991), p. 161.

50. Verkuyl, *Contemporary Missiology*, p. 63.

51. This booklet appeared in 1932 under the pseudonym Kjai Martawahana.

pounded the main points of the gospel in terms of the layout of the *kraton,* the palace of the monarch, whose many entrances and gates all had religious significance.

The crown of Bavinck's attempt to present the gospel contextually came with the appearance of his 1934 book, *Christus en de Mystiek van het Oosten (Christ and the Mysticism of the East).*[52] The work clearly showed his opposition to the popular contemporary concept of "continuity," which argued for a smooth, seamless attachment of the gospel to existing religions. Yet, Bavinck did not support the idea of rigid discontinuity either. Because of his strong inner bond with Christ, the Final Answer, he felt free to openly absorb and savor Asian thought. He observed striking similarities between the gospel and Javanese mysticism, pinpointed elements in Asian thinking that led to a deeper understanding of the biblical message, and discovered aspects of Asian experience that provided a point of contact for the proclamation of the gospel. At the same time, he made it clear that "the God of Asia is different from the God who appeared in Christ for our sake." The conclusion of the book states: "I am utterly convinced that there is only one means by which we can cause the difference to be deeply and truly felt, and that is by confronting Asia with the sacred figure of Jesus Christ."[53] J. van den Berg rightly points out that, in this book, Bavinck dealt with the communication between gospel and religion "innocently, as it were. After Tambaram, at which the question of 'continuity or discontinuity' was hotly debated, he approached this issue differently."[54]

Third, Bavinck showed a special concern for youth work. Bavinck noticed that young people in Solo's school circles were in a difficult position: their exposure to western science left them suspended between traditional folk beliefs and the Christian faith. Bavinck constantly emphasized the strategic position occupied by mission schools as institutions that could help youth deal with this culture shock. An article he wrote in 1931 urged mission-school education to become more attuned to Indonesian society, to develop

52. Cf. Verkuyl, *Contemporary Missiology,* p. 39; Verkuyl considered this work Bavinck's most important publication; it might be better termed his first important work in the area of applied elenctics. A later book that witnesses equally well to Bavinck's formidable knowledge of the Asian world is found in Johan Herman Bavinck, *De Psychologie van den Oosterling* (Loosduinen: Kleijwegt, 1942).

53. J. H. Bavinck, *Christus en de Mystiek,* p. 202; ET: *JHBR,* p. 410. Ed. note: The translations of passages from *Christus en de Mystiek* as well as other writings are those of the author (PJV). Page references to *JHBR* are provided as a convenience to the reader.

54. J. van den Berg, "De Wetenschappelijke," pp. 34-35.

according to distinctively Christian principles, and to work via closer cooperation with Christian churches to strengthen personal piety and cultivate Christian living.[55] Bavinck himself put these principles into practice at the Christian Teachers College in Solo, where he taught psychology and gave weekly lectures for the whole student body.

Another arm of Bavinck's youth-orientation was his initiative at setting up *pantja saudara,* "circles of five."[56] These were Bible-study groups that aimed to provide young people with support for their faith as they left the mission schools and found themselves confronted by difficulties and temptations in the environments to which they returned. Bavinck chose five *(pantja)* as the guiding number for these groups because in traditional Javanese culture that figure denoted a multiplicity that formed an unbreakable unity, like the five fingers of one hand. This link with the local culture proved effective, and this type of youth work became enormously popular.

In 1931 the Sower Library was established for the special purpose of facilitating the spiritual development of youth. Each year, five booklets were published, each dealing with a basic tenet of the Christian faith. Bavinck penned a number of these works,[57] which kept his leadership influential for a long time. After the war, in 1945, he underscored the purpose for this focus: "Education is one of the very best modes of mission; it is an excellent means of showing the Indonesian world that the gospel lays claim to the whole of life, including science."[58]

Finally, Bavinck showed sympathy for rising Indonesian nationalism and the cognate necessity of establishing the independence of the indigenous churches. In accordance with the stated principle of their Synod of Middelburg (1896) — to wit, that no church may be subordinated to another church — the mission agencies of the Reformed Churches in the Netherlands had, from the very beginning, given thought to the issue of the inde-

55. Johan Herman Bavinck, "De Crisis van het Zendingsonderwijs in Indië," *De Macedoniër* 36 (1932): 97-101, 129-33.

56. Cf. Johan Herman Bavinck, "Jeugdwerk: De Kringen van 5," *De Macedoniër* 37 (1933): 353-63.

57. Johan Herman Bavinck, *De Tien Geboden* (Magelang: Chr. Persvereeniging, 1932); *Hoe Kunnen wij den Heere Jezus Vinden?* (Magelang: Chr. Persvereeniging, 1933); *Het Licht des Levens* (Magelang: Chr. Persvereeniging, 1934); *Paulus de Grote Apostel* (Djokja: Ribbens, 1937).

58. Johan Herman Bavinck, "De zending nu!," foreword in *Historisch Document: Referaat van A. Kuyper over Zending* by Abraham Kuyper (Utrecht: Bootsma, 1940). This is a reissue of the address on mission delivered by A. Kuyper in Amsterdam in 1890 (no place name, 1945).

pendence of local missionary congregations. What was unique in Bavinck's case was his profound sympathy for the national awakening of Indonesia. Bavinck did everything he could to stimulate the growth of independence among the Javanese churches. He was deeply aware of an urgent desire among educated, indigenous Christians to fulfill tasks that, until then, had been presumed to belong to the missionaries. And though local believers were not always prepared for such a transition, Bavinck considered it important to transfer ecclesiastical authority and pastoral responsibility to them, especially to protect the mission from accusations of being a tool of colonialist power politics. If the church in Java was going to have a future, it would need to become a Javanese church; in order for missionary work to be successful in a nationalistic climate, it would have to be carried out in increasing measure by local believers. "Mission work stands or falls, humanly speaking, with the presence or absence of zeal for and love of the gospel among young indigenous Christians."[59]

Bavinck's work as a missionary youth pastor ended when he accepted an appointment as instructor at the Theological School in Jogjakarta, an academy for training Javanese evangelists and ministers. This school, founded in 1891, had evolved step by step to a higher level until it was as important for the indigenous churches in Central Java as Kampen Seminary and the Theological Faculty of the Free University were for the churches in the Netherlands.[60] To continue to improve its academic quality, administrators lengthened the school's course of study from two to three years and appointed two new instructors in 1931, Abraham Pos and J. H. Bavinck. Apparently, Bavinck had no doubt about his qualifications this time, although he did have his appointment postponed until he could arrange for a successor at Solo. After further study in Old Javanese and traditional Javanese religion at Leiden, he commenced his work at the Theological School in September 1934. He titled his inaugural lecture *De strijd des geloofs (The Struggle of Faith).*[61]

From the beginning, Bavinck felt comfortable in his new position. For one, he was on excellent terms with the other two instructors; besides, he was a gifted teacher. As one of his students later wrote, "He understood his

59. J. H. Bavinck, "Zending en crisis," p. 107.

60. William Breukelaar, "Berichten over Werkzaamheden van J. H. Bavinck," *Het Zendingsblad* 29 (1931): 240.

61. Though this lecture never appeared in print, a summary report of the inauguration was published in *Het Zendingsblad* 32 (1934): 172-73: "Verslag van inauguratie van dr J. H. Bavinck."

students and their thoughts and he brought them close to God. As a result, he had a great influence on the life of the Javanese and Chinese churches in Java."[62] Here again one of Bavinck's most important contributions consisted of giving much more attention to the cultivation of *theologia in loco,* i.e., the encouragement of indigenous theological expressions of the faith.[63] In addition to teaching, the instructors were also expected to produce textbooks and to maintain contact with alumni. Bavinck teamed up with F. L. Bakker to write *De Geschiedenis der Godsopenbaring (The History of Divine Revelation),* a commentary on the whole Bible published both in Dutch and in Javanese. The work was profound, yet simple, and so could be used profitably by both ordinary church members and theological scholars.

Without a doubt, Bavinck rendered a great service to the progress of mission work in Java. As his foremost student wrote: "In terms of mission, Bavinck's stay in Solo was the most fruitful period of his life."[64] It also constituted the initial impetus for his later missiological reflection. For himself Bavinck referred to his time at the Theological School as "the most wonderful years of my life."[65] He gained a veritable treasury of knowledge and experience, which he would put to use as a scholar and professor of missions. His work was so widely appreciated that he was named Officer in the Order of Orange Nassau by Queen Wilhelmina in 1938.[66]

Professor of Missions

Back in the Netherlands, many in the *GKN* sensed a growing need for improved training of missionary pastors, doctors, nurses, and teachers. A position in missiology was authorized at Kampen Seminary in 1938. The occupant was to teach the history and theory of missions and of missionary church polity, as well as furnish the church in the Netherlands with information and advice on missionary affairs.[67] Given that job description, the

62. Frederik L. Bakker, "In Memoriam Prof. Dr. J. H. Bavinck," *Algemeen Handelsblad,* 24 June 1964.

63. Verkuyl, *Contemporary Missiology,* p. 64.

64. Verkuyl, *Contemporary Missiology,* pp. 63-64.

65. Johan A. C. Rullmann, "Bij het Overlijden van Prof. Dr. J. H. Bavinck," *Nieuw Rotterdamsche Courant,* 24 June 1964.

66. Cf. *Het Zendingsblad* 36 (1938): 186.

67. Cf. Bernard J. Esser, "Ambt en Kerkelijke Positie der Missionair-Predikanten in de Gereformeerde Kerken en de Opleiding Daartoe," *De Macedoniër* 37 (1933): 106-11.

Synod faced a difficult task in finding the right person for the slot. As the secretary of the Mission Board noted: "We are thinking, in the first place, of a man equipped with first-rate academic abilities . . . who wholeheartedly reflects on the theory of mission, with all of its pressing problems, in the light of our principles, and who is capable of inspiring a sacred enthusiasm in our future ministers for the Lord's cause."[68] Certain people satisfied this description, the secretary continued, but "there is no one who could be withdrawn from his present duties without causing too much damage to the vital interests of the work in which he is involved."

If the secretary already had the erudite Johan Herman Bavinck in mind, some potential colleagues at Kampen Seminary were less than happy at the prospect. Professor Klaas Schilder and a member of the board of trustees, Rev. Geert Diemer,[69] privately grumbled that Bavinck's book *Inleiding in de Zielkunde (Introduction to Psychology)* unwisely yoked Reformed with unReformed thought. Schilder wrote: "Association with non-Reformed theories, however unintentional, can, in my view, be detected throughout this work."[70] He also argued that, in Bavinck's method, "Scriptural principles are mentioned only *a posteriori* and then related as best as possible to findings arrived at by other means."

Nonetheless, Bavinck received the Synod's nod in 1938 and immediately telegraphed his reply: "Am gladly willing in God's strength to accept appointment."[71] After one more year finishing his work in Jogjakarta, Bavinck arrived as the first Reformed professor of missions in the Netherlands. His inaugural address, *Christusprediking in de Volkerenwereld (Proclaiming Christ to the Nations)*,[72] dealt with a question dear to his heart, a question that would run like a thread through the whole of his missiological reflection: How can Jesus Christ be preached so that he does not remain an abstraction but rather becomes tangible and real for people?

Bavinck proceeded cautiously. He greatly preferred open dialogue to confrontation, so, soon after commencing his work at Kampen, he requested a special faculty meeting "to talk about a few questions in connection with

68. "Algemene berichten," *Het Zendingsblad* 34 (1936): 213.
69. Two undated letters dealing with this matter, one from Schilder and the other from Diemer, can be found among the personal papers of G. M. den Hartogh (at that time professor of church history), which are located in the archives of Kampen Seminary.
70. Letter from Klaas Schilder, 4; personal papers of G. M. den Hartogh, Kampen Seminary.
71. "Algemene berichten," *Het Zendingsblad* 36 (1938): 93.
72. Chapter 2 of this volume.

the subjects" he was teaching, matters that he wished to "submit to the judgment of his colleagues."[73] His paper on *The Phenomenon of Pseudo-Religion in Connection with General Revelation*[74] was well enough received for Bavinck to be asked to teach psychology the following year.

The discipline of missiology in the standard theological curriculum was divided into three parts: the history of missions in the Dutch East Indies, the theory of missions according to Reformed principles, and elenctics or missionary apologetics with specific reference to the non-Christian religions found on the *GKN's* Indonesian mission fields. Bavinck's surviving lecture notes reveal a great erudition, broad knowledge, and a global perspective. Under the history of missions, he dealt extensively with Indonesia but also with India and China. In his courses on mission theory, he taught from a Reformed perspective but also examined the development of missionary thinking across the centuries, including the more recent ecumenical views articulated at the International Missionary Conferences held since 1910. In missionary apologetics he focused on the history and phenomenology of religion.[75] In addition to his official lectures, Bavinck led well-attended missionary study groups in Kampen and Amsterdam at which he discussed important missiological publications — such as Hendrik Kraemer's *The Christian Message in a Non-Christian World* — with interested students. Bavinck was also commissioned to take part in the two-year certificate-training course for prospective missionary pastors and to set up a yearlong missionary training course for medical doctors and nurses.

On the whole, Bavinck maintained good relationships with his students. Many who studied under him remember him as an open, wise, and warm-hearted man. One of them later recalled: "Bavinck had something prophetic about him: when he spoke, it was with great inner authority. . . . What always struck me, too, was [his] unpretentious, thoroughly genuine humility and modesty. When you are sitting in class at the age of twenty, it is not only the subject matter that makes an impression, but also the whole attitude of your professor."[76] Another recalled: "It is impossible to say how many have been

73. Cf. the Minutes of the Meetings of Professors (Kampen), 21 February 1939.

74. *Het problem van de pseudo-religie en de algemene openbaring* (no place name, no year, bound separate issue of an article that appeared in *Orgaan van de Christelijke Vereeniging van Natuur-en Geneeskundigen in Nederland* [1941]: 1-16).

75. Cf. the Johan Herman Bavinck Archives of the Free University, Amsterdam.

76. Letter from B. J. Aalbers to R. van Woudenberg, 25 July 1992: "that the modesty which commanded such great respect sometimes proved to be something of a hindrance to Bavinck is illustrated by the following anecdote related to me by one of his former students,

gripped for life by the vision of God's worldwide work that was imparted to them by Bavinck."[77] Notably, it was often the students who rejected the antithetical attitude in the *GKN* who viewed Bavinck as a role model. These students observed that Bavinck, though he did not do violence to the truth, was able to do theology differently.

After World War II Bavinck began to move in broader circles. A sister denomination (the *Christelijke Gereformeerde Kerk*) decided to add missiology to its curriculum in 1945, and Bavinck was asked to teach this class. In October and November 1947 Bavinck traveled to the USA to lecture at Calvin College and Seminary in Grand Rapids. In the 1950s, at the request of the Theological Education Fund of the International Missionary Council, Bavinck visited South Africa three times (1952, 1953, 1963) to teach missiology at Potchefstroom Theological Seminary. Interest in these courses was reported to be "extremely great." In 1959, he was asked by the South African Committee on Science and Freedom to assess a proposal to establish separate faculties for blacks. In September 1960 he delivered a lecture at Presbyterian Theological Seminary in Louisville, Kentucky, and in 1961-62 he taught as guest professor at the Federated Theological Faculty of the University of Chicago. There, Bavinck's sensitive "analysis of the morphology of religions was so striking that the world's greatest scholar of the morphology of religions, Mircea Eliade, invited Bavinck to lecture."[78] Finally, because Bavinck was such a stimulating teacher he attracted many Dutch and international graduate students who received his intense, expert supervision.[79] "The stream of dissertations [eighteen in total] which flowed from the pens of his students"[80] was the measure of his encouragement of academic research and of his exceptional impact as professor.

Bavinck's own writing during this period was prolific, though he contributed less to international missiological journals than to various Dutch periodicals. He dealt there with fundamental missiological issues or ad-

L. J. Wolthuis: Once when a student had clearly failed an oral examination, Bavinck couldn't seem to find a way to tell him that. It remained quiet for a while until the student himself finally said: 'Shall I come back later and try again?'"

77. Abraham Pos, "Bij het Sterven van Prof. Dr. J. H. Bavinck," *Trouw* (24 June 1964).

78. Verkuyl, *Contemporary Missiology*, p. 40.

79. His foreign graduate students came from North America, South Africa, and China. Cf. Appendix II in Paul J. Visser, *Bemoeienis en Getuigenis. Het Leven en de Missionaire Theologie van J. H. Bavinck* (Th.M. thesis, University of Utrecht, 1987), p. 325.

80. Verkuyl, *Contemporary Missiology*, p. 40; for similar testimonial statements by other Bavinck students, cf. Pos, "Leven en Werk," pp. 25-26.

dressed practical problems faced by his denomination especially in light of the decolonization of Indonesia and the changing relationships between the indigenous churches and mission authorities.[81] He also began to reflect more and more on the task of church and mission amid postwar changes, calling attention to the difficulties of proclaiming the gospel in the spiritual vacuum created by rising nihilism and materialism. He continued to look critically at his own church to try to rouse it to revival and new expectations.

Bavinck's most important missiological works manifest a gradual deepening of insight, especially as they evolved from his theological reflection on the relationship of the Christian faith to other religions. Since the substance of these books will be dealt with later, brief mention of them will suffice here. Early in World War II there appeared *De Boodschap van Christus en de Niet-Christelijke Religies (The Message of Christ and Non-Christian Religions)*,[82] which summarized the argument of Hendrik Kraemer's *The Christian Message in a Non-Christian World* (written for the 1938 International Missionary Conference in Tambaram) with supplementary notes lightly criticizing Kraemer's radical view of Christianity and the notion of biblical realism. In *Alzoo wies het Woord (And Thus the Word Grew and Increased)*,[83] Bavinck reflected on the methods of Paul in an attempt to develop a responsible, contemporary discharge of the missionary calling. This book, especially the interpretation of Paul's speech on the Areopagus, reveals how intensively Bavinck had pondered the relationship between the gospel and other religions.

After the war Bavinck first produced *Zending in een Wereld in Nood (Mission in a World in Need)*,[84] intended as an introduction to the principles of mission for interested church members. *The Impact of Christianity on the Non-Christian World*,[85] the lectures that Bavinck delivered at Calvin Theological Seminary in 1947, form a solid reflection on missionary apologetics. In the Foreword, Calvin Seminary Professor Clarence Bouma states: "Though

81. Cf. the bibliography of these writings during the period 1945-1949 in van den Berg et al., *Christusprediking in de Wereld*.

82. Johan Herman Bavinck, *De Boodschap van Christus en de Niet-Christelijke Religies* (Kampen: J. H. Kok, 1940).

83. Johan Herman Bavinck, *Alzoo wies het Woord: Een Studie over de Voortgang van het Evangelie in de Dagen van Paulus* (Baarn: Bosch & Keuning, 1941).

84. Johan Herman Bavinck, *Zending in een Wereld in Nood* (Wageningen: Zomer en Keuning, 1946).

85. Johan Herman Bavinck, *The Impact of Christianity on the Non-Christian World* (Grand Rapids: Eerdmans, 1948).

not as wide in scope, as to spirit and content, this work should be classed with Hendrik Kraemer's *The Christian Message in a Non-Christian World.*"

Then came three titles that constitute the high point of Bavinck's work. In *Religieus Besef en Christelijk Geloof (Religious Consciousness and Christian Faith),*[86] one of his most engrossing works, Bavinck continued to elaborate on Kraemer's ideas but developed them according to his own thinking and insight. Particularly in light of Romans 1, Bavinck deals with questions about the reality of general revelation, the origin and content of religious consciousness, and God's revelation in Christ. This book's combination of theological reflection and psychological insight qualifies it as one of the "modern classics."[87] *Inleiding in de Zendingswetenschap (Introduction to the Science of Missions)*[88] served as a textbook, the first standard Reformed work in missiology to be published in the Netherlands. It gave expanded treatment to themes in many of Bavinck's other works and was translated into English in 1960. Finally, *The Church Between Temple and Mosque,*[89] his last important work, was a posthumous publication of Bavinck's lectures in Chicago that deals in a profound and detailed way with the content of religious consciousness in relation to Christian faith.

Nor were Bavinck's interests limited to missiology. He published studies in biblical theology that were marked by a deep pastoral concern: *De Bijbel, het Boek der Ontmoetingen (The Bible, the Book of Encounters)* and *De Mensch en zijn Wereld (Man and His World).*[90] He also produced an original exegetical study of the last book of the Bible, *En Voort Wentelen de Eeuwen: Gedachten over het Boek der Openbaring van Johannes (And Age Follows upon Age: Reflections on the Book of Revelation of John).*[91]

---

86. Johan Herman Bavinck, *Religieus Besef en Christelijk Geloof* (Kampen: J. H. Kok, 1949; reprinted with a foreword by J. Verkuyl and enlarged with "Algemene openbaring en de niet-Christelijke religies," a translation of "General Revelation and the Non-Christian Religions" [1955], ed. R. van Woudenberg (Kampen: J. H. Kok, 1989). Ed. note: The latter is Chapter 1 in this volume and the former is found in Chapters 3-5.

87. Cf. Verkuyl, "Woord vooraf," p. ix.

88. Johan Herman Bavinck, *Inleiding in de Zendingswetenschap* (Kampen: J. H. Kok, 1954); ET: *Introduction to the Science of Missions,* trans. David Hugh Freeman (Grand Rapids: Eerdmans, 1960).

89. Johan Herman Bavinck, *The Church between Temple and Mosque* (Grand Rapids: Eerdmans, 1966).

90. Johan Herman Bavinck, *De Bijbel, het Boek der Ontmoetingen* (Wageningen: Zomer en Keuning, 1942); *De mensch en zijn wereld* (Baarn: Bosch en Keuning, 1946).

91. Johan Herman Bavinck, *En Voort Wentelen de Eeuwen: Gedachten over het Boek der Openbaring van Johannes* (Wageningen: Zomer en Keuning, 1952).

As attested by many contemporary observers, all of Bavinck's published works are characterized by a combination of learnedness and lucidity, academic rigor and simplicity. This made them broadly attractive and accessible to both scholars and ordinary church members.

Bavinck in World War II

The Second World War broke out soon after Bavinck had taken up his position at Kampen and Amsterdam. As a direct consequence the connection between the Netherlands and the Dutch East Indies was broken, instigating a search for new ways of giving shape to the missionary task of the church. Bavinck played a prominent role in this search. One of his important activities was the intensive training of missionary ministers, teachers, doctors, and nurses for service after the war. In an interview, one of the graduates of this program, Anton G. Honig, future professor of missiology at Kampen, said: "Bavinck prepared us for missionary service in those years in a truly superb way." Gradually, the desire emerged to establish a center to better promote and support the church's missionary enterprise. A plan that Bavinck drew up was adopted by the Synod of Utrecht in 1943. The goal of the Center was not only to aid the work of foreign missions but to actively stimulate mission awareness at home so that churches would truly engage the cause. After finding a suitable building in Baarn, the Center for Mission opened in 1946 under the direction of Rev. Barend Richters.

Meanwhile, by order of the German authorities Bavinck's lectures in Kampen and Amsterdam were suspended from 1943 to 1945. Bavinck used most of this enforced free time for scholarship. He wrote in his war diary, "I drew up an outline for a new book, a kind of introduction to the history and phenomenology of religion [perhaps a first draft of *Religious Consciousness and Christian Faith*]. It will take a number of years before the book is finished, but the initial spadework has been accomplished in the time of war."

The war years brought Bavinck and his wife considerable anxiety. Their two sons, and also at one point their daughter, were actively involved in the Dutch resistance movement. Both sons were arrested within the same week in June 1944. The elder son was held in German custody until September 1944, and the younger was deported to Germany and imprisoned in the concentration camps at Sachsenhausen and Rathenau until June 1945.[92] Unfor-

92. This information is based on Bavinck's wartime diary referred to above.

tunately, the war years also saw a serious theological conflict flare up in the *GKN*, leading to a church schism, the so-called *Vrijmaking* (Liberation) in 1944. The conflict centered on the views of Kampen Seminary professor Klaas Schilder, who contested, *inter alia*, the Kuyperian notion that baptism presupposed regeneration. At the invitation of the Student Union, *Fides quaerens intellectum*, Bavinck gave a lecture at Kampen on 2 November 1942, titled *De Toekomst van onze Kerken (The Future of Our Churches)*.[93] In it he sketched the evolution of the spiritual currents within the *GKN* in an attempt to trigger open and fruitful discussion of the "Schilder controversy." The speech made a deep impression on the students; as one of them later wrote: "A probing, a warm and emotional appeal was made to us. Was it not true that, in our little church, in the midst of this big world, we were getting worked up about trifling matters, futilities?"[94] Schilder, who was sent a report of the speech, sharply contested Bavinck's argument at every point.[95] Bavinck chose not to reply to Schilder's letter. A much happier occasion came on 5 May 1945 when Allied forces liberated the Netherlands from the German occupation. On the following Sunday, Bavinck led a packed service at one of the largest churches in Utrecht, preaching on 1 Timothy 1:17: "Now to the King eternal, immortal, invisible, the only God, be honor and glory forever and ever. Amen."

The Postwar Years: Mission, Ecumenism, and Practical Theology

After the capitulation of Japan on 18 August 1945, the *GKN* sought ways to return as quickly as possible to Central Java and Sumba. During the war, a pool of potential missionary workers had been recruited who could now be sent out. On the very day the Japanese surrendered, Bavinck wrote a brochure titled *De zending nu! (Missions Now!)*,[96] in which he outlined the expected possibilities and challenges for mission in Indonesia. His approach to

---

93. For a summary of this important speech, see Paul J. Visser, *Heart for the Gospel, Heart for the World* (Eugene: Wipf & Stock, 2003), pp. 58-60.

94. Jacob Kamphuis and Klaas Schilder, *Zien in de Toekomst* (Groningen: De Vuurbaak, 1979), p. 31.

95. Cf. Kamphuis and Schilder, *Zien in de Toekomst*, pp. 39-58, which contains the complete text of Schilder's reaction.

96. In this brochure, Bavinck affirms the continuing significance of a celebrated speech that Abraham Kuyper gave on mission in 1890. However, Bavinck did state that "our opinions with respect to some points have changed somewhat."

the postwar and nearly postcolonial situation in Indonesia was thoroughly informed by a harmony between realism and conviction of faith. He emphasized the need for the mother-church to listen carefully to the daughter-churches and to serve them faithfully without being swayed by political considerations.

In 1946 Bavinck and two colleagues, F. L. Bakker and Abraham Pos, were commissioned by the Synod of the *GKN* to go to Indonesia to deliberate with the churches that had developed out of *GKN* missionary activities.[97] From this "Kwitang Conference" in 1947[98] Bavinck reported a greater-than-expected amount of distrust among the young Javanese churches toward new forms of western domination. "It was an almost painful revelation," he acknowledged. "Gradually, however, trust was completely restored. This was due to the fact that we argued emphatically at every turn that our only concern was the coming of the Kingdom of Jesus Christ."[99] After deep, intense discussion,[100] the *GKN* Synod unanimously accepted the proposals formulated by Javanese churches. In the future, missionary work would be carried out by Indonesian churches, and they would perform this task in close cooperation with other Javanese- and Malaysian-speaking churches.[101] Foreign churches would be allocated only an assisting role in mission. This new relationship would be a "partnership in obedience," a term that figured strongly at the 1947 International Missionary Conference at Whitby. Bavinck argued that this decision was in line with the conclusions of the 1896 *GKN* Synod of Middelburg, at which these principles of missionary work had already been formulated.[102] The 1948 Synod of the Javanese Churches in Magelang also

97. Cf. "Algemene berichten," *Het Zendingsblad* 44 (1946): 3; "Algemene berichten," *Het Zendingsblad* 45 (1947): 11.

98. This conference, held in Kwitang church in Batavia (Jakarta), took place from 19 to 24 May 1947. Though some of the attending Javanese churches had roots in the mission of the RCN, and others in that of the NRC, they had been officially cooperating with each other since May 1946.

99. Johan Herman Bavinck, "De conferentie in Kwitang," *Het Zendingsblad* 45 (1947): 40-42.

100. Herman N. Ridderbos reported that Bavinck was very deeply involved in this discussion since he felt that there was so much at stake; cf. Herman N. Ridderbos, "In Memoriam Prof. dr. J. H. Bavinck," *Gereformeerd Weekblad* 20 (1964): 2.

101. "Algemene berichten," *Het Zendingsblad* 46 (1948): 56-58.

102. "Algemene berichten," *Het Zendingsblad* 46 (1948): 21-22. "Since every local church is complete in itself and stands directly under King Jesus, the sending church, as mother church, may support and advise but may never take it upon itself to exercise authority over such a church."

adopted the report of the Kwitang conference. About this decision, Bavinck later wrote: "That such a thing was possible in these difficult and confusing times is something for which we can give God hearty thanks."[103]

The question of the independence of the indigenous churches was complicated by the conservative views on Dutch colonial policy held by the Anti-Revolutionary Party (ARP), to which most *GKN* members belonged.[104] Though Bavinck did not directly involve himself in political affairs, he did consistently resist this conservative bent both in the party and the church. Because of his calm and wise method of argumentation,[105] he was able to overcome many of the sharp differences that had arisen over the issue, and he convinced many of the appropriateness of his position.[106] His knowledge and insight did not remain unnoticed in broader circles, so that Bavinck was invited to be an advisor at the Round-Table Conference organized by the Dutch government to discuss Indonesian independence.

After the war the *GKN* gradually expanded its contact with other churches both at home and abroad. Bavinck hoped to stimulate this contact not only out of his personal interests but because he believed the church to be ecumenical by nature.[107] In 1946, the *GKN* joined the Dutch Missionary Council (DMC) and became affiliated with the International Missionary Council (IMC). In 1947 the *GKN* also took part in the inaugural meeting of the Reformed Ecumenical Synod (RES) in Grand Rapids, Michigan, at which various American, South African, and Western European Reformed churches were represented. Bavinck warmly supported a proposal to set up an international cooperative committee to study the implications of Reformed principles for mission. When he was back home again in the Netherlands, he made a passionate plea for this idea and outlined the benefits of

103. Johan Herman Bavinck, *Het Zendingsblad* 47 (1948): 24-25.

104. This was the Christian political party associated with the RCN at that time.

105. Cf. Johannes Verkuyl, *Gedenken en Verwachten: Memoires* (Kampen: J. H. Kok, 1983), pp. 142-43, where he relates that, at a pastors' conference where he had shared the platform with Bavinck, the chairman of the meeting had likened their differing styles of political and ecclesiastical criticism to the difference between wool (Verkuyl) and silk (Bavinck), a jacket and a jacquet. In conversation, Verkuyl indicated to me that this strong side of Bavinck was also his vulnerable side: his modesty and delicacy occasionally weakened his argument.

106. Cf. Jan A. Boersma, "Een Halve Eeuw Zending van de Gereformeerde Kerken (Vrijgemaakt) Tegen de Achtergrond van Middelburg 1896," *Documentatieblad voor de Geschiedenis van de Nederlandse Zending en Overzeese Kerken* 3, no. 2 (1996): 69.

107. Cf. Johan Herman Bavinck, *Inleiding in de Zendingswetenschap*, p. 207; ET: *Science of Missions*, p. 204.

such a collective effort. Bavinck was convinced that both church and missions would gain much from joint reflection on pressing missiological questions and from mutually sharing experiences and strengths.[108] The second assembly of the RES, held in Amsterdam in 1949, instituted the International Reformed Missionary Council.

In 1948 the World Council of Churches (WCC) was founded in Amsterdam. Various *GKN* Synods, since the 1930s, had rejected participation in the ecumenical movement because they feared it was pursuing unity at the cost of truth.[109] Bavinck, though recognizing the validity of this concern, regretted the Synodical vetoes. To him, the purpose statement adopted at the first assembly of the WCC in Amsterdam ("The World Council of Churches is a fellowship of churches which confess the Lord Jesus Christ as God and Savior according to the Scriptures") justified *GKN* membership in this body. Moreover, official participation in the WCC would make it possible for the *GKN* to render a positive contribution to the understanding of truth at the global-church level. It would be irresponsible to ignore this ecumenical calling, he argued, because of the strong and long-lasting influence such international gatherings had on the thinking and life of churches around the world.[110]

Following a long, wasting illness, Bavinck's wife died on 12 January 1953. Trientje's death was an unspeakable loss for Bavinck and his children. Her close interest in Bavinck's work had been a great support to him throughout the years. Her character had been stamped by sobriety, openness, and warmth, and her relationship with Christ was the wellspring of her life. After a few lonely years, Bavinck married Fennechine van der Vegt on 11 April 1956.

At the same time, Bavinck was appointed professor of practical theology at the Free University in Amsterdam in January 1954.[111] This appointment was made because Bavinck combined a high degree of religious-psychological expertise with homiletical and pastoral gifts.[112] Bavinck also continued to teach missiology at Amsterdam. This new phase in Bavinck's life was marked not so

108. Cf. "Algemene Berichten," *Het Zendingsblad* 46 (1948): 6-7.

109. Cf. Anne Wind, *Zending en Oecumene in de Twintigste Eeuw*, vol. 1 (Kampen: J. H. Kok, 1984), pp. 208-10.

110. Cf. Johan Herman Bavinck, "De Vergadering van de Wereldraad van Kerken," *Bezinning* 3 (1948): 276.

111. Pos, "Leven en Werk," p. 17.

112. Cf. Johannes van den Berg, "The Legacy of Johan Herman Bavinck," *International Bulletin of Missionary Research* 7, no. 4 (October 1983): 172.

much by a change in direction as by the addition of new interests.[113] As Abraham Pos wrote: "Twice we saw Bavinck switch to a new area of investigation without completely abandoning the old one. The publication of his *Inleiding in de Zielkunde* [*Introduction to Psychology*] in 1926 constituted the high point and the endpoint of his direct academic reflection in this field, though the results of this research continued to play an important, perhaps even a dominant, role in his practical and academic missionary activities. And the publication of his *Introduction to the Science of Missions* in 1954 was the crown of his professorship in mission, but the findings of this study continued to influence his work in practical theology. It was, thus, both psychology and missiology that qualified him for this new task."[114]

In his new position Bavinck taught homiletics, poimenics (pastoral theology and psychology), and evangelism. His lectures, delivered with love and dedication, were well attended and made an unforgettable impression on many of his students. The sermon sketches he offered in class were diligently copied down and inspired many a future preacher.[115] The lecture notes of one of his courses were posthumously published in 1967 under the title *De mens van nu (Contemporary Man)*.[116] This volume clearly demonstrates the psychological and missiological dimensions of Bavinck's work, attempting to analyze modern people in the context of their time in order to promote more effective preaching and pastoral care. He clearly recognized that, even within his own church, confessional faith was dwindling; the experience of sin and grace, the practice of leading a Christian life in the world, eschatological orientation, in short, a life lived in and according to the Holy Spirit was on the wane. In light of these developments, Bavinck wrote, in addition to various articles,[117] a discerning book titled *Ik geloof in de Heilige Geest (I Believe in the Holy Spirit)*.[118] It prophetically pointed to a great, cultural reversal, whereby God was becoming the great Absent One, a reversal that constituted a religious crisis for the church.

A serious kidney ailment sapped Bavinck's strength during the last two years of his life, increasingly limiting his activities. Just before the twenty-

---

113. Cf. van den Berg, "De Wetenschappelijke Arbeid," p. 40.

114. Pos, "Leven en Werk," p. 17.

115. This was corroborated in an interview I had with Bavinck's nephew, H. J. Bavinck, who had himself attended his uncle's classes.

116. Johan Herman Bavinck, *De Mens van Nu* (Kampen: J. H. Kok, 1967).

117. Cf. Johan Herman Bavinck, *Gereformeerd Weekblad* 11 (1956): 305, 314, 321, 329.

118. Johan Herman Bavinck, *Ik Geloof in de Heilige Geest* (Den Haag: J. N. Voorhoeve, 1963).

fifth anniversary of his appointment as professor, he was hospitalized in Amsterdam, where he died on 23 June 1964. On June 26, his body was sown in the earth of Zorgvlied cemetery in Amsterdam to await the day of God's great harvest. At Bavinck's own request, his funeral was sober and without speeches or flowers; even in death, he magnified the *gloria Dei,* the same theme that, in life, he had set as the goal of mission.

We can make the following summary assessments of Bavinck's life:

1. As the first *GKN* professor of missions, Bavinck engaged in careful reflection on the principles of missiology from the confessional perspective of the Reformed church. This reflection helped create a place for a Reformed model of mission both in the Netherlands and elsewhere.
2. Bavinck's fascination with the problem of God and the human soul lent a distinct color to his missiological reflection and equipped him in an outstanding way for his study in the field of practical theology.
3. Bavinck was more of a passionate thinker and prophetic seer than a systematic theologian; he was a man of great vision who thought along broad lines from the perspective of eternity. He attempted to illuminate the deep dimensions of human life and world history in light of Scripture, the source of ultimate truth, and he tried to communicate his message in clear language to as many people as possible. This is reflected in his publications, in which academic rigor and inner conviction go hand in hand.
4. Bavinck possessed an open disposition and developed an ecumenical attitude without compromising truth. Close friendships across denominational boundaries, such as his friendship with Hendrik Kraemer, contributed to this posture. Bavinck played a pioneer role in his church by helping it break out of its isolation and enter into ecumenical relationships.
5. Bavinck's personality was most notably characterized by a harmonious alliance of feeling, intellect, warmheartedness, and an almost hesitant modesty, all of which imparted a special authority to his words and actions. His prophetic vision was always accompanied by priestly concern.

3. The Content and Context of Bavinck's Thought

Johan Bavinck was the first *GKN* theologian in the Netherlands to try to construct a complete Reformed missiology. He set out its *prolegomena* in his handbook, *An Introduction to the Science of Missions*. Its broader *frame of reference* can be readily gleaned from his publications, which show how well-read Bavinck was in the scholarly domains relevant to missiology and how closely he integrated this research into his own work. The most salient parts of his theological context can be divided between his theology of religion *(theologia religionum)* and his theology of mission.

Missiology Defined

Bavinck divided the discipline of missiology into three main areas of concern: missions theory, elenctics, and missions history.[119]

First, following Gustav Warneck,[120] a leading authority in the field, Bavinck emphasized the need to develop a robust missionary theory — that is, rigorous reflection upon the biblical foundations, essence, approach, and aim of missions. Bavinck took as his point of departure the assumption that the Bible contains the "complete revelation of God valid for all times and all peoples."[121] Just as much, Bavinck was concerned to develop a biblically responsible approach to other religions. Citing Walter Holsten,[122] Bavinck argued that any serious missiology must engage in the development of a *theologia religionum* because the church's assessment of other religions is crucial in its perception of the missionary task.[123] Second, his body of work clearly indicates the importance of elenctics in Bavinck's missiological reflection and development. Third, in *Inleiding in de Zendingswetenschap* Bavinck dealt with the history of missions in light of scripturally derived missionary principles in hopes of learning lessons from history for use in contemporary practice.[124] He rejected François E. Daubanton's argument

119. Johan Herman Bavinck, *Inleiding in de Zendingswetenschap*, pp. 16-17; ET: *Science of Missions*, p. xxi. In *Zending in een Wereld in Nood*, a forerunner of *Inleiding in de Zendingswetenschap*, Bavinck employs only two divisions: theory of mission and history of mission.

120. Cf. Gustav Warneck, *Evangelische Missionslehre*, vol. 1 (Gotha: Perthes, 1894).

121. Johan Herman Bavinck, *Onze Kerk, Zendingskerk* (Kampen: J. H. Kok, 1948), pp. 8-9. Bavinck states in no uncertain terms that if biblical revelation is denied or if its truth is relativized, there is no basis for Christian mission.

122. Walter Holsten, *Das Kerugma und der Mensch* (München: Chr. Kaiser Verlag, 1953), p. 55: "Die Religionswissenschaft ist von hier aus gesehen nicht eine Hilfswissenschaft der Missionswissenschaft, sondern sie bedingt die Missionswissenschaft, wie sie von ihr bedingt ist; beide gehören zusammen als ein Ganzes."

123. J. H. Bavinck, *Zendingswetenschap*, p. 17; ET: *Science of Missions*, p. xxi.

124. J. H. Bavinck, *Zendingswetenschap*, pp. 280-81; ET: *Science of Missions*, p. 281.

that theory must entirely derive from history if missionary theology were to attain scientific quality. Just the reverse, Bavinck said: it is only upon the basis of a theory of missions that the history of missions can be studied as the work that God has accomplished in his church throughout the ages.[125]

Bavinck subsumed his three divisions of missiology under the term "science of mission," a common term among both Dutch and German missionary scholars.[126] He rejected the term "prosthetics" as introduced by Abraham Kuyper from the New Testament verb *prostithenai*: to add to (the community of believers), "addition" being understood in both a quantitative and a qualitative sense. Bavinck objected because the New Testament always used the verb *prostithenai* with God as the subject (cf. Acts 2:41, 47; 11:24), so that the proper study of mission consisted of the systematic reflection on *our* calling to preach the gospel.[127] "The church is a 'sent community,' just as Christ is the Sent One of the Father (cf. John 20:21). This means that the sending of the church is the object of the science of mission."[128] Bavinck used the term "science" instead of "theology" of mission because he did not want to distinguish between knowledge and faith. For Bavinck, the knowledge of God contained the highest degree of (scientific) objectivity.[129]

In his *Introduction,* Bavinck also defined the place of missiology within the corpus of theology. Viewing the church from the perspective of its missionary obligation means that missiology is primarily concerned with two realities: first, the divine calling and ordination of the church, and second, the actual realization of that calling in the course of history.[130] Consequently, Bavinck saw a close relationship between missiology and exegesis, dogmatics, ethics, homiletics, and church history; missiology was not an isolated discipline set apart from the rest of theological study. Yet, it was not to be subsumed under some other discipline either. With Gustav Warneck and Joseph Schmidlin before him,[131] Bavinck made a case for the independence

125. J. H. Bavinck, *Zendingswetenschap,* p. 282; ET: *Science of Missions,* p. 283.

126. E.g., the Protestants F. E. Daubanton, H. W. Schomerus, and W. Holsten, and the Roman Catholics A. J. M. Mulders and J. Schmidlin.

127. J. H. Bavinck, *Zendingswetenschap,* pp. 12-13; ET: *Science of Missions,* p. xvii.

128. J. H. Bavinck, *Zendingswetenschap,* p. 13; ET: *Science of Missions,* p. xvii; Bavinck already used the term "science of mission" in his inaugural address, *Christusprediking in de Volkerenwereld* (Kampen: J. H. Kok, 1940), p. 5; ET: *JHBR,* Chapter 2.

129. Cf. J. H. Bavinck, *Religieus Besef en Christelijk Geloof* (Kampen: J. H. Kok, 1948), p. 110; ET: *JHBR,* Chapters 3-6.

130. J. H. Bavinck, *Zendingswetenschap,* p. 15; ET: *Science of Missions,* p. xix.

131. Cf. Warneck, *Evangelische Missionslehre,* pp. 32-44, and Joseph Schmidlin, *Einführung in die Missionswissenschaft* (Münster in Westfalen: Aschendorff, 1925), pp. 8-11.

of missiology; with Kuyper,[132] he argued that missiology, as the reflection on an aspect of the *diakonia* (ministry) of the church, deserves a rightful place among the several subdisciplines of practical theology. Bavinck critiqued Kuyper, however, for classifying missiology among the didascalic subdisciplines of practical theology, those concerned with the ministry of the Word. While he recognized that the *didaskalia* — education and proclamation — lay at "the heart of the missionary task," he felt that this classification "limited the scope of the missionary task too much."[133]

Bavinck's Theology of Religion in Context

Bavinck's own theology of religion can be clarified by contrasting it to the many other Christian thinkers whom he studied in detail.

Already in *Christus en de Mystiek,* his first important publication in the theology of religion, Bavinck made connections to three elements of **Augustine**'s thought. First, over against the concept of an abstract Being into which human beings were reabsorbed at the end of life, Augustine stated that the essence of God finds its expression in the divine attributes or virtues, an important insight in the struggle against forms of mystical union.[134] Second, Augustine saw the being of God and the human soul to be inextricably tied together, making it impossible for human beings to disengage themselves from God; thus, in one way or another, humans are conscious of God. This insight served as the initial point in Bavinck's theological interpretation that the consciousness of God present in all human beings was initiated by God.[135] Third, Bavinck agreed with Augustine's rejection of the cosmological divine order in favor of a Trinitarian way of thinking, and he emphasized that the truth of existence can only be grasped through the revelation of God.[136]

As he developed his theology of religion, Bavinck clearly followed **John Calvin** in his *Institutes of the Christian Religion.* Here too, three points deserve special attention. First, according to Calvin, religion was not a human invention but resulted from God's continuing revelation in the world. This

132. Cf. A. Kuyper, *Encyclopaedie der Heilige Godgeleerdheid,* 3 vols. (Kampen: J. H. Kok, 1909), 3: 487.

133. Cf. J. H. Bavinck, *Zendingswetenschap,* pp. 15-16; ET: *Science of Missions,* p. xx.

134. Cf. J. H. Bavinck, *Christus en de Mystiek,* pp. 112-17; ET: *JHBR,* pp. 309-13.

135. Cf. J. H. Bavinck, *Christus en de Mystiek,* pp. 120ff.; ET: *JHBR,* pp. 317ff.

136. Cf. J. H. Bavinck, *Christus en de Mystiek,* 173ff.; ET: *JHBR,* pp. 362ff.

meant that religion was fundamentally a theological phenomenon.[137] Second, Calvin spoke about the *sensus divinitatis*, the sense of God experienced by every person, an awareness that could not be destroyed and that was stimulated by the revelation of God in nature and in the ordering of human life.[138] Finally, it was evident to Calvin that this endowed knowledge of God was always smothered or corrupted; consequently, his evaluation of all extra-biblical religion was negatively charged.[139] Though in general affirming Calvin's principles, over time Bavinck became more critical of Calvin's understanding of the *sensus divinitatis*, and came to consider the mode of this sensibility to be more relational than substantial.[140]

Bavinck had serious reservations about much of **Friedrich Schleiermacher**'s theology.[141] Yet, he was influenced by Schleiermacher's notion of religion as the "feeling of dependence" and wholeheartedly agreed with Schleiermacher's rejection of the rationalistic construct of *religio naturalis*, adopting this as a point of departure in his own work.[142] Likewise, early in his missiological studies, Bavinck supported many of the views articulated by **Rudolf Otto** in his 1922 publication, *Das Heilige*, including the idea that the religious feeling inherent in humans is activated by experiences of God.[143] Later on, Bavinck rejected this religious *a priori* on theological grounds, though he maintained sympathy for Otto's description of human sensitivity to religious impulses.

Within the neo-Calvinist tradition, Bavinck became thoroughly acquainted with **Abraham Kuyper**'s theology of religion. Kuyper developed his understanding of "non-Christian religions" primarily in light of Romans 1:18ff.[144] This Scripture passage became a point of departure in Bavinck's own reflection. Kuyper especially influenced Bavinck in his perception that

---

137. Cf. John Calvin, *Institutes of the Christian Religion*, trans. Ford Lewis Battles, ed. John T. McNeill (Philadelphia: Westminster, 1961), 1.3.2.

138. Calvin, *Institutes*, 1.3.1 and 1.5.1.

139. Calvin, *Institutes*, 1.4.1-2.

140. Cf. J. H. Bavinck, *Religieus Besef*, pp. 147-48; ET: *JHBR*, pp. 263-64.

141. Cf. Paul J. Visser, *Geen andere naam onder de hemel: De missiologie van Johan Herman Bavinck* (Th.M. Thesis, Utrecht, 1987), for a treatment of three of Schleiermacher's views with which Bavinck deeply disagreed, *viz.*, the image of God: absolute immanent causality; the Bible: a collection of religious experiences; Christian faith: a step on the way to pure monotheism.

142. Cf. J. H. Bavinck, *Religieus Besef*, pp. 99-102; ET: *JHBR*, pp. 223-25.

143. Rudolf Otto, *Das Heilige*, 16th ed. (Gotha: Leopold Klots, 1927); ET: *The Idea of the Holy*, trans. John W. Harvey (London/New York: Oxford University Press, 1958).

144. Cf. Kuyper, *Encyclopaedie*, 3: 446-48.

the witnessing Christian stands in the same position as his non-Christian auditor, in that the Christian, too, is naturally drawn to pseudo-religion.[145]

Bavinck thoroughly acquainted himself with his uncle **Herman Bavinck**'s dogmatic theology, especially as it was outlined in the *Reformed Dogmatics*.[146] In accordance with classical Reformed theology, Herman Bavinck made four main points that are relevant to theology of religion. First, religion exists because God is God and wishes to be served by his rational creatures. God is thus the *principium essendi* of all religion.[147] Second, because God wishes to be served, he reveals himself to humanity in nature, in history, and in the human conscience *(principium cognoscendi externum)*, rendering human beings subjectively capable of receiving this revelation *(principium cognoscendi internum)*.[148] Third, though the knowledge of God that is naturally present in human beings is inadequate, it sustains an awareness that humans are created in God's image and gives rise to yearnings for Christ.[149] Fourth, general revelation is the foundation upon which special revelation rests, and natural revelation provides a point of contact for the gospel message.[150] J. H. Bavinck initially followed Herman's thinking, albeit in a more psychological and less philosophical fashion. Gradually, however, his thinking became more theologically distant.

This shift stemmed indirectly from the influence of **Karl Barth**, for whom religion as such was not a theological phenomenon but "ein Angelegenheit des gottlosen Menschen" (a concern of godless men).[151] While Bavinck's interpretation of Romans 1:18ff. led him to fundamentally disagree with Barth on this point, Bavinck was influenced by Barth via Hendrik Kraemer,[152] who conveyed to him Barth's insistence on employing the Word of God as the sole point of departure for theological reflection. Bavinck rec-

145. Cf. Kuyper, *Encyclopaedie*, 3: 449.

146. The first edition of this four-volume work appeared between 1895 and 1901; the second revised and enlarged edition was published between 1906 and 1911. Subsequent editions are unaltered in content though the pagination varies.

147. Cf. Herman Bavinck, *Reformed Dogmatics*, vol. 1, *Gereformeerde Dogmatiek* (Kampen: J. H. Kok, 1906), p. 287.

148. Cf. H. Bavinck, *Reformed Dogmatics*, 1: 286-90.

149. Cf. H. Bavinck, *Reformed Dogmatics*, 1: 334-35.

150. Cf. Herman Bavinck, *Reformed Dogmatics*, vol. 3, *Gereformeerde Dogmatiek* (Kampen: J. H. Kok, 1910), p. 248.

151. Karl Barth, *Die Lehre vom Worte Gottes* (München: Kaiser, 1927), p. 329.

152. Kraemer also influenced Bavinck in terms of his departures from Barth, e.g., when on the basis of Scripture he argued, contrary to Barth, for a link between religious awareness and general revelation.

ognized the importance of Barth's emphasis and agreed wholly with this strict orientation toward Scripture.[153] Likewise, while Bavinck refers only summarily to **Emil Brunner**, there are clear similarities between Brunner's notion of the divine-human relationship as dialectical and Bavinck's concept of it as "dialogical."[154] It is possible, in this regard, that Brunner had more of an influence on Bavinck than the latter admitted.[155]

From the beginning of his missiological career, Bavinck had intensive contact with the Reformed missionary theologian **Hendrik Kraemer**. They had known each other since their student days, but became better acquainted in Solo, Indonesia, where, between 1930 and 1934, Kraemer introduced Bavinck to the secrets of Javanese literature and mysticism. Bavinck's 1934 publication, *Christus en de Mystiek van het Oosten,* was at least in part a fruit of Kraemer's tutelage. At a later stage, Kraemer had a decisive influence on Bavinck's theology of religion. Kraemer's study, *The Christian Message in a Non-Christian World,* written for the International Missionary Conference in Tambaram (1938), led Bavinck to alter his understanding of other religions: he shifted from a more psychological to a radical theological approach. Conversely, Kraemer appreciated the way Bavinck, with his psychological insight, interpreted Romans 1:18ff.[156]

Bavinck's Theology of Mission

Bavinck's theology of mission began by interaction with his Dutch Reformed predecessors; he then closely engaged other, particularly Protestant, missionary theologians at home and abroad.

Bavinck spoke appreciatively of the first Reformed theologian to elabo-

---

153. Cf. J. H. Bavinck, *Religieus Besef,* p. 156; *JHBR,* p. 271.

154. Cf. Emil Brunner, *Natur und Gnade* (Tübingen: Mohr, 1934) and *Der Mensch im Widerspruch: Die Christliche Lehre vom Wahren und vom Wirklichen Menschen* (Zürich: Zwingli-Verlag, 1941). For Brunner there is continuity in the divine-human relationship in consequence of the fact that man as *imago Dei* is always orientated toward God and possesses "Wortmächtigkeit" or "Sprachfähigkeit" vis-à-vis God, which makes it possible to speak with people about God. But this relationship also exhibits discontinuity, which lies in the fact that it exists in a loveless or hostile world and that man answers God accordingly.

155. An indication of this is Bavinck's somewhat offhand but, in view of its context, nevertheless important question: "Or is it . . . better to speak only of 'Wortmächtigkeit,' but then what do we mean by that?" J. H. Bavinck, *Religieus Besef,* p. 160; *JHBR,* p. 275.

156. Cf. Hendrik Kraemer, *Religion and Christian Faith* (Philadelphia: Westminster, 1957), pp. 79-81.

rate a number of missionary principles, **Gisbertus Voetius**.[157] Voetius's authority in the *GKN* became evident at the Synod of Middelburg in 1896, where the denomination laid out a biblical view of mission on the basis of his thought.[158] Voetius influenced Bavinck on five points. First, Voetius's theocentricity, which cast mission as primarily God's work and secondarily that of the church, always remained basic for Bavinck. Second, Bavinck followed Voetius's ecclesiocentric conception of mission, rendering mission not the affair of special societies or sodalities but a task that belonged exclusively to the church.[159] Third, Bavinck adopted Voetius's understanding of the threefold aim of missions: the conversion of unbelievers *(conversio gentilium)*, the establishment of the church *(plantatio ecclesiae)*, and the glorification of God *(gloria gratiae divinae)*.[160] Fourth, Voetius made a distinction between the ecclesiastical missionary work of ordained ministers of the Word and the ancillary services of medical personnel and teachers. This distinction was reflected in Bavinck's distinction between the *cardinal* ministry of mission, consisting of the proclamation of the gospel, and *auxiliary* missionary ministries, including medical care, education, and social services. Fifth, particularly under the influence of Abraham Kuyper, Bavinck gave Voetius's *theologia elenctica*[161] a prominent place in his handbook on missiology.[162]

The basic guidelines that the *GKN* drew up at the **Synod of Middelburg** in 1896 influenced Bavinck's missionary reflection from start to finish. His writing contains scores of references to the *Acts* of this Synod, and he ex-

---

157. Cf. J. H. Bavinck, *Zendingswetenschap*, pp. 8, 21; ET: *Science of Missions*, pp. xiv, 6; *Zending*, p. 31. For Voetius's writings on the theology of mission, see Huibert A. van Andel, *De Zendingsleer van Gisbertus Voetius* (Kampen: J. H. Kok, 1912); Jan A. B. Jongeneel, "Voetius' Zendingstheologie: de Eerste Protestantse Zendingstheologie," in Johannes van Oort et al., *De Onbekende Voetius: Voordrachten Wetenschappelijk Symposium Utrecht 3 Maart 1989* (Kampen: J. H. Kok, 1989), p. 123; ET: "The Missiology of Gisbertus Voetius: The First Comprehensive Protestant Theology of Missions," trans. John Bolt, *Calvin Theological Journal* 26 (1991): 47-79.

158. Cf. Jongeneel, "The Missiology of Gisbertus Voetius," p. 74; Van Andel, *Voetius*, pp. 142-43.

159. Cf. J. H. Bavinck, *Zending in een Wereld in Nood*, pp. 32ff. Bavinck points out here that it was not actually Voetius but Adrianus Saravia (1531-1613) who was the first Protestant theologian to argue on the basis of the missionary mandate in Matt. 28:18-20 that mission is a church matter; cf. also J. H. Bavinck, *Science of Missions*, pp. 57-62.

160. Cf. J. H. Bavinck, *Science of Missions*, pp. 155-59.

161. Cf. Jongeneel, "The Missiology of Gisbertus Voetius," p. 53, n. 12; Van Andel, *Voetius*, p. 121, n. 8.

162. Cf. J. H. Bavinck, *Science of Missions*, pp. 221-72.

pressed great appreciation for "the depth of insight" they reflected.[163] At the same time he recognized that these guidelines were a product of their era and thus subjected them to critical discussion from a biblical-theological point of view. He especially objected to the Synod's assumption about the possible presence of elements of truth in non-Christian religions and to its teaching that the so-called auxiliary missionary services merely served as preparation for the gospel. Bavinck also interacted fruitfully with the *GKN* scholars who followed him in the field. Over the years, particularly a number of his former doctoral students — J. Verkuyl, J. Blauw, A. G. Honig, and J. van den Berg — made significant contributions studying missiology, as Bavinck noted in regularly referencing them in his publications.

The most important figure for Bavinck's missions theology outside his own tradition was **Gustav Warneck**. Bavinck called Warneck's *Evangelische Missionslehre* (1892) "one of the most important sources for the academic study of mission,"[164] and stated that Warneck's missionary research "has exercised a great influence upon all who have subsequently dedicated themselves to the study of the theory of mission."[165] There are obvious similarities between the two, particularly with respect to the biblical foundation of mission.[166] Nonetheless, Bavinck was critical of Warneck on two core issues. He disagreed with Warneck's notion of a historical and ethnological basis for mission, and he disagreed with Warneck's belief that, in practice, the missionary task can be sufficiently carried out by an active, mission-minded fellowship within the church, an *ecclesiola in ecclesia*. Bavinck flatly rejected this idea: "The Bible knows nothing of an inner circle within the church having a special calling to assume responsibility for mission."[167]

Beyond Warneck, Bavinck's oeuvre demonstrates thorough familiarity with the works of other leading Protestant and Roman Catholic missiologists such as the Netherlanders Johannes C. Hoekendijk, Albert C. Kruyt, and Barend M. Schuurman; the Germans Walter Freytag, Bruno Gutmann, Karl Hartenstein, Walter Holsten, Christian Keysser, Julius Richter, Joseph Schmidlin, and Johannes Thauren; the Britons William Carey, Roland Allen, G. E. Phillips, Stephen Neill, and M. A. C. Warren; the Dutch-American Harry R. Boer; the Indian Vengal Chakkarai; and the Japanese Toyohiko Kagawa. While it is difficult to discern the influence these figures had on

---

163. Cf. Bavinck's foreword to Kuyper, *Historisch Document*, pp. i-iii.
164. J. H. Bavinck, *Zending*, p. 31.
165. J. H. Bavinck, *Science of Missions*, p. 7.
166. J. H. Bavinck, *Science of Missions*, pp. 71, 299.
167. J. H. Bavinck, *Science of Missions*, pp. 58-59.

Bavinck, or to determine precisely where he distinguished between their perceptions and his own, their thinking helped shape and sharpen his own positions.

Bavinck and Ecumenical Missionary Theology

The awareness of the need for ecumenical cooperation in missions in the later nineteenth century led to the organization of the first international missionary conference at Edinburgh in 1910 and to the establishment of the permanent International Missionary Council (IMC) thereafter. During Bavinck's lifetime, the IMC organized a series of additional international missionary conferences: at Jerusalem in 1928; Tambaram, India, in 1938; Whitby, Canada, in 1947; Willingen, Germany, in 1952; Achimota, Ghana, in 1958-59; and Mexico City in 1963.

Bavinck acknowledged that mission should be approached ecumenically both for the credibility of the gospel and for the advantages derived from working cooperatively.[168] Though he recognized the tendency of ecumenical conferences to produce disparate views and statements, he considered the diversity of such conferences to be a great strength. In response to the founding of the WCC in 1948, he offered the following evaluation of ecumenical meetings: "In short, a process of fermentation takes place that often continues for many years. Therefore, it is very naïve for some, with a certain air of condescension, to look down upon such international gatherings as something not worth the time and money. Those who talk in this way display a sore lack of vision with respect to the supranational character of the Church and the tremendous strengths revealed in the life of the various churches."[169]

Yet Bavinck always responded to conference themes in terms of his own principles. Thus, in regard to the *missio Dei*, he subscribed wholeheartedly to the statement made at Willingen in 1952 that the Trinitarian God is "a missionary God." "Out of the depths of His love for us, the Father has sent forth His own beloved Son to reconcile all things to Himself, that we and all men might, through the Spirit, be made one in Him with the Father in that perfect love which is the very nature of God."[170] The importance of a Trini-

---

168. Cf. J. H. Bavinck, *Science of Missions,* pp. 199-204.

169. J. H. Bavinck, "De Vergadering," p. 276; cf. also J. H. Bavinck, *Zending,* p. 200, where Bavinck terms ecumenical reflection and cooperation "a cause for joy."

170. Norman Goodall, ed., *Missions Under the Cross: Address Delivered at the Enlarged*

tarian foundation, Bavinck noted, had been affirmed already at the *GKN* Synod of Middelburg in 1896. Likewise, Bavinck welcomed the generally accepted notion in the ecumenical movement of *missio ecclesiae* — that mission belonged to the very essence of the church — as commensurate with the *GKN* understanding.[171] Bavinck firmly rejected, however, the view that grew up in post-Willingen missionary theology under the influence of J. C. Hoekendijk. In this conception the church gradually came to be seen as a "function of the apostolate," and *missio ecclesiae* became defined in terms of the coming of God's kingdom rather than as the task of church-planting.[172] For Bavinck the *raison d'être* of the church was not defined exclusively by the apostolate but also by its doxological calling and nurturing task.[173] The advent of God's kingdom was to be realized through the conversion of people to the Christian faith and the planting of the church.[174]

Although not everyone agreed with Hoekendijk, after Willingen many missionary theologians began to explicate the concept of *missio ecclesiae* within the eschatological framework of the already and not-yet of God's kingdom. It is striking that, from this time on, Bavinck's missiology does bear traces of this emphasis. He not only began to use the term "Kingdom of God" more frequently (in *Inleiding in de Zendingswetenschap*, published just two years after Willingen, he even included it in his definition of mission), but he also expressed appreciation that "the eschatological moment is being given a place of great importance in more recent thinking on mission."[175]

In terms of *church partnership*, the IMC conference at Jerusalem in 1928 made great strides with respect to the perception and clarification of the relationship between "sending churches" and "mission field." Traditional nomenclature was replaced with the new designations of "older" and "younger" churches; employing the terminology of partnership indicated the fundamental equality of the two types of churches.[176] At Whitby in 1947 the term was expanded to "partnership in obedience." Since the *GKN* had al-

---

Meeting of the Committee of the International Missionary Council at Willingen in Germany, 1952 (London: Edinburgh House Press, 1953), pp. 189ff.

171. Cf. J. H. Bavinck, *Science of Missions*, p. 59.

172. Cf. Wind, *Zending*, 1: 221ff.

173. Cf. J. H. Bavinck, *Science of Missions*, pp. 68-69; it is clear that Bavinck was reacting here to both Kraemer and the discussions that took place at and subsequent to the International Missionary Conference held in Willingen in 1952.

174. Cf. J. H. Bavinck, *Science of Missions*, pp. 155ff.

175. J. H. Bavinck, *Science of Missions*, p. 50.

176. Cf. Wind, *Zending*, 1: 77; J. H. Bavinck, *Science of Missions*, p. 319.

ready declared at Middelburg that churches in the mission field were equal to sending churches, Bavinck adopted these new terms without reservation. He said: "Both [younger and older churches] must try to think in terms of a higher, more ecumenical, more catholic perspective: namely, that they are doing the mission work together in service of the same Lord and King."[177]

On the other hand, the Jerusalem conference also defined a "comprehensive missionary approach," which consisted of proclamation, education, medical care, and social-economic aid. From this point on, it became customary to speak of mission as having a four-dimensional character that embraced the whole of life.[178] Whereas the Jerusalem convention directed concern mainly toward change at the level of microstructures, the delegates at Tambaram in 1938 emphasized the need to transform the macrostructures of human society as well.[179] A number of observers in the *GKN* immediately criticized this proposition;[180] Bavinck, too, had his doubts about it. He did not reject the notion of a "comprehensive approach" as such — in fact, he made use of this concept in his writings — but he worried that the four-dimensional approach could easily lead to an attenuation of the decisive significance of the proclamation of the gospel in mission.[181]

The ecumenical movement also had to consider a theological response to non-Christian religions; especially at Tambaram, conference participants were divided over the "continuity and discontinuity" between Christianity and other religions, and on a proper approach to interreligious relationships.[182] Bavinck was deeply involved in these conversations, which spurred his further thinking on the topic. He made a modest contribution to the discussion in the form of a booklet, *The Faith by Which the Church Lives*,[183] in which he delineated the model of divine revelation vis-à-vis that of the cosmic apprehension of life. In the process he was drawn to take a more theological rather than psychological approach to these issues.

177. Cf. J. H. Bavinck, *Science of Missions*, pp. 207ff.

178. J. H. Bavinck, *Science of Missions*, p. 108.

179. Cf. Wind, *Zending*, 1: 77, 152.

180. Cf. e.g., Huibert A. van Andel, "De conferentie op de Olijfberg," *De Macedoniër* 23 (1929): 72. Van Andel wrote: "Mission as proclamation of the gospel plants the seed in people's hearts from which a Christian social and political life can take its rise, but it does not provide an agenda for social reform or a program of political action."

181. J. H. Bavinck, *Science of Missions*, pp. 107ff.

182. Cf. Wind, *Zending*, 1: 71ff., and Jerald D. Gort, "Van Edinburgh 1910 naar San Antonio 1989, Een Doorlopend Verhaal," *Wereld en Zending* 18, no. 4 (1989): 26off.

183. This booklet, which can found in the archives of the WCC in Geneva, also appeared in Dutch, titled "Het Geloof Waaruit de Kerk Left," *De Opwekker* 82 (1937): 520-47.

4. Religious Consciousness in Biblical Perspective

The question of the relationship between religious experience and God's revelation in Christ was *the* theme that governed the whole of Bavinck's missionary theology.[184] This question goes to the essence of missions and governs the whole methodology of missionary work. Bavinck's understanding of religion evolved gradually, in two distinct phases. Initially, he took his departure from the conceptual resources of the psychology of religion, which he then tried to substantiate theologically. Later on, he reversed his approach: biblical-theological inquiry became his primary concern, and out of that concern he began to elucidate the psychological processes involved in the emergence of religiosity. This shift resulted from Bavinck's reflection on Kraemer's *The Christian Message in a Non-Christian World*, a book that can be summarized in a single statement: Revelation in Christ is not the fulfillment of all religious aspirations; rather, it constitutes God's judgment over these endeavors, and it precipitates radical conversion.

As Bavinck's psychological phase is treated thoroughly in another place,[185] we focus here on Bavinck's second approach, also because of its enduring theological value. Bavinck wrestled most with two subjects in this regard, *general revelation* and *religious consciousness*, but approached both under his basic principle of submission to Scripture.

Religion as a Response to General Revelation

Bavinck put the issue in a pointed question: "Where does religion originate, with man or with God? What is religion actually? Is it a word, an attitude toward life, a conviction, a collection of thoughts and sentiments born in the human heart? Or does it consist, in its deepest essence, of an answering, a reply to what God said first, a response to what God did first, a reaction to God's action?"[186] Concepts of the origin and essence of religious consciousness can never be proved scientifically, he maintained, but can only be pos-

---

184. J. van den Berg, "The Legacy of Johan Herman Bavinck," p. 173; cf. also Johan Herman Bavinck, *The Impact of Christianity on the Non-Christian World* (Grand Rapids: Eerdmans, 1948), p. 81, where Bavinck refers to this as the "ruling problem for missiology."

185. Paul J. Visser, *Heart for the World, Heart for the Gospel: The Life and Thought of a Reformed Pioneer Missiologist Johan Herman Bavinck [1985-1964]* (Eugene, OR: Wipf & Stock, 2003), pp. 105-13.

186. J. H. Bavinck, *Religieus Besef,* p. 112; ET: *JHBR,* p. 234.

ited on the basis of presuppositions. When speaking of religious consciousness we touch on the deepest foundations of human existence, foundations that humanity is unable to fathom. The entire cosmos, our being and our inner life, is rooted in mystery. This does not render them unfit for academic investigation; on the contrary, "whoever does not experience that mystery is not yet ready for real scientific endeavor."[187]

Bavinck endorsed Kraemer's thesis that, philosophically speaking, the theological approach to religion is as valid as that of the history and phenomenology of religion. Since the latter do not operate without "prescientific" opinions and choices, the theological approach cannot be disqualified for its own subjective biases.[188] Moreover, the "scientific" approach includes another presupposition, namely, that religion is nothing more than a historical phenomenon and that the deepest questions of life are unanswerable. For the Christian, a foundational presupposition is the absolute truth of God's revelation in Scripture. This implies that human beings must listen to God. God alone can help us understand the religious consciousness — what it is, where it comes from, and where it ends.[189] This belief is more than a subjective value or a choice that could be exchanged at will for another; rather, it is a result of the witness of the Holy Spirit in our hearts and is, therefore, in its essence, of the highest objectivity.[190]

Within this understanding of the primacy of Scripture, Bavinck moved on to consider the missiologically significant issues around the concept of general revelation. He began on a traditional Reformed understanding of the term. God does not abandon the fallen human race but reveals himself to them. "It should be noted that all human persons, no matter how deeply they have fallen or how far they have gone astray, remain within the reach of God's general revelation."[191] Further, "The history of mankind is more than just a long account of what man has done, created and invented; its deepest mystery is the story of God's concern with man and man's response to God's

187. J. H. Bavinck, *Religieus Besef*, p. 110; ET: *JHBR*, p. 232.

188. Johan Herman Bavinck, "Religie en het Christelijk Geloof," *Bezinning* 12 (1957): 66-67. Cf. Hendrik Kraemer, *Religion and the Christian Faith* (Cambridge: James Clarke Co., 1956), p. 143.

189. J. H. Bavinck, *Religieus Besef*, p. 110; ET: *JHBR*, p. 232.

190. Johan Herman Bavinck, *De Boodschap van Christus en de Niet-Christelijke Religies* (Kampen: J. H. Kok, 1940), pp. 80-81. Ed. note: These pages are not included in the translation in this volume.

191. J. H. Bavinck, *Science of Missions*, p. 227.

revelation."[192] This truth is evident in Scripture: while it may seem as if, in his concern for the nation of Israel, God abandoned the other nations to their fate, this is by no means the case. God continued to deal with the other peoples.[193] In this regard, Bavinck referred to Job 33:14-18, John 1:4-9, Acts 14:15-17, Acts 17:26, 27, and especially Romans 1:19, 20.[194] For Bavinck, the last pericope constituted the most important testimony on human religious consciousness; he subjected it to close exegesis, and it formed the enduring basis of his thought on general revelation.[195]

Based on Scripture, Bavinck came to the conclusion that human life is never two-dimensional but always includes a third dimension in one form or another. Besides our fellowship with other human beings and with the cosmos, we also have a permanent fellowship with God, even when we are not aware of it. Human life consists of a continual dialogue with God, a conversation that God continues to initiate. This I-Thou relation comprises the core of our existence.[196]

Bavinck rejected the meaning given to the concept of general revelation throughout much of the history of theology. He did not consider it to be a disclosure of divine truths discovered by reason but a person-directed, relevant, impinging expression of God's will. "When the Bible speaks of 'general revelation' . . . it is divine concern for men collectively and individually. God's deity and eternal power are evident; they overwhelm man; they strike him suddenly in moments when he thought they were far away. They creep up on him; even though man does his best to escape them, they do not let go of him."[197] This definition was close to Kraemer's, who similarly wrote that revelation is not an object but an action, a divine movement.[198]

General revelation is always concrete and real: "It often pounces on man, as it were, suddenly confronting him with the reality that God exists

192. Johan Herman Bavinck, *Church between Temple and Mosque* (Grand Rapids: Eerdmans, 1966), p. 19.

193. J. H. Bavinck, *Science of Missions*, pp. 12-13.

194. Cf. Visser, *Heart for the World*, pp. 120-23.

195. Cf. J. H. Bavinck, *Religieus Besef*, p. 122; ET: *JHBR*, p. 242.

196. Cf. Johan Herman Bavinck, *Religies en Wereldbeschouwingen in Onze Tijd* (Groningen: Wolters, 1958), p. 137; "De Onbekende God," in Johan Herman Bavinck et al., *Het geloof en Zijn Moeilijkheden* (Wageningen: Zomer & Keuning, 1946), p. 11; ET: *Faith and Its Difficulties*, trans. William B. Eerdmans Sr. (Grand Rapids: Eerdmans, 1959); cf. *Church between Temple and Mosque*, pp. 123-24; *Religieus Besef*, p. 124; ET: *JHBR*, p. 243.

197. Cf. J. H. Bavinck, *Church between Temple and Mosque*, p. 124.

198. Hendrik Kraemer, *The Christian Message in a Non-Christian World* (Grand Rapids: Kregel, 1969), pp. 118-19.

and that, despite all our efforts at resistance, we can never radically push Him away."[199] Thus, at heart general revelation bears an existential character: it is less "an entity appealing to human philosophical instincts" and more "a power that man encounters in the various relationships of his life."[200] This does not mean that elements of scrutiny and reflection are absent in one's encounter with this form of divine self-disclosure. On the contrary, the structured religions demonstrate this reflection.

As to the foundations of general revelation, Bavinck had to pursue the typically Reformed question of whether it was grounded, theologically speaking, in the common grace of the Creator or in the grace of Christ. Calvin was convinced of the first; God both sowed the seed of religion in the human mind and daily disclosed himself in the workmanship of the whole universe. As a consequence, when people open their eyes, they are compelled to see him.[201] Bavinck followed Calvin's line for a long time, based on the notion of God's voice sounding throughout the creation and on God's enduring providence and reign. He believed that, based on his status as Creator, God lays claim to the entire world and maintains full jurisdiction over it. On the Areopagus Paul said that "in Him we live and move and have our being" (Acts 17:28).[202] Yet, in his posthumous book, *The Church Between the Temple and Mosque*, Bavinck adduced a Christological foundation for general revelation instead: "God's self-disclosure in Jesus Christ is the root of His search for man and His ceaseless speaking to him."[203]

Bavinck then moved on to the manner in which God effects his self-disclosure. Its first site was nature, the whole universe. The overwhelming grandeur of creation compels us, as it were, to come to a recognition of God. We do not reach this awareness by means of logic or carefully constructed argumentation but arrive at it directly and spontaneously,[204] as stated in Psalm 19:2-3: "The heavens declare the glory of God; the skies proclaim the work of His hands. Day after day they pour forth speech; night after night

199. J. H. Bavinck, *Religies en Wereldbeschouwingen*, p. 138.
200. J. H. Bavinck, *Religieus Besef*, p. 165; ET: *JHBR*, p. 278.
201. Calvin, *Institutes*, 1.1.1.
202. Cf. J. H. Bavinck, *Religieus Besef*, p. 113; ET: *JHBR*, p. 235; earlier in his life, Bavinck used this text in reference to religious yearnings in the human heart. Cf. Johan Herman Bavinck, *Zielkundige Opstellen* (Bandoeng: Javasche Boekhandel & Drukkerij, 1925), p. 103.
203. J. H. Bavinck, *Church between Temple and Mosque*, p. 19; Bavinck never thoroughly developed this insight, borrowed from Kraemer.
204. Cf. J. H. Bavinck, "De onbekende God," p. 8; *Church between Temple and Mosque*, p. 124.

they display knowledge." This proclamation bears a paradoxical character: "There is no speech, nor are there words; their voice is not heard; yet their voice goes through all the earth, and their words to the end of the world" (vv. 4, 5). This revelation consists of wordless witness; it is a power that enfolds us on all sides in quiet majesty.[205] God meets us in the order of creation, in the seasons, in the wind, in thunder and lightning, and in the "radiant beauty of a glorious summer morning."[206]

Second, God reveals himself in human conscience. "God occupies Himself with man's . . . innermost being. God reminds man again and again that responsibility and guilt do exist."[207] Even though the term "conscience" does not occur in the Old Testament, it has an implied presence there. For example, one could turn to Amos 4:13: "He who . . . declares to man what is his thought . . ." or to Psalm 139, which clearly witnesses to "the presence of God in the depths of our inner life, in [our] conscience."[208] In the New Testament this notion comes to new expression in the writings of Paul, for example, in Romans 2:14, 15: "Indeed, when Gentiles, who do not have the law, do by nature things required by the law, they are a law for themselves, even though they do not have the law, since they show that the requirements of the law are written on their hearts, their consciences also bearing witness, and their thoughts now accusing, now even defending them." This passage also clearly witnesses to the hidden action of God in the human heart.[209] Human self-consciousness, the observing and critical inner eye, originates in this divine action. "Man is always at the same time actor, observer, and judge. He acts, but also knows that he acts, and he also judges what he does." Humans both see themselves and view themselves critically. "In that great mystery of the duality in our consciousness there is something of God."[210]

Finally, God also reveals himself in the history of peoples and individuals. "There are good and bad days, there are all sorts of vicissitudes and fortunes,

205. Cf. Johan Herman Bavinck, "General Revelation and the Non-Christian Religions," *Free University Quarterly* 4 (1955): 53; *JHBR*, p. 107; *Religieus Besef*, p. 114; ET: *JHBR*, p. 235.

206. J. H. Bavinck, *Church between Temple and Mosque*, pp. 123-24; cf. J. H. Bavinck, *Religieus Besef*, p. 114; ET: *JHBR*, p. 235.

207. J. H. Bavinck, *Church between Temple and Mosque*, p. 124.

208. J. H. Bavinck, *Religieus Besef*, pp. 115-16; ET: *JHBR*, pp. 236-37. This exegesis is questionable because in both cases it is said to believers. On the other hand, it says something about the possible ways God can work in the human mind.

209. Cf. Johan Herman Bavinck, *Het Probleem van de Pseudo-Religie en de Algemene Openbaring* (no place name, 1941), pp. 10-11. Strangely, Bavinck did not employ this text in *Religieus Besef en Christelijk Geloof*.

210. J. H. Bavinck, *Religieus Besef*, p. 115; ET: *JHBR*, p. 236.

and in all of them the great Ruler of our lives speaks to us."[211] The Old Testament, in particular, clearly teaches that God is present in world affairs and shows that in human life, fortune and misfortune are tethered to deeds. In this regard, Bavinck cites a number of texts from the book of Proverbs (1:31; 5:22; 14:34) that may seem to have a karma-like ring to them, but which, "in reality, always bear a theological significance": they teach something about God's righteous judgment on the sin that is visible and tangible in personal and public life.[212] "In all punishment," Bavinck contended, "something of God is present; God himself is involved in it. Even when sin seems to bring its own punishment, God still has a hand in it."[213] This is so because we are created with human limits, which we cannot transgress without negative consequences.

As to the instrumental mode of general revelation, Bavinck gave striking emphasis to the pneumatological aspect interior to revelation. That is, people cannot be reached by God's revelation — not even by so-called general revelation — apart from the working of the Spirit. "There is . . . always the silent activity of the Holy Spirit inside [natural] man, even if he resists Him constantly."[214] Bavinck referred to the work of the Holy Spirit more often implicitly than explicitly.[215] For example, "It is true that the majesty of God is universally revealed throughout the entire world, but every time a person begins to see that majesty, every time his eyes are opened to it, that general revelation takes on the character of a highly individual intervention."[216] On this score Bavinck turned away from his uncle Herman, who spoke philosophically about a *principium internum* (interior feeling for God) and *principium externum* (general revelation of God).

General and Special Revelation

Because God reveals himself in a general way to very different characters and in very different circumstances, the content of general revelation varies greatly. This does not mean, Bavinck cautioned, that nothing can be said

---

211. J. H. Bavinck, "De onbekende God," p. 8.

212. J. H. Bavinck, *Religieus Besef*, pp. 116-17; ET: *JHBR*, pp. 237-38.

213. J. H. Bavinck, *Christus en de Mystiek*, p. 186; ET: *JHBR*, p. 373.

214. J. H. Bavinck, *Church between Temple and Mosque*, p. 125.

215. Cf. Johan Herman Bavinck, *Alzoo wies het Woord: Een Studie over den Voortgang van het Evangelie in de Dagen van Paulus* (Baarn: Bosch & Keuning, 1941), p. 186: ". . . I do not wish to deny that the Spirit of God has worked among the heathen more than we often suspect."

216. J. H. Bavinck, *Religieus Besef*, p. 117; ET: *JHBR*, p. 238.

about its substance. In Romans 1:20, Paul speaks about "eternal power" to indicate the Almighty and "divine nature" to indicate the Holy, concepts that manifest themselves in multiple ways and place human beings in a moral relationship with God. On the basis of Romans 1:19 Bavinck argued that general revelation is both overwhelming and very limited. There Paul speaks of "what may be known about God," simultaneously defining the possible knowledge of truth and implying its enormous limitation.[217]

General revelation consists of the great self-manifestation of God, and so, in principle, it cannot be different from special revelation. God does not have two faces; God is One. In a long and beautiful statement Bavinck said: "We must understand that the Ground of the world, out of Whom the overwhelming multitude of suns and stars has been born, is the same as the Regent of our lives who holds us by the hand and leads us forward step by step. And we must learn to see that this Director of our lives, who holds all that ebbing and flowing of our fortunes in His hands, is the same as the God who turned His Face to us in Jesus Christ. We need to learn to understand that the Unknown God is the same as the Known God, Whose holy will to redemption we behold in Jesus Christ."[218]

Yet, Bavinck's Christological approach gave rise to a tremendous tension, because it is difficult to hear the same word spoken in general revelation as is spoken in special revelation. Here Bavinck followed the track laid by Kraemer, who spoke of the "broken and troubled way" in which revelation breaks through "in this fallen world."[219] On this score Bavinck distanced himself from the optimism to which neo-Calvinism was sometimes given regarding the possibility of gaining saving knowledge from general revelation.

Since God deals with every human life for a purpose, Bavinck postulated that the goal of general revelation is to coax a response from us, to provoke us to become religiously active. He appealed repeatedly in this connection to Acts 17:27: "God did this so that men would seek Him and perhaps reach out for Him and find Him. . . ." Whether this goal is achieved, whether the peoples really seek and find God, remains an open question according to Bavinck. Nonetheless, such constitutes God's purpose for the human race. Remarkably, Bavinck does not refer to the other goals often stipulated for general revelation, including keeping the world livable and, with respect to the final clause of Romans 1:20, "so that men are without excuse." John Cal-

---

217. J. H. Bavinck, *Religieus Besef*, p. 122; ET: *JHBR*, p. 242.
218. J. H. Bavinck, "De onbekende God," p. 8.
219. Kraemer, *Christian Message*, p. 120.

vin, who thought that *gloria Dei* was the final aim of all God's actions, emphasized in connection with this verse that God revealed himself, on the one hand, because "the final goal of life rests in the knowledge of God," and on the other, so that men "might be condemned by their own testimony."[220]

From all this it is clear that general and special revelation are intimately connected, for both consist of the self-manifestation of God.[221] Because God and Christ are one, there is a fundamental and material unity between both sources of revelation: both are Christologically qualified.[222] And yet they also differ substantially. General revelation does not have the capacity to bring people to a true knowledge of God, nor does it possess δύςαμις (power) for salvation (Rom. 1:16), which belongs exclusively to the gospel of Jesus Christ. Although God has not left himself without witness, it is only through special revelation that he makes himself known in the "most intimate way possible."[223] Further, general and special revelation align in terms of instrumental mode: it is the Holy Spirit who is active in both forms of divine self-disclosure.[224] Finally, general and special revelation show similarity in essence. Both have the character of God's personal involvement in the lives of fallen human beings.

Without detracting from the basic difference between general and special revelation, however, Bavinck noted that there are "numerous moments in which it is difficult to tell whether one is dealing with *general* or *special* revelation."[225] In the Bible we find accounts of situations in which "God bends himself low, down to the level of heathendom . . . to reveal his judgment to people via dreams, or to make known through the stars that a great King has been born in Israel."[226] Today, too, "in the mission field, we are . . .

---

220. Calvin, *Institutes*, 1.3.1.

221. Cf. J. H. Bavinck, *Religieus Besef*, pp. 180-88; ET: *JHBR*, pp. 291-97.

222. Johan Herman Bavinck, *Levensvragen* (Magelang: Colportage-Boekhandel, 1927), pp. 23-28. Here one finds a striking example of this when Bavinck argues that the principle of service present in the creation order is revealed fully in Christ.

223. Bavinck refers here to Ps. 147:19, 20: "He has revealed His word to Jacob, His laws and decrees to Israel. He has done this for no other nation; they do not know His laws." Also to Eph. 3:5: "The mystery of Christ was not made known to men in other generations, but has now been revealed by the Spirit."

224. This means that general revelation, too, is an act of God in the fullest possible sense, and that the distinction made by H. Bavinck between *revelatio naturalis* and *revelatio supranaturalis* no longer holds for J. H. Bavinck. Cf. *Reformed Dogmatics*, 1: 303.

225. J. H. Bavinck, *Religieus Besef*, p. 180; ET: *JHBR*, p. 291.

226. Johan Herman Bavinck, *Het Woord Voor de Wereld* (Baarn: Bosch & Keuning, 1950), pp. 55-56.

continually confronted by the surprising fact that God leads people to the gospel by means of dreams and visions, and in such cases we constantly ask ourselves whether we are dealing with general revelation or something very special."[227] Thus, Bavinck concluded, general and special revelation can be distinguished but can be divided only with difficulty.

The Paradox of Religious Consciousness

The question of revelation thus raises the question of religious consciousness. If God initiates a dialogue with every human person by means of general revelation, people must have some capacity for hearing God's sound if there is to be a real encounter. The crucial issue is whether such a capacity exists and, if so, what it means. The answer given to this twofold question will be decisive for the entire corpus of missionary theology.[228] Bavinck rightly concluded: "this is where it becomes prickly, here lies the core of the whole problem."[229]

The issue breaks down into several subsidiary questions. First, does humankind have the ability to hear God's sound? Historically in the Reformed tradition, this question was never in doubt; ever since Calvin wrote about a *sensus divinitatis* (feeling for God) and a *semen religionis* (seed of religion), the existence of a human faculty for receiving divine revelation was simply assumed as a philosophical certainty. In Bavinck's time, however, owing to the influence of Barth, the matter had become an open issue. Barth thought that, though it is possible to speak of divine revelation apart from the Word, it is clear from God's revelation in Christ that people have never been able to hear the voice of God "by means of this intelligence."[230] Humans merely hear the voices of the elements of creation, which they wrongly clothe with divine dignity. General revelation does not lead to genuine encounter with God[231] but only to human religion.

227. J. H. Bavinck, *Religieus Besef*, pp. 180-81; ET: *JHBR*, pp. 291-92.

228. Cf. J. H. Bavinck, "General Revelation," p. 49; ET: *JHBR*, p. 100; here Bavinck writes that these questions were of preeminent importance to mission: all depends on the question how one estimates the religion of the people with whom the missionary is working.

229. Bavinck, *Religieus Besef*, p. 168; ET: *JHBR*, p. 281.

230. Karl Barth, *Het Christelijk Openbaringsbegrip*, trans. H. C. Touw (Nijkerk: Callenbach, 1937), pp. 21-22.

231. Johannes Witte, *Die Christus-botschaft und die Religionen* (Göttingen: Vandenhoeck & Ruprecht, 1955), p. 40. Witte summarizes Barth's standpoint here as follows: "Gott hat sich wohl in der Schöpfung und im Gewissen offenbart. Aber die Menschen waren

It was against this backdrop that Bavinck developed his own position. He aligned himself with Kraemer, who stated that "the world is still the creation of God, that God does not abandon the work of His hands, but continues working in it,"[232] so that "the living religions inevitably precipitate the beginning of the drama that takes place between God and man."[233] Bavinck wrote: "I am prepared to go along with Barth's negative assessment of man, but on this one point I am definitely opposed to him. Barth does not understand that man, also fallen man, sinful man, can and may never be conceptualized apart from the revelation of God."[234] Particularly in Romans 1:18ff. Paul repeatedly states that revelation does not merely slide off people's backs but actually reaches them.[235] An "internal religious principle" does exist.

But what kind of capacity is this? Investigation of Bavinck's understanding of the *principium internum* reveals a long, gradual development in his thought. During his psychological phase, and following in the line of Schleiermacher and especially of Otto, Bavinck placed strong emphasis on the *principium internum* as a yearning after God. After coming into contact with Kraemer's radically biblical approach, however, particularly Kraemer's understanding of the anthropological consequences of humanity's fall, Bavinck gradually abandoned this understanding. He came to argue that, theologically speaking, there was no thirst for God originating on the human side. Thus, in 1941 he rejected what he had written in 1928: "Earlier I referred now and again to the concept of *Suchen im Fliehen* [a searching for God while simultaneously fleeing from Him]. Now I would like to express the matter differently. No one seeks God on his or her own, not even one (Rom. 1:11). If there is any kind of seeking anywhere, it exists by reason of the *horismos,* the divine purpose and guidance which does not relinquish its hold on a deeply sunken humankind."[236]

---

infolge ihrer Sünde ausserstande Gott in dieser Offenbarung zu erkennen." (God did reveal himself in creation and in the conscience. But as a result of their sin, people were not in a position to recognize God in this revelation.)

232. Kraemer, *Christian Message,* p. 120.

233. Hendrik Kraemer, *Godsdienst, Godsdiensten en het Christelijk Geloof* (Nijkerk: Callenbach, 1958), p. 161. On this point, the thinking of the father of modern dialectical theology is decidedly un-dialectical and rationalistic. Cf. J. H. Bavinck, *Religie en Christelijk Geloof,* pp. 67-69.

234. J. H. Bavinck, *Religieus Besef,* p. 176.

235. J. H. Bavinck, "General Revelation," p. 53; ET: *JHBR,* p. 107; cf. also J. H. Bavinck, *Church between Temple and Mosque,* p. 120, and *Religieus Besef,* p. 125; ET: *JHBR,* p. 244.

236. J. H. Bavinck, *Probleem van de Pseudo-Religie,* p. 18.

From this time on, Bavinck placed full accent on revelation and spoke extremely cautiously about any "internal principle."[237] He inferred the existence of such an organ from Romans 1:20, where, in his view, its presence is connoted by the Greek passive participle νοούμεϛα (being understood or apprehended). He insisted emphatically that this principle may not be sought via human reason, since the term νοούμεϛα in Romans 1:20 signifies the idea of "becoming aware, sensing, observing, noticing." The combination of νοούμεϛα with the word καθορται (are clearly seen) suggests "an almost visionary happening . . . suddenly man catches sight of things."[238] This seeing is more than a rational process; it pertains to a person in the depths of her being. Just as the eye cannot see itself, the inner principle does not see itself; it may only see God. Even the keenest reflection will never succeed in discovering it.

It seems that, on one hand, Bavinck wished to maintain the notion of an "internal principle" in line with Reformed tradition. On the other hand, he turned more and more to the I-Thou relationship for an explanation of this phenomenon: "Personally, I am inclined to view this one thing as an extremely important matter, namely, that man can assume life solely in the form of communicative interchange. It is only in this way that he can exist as a living person. . . . I am deeply mindful of the fact that man can do no other than speak continually with that Someone who stands before him every day anew."[239] By the time of his last publication on this topic, *The Church Between Temple and Mosque,* Bavinck's view had become purely relational: people do not understand God's revelation on their own account but as a result of "the silent activity of the Holy Spirit inside man."[240] As a reactive being, a person always has to answer to God's wordless speech, "either in a positive or in a negative sense."[241]

We are thus in a paradoxical position. If general revelation does not simply slide off our backs "like a raindrop glides off a waxy tree leaf," it turns each of us into a knower; as Bavinck put it: "The juridical position of man is that of one who knows."[242] At the same time the Bible paints a picture of humankind as people who do *not* know, as it is written in Acts 17:23: "What you

237. Cf. J. H. Bavinck, *Probleem van de Pseudo-Religie,* p. 7.
238. J. H. Bavinck, *Religieus Besef,* pp. 168-70; ET: *JHBR,* pp. 281-83; cf. also *Church between Temple and Mosque,* p. 120.
239. J. H. Bavinck, *Religieus Besef,* p. 170; ET: *JHBR,* p. 283.
240. J. H. Bavinck, *Church between Temple and Mosque,* p. 125.
241. J. H. Bavinck, *Religieus Besef,* pp. 19, 32; ET: *JHBR,* pp. 157, 167-68.
242. J. H. Bavinck, *Religieus Besef,* p. 171; ET: *JHBR,* p. 283.

worship as unknown. . . ." The paradox resides in humanity itself. Thus the question becomes: Who is man? It is not psychology — valuable though it may be — but theology that must supply the decisive answer to this question, Bavinck averred.[243] To cultivate right judgment, one must be freed from the spell of self-speculation and assume a listening stance vis-à-vis God. How does God view us? How does he judge our lives? It is only through faith in the Word of God that the motifs of the embroidery that is the work of our lives can be finally explained.

Genesis 3 speaks of a pervasive, decisive act by which humanity became what it now is. It speaks of an act of doubting God's word, of greedily heeding the slanderous talk of the evil one, of exiting the safe confines of the knowledge that God is love, and of desiring to be like God.[244] Since then, all people have rebelled against God down to the deepest layers of their existence. There is no "unsullied piece of ground" of which we can say, "here is the inner sanctum." From our created condition as a "son of God" we have degenerated into a "slave of demonic powers."[245] In this regard, Bavinck turned to Romans 3:9-20, where the reality of man's condition is trenchantly portrayed.[246] He concluded that a biblical anthropology can do nothing but recognize that, at the integrating core of our being, we are rebels who are frightened of God, avoid God, push God away, and resist God.[247]

Knowers who do not know, perceivers who does not perceive: that is the human plight.[248] But even that does not end the story. Bavinck dug deeper by explicating two particular phrases from Romans 1:18ff.: "men who suppress the truth by their wickedness" (v. 18); "they exchanged the truth of God for a lie" (v. 25). He exegeted these words literally but also analyzed them from a psychological angle. Thus, whenever God's truth grasps us, we grasp that truth but subject it to a process of suppression (κατεχόϛτως). The term connotes violence, the idea of "pushing something down" or "holding some-

---

243. Cf. J. H. Bavinck, "Het raadsel mensch," in J. H. Bavinck, J. de Groot, and M. J. A. de Vrijer, *Het geloof en zijn Moeilijkheden* (Wageningen, 1940), p. 65. Bavinck writes that "psychology can unravel a few threads from a tangled skein, it can open our eyes to the knots, but it can never disclose the deepest grounds of man's condition or behaviour."

244. Cf. J. H. Bavinck, *Woord Voor de Wereld*, p. 181.

245. J. H. Bavinck, *Woord Voor de Wereld*, pp. 161, 163.

246. Strangely enough, nowhere in his biblical argumentation does Bavinck refer to Rom. 5:12-21, where Paul forges an explicit link between the "trespass of the one man" and the sin of all.

247. Cf. J. H. Bavinck, *Science of Missions*, p. 122.

248. J. H. Bavinck, *Religieus Besef*, p. 172; ET: *JHBR*, p. 285.

thing under," as a soldier might hold the head of his opponent under water.[249] Bavinck equated this term with the contemporary psychological concept of "repression," which taught, much like traditional Calvinism, that human cognitive functions operate throughout the whole of the personality; these do not function on their own but are inherently connected to emotional and voluntary forces.[250] A person never views life with complete objectivity; we perceive what interests us, we discern what we want to discern, or, obversely, do not see what we do not wish to see.[251] As a rule, Bavinck noted, while this repression takes place unconsciously, it is very real. Furthermore, it occurs so immediately and spontaneously that, at the very moment one sees, one no longer sees, and at the very moment one knows, one no longer knows.[252] By his use of the term *in unrighteousness* (εν αδικία — the preposition "in" being used here to mean "within the sphere of"), Bavinck signified the immoral stance that fallen humanity continually assumes vis-à-vis God. Repression, therefore, originates from our "hidden, invariably unvoiced, often totally unconscious motive to stand in moral opposition to God."[253]

Immediately connected to this repression is the act of "substitution," the Greek terms for which, ἤλλαξαν (αλλασσω) and μετήλλαξας (μεταλλάσσω), occur three times in Romans 1 (vv. 23, 25, 26). Bavinck observed that substitution is also a well-known principle in psychology; by using this word, Paul "once again touches upon one of those very remarkable phenomena to which current psychology points."[254] Psychology has shown that stifled impressions and repressed experiences continue to operate in a person's unconscious life: they remain strong and try to reassert themselves again and again, succeeding in showing every now and again that they still exist. These insights can be applied theologically, Bavinck argued: though God's truth may be suppressed, it has not been destroyed. On the contrary, it continues to press itself upon the

249. Cf. J. H. Bavinck, *Probleem van de Pseudo-Religie*, p. 8.

250. J. H. Bavinck, *Probleem van de Pseudo-Religie*, p. 15.

251. J. H. Bavinck, *Church between Temple and Mosque*, p. 118. Bavinck cites Webster's *New Collegiate Dictionary* definition of "repression" as the process by which unacceptable desires or impulses are excluded from consciousness and thus being denied direct satisfaction are left to operate in the unconscious, adding that post-Freudian psychology shows that impulses or desires that are repressed may be very valuable.

252. Cf. J. H. Bavinck, *Church between Temple and Mosque*, pp. 118-22, and *Religieus Besef*, pp. 172-79; ET: *JHBR*, pp. 285-89.

253. J. H. Bavinck, *Religieus Besef*, p. 173; ET: *JHBR*, p. 285.

254. J. H. Bavinck, *Church between Temple and Mosque*, p. 121.

conscious mind in fragmentary ways; it "forms nuclei around which conceptual complexes of a totally deviant nature crystallize."[255]

While Bavinck maintained that, in principle, all religions must be judged with this perspective, he noticed different degrees of repression and substitution among their practitioners. Some people have so repressed the truth that they consider God unreal and never have devoted a thought to him.[256] In other cases, the process of repression moves with much greater difficulty or breaks down completely. "Sometimes it appears that God's presence obtrudes so self-evidently in a person's life that he or she is totally incapable of escaping it, is given no chance to repress it, is simply overwhelmed by it."[257] Bavinck wrote: "We meet figures in the history of non-Christian religions who feel that God wrestled with them in a very particular way. We still notice traces of the process of suppression and substitution, but occasionally we observe a far greater influence of God than in other human religions. The history of religion does not present a monotonous picture of only folly and degeneration. There are culminating points in this history, especially in Buddhism and Islam."[258] This moderation of the process of repression and exchange occurs "not because certain human beings are much better than others, but because every now and then divine compassion interferes, compassion which keeps man from suppressing and substituting the truth completely."[259]

On Bavinck's reading, Romans 1 reveals that there is "something thoroughly tragic" about the process of suppression and substitution. The passive expressions in verse 21 ("their thinking became futile and their foolish hearts were darkened") indicate that this is a process that escapes us at a given moment, a mechanism over which we have no control. Not only are we rebels, we are simultaneously victims, unable to stop ourselves. We are both responsible for our suppression and simultaneously unable to resist it.

The continual process of rejection and replacement of God's truth causes people to become less and less receptive to general revelation: "The aerial of man's heart can no longer receive the wave length of God's voice,

---

255. J. H. Bavinck, *Religieus Besef,* p. 179; ET: *JHBR,* p. 290.

256. J. H. Bavinck, *Religieus Besef,* p. 179; ET: *JHBR,* p. 290.

257. J. H. Bavinck, *Religieus Besef,* p. 174; ET: *JHBR,* p. 286.

258. J. H. Bavinck, *Church between Temple and Mosque,* pp. 125-26. In "General Revelation," pp. 51-52; ET: *JHBR,* pp. 140-42, he takes into account the possibility (Buddhism) and the reality (Islam) of the influence of special revelation (Scripture) at the basis of these religions.

259. J. H. Bavinck, *Church between Temple and Mosque,* p. 126; cf. J. H. Bavinck, *Religieus Besef,* p. 174; ET: *JHBR,* p. 286.

even though it surrounds him on all sides. In his innermost heart, he has turned away from God and God has now vanished from sight."[260] This dramatic aspect of human defiance is clearly reflected in the thrice-repeated statement, "God gave them over" in verses 24, 26, and 28, itself harkening back to "the wrath of God" in verse 18.

In short, Bavinck agreed in principle with the Calvinist tradition,[261] but he worked its idea out in an unique way, through the combination of theology, anthropology, and psychology.[262]

The Magnetic Points in Religious Consciousness

From the previous discussion, it is clear that the origin of religious consciousness is not primarily human but divine. Moving to the human side, however, Bavinck noted four ancillary factors that play a role in the formation and nature of religious life. First, he spoke of the proto-word revelation, a primeval divine self-disclosure that took place before humanity became defiled and tainted and that remained in human memory with its own dynamic.[263] Second, he pointed to the possibility of the radiation or inflow of special revelation into different religions at different times and places: "the interesting datum that the non-Christian religions are not truly religions that bloomed fully outside the sphere of special revelation, but that a certain

260. J. H. Bavinck, *Church between Temple and Mosque*, pp. 120-21.

261. Cf. Calvin, *Institutes*, 1.1.3-5. In 1.5.15 Calvin concludes: "It is therefore in vain that so many burning lamps shine for us in the workmanship of the universe to show forth the glory of its Author. . . . Surely they strike some sparks, but before their fuller light shines forth, these are smothered. . . . They do not cease on this account to follow their own ways, that is, their fatal errors." Cf. J. H. Bavinck, *Religieus Besef*, p. 146; ET: *JHBR*, p. 262.

262. Johannes van den Berg, "The Legacy of J. H. Bavinck," *International Bulletin of Missionary Research* 7, no. 4 (October 1983): 174 and Johannes Verkuyl, *De Kern van Het Christelijk Geloof* (Kampen: J. H. Kok, 1992), p. 17. His student J. van den Berg called Bavinck's exegesis of Rom. 1:18ff. "a masterly analysis," and J. Verkuyl said that Bavinck "provided a profound analysis of the process of enlightenment, repression, and substitution." For a discussion on whether this interpretation of Rom. 1 is too colored by psychological categories, see Visser, *Heart for the Gospel*, pp. 150-52.

263. Cf. J. H. Bavinck, *Christus en de Mystiek*, p. 3; "Het problem der 'Anknüpfung' bij de Evangelieverkondiging," in René van Woudenberg, ed., *J. H. Bavinck: Een Keuze uit Zijn Werk* (Kampen: J. H. Kok, 1991), p. 65; "Phaenomenologische Classificatie der Religieuze Structuren," *Vox Theologica* 13 (1941-1942): 28-32; *Zending*, p. 70; *Probleem van de Pseudo-Religie*, p. 13; "General Revelation," p. 51; ET: *JHBR*, p. 105; and *Introduction to the Science of Missions*, pp. 234-36.

measure of influx has to be regarded as a probability in several cases."[264] Bavinck thought this possibility definitely existed in the modern period. Third, Bavinck called attention to the role played by demonism in all non-Christian religion: "An endless multitude of men and women all over the world are daily oppressed by the powers of . . . darkness," as is often witnessed by the frequency with which newly converted Christians themselves mention the devil (see, e.g., Eph. 2:2, 3).[265] Finally, Bavinck noticed that the answers given in response to God's revelation are always developed within an existing religious context. People are always part of a community and not merely isolated individuals. For example, people obtain their view of God from their parents and grow up within a particular religious situation. Therefore, religious context exercises great influence upon a person's response to God's revelatory call.[266]

Moreover, in the complex diversity of religions Bavinck distinguished "a sort of framework within which the religious thought of humankind must move. . . . There appear to be certain intersections around which all sorts of ideas crystallize . . . so-called *magnetic points* to which the religious thinking of mankind is irresistibly attracted."[267] He delineated — again in a very unique way — five of these magnetic points. Each of them corresponded to a primal human question.

1. *A sense of belonging to the whole; an awareness of cosmic relationship.* Human beings have always felt a mysterious affinity with the totality of things; we are given meaning in life because we are each "a tiny cell in the colossal body of the universe" and part of a divine world.[268] All of this is reflected in the idea of macrocosm (the universe) and microcosm (human life) bound up with each other and yielding an ethic of harmony: human behavior must be brought into conformity with cosmic laws.

2. *A sense of transcendent norms.* In all contexts, people realize that what is, is "not the way it's supposed to be."[269] In everything we think and do, we are confronted with the mysterious awareness that we could have acted differently, that we had a choice. Everywhere in the world, people know themselves to be subjected to norms and rules, norms that they feel "have a divine

---

264. Cf. J. H. Bavinck, "General Revelation," pp. 51-52; ET: *JHBR*, pp. 105-6.

265. J. H. Bavinck, *The Impact of Christianity*, p. 151.

266. Cf. J. H. Bavinck, *Church between Temple and Mosque*, pp. 19, 124.

267. J. H. Bavinck, *Religieus Besef*, p. 103; ET: *JHBR*, p. 226.

268. J. H. Bavinck, *Church between Temple and Mosque*, p. 54.

269. Cf. the title of Cornelius Plantinga Jr.'s book, *Not the Way It's Supposed to Be: A Breviary of Sin* (Grand Rapids: Eerdmans, 1995).

origin" and hence constitute "a divine institution."[270] This sense of norm is often closely identified with the cosmic order. Adherence to or disregard of norms bears far-reaching consequences for humankind and the cosmos.

3. *A sense of existence being governed by a providential or destining power.* At all times and in all places, people have experienced a tension between deed and destiny: people *lead* their lives, but they are also *led*.[271] We are continually confronted with powers that are far greater than ourselves, and that confrontation always registers as a religious reality. If they live in an all-embracing cosmic whole, people will tend to be passive rather than active in response.

4. *A recognition of the need for redemption.* As people have always been aware that life is not what it was meant to be, they have unremittingly sought ways to rectify this deficiency, to elevate life to a higher plane so as to live in true fullness. People have a sense of "paradise lost," a deeply rooted feeling that the ties between heaven and earth were severed long ago. In "the time before all times, something must have happened that caused man's struggle with numberless insurmountable difficulties, and especially death."[272] Hence the continual attempts to endow life with "an additional dimension of sacredness" so that it might "be worth living and beneficial."[273] In many religious traditions redemption is closely related to the cosmic whole and consists of the loss of the "I," the forfeiture of all human passion, to the divine order. In religions where "redemption is regarded as a fruit of man's own labor," by contrast, there is a strong emphasis on synergism between man and god.[274]

5. *A sense of relatedness to a Superior or Supreme Power.* In all these facets of religious consciousness, people experience a Higher Power to which their life is subject. The history of religion demonstrates that people have always tried to gain knowledge and lay hold of that Power, the great Unknown behind and under everything, "the deepest being of all being, the hidden, impersonal background of all things."[275] We perceive the "unapproachable distance" of this divine Power,[276] yet simultaneously identify it with the surrounding celestial and natural world — the sun, moon, and stars, various

---

270. J. H. Bavinck, *Religieus Besef,* p. 27; ET: *JHBR,* p. 163; and *Church between Temple and Mosque,* p. 54.

271. J. H. Bavinck, *Church between Temple and Mosque,* p. 67.

272. J. H. Bavinck, *Church between Temple and Mosque,* p. 83.

273. J. H. Bavinck, *Church between Temple and Mosque,* p. 84.

274. J. H. Bavinck, *Church between Temple and Mosque,* p. 90.

275. J. H. Bavinck, *Church between Temple and Mosque,* p. 101.

276. J. H. Bavinck, *Church between Temple and Mosque,* p. 97.

phenomena and events. The border between the natural and the supernatural is often little more than an obscured line.

Bavinck emphasized that, though they can be distinguished, these five features of religious consciousness are always "completely intertwined, the one being subject to conditioning by the other."[277] Taken as a whole, one can say that religious consciousness has two main dimensions. The first is a combination of the cosmic and fatalistic feeling that life is not more than a minute ripple in the boundless ocean of total reality and that all of life is determined by that reality. The second is the combination of an unattainable norm and the need for redemption: we feel accountable and guilty in the face of an existing moral norm and seek to be redeemed from a curse. If these two dimensions are pictured as a pair of intersecting lines, then the point at which they cross may be viewed as the human feeling of relatedness to a Higher Power, the core of all religion.[278] The wide variety of religions has resulted from this intersection. Bavinck noted: "We see that the history of religion depicts a great variety of divine forms and myths. When examining its searching and groping, we encounter so many different ideas. They are sometimes bizarre, unbelievably childlike and foolish; yet sometimes they strike us as being sublime and imposing. At times these ideas led to inhuman deeds and dreadful wars, but also to self-denial and neighborly love."[279]

Bavinck's theological assessment of religious consciousness ran parallel to the change in his view of the essence of that consciousness. Initially, in his psychological approach, he had spoken of our search for God *in* our flight from God.[280] In his later radical-theological approach, he thought that our flight and our search coincided: every search for God is at bottom a flight from God.[281] The first word in the divine-human dialogue is true precisely to the same degree that the second word is false. This dialogical relationship can be likened to a person standing before a carnival looking-glass: the curved mirror reflects the form in front of it, but the image it displays is misshapen in every detail; it is altogether false.[282] This metaphor could give the impression that what emerges from the warped human response to general revelation is simply an *erroneous concept* of God and not a *different* God. But

277. J. H. Bavinck, *Religieus Besef,* p. 72; ET: *JHBR,* p. 201.
278. J. H. Bavinck, *Religieus Besef,* pp. 72-75; ET: *JHBR,* pp. 201-4.
279. J. H. Bavinck, *Church between Temple and Mosque,* p. 111.
280. Cf. J. H. Bavinck, *Persoonlijkheid en Wereldbeschouwing,* pp. 165ff.
281. Cf. J. H. Bavinck, *Probleem van de Pseudo-Religie,* p. 18.
282. J. H. Bavinck, "Het Evangelie en de Andere Godsdiensten," *Het Zendingsblad* 39 (1941): 166.

that impression would be mistaken. Anyone who views God differently from the way God has revealed himself in Jesus Christ does not merely have a divergent notion of God but another god altogether.[283] Bavinck stated that he could not "express this better and more deeply than Calvin did" in the *Institutes:* "Indeed, vanity joined with pride can be detected in the fact that, in seeking after God, men fly off into empty speculations. They do not therefore apprehend God as he offers himself, but imagine him as they have fashioned him in their own presumption."[284] In the light of Scripture, all religions are revealed as forms of spiritual degeneracy and apostasy;[285] they are called vanity, profligacy, darkness, ignorance.[286]

Does the radical judgment imply that non-Christian religions have no positive significance whatsoever? Bavinck answered this question negatively. Following J. Witte's line of thinking,[287] he made a distinction between the "thatness" and the "whatness" of religion. The "thatness" is the basic consciousness that there must be a Higher Power, a transcendent norm, and something like redemption; the "whatness" is the manner in which people interpret and give substantive form to this consciousness.[288]

Bavinck wished to give full weight to the significance of the compelling power of God's plan for fallen humanity. "We may thankfully state *that* they believe in God."[289] Without the "thatness," this *fides qua creditur,* missionary communication would be utterly impossible.[290] At the same time these primary feelings are always enveloped by the fallacious "whatness," the mistaken *fides quae creditur* and erroneous praxis of religion. Therefore, the notion "elements of truth" must be used judiciously. If the term is taken in a vague and general sense, it must be admitted that such elements are found in non-Christian religions. If taken in a more special and defined meaning, it is untenable. All central ideas involved in Christian belief, such as God, cre-

283. Cf. Johan Herman Bavinck, "Het Eerste Gebod," in Thomas Delleman, ed., *Sinaï en Ardjoeno, Het Indonesische Volksleven in Het Licht der Geboden* (Aalten: De Graafschap, 1946), p. 91.

284. Calvin, *Institutes,* 1.1.5.

285. Cf. J. H. Bavinck, *Probleem van de Pseudo-Religie,* p. 10.

286. In this connection Bavinck refers in *Science of Missions,* p. 54, to Eph. 2:18, 19; 4:17; 5:8; Rom. 1:24, 31; and in *Religieus Besef,* p. 129; ET: *JHBR,* p. 247, to 1 Cor. 2:8.

287. Witte, *Die Christus-Botschaft,* pp. 37-40.

288. Cf. Johan Herman Bavinck, "Het Probleem der Anknüpfung bij de Evangelieverkondiging," *Vox Theologica* 11 (1939-1940): 64-68; "Het Evangelie," pp. 67-68; *Science of Missions,* p. 228; and *Church between Temple and Mosque,* pp. 13-14.

289. J. H. Bavinck, "General Revelation," p. 53; ET: *JHBR,* p. 107.

290. J. H. Bavinck, *Church between Temple and Mosque,* p. 14.

ation, man, sin, salvation, law of life, and the goal of the world, are found in most religions, but they are all understood in a fundamentally different sense and applied in a different connection.[291]

In the end, however, they may not in themselves be viewed as pure "hypocrisy" or be considered "untrue."[292] A negative theological judgment does not rule out a positive evaluation from a cultural point of view. According to Bavinck, general revelation has had a felicitous, salvific effect on the life of peoples everywhere: "There is some effect on human conscience, something causing Paul to say that gentiles who have no law 'do by nature the things of the law'" (Rom. 2:14).[293] Bavinck also pointed to a number of positive products of non-Christian religion: a strong social drive that engenders community and creates a sense of mutual responsibility and security; a wholistic, religious experience of life, obviating any duality between the sacred and the profane; and a fervent religious devotion.[294]

Christianity, Other Religions, and the Future of Religion

For Bavinck, the relationship between Christianity and the extra-biblical religions was the life-and-death problem with which the church dealt in all the centuries of its existence.[295] In his opinion, there was a formal similarity between the two. Both the "whatness" of religious consciousness and of the Christian faith constitute subjective answers to the self-manifestation of God;[296] in this regard, all religions are alike, for "religion by its very nature is a response . . . a communion, in which man answers and reacts to God's revelation."[297] Further, the central religious questions remain the same for every

---

291. J. H. Bavinck, "General Revelation," p. 54; ET: *JHBR*, p. 108.

292. J. H. Bavinck, *Impact of Christianity*, p. 97; *Church between Temple and Mosque*, p. 203.

293. J. H. Bavinck, "General Revelation," p. 53; ET: *JHBR*, p. 107.

294. Cf. Johan Herman Bavinck, *In de ban der Demonen* (Kampen: J. H. Kok, 1950), pp. 24-26, and "Het Evangelie," pp. 3-4. Bavinck also calls attention, in these same publications, to the theological, less attractive reverse side of these characteristics; cf. respectively "Het Evangelie," pp. 35-37, and *In de ban der Demonen*, pp. 26-29.

295. Johan Herman Bavinck, "Uitkomsten der studie van buitenbijbelse religies," in Jan Waterink et al., *Cultuur Geschiedenis van het Christendom*, part 4 (Amsterdam-Brussels: Elsevier, 1951), p. 337.

296. J. H. Bavinck, *Religieus Besef*, pp. 188-89; ET: *JHBR*, p. 298.

297. J. H. Bavinck, *Church between Temple and Mosque*, pp. 18-19.

religion; all religious answers focus around the same five "magnetic points," *the* great life-and-death questions that concern every single human being.

Bavinck even thought that sometimes other religions contain elements that, after conversion to the gospel, can lead to a deeper encounter with the biblical message: "The Oriental way of thinking can help us to place the wealth of biblical ideas in an even purer and fuller light. . . . The Oriental is more strongly convinced of the omnipresence of the divine . . . is not so far removed from the miracle . . . is capable of waiting more quietly for the voice of God and can submit to Him with a greater degree of passivity . . . is more aware that the form of this world is passing away."[298]

But Bavinck also stressed the substantial difference between religious consciousness and Christian faith. The two are separated by a wide rift — they "live in one house, but are . . . dogged enemies."[299] For Bavinck, Christian faith comes into existence when the truth of God's revelation in Christ breaks through the process of suppression and substitution and the Spirit leads people into the truth.[300] The discrepancy between religious consciousness and Christian faith becomes most apparent in the crucifixion of Christ by the "rulers of this age" (1 Cor. 2:8). "The crucifixion of Christ is the concentration point of that continual turning away from the truth, which is the tragic secret of every person's life."[301] Conversely, Christ's crucifixion also signifies God's ultimate judgment over all human life, including religious life.

Bavinck emphasized that this fundamental difference does not permit Christianity to assume an air of superiority vis-à-vis religious consciousness and other religions. Christians, too, have often been guilty of suppressing and replacing the truth. Indeed, in this respect the guilt of Christians is much greater than those of other religions, for Christians have often obscured the clear and revealed gospel of Jesus Christ.[302] Further, repression and substitution within the Christian have not only taken place in the past: "in the Christian, too, the pagan continues to live and breathe."[303] This makes it impossible to speak of the absolute truth of Christian faith; it never constitutes an adequate reflection of the content of the gospel. Absolute truth holds only for God's revelation in the gospel of Christ.[304]

298. J. H. Bavinck, *Christus en de Mystiek*, pp. 9, 232; ET: *JHBR*, p. 411.
299. J. H. Bavinck, *Religieus Besef*, p. 190; ET: *JHBR*, p. 299.
300. J. H. Bavinck, *Religieus Besef*, p. 188; ET: *JHBR*, p. 298.
301. J. H. Bavinck, *Religieus Besef*, p. 129; ET: *JHBR*, p. 247.
302. J. H. Bavinck, *Church between Temple and Mosque*, p. 200.
303. J. H. Bavinck, *Religieus Besef*, p. 189; ET: *JHBR*, p. 298.
304. Cf. Johan Herman Bavinck, *De Absoluutheid van het Christendom* (Bandoeng:

Finally, Bavinck asked himself whether religious consciousness was a thing of the past, dying off in the face of the global secularization of culture, or, conversely, whether it remained alive and well and would continue to figure strongly in the future.[305] He offered a twofold answer to this question. On the one hand, he acknowledged the massive, pervasive loss of a sense of transcendence brought about by the advancement of positivist science and technology.[306] "The process of *Entgötterung*[307] of the [western] worldview and the secularization of life in general continues apace."[308] Bavinck thought that the American-British poet T. S. Eliot (1888-1965) was right in a certain sense when he wrote: "Men have left God not for other gods, they say, but for no God: and this has never happened before."[309] From a religious viewpoint, the development of modern culture is disastrous, Bavinck declared: "Something in our thinking has been irreparably broken."[310] The core of religious consciousness is fading away. Any answers that are given to existential questions of life and death are losing their religious tone and becoming businesslike, sterile, paltry, meager, and bitter.[311] "God is dead, we have murdered Him. A generation is growing up for whom God is in fact not much more than a long forgotten word found in ancient writings, a generation that doesn't feel the slightest twinge of sorrow that it has lost Him."[312] The altar has been replaced by the mirror; we sees nothing but ourselves.[313]

One should not forget, however, that even after the disappearance of religion itself, all sorts of religious feelings continue to impinge on the human soul, "like the lingering twilight after the sun has already set," retaining their compelling "power throughout many generations."[314] This post-Christian

---

Javasche Boekhandel & Drukkerij, ca. 1936), pp. 10-15, and *Religieus Besef*, p. 189; ET: *JHBR*, p. 298.

305. Cf. J. H. Bavinck, *Religieus Besef*, p. 76; ET: *JHBR*, pp. 204-5.

306. Cf. J. H. Bavinck, *Religieus Besef*, p. 5; ET: *JHBR*, p. 145.

307. Literally "un-god-ing," which means: alienation of, estrangement from, disposal of the gods.

308. J. H. Bavinck, *Religieus Besef*, p. 6; ET: *JHBR*, p. 146.

309. T. S. Eliot, "Choruses from 'The Rock,'" in *The Complete Poems and Plays, 1909-1950* (New York: Harcourt, Brace, 1952), p. 108. Cf. J. H. Bavinck, *Church between Temple and Mosque*, p. 25; "General Revelation," p. 53; ET: *JHBR*, p. 107.

310. J. H. Bavinck, *Religieus Besef*, p. 83; ET: *JHBR*, p. 210.

311. Cf. J. H. Bavinck, *Religieus Besef*, pp. 83-91; ET: *JHBR*, pp. 210-17.

312. J. H. Bavinck, *Religieus Besef*, p. 91; ET: *JHBR*, p. 217.

313. Cf. J. H. Bavinck, "De onbekende God," p. 20.

314. J. H. Bavinck, *Religieus Besef*, p. 9; ET: *JHBR*, p. 149.

religious consciousness is of a peculiar nature in that it is influenced by Christianity but also strongly opposed to it.[315] At any moment, these residual religious feelings can become embodied in all manner of movements, such as nationalism, National-Socialism, and Communism, causing them to evince a wondrous religious glow.[316] At a later stage, Bavinck observed that these forms of religiously tinted idealism were also disappearing. He pointed out that an impersonal pattern of mass existence was emerging in which existentialism and nihilism were burgeoning; life was becoming bereft of spiritual and moral values, and increasingly characterized by hedonism and the incessant search for sensation.[317]

If this were the lone earmark of contemporary life, it would mean that modern culture was witnessing the final death spasms of a few attenuated religious feelings. Man under modernity would be turning into an a-religious being. Bavinck refused to draw this conclusion, however, since he did not consider secularization to be the sole characteristic of existence in the twentieth century. He remained fundamentally convinced that no human being could peremptorily withdraw from the existential relationships through which God revealed himself. "Whether we know it or not, we remain caught in the clasp of the religious questions of humankind,"[318] and our lives constitute an answer to those questions. Everyone responds in some way to the elemental riddles of existence. Thus, every human life, even the life of a secular person, "is essentially a choice and a decision." The five questions involved in religious consciousness remain operational in nonreligious modern people, who "must respond [to these questions] in some way or other. This need not be done philosophically — the answer to these basic problems can be given in the course of everyday life."[319] As a result of radical suppression of God's wordless speech, this answer can also assume the nature of a denial of God and thereby take on a totally secular cast.[320] Nevertheless, even then, this answer remains a *religious* response, a response given within the framework of

315. Cf. J. H. Bavinck, *Religieus Besef,* p. 9; ET: *JHBR,* p. 149.

316. Cf. J. H. Bavinck, *Religieus Besef,* pp. 7-9; ET: *JHBR,* pp. 146-49.

317. Cf. J. H. Bavinck, *De Toekomst van onze Kerken* (Bruinisse: J. van der Wal, 1943), pp. 38-47.

318. J. H. Bavinck, *De Toekomst,* p. 84.

319. Cf. J. H. Bavinck, *Church between Temple and Mosque,* pp. 111-12.

320. Cf. Johan Herman Bavinck, *Christus en de Wereldstorm* (Wageningen: Zomer & Keuning, 1944), where Bavinck deals with contemporary secularized man under four rubrics: man and community (p. 8), instinct and reason (p. 14), hesitation regarding moral norms (p. 21), and the riddle of history (p. 26).

the mysterious, veiled dialogue between God and man, for "it touches the deepest religious realities with which man is confronted."[321]

Thus, "modern culture, too, is a religious phenomenon, either in the positive or in the negative sense,"[322] and the bearers of this culture can never be a-religious in the full sense of the word. Even when a man is inclined to abandon belief in "the reality behind reality . . . and to become an atheist in the full sense of the word, he is often still overwhelmed by it, as it were: the idea that there is a *Supreme Power* to which he is related is something that he can never get rid of."[323] Even when "he renounces the ideas and religious doctrines of earlier generations, the very intensity and rancorous bitterness of this renunciation resonates religiously in his breast. . . . Everywhere, one runs up against this peculiar reality of religious sentiment that fills and vibrates in everything."[324]

Despite societal changes, then, Bavinck believed that the deeper layers of human existence remain constant.[325] Indeed, the existential questions with which people try to deal "autonomously," i.e., without recourse to God, can at any moment become "intensified to such a degree that they regain the religious pitch they have always had throughout the ages."[326] This can happen, for example, in despair and hopelessness, which will be the price modern culture will pay for its godlessness. In the midst of this bleakness, nostalgia for lost religious values will arise, and repressed religious feelings will well up from the inscrutable depths of the heart.[327] Since God's wordless speech continues unabated, this means that the revival of religious consciousness is always a realistic possibility. However, Bavinck also observed with reference to Revelation 13 that in the last days the religious dimension in human life can take on dramatic forms. That chapter paints a vivid picture of a symbiosis between religious experience and religious degeneracy, an unadulterated

---

321. J. H. Bavinck, *Church between Temple and Mosque*, p. 111.
322. J. H. Bavinck, *Church between Temple and Mosque*, p. 23.
323. J. H. Bavinck, *Church between Temple and Mosque*, p. 33.
324. J. H. Bavinck, *Church between Temple and Mosque*, p. 111.
325. Cf. J. H. Bavinck, *Religieus Besef*, p. 76; ET: *JHBR*, pp. 204-5.
326. J. H. Bavinck, *Religieus Besef*, p. 84; ET: *JHBR*, p. 211.
327. Cf. *Religieus Besef*, pp. 7, 92; ET: *JHBR*, pp. 146, 217. See also Johan Herman Bavinck, "Worden Wij Weer Primitieve Menschen?" *Horizon* 7 (1940), where Bavinck, following Gerardus van der Leeuw, *De Primitieve Mensch en de Religie: Anthropologische Studie* (Groningen-Batavia: Wolters, 1937), argues that modern abstract thought does not satisfy because it clashes with the reality of life, resulting in the rise of a new primitiveness with religious tendencies.

process of repression and substitution in connection with the beast rising out of the earth.[328]

5. Bavinck's Missiology

From 1930 onward, Bavinck began to reflect more intensively on matters of missionary theology, publishing several works on the topic, including books and a large number of articles. The most systematic of his books was *Inleiding in de Zendingswetenschap* (1954) (*Introduction to the Science of Missions*, 1960) in which he brought together much of what appeared in his earlier writings. The volume thus provided a survey of his cumulative missiological thought, including its biblical foundation and his concept of the essential character and purpose of missions.

The Biblical Foundation of Mission

In all missionary questions, Bavinck began, he turned to Scripture as the essential guide: "For the work of mission is so much a work of God, which takes place in his service, that it is not permissible for us to engage in independent improvisation. At every step we will have to ask what God requires of us." At the same time, however, Bavinck realized that the Bible does not furnish a direct answer to all current problems and questions: "It will not always be easy to find the right course in the midst of stubborn, everyday practice."[329] Bavinck therefore tried to be biblical without becoming a biblicist. In that spirit the *Introduction* examined the Old Testament, the intertestamentary period, and the New Testament to determine the proper foundation for missions.

Missionary Principles in the Old Testament   For Bavinck it was obvious that "from the first page to the last, the Bible is a book which has the whole world in view and which unfolds the divine plan of salvation with respect to that world. . . . In the Bible, God is wrestling with the world, persuading, re-

---

328. Cf. Johan Herman Bavinck, *En Voort Wentelen de Eeuwen: Gedachten over het Boek der Openbaring van Johannes* (Wageningen: Zomer en Keuning, 1952), pp. 169-96, esp. 188-96; here Bavinck deals at length with the demonic aspect of religion.

329. J. H. Bavinck, *Science of Missions*, p. 5.

proving, admonishing, beseeching the various people of the world to accept the truth and be reconciled to God."[330] It is essential, therefore, that the witness of the Old Testament be included in the development of a biblical foundation of the missionary calling. Bavinck found eight elements in the Old Testament that provided part of that foundation.[331]

1. In Genesis 1, the God of Israel is revealed as the creator of heaven and earth. This God is not a god with limited functions like foreign gods but is Lord of all humankind and ought to be served as such. Genesis 1–3 shows that all people share the same glory and the same misery, while the "table of nations" in Genesis 10 confirms that God's reign encompasses the whole earth. Bavinck concluded: "Without this basis, the great commission of Matthew 28:19 could not exist."

2. Though God is focused on working out his plan of salvation through a particular people, the nation of Israel, God continues to be concerned with all nations. According to several psalms and many prophetic words, the whole world remains an "object of His care." For example, Psalm 33: "The Lord looks from heaven, He beholds all the sons of men; from His dwelling place He looks upon all the inhabitants of the earth. He Who fashions the hearts of them all, Who considers all their doings . . . !"

3. In the Old Testament, the idea that YHWH alone is God leads to the unconditional condemnation of all idolatry (cf. Deut. 4:39; Jer. 10:10). There is no place in the Old Testament where God tolerates honor given to other gods. This implies the possibility and necessity of a missionary mandate.

4. It is precisely Israel's isolation, an isolation that begins with the call of Abraham, which is fundamental to the missionary task. On the one hand, the covenant, with its embedded legislation, served as the framework for the utterly unique place of Israel in the midst of the nations ("You only have I chosen of all the families of the earth" — Amos 3:2). On the other hand, from the very beginning this isolation is presented as temporary, as an essential part of God's plan of salvation for the whole world. Three times Abraham was assured that, through his descendants, all the nations of the earth would be blessed (Gen. 12:3; 18:18; 22:18).

5. The covenant structure contained room for mission. It allowed no exclusive identification: of YHWH as a tribal god, nor any special claim on God by Israel. The relationship with Israel was rooted entirely in God's elect-

---

330. J. H. Bavinck, *Science of Missions*, p. 8.

331. Cf. J. H. Bavinck, *Science of Missions*, pp. 8-23; what follows is taken from these pages without further reference. Cf. Visser, *Heart for the Gospel*, pp. 190-94.

ing love, and the possibility remained for other nations to share in the blessing of the covenant.

6. Israel continually viewed its history as enacted on the stage of the world, "before the eyes of the surrounding nations." Repeatedly, Israel prayed that God might intervene in his merciful power so that the nations would acknowledge his Name (Exod. 32:12; Num. 14:16; Josh. 7:9; Isa. 37:20). Israel realized "that its history was not a private affair which was of no concern to anyone else; it knew that God pleaded His case with the other nations through its history and hence that in the ups and downs of that history God extended the concerns of His heart to the whole world." Although one cannot speak of a missionary passion in the Old Testament, there is a theocentric yearning for the whole world to recognize that YHWH is the true God.

7. Though Israel's separation excluded official missionary activity toward the surrounding peoples, there were missionary moments in Israel's history. From time to time there were people who bore witness to YHWH in foreign lands (2 Kings 5:1-3; Daniel 1-3). These missionary moments, however, remained an incidental phenomenon. According to Bavinck, not even Jonah's journey to Nineveh was mission in the true sense because Jonah's purpose was not "to found a congregation of God in Nineveh." In light of the examples mentioned earlier, this argument is inconsistent.[332]

8. Bavinck devoted much attention to the missionary perspective of the prophetic writings, especially to what was written in Ezekiel 36 and Jeremiah 31 about the new covenant that promised a fulfillment of salvation for Israel and the world. This renewal constantly centered on the figure of the coming Messiah and was linked to the outpouring of the Holy Spirit upon all flesh (Joel 2:28). All the emphasis in these texts, however, falls on a spontaneous coming of the nations to the salvation revealed in Israel. Only in Isaiah 55:5 is there a mandate[333] to engage in missionary activity: "Behold, you (Israel) shall call nations that you do not know, and nations that do not know you shall run to you because of the Lord your God." But one thing is very clear:

332. This is remarkable. Johannes Verkuyl, Bavinck's successor, rightly calls the book of Jonah profoundly meaningful for the biblical foundation of the missionary task because of its universal character.

333. J. H. Bavinck, *Science of Missions*, p. 22. It is strange that in searching for centrifugal mission ideas in the Old Testament, Bavinck refers to Isa. 55:5, but not to Isa. 42:4 and Isa. 49:6; cf. Cornelis Graafland, "De Bijbelse Fundering van het Zendingswerk," in Johannes P. Versteeg et al., *Gij die Eertijds Verre Waart: Een Inleiding tot de Gereformeerde Zendingswetenschap* (Utrecht: De Banier, 1978), p. 25.

God makes a worldwide name for himself and proclaims the eschatological perspective of an all-embracing shalom for the whole earth at the end of time (Isa. 11:5-9).

In sum, according to Bavinck, mission did not begin in the New Testament but was rooted in God's heart from the very beginning. This mission came to full development in God's own time, despite the resistance of the fallen world.

Missionary Motifs in the Intertestamentary Period Bavinck stated that, in principle, nothing changed during the intertestamental period. Theologically, Israel continued to think of itself as a separated people, and there remained a wall between Jew and Gentile. Due to changing political and cultural factors, however, breaches began to open in this wall. Politically, Israel was incorporated into the Roman Empire; they came into closer contact with the surrounding nations and encountered interested gentiles.[334] Culturally, there emerged a Jewish diaspora in Asia (because the majority of Jews did not return from captivity) and in the West (as a result of the establishment of trade colonies in the Hellenistic world).

Even though the Jews were initially treated with contempt and misunderstanding by the Greek world, their monotheistic faith and high moral standards gradually made them more appreciated, and many "proselytes" began to join the Jewish faith. As a result, a strong missionary zeal slowly developed in some Jewish circles (cf. Matt. 23:15). Later on, the Jewish concept of God began to resonate with the Greek intellectual world, which had begun to distance itself from ancient religious myths. The translation and distribution of the Old Testament into Greek (the Septuagint) played an important role here. Finally, Jewish communities were politically and socially attractive because they came to occupy an important place in the social order of that time.

Missionary Principles in the New Testament The Old Testament prophets viewed messianic salvation as a comprehensive event that would be realized in the last days, an event that would include the spiritual renewal of Israel, the spontaneous coming of the nations to the Lord, and the radical transformation of the world order. The messianic message proclaimed in the Gospels therefore was at first puzzling, Bavinck said, because it did not follow

---

334. J. H. Bavinck, *Zending*, pp. 13-14. In *Science of Missions*, this aspect is barely mentioned.

the expected pattern.[335] Further reflection reveals that, while the manner of the fulfillment differed from Old Testament expectations, the content of those expectations remained the same. In other words, the unexpected ways in which Jesus fulfilled the Old Testament were already foreshadowed in Old Testament prophecy.

Bavinck traced, step-by-step, the development of the missionary mandate *in the Gospels*. He rejected the idea of an evolution in Jesus' stance from particularism to universalism, emphasizing that the Gospels as a whole have a universal tenor. He pointed especially to the song of Simeon (Luke 2:32), the coming of the wise men (Matt. 2:1-12), and a variety of Jesus' sayings (cf. Matt. 8:11; John 3:16). Bavinck concluded: "Thus we see throughout the gospel that Jesus always saw his life in the broad context of the ancient prophecy of salvation."[336] This universal tenor does not deny that Jesus' early ministry was characterized by particularism. For example, Jesus initially sent out his disciples with the emphatic instruction *not* to go among the Gentiles or to enter any town of the Samaritans (Matt. 10:5). Thus, Jesus did not immediately end the separation between Jews and Gentiles and did not immediately inaugurate the great unfolding of salvation for the whole world.

Instead, Bavinck pointed out, Jesus gradually made it clear that the ultimate *parousia* of redemption runs via the detour of the Cross and Resurrection, a detour that Israel did not expect.[337] This detour had two sides. First, it brought a great delay before the full manifestation of God's kingdom, a delay resulting from the rejection of Jesus by the spiritual representatives of Israel (cf. Luke 14:15-24; Matt. 21:33-46). As a consequence, the kingdom was given to a different nation, an interim period was inaugurated, and the final kingdom events were extended in time. Second, because the Cross and Resurrection had universal significance, they formed the foundation for the worldwide missionary task that was to begin in Jerusalem (Matt. 28:19; Luke 24:47; John 20:21; Acts 1:6-8). The interim served as a period for the Scriptures to be fulfilled: the nations would finally come to salvation through the missionary activity of Jesus' *Jewish* followers. Bavinck concluded that, in the teaching of

335. J. H. Bavinck, *Science of Missions,* pp. 29-30. Bavinck even chose as heading "The Riddle of the Gospels."

336. J. H. Bavinck, *Science of Missions,* pp. 32-33.

337. J. H. Bavinck, *Science of Missions,* p. 30, speaks here of two lines in the prophecies of Jesus: one that ends in Jesus' death and resurrection, and one that ends in his *parousia,* two lines that ultimately join in the one line of the coming Kingdom by way of the suffering Servant; he is following Herman N. Ridderbos, *The Coming of the Kingdom,* trans. H. de Jongste, ed. Raymond O. Zorn (Philadelphia: P. & R. Publishing, 1962), pp. 456ff.

Jesus, the idea of mission slowly and cautiously emerged from the totality of messianic expectations. The dividing walls of history were broken down by mission.[338]

Did this course of events create a contradiction between the Old Testament promises and the New Testament realization of salvation? Bavinck answered with reference to Galatians 3:8-16: the Old Testament promises had been fulfilled, albeit in a different manner "than the Israelites had dreamed of." Bavinck concurred with Paul that this tension between promise and fulfillment gave cause for worship (Rom. 11:33).[339] "The coming of the kingdom is no longer an end*point* on the time line of history; rather, this endpoint has itself become a *line* leading toward a later, definitive endpoint."[340]

Bavinck clearly viewed the book of Acts as an important source for missiological reflection, the place where the missionary mandate was implemented.[341] He distinguished six elements in the book that contributed to the foundation of mission. First, the entire book of Acts conveys the idea that mission is a concern of the exalted Christ, who continues in the world what he began in Israel. Second, mission is viewed, in direct continuity with Old Testament prophecy, as an eschatological event, a sign of the end time, a phenomenon of the Last Days (Acts 2:17). The promised messianic redemption is realized in this way until the day of Christ's return. Third, in the course of Acts, it becomes increasingly clear that mission is a responsibility of the church. In Acts 13, Paul and Barnabas are sent by the church of Antioch, and Acts 15 and 21 emphasize the leading role of the church of Jerusalem in the missionary task. Fourth, the church is mission-oriented in its very essence. The spread of the gospel happens spontaneously through church members in their daily contact with others and through lay preachers from among persecuted church members (Acts 8:4; 11:19-20). Fifth, while centrifugal movement is dominant, centripetal movement also clearly continues: the book mentions "the spontaneous coming of outsiders, who are simply attracted to the new life that finds embodiment in the church" (Acts 2:47; 5:13). Sixth, missionary work follows the course of first Jews and then Gentiles (Acts 13:46). With all these insights, Bavinck neglected what is perhaps the most important message of the book, which even determined its structure,

---

338. J. H. Bavinck, *Science of Missions*, pp. 32-36.

339. J. H. Bavinck, *Zending*, pp. 17-18. Cf. also J. H. Bavinck, *Science of Missions*, p. 50.

340. Cf. Johannes Blauw, *Gottes Werk in dieser Welt, Grundzüge Einer Biblischen Theologie der Mission* (München: Kaiser, 1961), p. 84.

341. Cf. J. H. Bavinck, *Science of Missions*, pp. 36-40.

that the gospel goes from Jerusalem, the center of Israel, to Rome, the center of the world.[342]

In the letters of the apostles, the missionary mandate was elaborated. The New Testament epistles were all written in a missionary context, Bavinck noted, and feature seven themes that go to the heart of the missionary calling.[343] In the first place, all missionary work has its origin in God's miraculous work of making every object a subject. God's personal turning toward people serves a worldwide goal. Then, too, the church represents Christ in the execution of the missionary task and so must exhibit both strength and humility. Third, missionary work depends on the work of the Spirit, a theme that Paul repeatedly emphasizes, especially when speaking about the need for God to open doors in this world and in his Word (1 Cor. 16:9; 2 Cor. 2:12; Col. 4:3) and for giving growth (1 Cor. 3:7).

The fourth theme Bavinck found was more complex: as churches grow qualitatively, they increasingly discover their missionary task. They do so in three ways. They discover their important task of intercession, "that the message of the Lord may spread rapidly and be honored" (2 Thess. 3:1; Eph. 6:19; Col. 4:3). They are given the centripetal task of behaving as children of light, so that unbelievers may be drawn to Christ as bees to flowers (cf. Phil. 2:14-15). Since the church lives before the eyes of the world, it must not give offense (cf. 1 Cor. 10:32-33), but rather, "by doing good . . . should silence the ignorant talk of foolish men" (1 Peter 2:15; cf. 1 Thess. 4:12; Col. 4:5). Finally, they are called to continual witness, striving, with one mind, for the faith of the gospel (cf. Phil. 1:27). The church is "involved in a permanent discussion with the world around it," so its "feet must be fitted with the readiness that comes from the gospel of peace" (Eph. 6:15). It must make the most of every opportunity (Eph. 5:16), ensuring that its speech is always full of grace, seasoned with salt (Col. 4:6).

The epistles' final three missiological themes put the task in broader perspective. Mission work is marked by the all-encompassing character of salvation. Everything changes in those places where Christ has placed his hand upon humankind (2 Cor. 5:17; Gal. 6:15). There is no neutral area in human life, nothing that falls outside the power of sin, and nothing that is excluded from God's redemption. Further, the whole of the missionary task stands in

---

342. Cf. Blauw, *Gottes Werk in dieser Welt*, p. 84.

343. J. H. Bavinck, *Science of Missions*, pp. 42-49, and *Zending*, pp. 20-31. In *Zending*, Bavinck deals only with Paul's missionary activity, discussing first its unique, time-specific, and local nature and then mentioning three facets of its permanent significance: the call to and the goal and plan of his work.

an eschatological perspective. Through mission, God is at work preparing for the fullness of time "to bring all things in heaven and on earth together under one head, even Christ" (Eph. 1:10). The goal of all missionary work is "the realization of what will take visible shape in the age to come, beyond the horizon of history." Finally, in missionary work Israel and the Gentiles are in the same theological position: both are called to conversion to Christ, and both are blessed by him without difference (Rom. 10:12, 13). At the same time, their relation to each other has changed: because they rejected the Messiah, Israel has experienced a hardening of heart until the full number of the Gentiles has come in. The first has become the last.[344] Nevertheless, God's promises are irrevocable, so mission among the people of Israel must be intensified. Notably, that task can only be done via witnessing dialogue.[345]

The Essence of Mission

From these biblical foundations, Bavinck took important structural elements for framing his theory of missions: a Trinitarian basis, a profound salvation-historical orientation, and a balanced ecclesiocentric approach that maintained a basileia-centered focus.

Bavinck considered mission first and foremost as God's work: it "has its origin in divine compassion and is realized in the sending of the Son (John 3:16)."[346] Thus, missionary work is exclusively grounded in the gracious pleasure of God in Christ Jesus.[347] In this regard, Bavinck rejected the concept of a "double missionary foundation" espoused by the Protestant missiologist Gustav Warneck and the Roman Catholic missiologist Joseph Schmidlin,[348] according to whom the impetus for mission lies both in God's pleasure and in human desire.[349] Bavinck considered this idea's traditional appeal to Haggai 2:7 (Christ as the Desire of all nations) — also made by H. Bavinck — to be a false interpretation of the text. "Viewed objectively, it is true that the nations need Christ and cannot find peace without him, but that does not mean that

344. J. H. Bavinck, *Science of Missions*, pp. 51-52.
345. See J. H. Bavinck, *Science of Missions*, p. 73, n. 20.
346. J. H. Bavinck, *Zending*, p. 7.
347. J. H. Bavinck, *Science of Missions*, p. 62.
348. Cf. J. H. Bavinck, *Science of Missions*, pp. 62-65.
349. Warneck, *Evangelische Missionslehre*, 1: 240-304. Joseph Schmidlin, *Katholische Missionslehre im Grundriss* (Münster: Verlag der Aschendorffschen Verlagsbuchhandlung, 1925), p. 96. Cf. J. H. Bavinck, *Science of Missions*, p. 64.

they long for him and seek him on their own initiative. The gospel of Christ is 'not something that man made up' (Gal. 1:11), nor is it the message of redemption to which the nations have eagerly looked forward."[350]

At the same time, mission is a task of the church. This part of God's work includes rather than excludes human work; mission cannot exist without both a Sender and those who are sent. Thus, missionary work is "the human side of a great, divine seeking and speaking that continues through all ages of history."[351] Reconciliation in Christ was God's work, but the administration of this reconciliation has been entrusted to us, Bavinck stated. "The Scriptures make it absolutely clear that it is the church, the body of Christ, that constitutes the organ through and in which the glorified Christ wants to reveal his great redemptive work to the world."[352] He also wrote: "We will have to apply this principle to our own situations in our own way."[353] Bavinck's ecclesiological emphasis here is not surprising, since the GKN had played a pioneering role in the area of church-based mission work.

Yet in contrast to Kraemer and Hoekendijk, Bavinck consistently refused to define the church exclusively in terms of its missionary calling. Kraemer said: "In my view, the *raison d'être*, the reason for the existence of the church, is that it is present *because of* and *in* the distress of the world."[354] But Bavinck was not prepared to turn the church into a function of the apostolate. On the contrary, he argued that the church has a threefold significance. First and above all, it has a doxological function: "The Church does not exist in the first place because of the world or because of the distress of the world, but it exists in the first place because of God for the glory of God." Second, the church has a nurturing task: "The Church continues to work on itself; it proclaims the Word of God to the generations to come." Third, following these other functions, the church also has a missionary task: "The same God who preserves his church also gives it increase."[355]

From the very beginning of his missiological reflection, Bavinck emphasized the twofold nature of the missionary mandate. As early as 1934 he described mission as both "an attempt to lead human souls to the Light of Jesus

---

350. Cf. J. H. Bavinck, *Alzoo wies het Woord*, p. 120.

351. Johan Herman Bavinck, *Onze Kerk, Zendingskerk* (Kampen: J. H. Kok, 1948), p. 10.

352. J. H. Bavinck, *Science of Missions*, p. 59.

353. Johan Herman Bavinck, "Kerk en Zending," *Het Zendingsblad* 50 (1952): 100.

354. J. H. Bavinck, "Kerk en Zending," p. 15. Cf. Kraemer, *Christian Message*, p. 30: "The church is a fellowship of believers, rooted in God and his redemptive order, and therefore committed to the service and the salvation of the world."

355. J. H. Bavinck, *Science of Missions*, pp. 68-69.

Christ, so that they surrender to Him and rest in Him in life and in death," and also as a "wrestling with other cultures."[356] In 1947 he applied to mission the Kuyperian concept of the implementation of the Christian principle in all areas of life.[357] Bavinck called this the Christocentric idea and grounded it in the great commission (Matt. 28:19): "Go and make disciples of all nations, teaching them to obey everything I have commanded you." From this, Bavinck concluded, "if one is a disciple, he must become a whole disciple, he must follow Christ in his personal life as well as in his social, economic, and political life." Bavinck stressed that the struggle between the gospel and culture always presupposes pluriformity: one may not "force one's own culture on other nations" but seek to give form to the rule of Christ in "living relationship to that which is central to the culture" of a given people.[358]

Gradually, Bavinck began to use the concept of the kingdom of God in a more consciously theological manner. Thus, he wrote in 1961: "The idea of the coming Kingdom of the Lord, with its immense blessing of *shalom* (peace), is by far the most dominant theme in both the OT and NT." Mission takes place in the service of the coming of God's kingdom "and in that immense work of God we are his hands."[359]

Extending his theme of salvation history, Bavinck kept mission in *eschatological perspective;* it is part of the sequence of the last things.[360] Bavinck made this point on biblical-exegetical grounds,[361] noting that already the Old Testament prophets looked forward to the coming of the nations to Mount Zion as a sign of a new age in which the salvation of the Messiah would permeate all of life. This continued in the New Testament, as in the missionary mandate of Matthew 28:18-20, where the church is called to mission on the basis of the Cross and Resurrection with a view to the end of the age. The missionary mandate, thus, is implemented between the initial fulfillment and the final culmination of the Kingdom, the period in which sal-

356. J. H. Bavinck, *Christus en de Mystiek,* p. 5.

357. J. H. Bavinck, *Zending,* pp. 8-9. It is remarkable how easily Bavinck linked this Kuyperian principle with the Barthian principle that the preaching of the kingdom of heaven critically permeates all of existence.

358. J. H. Bavinck, "Zendingsbegrip en Zendingswerkelijkheid," *De Heerban* 2 (1949): 4-6.

359. J. H. Bavinck, "Theology and Mission," *Free University Quarterly* 8 (October 1961): 64-65; on p. 63, he speaks of the Kingdom as "that almost always forgotten chapter of doctrinal theology, that is one of the most dominant ideas when we are dealing with missions."

360. Cf. J. H. Bavinck, *Science of Missions,* pp. 61-62.

361. Cf. J. H. Bavinck, "Zendingsbegrip en Zendingswerkelijkheid," p. 3; Bavinck refers to Walter Freytag, "A Mission im Blick aufs Ende," *Evangelisches Missions Zeitschrift* (1942): 321ff.

vation takes the provisional form of a balance between *already* and *not-yet*. In this light, Bavinck warned against too great an optimism concerning the realization of redemption in the present age. He pointed to 1 Corinthians 7:29-31, where Paul emphasized that redemption is tentative because the form *(schema)* of this world is passing away.[362]

Bavinck further drew a clear distinction between mission and evangelism. Evangelism is directed toward those members of the covenant who have strayed in order to bring them back to the Lord Christ and to his church. This raised an old problem from Dutch Reformed history, however, for, not knowing who belongs to the covenant, it is difficult to say where the boundaries of evangelism should be drawn.[363] One way to resolve the puzzle is to say that mission has to do with the "not yet" and evangelism with the "no longer," but such a definition of these terms cannot be clearly derived from Scripture. In the New Testament, the verb *euangelizesthai* (proclaiming the gospel) is not used in the narrower sense of evangelism but in a general sense. Further, according to Bavinck, a parallel can be drawn between evangelism and the preaching of the prophets, Jesus, and the apostles to the apostate and strayed among Israel, because that preaching included a call to return to a life under the covenant of God. Definitely, mission and evangelism are both expressions of the merciful love that reaches out to all who are as sheep without a shepherd, Bavinck concluded. He added, however, that the call to evangelism has priority because it involves people who "live in the same place, who in the past belonged to the same church, who in part still bear the mark of baptism on their forehead, and who are, therefore, to a high degree, still our responsibility."[364]

In this context, Bavinck retained the distinction between the objective meaning of the covenant and people's subjective knowledge of it. Though many belong to the seed of the covenant, innumerable people have never been in a church and know nothing of the basic truths of the gospel. If de-Christianization continues, evangelism will increasingly acquire the character of missionary work.[365] Bavinck noted that, in such a post-Christian at-

---

362. Cf. J. H. Bavinck, "Zendingsbegrip en Zendingswerkelijkheid," p. 3; "Theology and Mission," p. 66: "we are always in danger to stress too much the *already* or the *not-yet.*"

363. Cf. J. H. Bavinck, *Science of Missions,* pp. 74-76. Johannes Verkuyl, *Inleiding in de Evangelistiek* (Kampen: J. H. Kok, 1978), pp. 69-70, gives a brief summary of Bavinck's views on this matter.

364. Cf. J. H. Bavinck, "Zending en Evangelisatie," *Het Zendingsblad* 42 (1944): 19.

365. Johan Herman Bavinck, *De Mens Van Nu* (Kampen: J. H. Kok, 1967), published posthumously, is a telling testimony of this; cf. esp. pp. 38-47.

mosphere, missionary work will also often face "a deep-seated distrust of Christianity resulting from all manner of negative experiences people have had with Christianity." Thus, de-Christianization has methodological consequences: to confront this decayed society with the message of the gospel, one's point of departure must be found in this present apostate and secularized reality.

Over the years, Bavinck gave four different definitions of mission.[366] The best of them is found in his 1949 article, "Zendingsbegrip en Zendingswerkelijkheid" (The Concept and Reality of Mission): "Mission is that activity of the church throughout the whole world — which in deepest essence is an activity of Christ himself — through which the church calls the nations in their diversity to faith in and obedience to Jesus Christ, demonstrates to them by the signs of its service and ministry how the salvation of Christ encompasses all of life, and at the same time teaches them to look forward to the perfection of the Kingdom, in which God will be all and in all."[367]

In sum, Bavinck's concept is Christocentric, ecclesiocentric, comprehensive, and eschatological. It is ecumenical in involving the church throughout the whole world, and pluriform by taking the nations in their wide diversity. He agreed with the threefold goal of mission formulated by Voetius: *conversio gentilium, mohammedistarum et judaeorum* (conversion of unbelievers, Muslims, and Jews), *plantatio ecclesiae aut ecclesiarum* (planting of the church or of churches), and *gloria et manifestatio gratiae divinae* (glorification and revelation of the divine grace).[368] Bavinck interpreted Voetius's goals as three aspects of the one mighty purpose of God, namely, the coming of the kingdom of God. "That coming of God is about his glory, his greatness, and his grace. That coming includes the spread of the church over the whole earth. And that coming is realized in the conversion of sinners."[369] Bavinck examined the three aspects in this different order — the inverse of Voetius's — because he connected God's glory more closely to humanity's salvation in the present than to God's judgment in the end.

366. Cf. Visser, *Heart for the Gospel*, pp. 216-17.
367. Visser, *Heart for the Gospel*, pp. 7-8.
368. Cf. van Andel, *Voetius*, pp. 141-50.
369. J. H. Bavinck, *Science of Missions*, p. 155.

6. Missions Approach and Method

All of Bavinck's missiological efforts were meant to serve the proclamation of God's living Word to lost people. Thus, in this section we come to the climax of his thinking. We will trace the biblical theological support for and the methodological considerations proceeding from Bavinck's twofold missionary approach — one a broader and comprehensive approach, the other narrower and kerygmatic. The latter entailed what emerged as his characteristic method, that of persuasion or elenctics.

Bible and Method

Bavinck repeatedly emphasized that one must avoid the pretense of simply deriving missionary practice directly from the Bible. It would be shortsighted to reflexively apply Paul's method to the present, for example, since so ahistorical a move could actually lead to an *un*biblical approach.[370] Methodological principles must be discerned in Scripture very cautiously, functioning only as guidelines and boundary markers for our own work. In this sense, missions method was to be grounded in theological reflection and not be merely biblicistic.

At the same time, Bavinck protested against the secularized missions method that took only anthropology, ethnology, sociology, and psychology into consideration. The content and the method of mission are inextricably linked, he insisted. Since mission involves the voice of Christ himself, the work of mission is in principle an encounter between the living Christ and people who are imprisoned in all manner of foolish thoughts. Christ must recognize himself in any missionary approach.

The incarnation provided Bavinck with the cardinal argument for a personal and intensive approach to mission: "The revelation of God has never kept floating somewhere at a distance, has never come down to us as a general truth, but has entered into our history, has taken on bodily form and dwelt among us. Because the incarnation of the Word is the heart of revelatory history, revelation always has the character of a living, concrete encounter."[371]

---

370. Cf. J. H. Bavinck, *Science of Missions,* pp. 80-83. Bavinck states that facile conclusions drawn from apostolic missionary methods have proved to be "foolish" in contemporary situations.

371. J. H. Bavinck, *Science of Missions,* p. 83.

How then does theology relate to anthropology, ethnology, sociology, and psychology? On the one hand, theology leaves room for these disciplines because there are no "abstract, incorporeal, and ahistorical sinners, but only concrete sinners, whose sinful life is, among other factors, determined by various cultural and historical factors, by poverty, hunger, superstition, tradition, chronic illness, tribal customs, and a thousand other things."[372] On the other hand, theology limits the use and application of these disciplines. With reference to Karl Barth, Bavinck argued that theology will always "raise an admonishing finger in warning so that the purity of the gospel will not be sacrificed in the desire to come as close to one's audience as possible."[373]

The Comprehensive Approach

Bavinck thought that a missionary approach that revolved exclusively around proclamation was "naïve."[374] It is clear, both from Scripture and from the history of the church, that missionary activity must involve the totality of existence. The kerygmatic approach is always accompanied by the comprehensive approach, which finds expression in individual behaviors and in collective forms of assistance and development.[375] Though Bavinck did not reflect deeply on the kingdom of God as a theological theme,[376] it is clear that this biblical reality formed the foundation for his twofold approach. Thus, *all* deeds stand in close relationship to the kingship of God and belong to the new world order revealed in Christ.

In this matter, Bavinck distanced himself from the declarations of the Synod of Middelburg, which regarded this broad approach as a mere, if necessary, preparation for the real missionary task of proclaiming the gospel.[377] This perspective led to a distinction between the "primary ministry" of Word and sacrament and "subsidiary ministries" such as educational and medical work. This terminology clearly expressed a hierarchical view that Bavinck faulted. He maintained instead that the two types of ministry constitute an

---

372. J. H. Bavinck, *Science of Missions*, p. 81.

373. J. H. Bavinck, *Science of Missions*, p. 80.

374. J. H. Bavinck, *Science of Missions*, p. 87.

375. Cf. J. H. Bavinck, *Science of Missions*, pp. 87-89, 90-120; and *Zending*, pp. 45-46, 49-50.

376. Cf. Visser, *Heart for the Gospel*, pp. 234-39, which gives a summary of Bavinck's theology of the Kingdom.

377. Extract from the *Acta der Generale Synode* (Middelburg, 1896), p. 34.

indivisible whole that cannot be divided in missionary practice. He preferred the terminology of "core ministry" and "ancillary ministries."[378]

Bavinck, however, distinguished his position from the sort of "comprehensive approach" introduced at the International Missionary Conference held at Jerusalem in 1928. On the premise that "Man is a unity, and his spiritual life is indivisibly rooted in all his conditions — physical, mental and social,"[379] the International Missionary Council (IMC) postulated a four-dimensional missionary approach in which gospel proclamation, education, medical care, and social-economic aid stood side by side on equal footing. Bavinck criticized this concept for its anthropological (the "unity of man") and materialist foundations (the spiritual life is "rooted in all his conditions"). He also feared the dualistic secularization of these ministries common in western Christianity.[380] In light of his understanding of Scripture, the four-dimensional approach was "extremely misleading," Bavinck said, because "Christ only commanded us to preach the gospel to all nations."[381] Accordingly, the proper missionary approach is primarily one-dimensional. "All these other ministries only have meaning to the extent that they clarify, concretize, and give focus to that one thing: the preaching of the gospel."[382] We can only speak of a renewal of the totality of things from the perspective of the atonement;[383] there is but one door to the Kingdom, not four.

The Kerygmatic Approach

Bavinck used the concept of "encounter" to characterize the heart of his preferred approach: an encounter between preacher and hearer in which a confrontation takes place between the Word of God and the person. This encounter has psychological, theological, and pedagogical components, especially because human rebellion is hidden under both cultural and reli-

---

378. J. H. Bavinck, *Zending*, pp. 53-54. He already used these terms in *Ons Zendingsboek* (no place name, 1941). It is difficult to explain why he did not employ them in *Inleiding in de Zendingswetenschap*, in which he clearly rejected the terminology advanced by Middelburg.

379. William Paton, Samuel Guy Inman, and Harold Grimshaw, *Jerusalem Meeting of the International Missionary Council March 24–April 8, 1928*, vol. 5: *The Christian Mission in Relation to Rural Problems* (International Missionary Council, 1928), p. 287.

380. Cf. J. H. Bavinck, *Science of Missions*, pp. 100-107.

381. J. H. Bavinck, *Science of Missions*, p. 109.

382. J. H. Bavinck, *Science of Missions*, p. 109.

383. Cf. J. H. Bavinck, *The Impact of Christianity*, pp. 175-83.

gious shells. Bavinck caught the essence of the encounter in a striking comparison: we are not mail carriers who have completed our task "when we have simply spoken the right word" but envoys who, as *chargés d'affaires,* must look after Christ's business among the nations. In this context, Bavinck rejected three possible missionary methods.[384] He rejected the antithetical method, which works with apologetic rational argumentation, as psychologically insufficient. He rejected the sympathetic method, which links religion and gospel as partners in the truth, as theologically irresponsible. And he rejected the thetic method, which starts with the direct unfolding of the biblical message, as pedagogically inadequate.

Instead, Bavinck opted for the confrontational method as superior on all three scores, and he unfolded this existential encounter in three phases.[385] First, there must be a true seeing of the person encountered, in the sense of seeing through him. "Again and again we read in the gospels that Jesus *saw* an individual, and in each case, this means that he sees through all disguises and penetrates to the one thing that controls the entire life of that individual." The missionary is called to recognize, by careful exploration, the deepest intentions that lie hidden in the cultural and religious life of a person: What does this person do with God, and why? Next, one must adopt a stance of loving accommodation. Having come to recognize the deepest motivation of the other, one must approach her with patience, in "true awareness of our collective guilt before God and sincerely desiring to do for the other what Christ has done for me." Finally, this solidarity must result in an encounter in which the Word of God is active both in judging and in liberating the person encountered.

Of this approach Bavinck concluded: "it is not antithetic, for it does not seek its power in ridicule . . . nor is it sympathetic, for it does not view paganism as a precursor to the gospel . . . nor is it thetic, because it attempts to come as near as possible to the life and thought of those to whom the message is being presented."[386] It is clear that, though this method is kerygmatic in theory, it will always be dialogical in practice. In fact, Bavinck declared: "Missionary work is in practice always discussion and cannot be anything but discussion."[387]

But discussion can only proceed via a point of contact, a matter that

---

384. J. H. Bavinck, *Zending,* pp. 65-69. Cf. J. H. Bavinck, *Science of Missions,* pp. 134ff., 149.

385. Cf. J. H. Bavinck, *Science of Missions,* pp. 122-29.

386. J. H. Bavinck, *Zending,* p. 71.

387. J. H. Bavinck, "Het Evangelie," p. 54.

Bavinck gave its full due consideration.[388] Following Johannes Witte,[389] he drew a distinction between the substantive and formal contacts between Christianity and other religions. Substantive engagement is impossible because these religions replace the truth with a lie. Formal engagement with them, on the other hand, is unavoidable and proceeds through three movements. The first movement is theological; the other two, practical.

Theologically, we encounter in every non-Christian religion "vague and general intuitions" that have their origin in the revelation of God. God has not left himself without witness (Acts 14:15-17), and it is precisely this fact that constitutes the great point of contact available to the church for her work in service of the gospel. It is God's prior involvement in the lives of non-Christians that gives the missionary a starting point. She does not open the dialogue between God and her listeners; rather, she opens a new chapter in the existing dialogue. Revelation fastens on to revelation. Because of the radical difference between the gospel and the non-Christian religion, however, this point of contact can only be established by way of antithesis — an antithesis that "is not meant to condemn, but to provide a deeply positive way of dealing realistically with the dialectical reality" of human religion.[390]

Practically, missionaries are forced to adopt a variety of existing words and idioms to express their hearers' preexisting intuitions. Only thus could one make oneself understood. "Paul and the other apostles did not hesitate to use numerous, highly specific words and expressions from Hellenistic culture, such as *logos* and *soteria,* which were, of course, loaded with wrong connotations, in the preaching of the gospel."[391] Bavinck spoke in this context of "stepping stones";[392] the content of these words and concepts could be gradually purified through use in a different context. Further, it is necessary that, in these forms of expression, we seek a "very thorough adaptation to the nature and possibilities of the peoples to whom we preach." Bavinck cited the Javanese preference for allegory and late-night conversations. Such connecting with the indigenous culture clearly results from mission's unavoidable contextualization, which Bavinck still labeled *possessio* (take possession of).[393]

---

388. Cf. J. H. Bavinck, "Het probleem der Anknüpfung," p. 59; *Science of Missions,* pp. 134-41.

389. Cf. Johannes Witte, *Die Christusbotschaft und die Religionen* (Göttingen: Vandenhoeck & Ruprecht, 1936).

390. Cf. Kraemer, *Christian Message,* p. 139.

391. J. H. Bavinck, "Het probleem der Anknüpfung," p. 67.

392. J. H. Bavinck, "General Revelation," p. 54; ET: *JHBR,* p. 108.

393. J. H. Bavinck dealt with this challenge extensively. An overview of his theoretical

Bavinck also spoke of an existential entry point, a so-called "point of attack," particularly amid modernization's climate of spiritual poverty, dissatisfaction, emptiness, and fear. The Christian witness could relate to these feelings and experiences and use them as a means to penetrate to a person's deeper need, the need for God. "God can use this as a means to lay bare the heart and make it aware of the much greater misery, the deepest ground of all misery, the fact that we are sinners."[394]

Missionary Elenctics

The International Missionary Conferences in Edinburgh, Jerusalem, and Tambaram made the relationship with and witness to non-Christian religions preeminent and persistent topics of discussion. Bavinck dealt with them in his own way. Though he connected these topics closely to his theological understanding of universal religious consciousness, he devoted a separate section in his *Introduction to the Science of Missions* to missionary apologetics under the heading "elenctics." The word derives from the Greek verb *elenchein,* to persuade; Bavinck called it the discipline of persuasion and understood it as a two-pronged activity: scholarly reflection on religion, and theological reflection on the apologetic approach to the religious person. Though thus distinguished, Bavinck did not think these two elements could be detached from each other. They served each other or formed two sides of the same coin. Here we will focus especially on the theological aspect.

The confrontational notion of elenctics was first used in a missionary framework by Gisbertus Voetius, who derived it from Titus 1:13: "rebuke *(elenche)* them sharply, so that they will be sound in the faith." Abraham Kuyper revived the term to denote the antithesis to pseudo-religion, as polemics was the antithesis to heresy and apologetics to pseudo-philosophy.[395] Bavinck, in turn, linked the term to missiology: elenctics is the discipline that directly confronts non-Christian religions in order to convince non-Christians of sin and to move them to repentance and conversion.[396]

The Greek verb *elenchein* initially meant "to disgrace" or "to bring

and practical efforts in the area of *contextualization* or *possessio* is found in Visser, *Heart for the Gospel,* pp. 282-92.

394. J. H. Bavinck, *Science of Missions,* p. 140.

395. Cf. Jan A. B. Jongeneel, *Missiologie: Missionaire Theologie,* part 2 ('s-Gravenhage: Boekencentrum, 1991), p. 332, and Kuyper, *Encyclopaedie,* 3: 365.

396. J. H. Bavinck, *Science of Missions,* p. 232.

shame on someone." In New Testament Greek it acquired the meaning "to prove guilt, to refute," or "to hold someone's sin before him and to challenge him to turn around."[397] Bavinck cited a number of biblical references to the verb (Jude 14-15; Rev. 3:19; John 16:8; 1 Tim. 5:20; Matt. 18:15), noting its varying subjects — whether the Lord, the Holy Spirit, the office bearer, or the brother — demonstrated that *elenchein* refers to human activity but also has a divine dimension.[398]

For Bavinck the pursuit of elenctics had biblical foundations, not only because the term was used in numerous texts but primarily because the Bible itself is an elenctic book.[399] "The Bible is from first page to last one immense defense against paganism, against paganizing tendencies within Israel, in short, against all degeneration of religion."[400] As an elenctic text, Bavinck said, the Bible had five fundamental differences from other holy books: it did not identify God with the creation, it made central the kingdom of heaven and not the cosmic order, it embedded ethical norms in a relationship of love, it replaced a cyclical with a progressive-salvation view of history, and it cast the resurrection of Christ as inaugurating a new age with the promise of the restoration of all things.[401] In the Bible, God wrestles with the world, persuading, reproving, admonishing, and beseeching its various peoples to accept the truth and be reconciled to God.[402]

Founded in Scripture though it was, elenctics still required one to consult a variety of disciplines from outside the theological curriculum, the better to understand non-Christian thought and life.[403] Thus, such fields as the history of religion, science of religion, psychology of religion, phenomenology of religion, and philosophy of religion were ancillary disciplines to elenctics that Bavinck frequently consulted, as is apparent in some of his own publications and from the record of his reading.[404]

---

397. J. H. Bavinck, *Science of Missions*, p. 21; Bavinck quotes here from Gerhard Kittel, *Theologisches Wörterbuch zum Neuen Testament*, vol. 2 (Stuttgart, 1935), p. 471.

398. It is striking that he doesn't mention in this connection Titus 1:13, which inspired Voetius to introduce the term *elenctics*.

399. J. H. Bavinck, *The Impact of Christianity*, p. 132.

400. J. H. Bavinck, *Science of Missions*, p. 245.

401. J. H. Bavinck, *Church between Temple and Mosque*, pp. 29ff.

402. J. H. Bavinck, *The Impact of Christianity*, pp. 139-40.

403. J. H. Bavinck, *The Impact of Christianity*, pp. 234-40, and *Science of Missions*, pp. 233-39. On the one side, these disciplines must be pursued in their own right; on the other side, viewed in the light of biblical revelation, they concretize and intensify the missiological reflection.

404. Cf. Johan Herman Bavinck, *Het Primitieve Denken: De Discussie Over de Plaats der*

Bavinck's work in elenctics continued the neo-Calvinist tradition's ongoing suspicion of traditional rationalistic apologetics. In the early church and in the Roman Catholic tradition, *ratio* was considered to be a reflection of the Logos, the source of natural knowledge of God, the gateway to the Christian faith. John Calvin, Bavinck pointed out, was the first to critique this position,[405] regarding even the most sophisticated thinkers as "worse than obtuse and blind" in their thinking about God, so that for them any sparks of light "are extinguished before they emit a brighter radiance."[406] Thus, Calvin argued that reason itself could no longer serve as the starting point in apologetics. "It is nevertheless remarkable," Bavinck observed, "that missiology in the churches of the Reformation remained captive to the ideas of earlier Roman Catholic theology" in this regard. Bavinck referred particularly to Voetius, who emphasized the possibility of philosophical persuasion.[407] It was Kuyper who created a shift in thinking on this score. Though he saw value in using philosophical argumentation to refute pseudo-religion, Kuyper subordinated philosophical argumentation itself to its pre-philosophical set of assumptions. For Kuyper, the center of *elenchein* lay in the revelation of God: sinners can be convinced of the error of their ways only "if the Light *(Photos)* beams from Christ into the darkness *(skotia)*, and if they, who were given over in the sinful desires of their hearts, are seized by the mercies of God."[408]

When Bavinck began to articulate his own position on this matter, he repeated emphatically that philosophical argumentation, though having its place, can never lead to conversion. Religious aberrations do not simply involve errors in thought but secret flight from God; even if people see clearly, they love darkness instead of light (John 3:19).[409] "The rational life of man is too closely intertwined with his instinctive passions, with his emotional and volitional life, for reasonable arguments to be able to truly change him. Be-

---

Medische Zending (no place, no date); *De Godsdienst van Java* (no place: s.n., 1937-1971); "Het Hindoeïsme en Syncretisme als Zendingsprobleem," in Johan Herman Bavinck, *Hoofdmomenten uit de Zendingsgeschiedenis en Andere Referaten,* stenciled manuscript (Putten, 1944); "Phaenomenologische classificatie"; *De psychologie van de Oosterling* (Loosduinen: Kleijwegt, 1942); *Uitkomsten der Studie van Buitenbijbelse Religies* (no place, no date); and *De absoluutheid van het Christendom* (no place: Javasche Boekhandel & Drukkerij, 1936).

405. Cf. J. H. Bavinck, *Science of Missions,* p. 224.
406. J. Calvin, *Institutes* 1.5.12-14.
407. J. H. Bavinck, *Science of Missions,* p. 225.
408. Kuyper, *Encyclopedia,* 3: 449.
409. J. H. Bavinck, *Science of Missions,* p. 226.

hind folly lies rebellion against God. The deliberations of reason come to nothing, because people always suppress the truth by their wickedness."[410] Already early in his career he asked: "Is it sufficient to know the truth, to have the road to salvation outlined for us? No, because we don't follow that road. No matter how well I know what I must do, there is a power in me that always pushes me toward evil."[411]

Like the other disciplines, then, reason itself can provide auxiliary service in elentics but can never serve as the point of departure. But neither can the Bible, simply taken. Given his understanding of religious belief, Bavinck opted to begin with the inevitable communication that takes place between God and humanity. This led to a threefold point of departure.

In the first place, Bavinck argued, the missionary must realize, before initiating elentic contact, that God has already been present with his truth, so that what can be known of God is already plain to see (Rom. 1:19). Because people continually repress and replace the truth, they are inwardly restless. "There is, deep in the heart of men, a very vague awareness that one is playing a game with God and is always secretly busy running away from him."[412] Elentic argument must connect to this continuing divine-human conversation and appeal to people's existential insecurity. Bavinck's metaphor was striking: "This is the only chink in the Goliath-armor of pseudo-religion, where the shepherd boy with his stone — if God guides his hand — can hit people."[413] In the depths of our heart, we have a vague sense that we are trying to fool God and that we are guilty before God.[414]

In the second place, Bavinck pointed out that the revelation of God in Jesus Christ must stand at the center of the elentic approach so that the unmasking of untruth takes place in the light of the real truth. Prophetic-elentic arguments reveal all religious striving to be a "revolt against the one true God . . . self-deification, pulling God down to the world, and the horrifying attempt to make God subservient to oneself." The main question is always: What did you do with God? In response to this question, religion offers two possible answers, both of which the *elenchein* has to confront. One option comes in traditional and modern forms of mysticism in which people deify themselves by viewing God pantheistically. Here, elentics has to struggle with the original sin of wanting to be God. The other option is ap-

410. J. H. Bavinck, *Science of Missions*, p. 228.
411. J. H. Bavinck, *Levensvragen*, p. 88.
412. J. H. Bavinck, *Levensvragen*, p. 88, and *Science of Missions*, p. 227.
413. J. H. Bavinck, *Probleem van de Pseudo-Religie*, p. 19.
414. J. H. Bavinck, *Church between Temple and Mosque*, pp. 200-201.

parent in types of religion where people try to stimulate or appease super-natural forces through magic rituals or adherence to a moral code. Though based on love, this finally amounts to an endless power struggle with the Higher Being and indicates a disturbed, hostile relationship with it/him. Here, elenctics must counter hidden, rebellious attempts to manipulate God in one way or another.

In the third place, Bavinck pointed to the decisive importance of the Holy Spirit as the subject of *elenchein*. "The Holy Spirit himself creates the starting point, he awakens in man that deeply hidden awareness of guilt. . . . The Holy Spirit uses the word of the preacher and the Spirit himself creates in man's heart the receptivity that allows the word to enter." Elenctics as a purely human undertaking would be "a rather hopeless affair," but the Spirit "makes us powerful in Christ."[415] The messenger has only one powerful weapon, to trust in God's help and in the Spirit that the gospel will somehow touch the heart of man. "Then the engines of repression are stopped, as it were, and only then the hearer clearly sees who he is, and who God is."[416]

Elenctic Method

Because of the wide variety of religions, Bavinck did not think that there was a single, generally valid method for elenctics. Since *elenchein* can only be practiced in living contact with the adherents of other religions, any stan-dardized approach threatens to do injustice to a living person. In practice, one never deals with Islam as such but always with *a* Muslim and *his* or *her* Islamic beliefs. Initially, therefore, the elenctic approach involves more ex-ploration than proclamation. This does not mean that we cannot establish some basic methodological principles from Scriptures, however, especially from Paul's missionary work to the Gentiles (for example, Acts 17:23).[417]

Bavinck reiterated that, in the elenctic situation, we must never stand above but next to the other. The missionary, too, flees from God and pushes him aside, albeit in a more cunning way. Bavinck stated: "In all your elenctic efforts, you can view things from the point of your own life, in which God's grace has done its miraculous work, despite your stubborn recalcitrance,

---

415. J. H. Bavinck, *Science of Missions*, pp. 229, 231.

416. J. H. Bavinck, *Church between Temple and Mosque*, p. 206.

417. J. H. Bavinck, *Alzoo Weis het Woord*, pp. 121ff. Bavinck describes in an impressive way this important elenctic encounter. Cf. Visser, *Heart for the Gospel*, pp. 269ff.

and in which he still continues to work with infinite patience. Elenctics is only possible on the basis of that true self-knowledge by the Holy Spirit . . . which enables us to engage in authentic witness. Here emerges the heart-to-heart conversation, a dialogue in which the Holy Spirit can persuade both of us of the same sin and grace. For that reason, there is no more humbling work in the world than elenctics . . . for one realizes at every moment that the weapon he points at the other has wounded himself as well."[418] It thus becomes apparent that Bavinck attached great value to dialogue in both the exploratory and the proclamatory phases of the elenctic approach. His *elenchein* bears a dialogical character in the service of witness. "The church cannot avoid dialogue with the temple and mosque, because the church will have to state its opinion of those other religions."[419]

Bavinck regularly pointed out the complications attending the actual practice of elenctics. He particularly called attention to a strong tendency toward syncretism in all nations and the difficulty it poses for the proclamation of the gospel. It is "much easier to work among people who resist antithetically, than among people who say yes to everything, but understand [the gospel] in a syncretistic manner."[420] In his first elenctic study, *Cristus en de Mystiek van het Oosten (Christ and the Mysticism of the East)*, Bavinck illustrated the problem by demonstrating how certain aspects of the gospel appeal to the Javanese. As a consequence, the Javanese do "give Jesus a place of honor, provided that they are allowed to interpret him in the Asian spirit and to recognize Asian ideas in him." When the radical difference between the Christian faith and Javanese mysticism is emphasized, "a knowing smile will often appear on the face of the listener, because he thinks he understands Christianity much better than the Western preacher does."[421] Likewise, in his last book, *Church Between Temple and Mosque*, Bavinck wrote: "It is very possible that the opposition the Church faces is not as dangerous as the seeming recognition it receives from syncretistic movements."[422]

The syncretistic tendency is reinforced in two ways, Bavinck explained. First, missionaries, whether from false modesty, a lack of theological knowledge, or respect for religious differences, occasionally go too far in assimilating the Christian faith to non-Christian traditions.[423] Once this has oc-

418. J. H. Bavinck, *Science of Missions*, pp. 222 and 272.

419. J. H. Bavinck, *Church between Temple and Mosque*, p. 199.

420. J. H. Bavinck, "Syncretisme als Zendingsprobleem," p. 11.

421. Cf. J. H. Bavinck, *Christus en de Mystiek*, pp. 209-16; ET: *JHBR*, pp. 390-96.

422. J. H. Bavinck, *Church between Temple and Mosque*, p. 199.

423. Cf. J. H. Bavinck, *Church between Temple and Mosque*, pp. 229-30, and "Syncre-

curred, an elenctic call to conversion becomes extremely difficult because listeners believe they have already mastered the Christian faith.[424] Second is the challenge of religious revitalization, typically in the context of nationalism or rising anti-colonialism. This makes one's religious heritage seem too valuable to give up, inviting a synthesis between that heritage and the gospel.[425] Yet syncretism as a transitional phase in conversion is unavoidable, Bavinck observed; it simply calls for persistence in the elenctic approach. Conversion to the gospel takes time, making *elenchein* often a long-term undertaking. In this struggle the church is called to continually clarify the profound distinction between pagan belief and what God has revealed in Christ.[426]

More problematic than religious revitalization was the challenge of religious decay. Almost prophetically, already before World War II, Bavinck observed a great spiritual vacuum emerging on the cutting edge of western development. Religious awareness and experience were being undermined by scientific, technological, and economic developments. The divine was giving way to the secular, and the process of secularization was coming to harvest in its godless and normless tendencies.[427] Bavinck recognized that *elenchein* is much more difficult in the context of a crumbling religious awareness where it is difficult to find a point of contact. In 1948 he concluded: "If there has ever been a moment in world history that, in our opinion, must be viewed as extremely unfavorable to the spread of the gospel, it is this moment. Both those who bring the gospel and those who hear it find themselves in extremely perilous circumstances; there is virtually no time for quiet reflection on the truth of God, for earnestly seeking the peace of God."[428] Even so, he wrote in his *Introduction,* it can be expected that, "thanks to the miraculous work of God, the present whirl of developments will eventually break, and at

---

tisme als Zendingsprobleem," pp. 14-15, where Bavinck refers in this connection to the pluralistic missionary C. F. Andrews, who wrote in a reaction to Tambaram in 1939: "The inclination in Hinduism to bring all religions into harmony with one another is to be preferred by far over the rough and fanatical way in which many Christians condemn other religions." To support his view theologically Andrews quotes the words of Jesus, "Whoever does the will of God is my brother and sister and mother" (Mark 3:35).

424. Johan Herman Bavinck, "Christus en de Wereld van het Oosten," in Frederick W. Grosheide et al., *Christus de Heiland* (Kampen: J. H. Kok, 1948), pp. 233-34.

425. J. H. Bavinck, "Syncretisme als Zendingsprobleem," p. 13.

426. J. H. Bavinck, *Christus en de Mystiek,* p. 107; ET: *JHBR,* p. 304.

427. Johan Herman Bavinck, *De Psychologie van den Oosterling* (Loosduinen: Kleijwegt, 1942), p. 24.

428. J. H. Bavinck, "Christus en de Wereld," p. 211.

that time, the quest for inner stability, for a philosophy of life, and for permanence will come to the fore with overpowering force."[429]

Amid this emerging spiritual vacuum, *elenchein* gave way in Bavinck's thought to the verbal proclamation of Christ as the Way, the Truth, and the Life.[430] In witnessing, we are "more powerless than ever before, and are entirely thrown back on the last resources of power that are available to us: the firm confidence that God is King and that prayer is able to accomplish much."[431] Meanwhile, "In the struggle of the present time, when from all sides new, spiritual powers throw themselves upon us, it is important for us to enter more deeply into elenctics."[432]

In light of Scripture, Bavinck's emphasis on elenctics is justified and necessary. The call to faith in Jesus Christ may not be replaced by "an exchange of spiritual experiences, a mutual influencing of one another, and a strengthening of the spirit of brotherhood."[433] Anyone who opts for "mission *as* dialogue"[434] must remember that if missionary witness is redundant, then the Bible is wrong, and the missionary mandate that is found in all four Gospels and that is fulfilled in the works of the apostles is based on a mistake. Any *theologia religionum* that leads to this conclusion represents nothing less than a boycott of the Spirit-driven calling of the church.[435] Thus, *elenchein* constitutes an essential focus in missionary reflection and practice, particularly now as the church finds itself confronted and immersed in societies that are becoming both more thoroughly secular and increasingly irreligious.

7. Conclusion

Properly speaking, the whole of Bavinck's missiology can be qualified as original. As the first missionary theologian of the Reformed Churches in the

429. J. H. Bavinck, *Science of Missions*, p. 309.

430. Cf. Johan Herman Bavinck, *The Riddle of Life*, trans. J. J. Lamberts (Grand Rapids: Eerdmans, 1958), and *Christus en de wereldstorm*.

431. J. H. Bavinck, *Science of Missions*, p. 309.

432. J. H. Bavinck, *Science of Missions*, p. 246.

433. J. H. Bavinck, *Religieus Besef*, pp. 149-56; ET: *JHBR*, pp. 264-71.

434. Cf. D. C. Mulder, "Dialoog als Zending," in Johannes Verkuyl et al., *Zending op weg Naar de Toekomst: Essays Aangeboden aan Prof. Dr. J. Verkuyl*, ed. J. D. Gort and H. J. Westmaas (Kampen: J. H. Kok, 1978), pp. 137-45.

435. Johannes Verkuyl, *Inleiding in de Nieuwere Zendingswetenschap* (Kampen: J. H. Kok, 1975), p. 485.

Netherlands, he offered a biblical examination of the fundamental questions of the Christian missionary calling and task. For the Protestant tradition in general and the Reformed tradition in particular, he contributed to the deepening of existing missionary principles and themes. Bavinck's work presents a powerful and authoritative starting point in the cultivation of Reformed missiology. His freshness and originality are evident in the way he developed any number of topics and issues. Two of these themes are of particular value, both now and in future.[436]

In his understanding of the relationship of the Christian faith to religious consciousness and of the gospel to non-Christian religions, Bavinck provides a thoroughgoing approach. He integrated theological reflection with psychological insight in a truly original way. His approach is based on the deep conviction that the Bible is the Word of God, the source of all theological thinking and psychological reflection alike. He carefully analyzed the psychological reality of theological verities in a quest to ascertain, in both missions and the pastorate, what occurs in the human heart when it encounters God's revelation through the work of the Holy Spirit. This urge to understand the mystery of *homo religiosus* was not an isolated theme in Bavinck's work but always served his primary goal, the effective communication of the gospel. The enduring significance of Bavinck's missiological reflection is found in this combination of theological and psychological approaches. It is primarily due to this treatment of religious consciousness — and subsequently of elenctics — that Bavinck's works can be considered "modern classics," retaining their importance in the present post-Christian era. Bavinck offers a genial concept of dialogical encounter, a concept that manifests both its Reformed origin and its honest, kind Christian praxis.

Bavinck also made an important contribution in his understanding of the relationship between word and deed and in finding a biblical balance between these two types of ministry. Using biblical arguments, he rejected the traditional position that drew a distinction between "primary" and "secondary" missionary tasks and that relegated deed ministries to a nonessential role in missions. At the same time, Bavinck distanced himself from the four-dimensional "comprehensive approach" espoused by the ecumenical move-

---

436. It is with good reason that Johannes Verkuyl, the second Reformed professor in missions in the Netherlands, worked these two themes out in his own way. He incorporated Bavinck's view on *theologia religionum* and elenctics into his discussion of what he called "trialogue." And he expanded on Bavinck's understanding of a comprehensive approach by defining the essential task of mission in terms of the vertical and horizontal dimensions of the kingdom of God.

ment of his day. Aware of both the comprehensive character of the kingdom of God and the irreducible necessity of preaching the gospel, he developed a new concept of a one-dimensional approach that includes the whole of life and society. He preferred to speak of the kerygmatic core missionary task, consisting of the preaching of the gospel, and auxiliary missionary ministries, consisting of life-renewing deeds. He subsumed both types of ministry in a single category, "missionary proclamation." In my opinion, from a Reformed perspective, Bavinck's approach remains valid — if anything, it should be enlarged according to the biblical data regarding the kingdom of God.

Bavinck was a firm proponent of ongoing reflection on missions, a missiologically appropriate application of the Reformation principle *reformata, semper reformanda*.[437] Bavinck's missionary theology clearly retains its relevance for the present and represents an excellent point of departure for the further development of a Reformed theology of mission in the contemporary world. In this regard, one of the closing sentences of his *Introduction to the Science of Missions*, a sentence that reflects both his realistic faith and his buoyant spirituality, is as applicable now as when he wrote it: "When we look at the world of our day, we must take clear-eyed account of the immense resistance to the Gospel which manifests itself everywhere. But we may also rejoice to note that, time and again, often at totally unexpected moments, by God's grace, doors are opened that offer access to a new, hopeful future."[438]

PAUL J. VISSER

437. Cf. J. H. Bavinck, *Zending*, p. 223, and *Science of Missions*, pp. 306-9.
438. J. H. Bavinck, *Science of Missions*, p. 308.

I. God's Revelation to the Nations

1 General Revelation and the Non-Christian Religions

The connection between general revelation and the non-Christian religions[1] is not a new issue for the church but something it has wrestled with throughout history. It first arose as a serious concern within the early church due to its constant interactions with the prevailingly pagan culture of its day. Thus, it was natural for the church fathers to reflect on the content and value of other religions and how to properly understand them.

As the church fathers reflected on other religions, remarkably they made an important distinction between religious myths and Greco-Roman philosophy; in general they condemned the former because they understood these myths as being the result of the voice of the Tempter. Although some myths shared a few similarities with biblical teachings, these common teachings did not mitigate their harsh judgment. The fathers remained convinced that the apparent similarities were the result of the Devil patterning religious teachings after the beliefs of Israel in order to abate the influence of Chris-

---

1. Ed. note: We are retaining the expressions "non-Christian religions" and "world religions" as they are used by Bavinck himself, even though there are solid arguments to be made against the use of "religions" in the plural as a general description.

Ed. note: This essay was initially published in the *Free University Quarterly* 4 (1955): 43-55; then translated into Dutch and published with the new edition of *Religieus Besef en Christelijk Geloof* (1989) and in *J. H. Bavinck: Een Keuze uit zijn Werk*, ed. René van Woudenberg (Kampen: J. H. Kok, 1991). Used here with permission from the VU, Amsterdam. The essay has been significantly edited for clarity of English style by Gayle Doornbos, John Bolt, and James Bratt.

tian faith. Thus, according to the fathers, even the most sublime myths must be considered as the Devil's work.

However, their view of Greek philosophy was quite different. Many of the fathers held the ideas of Socrates, Plato, and Greek philosophers in high regard throughout their writings, a perspective thoroughly articulated in the work of Justin Martyr in his *Apologies*. At the beginning of the *First Apology*, he observes continuity between Christian teaching and the writings of the Greek poets and philosophers. He writes: "For while we say that all things have been produced and arranged into a world by God, we shall seem to utter the doctrine of Plato."[2] He explains these similarities by proposing that Greek philosophy derived its ideas from the various teachings of Israel's prophets. Thus, many "seeds of truth" could be found in Greek writings; however, he also observed that these "seeds" were often scattered randomly throughout Greek poetry and philosophy.

Later in the *First Apology*, Justin Martyr emphasizes the divine Logos as a possible reason for the striking continuity. For Christ was the Word [Logos] made flesh, and did not this same Logos work in the hearts of gentiles even before his coming? He writes: "and those who lived reasonably [with the Word] are Christians, even though they have been thought atheists; as, among the Greeks, Socrates and Heraclitus."[3] And, for Justin it was demons who enticed the Greeks to kill Socrates.[4] Furthermore, the Greek poets wrote of excellent things "on account of the seed of reason [the Logos] implanted in every race of mankind."[5] Before his conversion, Justin was fascinated by Plato, and he reflects on his conversion, noting that this was "not because the teachings of Plato are different from those of Christ, but because they are not in all respects similar."[6]

Clement of Alexandria had a similar approach to non-Christian religions as Justin Martyr. He too supposed that the Logos was reflected in human thought and guided the Greek philosophers and poets. Clement wrote: "Perhaps philosophy too was a direct gift of God to the Greeks before the Lord extended his appeal to the Greeks. For philosophy was to the Greek world what the Law was to the Hebrews, a tutor escorting them to

---

2. Justin Martyr, *First Apology*, 20, in *Ante-Nicene Fathers* (hereafter *ANF*), ed. Rev. Alexander Roberts and James Donaldson, 10 vols. (Grand Rapids: Eerdmans, 1975-1978), pp. 169-70.

3. Justin Martyr, *First Apology*, 46, in *ANF*, 1: 178.

4. Justin Martyr, *First Apology*, 5, in *ANF*, 1: 164.

5. Justin Martyr, *Second Apology*, 8, in *ANF*, 1: 191.

6. Justin Martyr, *Second Apology*, 13, in *ANF*, 1: 193.

Christ."[7] Thus, with Clement too, general revelation assumed a place of great importance because he based the many true and profound sayings found in ancient Greek philosophical writings in general revelation.

After the gospel had spread among the gentiles, the need to pursue the issue of general revelation and the non-Christian religions significantly diminished. Similarly, later interaction between the church and less intellectually developed tribes did not spur the church to further reflection concerning general revelation. It was only mission work among Muslims in East Asia that compelled the church to address this issue once again.

Thomas Aquinas reflects on this issue in his famous *Summa contra Gentiles* where he clearly distinguishes between truths that can be understood through the natural light of human reason and those that must be revealed to humans as mysteries of faith. He proposed that missionaries should first build on general concepts that could be derived from natural theology when they encountered paganism and then seek ways to teach the mysteries of faith from this foundation. This framework, developed by Aquinas, remained the major theological paradigm for missionary engagement for a long time.

From the outset, the Reformers perceived what was at stake in this discussion. They did not deny the truth of general revelation; on the contrary, they emphatically taught that God revealed himself in creation. They also fervently taught that all humans have a *semen religionis,* a seed of religion,[8] which can never be fully destroyed. However, they vehemently denied that this innate religious sense could ever bring humans to understand the glory and greatness of God. Calvin wrote: "It is therefore in vain that so many burning lamps shine for us in the workmanship of the universe to show forth the glory of its Author."[9] These shining lights have some effect on the human mind, but instead of arousing adoration of the true God, they cause humans to invent idols and create new religions.

Since the Reformation, the western world has become increasingly connected to other cultures and people around the world. Early on, explorers came into contact with people in Africa, Asia, and the remote islands of the

7. Clement of Alexandria, *Stromateis: Books One to Three,* trans. John Ferguson, in *The Fathers of the Church,* vol. 85 (Washington, DC: Catholic University of America Press, 1991), 1.5.28.

8. Cf. John Calvin, *Institutes of the Christian Religion,* ed. John T. McNeill, trans. Ford Lewis Battles, The Library of Christian Classics, vol. 20 (Philadelphia: Westminster, 1960), 1.3.1.

9. Calvin, *Institutes,* 1.5.14.

Pacific. Explorers often saw these regions as places of commercial interest, but they were also seen as objects of scientific investigation.

It was through these explorations and new mission endeavors that the church in the West first learned about East Asian religions. The first reports came from Jesuit missionaries working among the Chinese, and these accounts left a deep impression on the western church.[10] [Kong Fuzi (K'ung Fu-tzu), known in English as "Confucius," was venerated (1) for his transmission of the tradition of former sage kings, a tradition having both religious and political dimensions, and (2) for his urging cultivation of inner kindness of heart to accompany outward learned erudition in the tradition. For both Chinese and non-Chinese alike, the transmitted, scribal records of conversations that Kong Fuzi had with his students seem to indicate that Kong Fuzi focused more on the moral implications of received teachings than "spirits" and "divine beings," about which Kong Fuzi himself said little could be known. Kong Fuzi's apparent preference for the practical and moral impact of received teachings seemed to the Jesuits and to leading western philosophers well suited to the practical and moral concerns of modern "Europe in transition," a Europe in the midst of intriguing changes happening as a result of its self-designated "age of Enlightenment."] Educated circles were quickly turning away from the abstract and lengthy teachings of the church and were increasingly interested in understanding and practicing a natural religion, which was supposed to be the root of all religion and religious practice. As the concepts of Chinese religions and moral practice began to spread through Europe, the philosopher Leibniz made these approving remarks: "Certainly the condition of our affairs, slipping as we are into ever greater corruption, seems to me such that we need missionaries from the Chinese who might teach us the use and practice of natural religion, just as we have sent them teachers of revealed theology."[11]

---

10. Ed. note: The material that follows in square brackets is a significant rewriting of three sentences in the original: "The works of the great religion founder Confucius seemed to present a sober, reasonable form of practical religion that suited the modern world extremely well. No lengthy dogmatic treatises, but practical moral rules of life were the heart of their reverence to divine powers. This information reached a 'Europe in transition,' namely in the highly interesting period going by the name of 'Enlightenment.'" In keeping with our editorial decision to use the Pinyin system of Romanizing Chinese spelling and to acknowledge current scholarship that no longer thinks of Kong Fuzi (Confucius) as the "founder" of a religion, Diane Obenchain prepared the expanded rewrite.

11. Gottfried Wilhelm Leibniz, *The Preface to Leibniz' Novissima Sinica: Commentary, Translation, Text*, trans. Donald F. Lach (Honolulu: University of Hawaii Press, 1957), § X,

It is plain that this approach to other religions was quite different from the approach taken by the Reformers. The starting point of engagement for Enlightenment philosophers was the belief that the standard of morality and religion rested in "natural religion," which was a hidden treasure present deep in the consciousness of all humans. Thus, they developed systems of thought based on this idea of "natural religion." While these systems themselves are not quite relevant to our subject, they do serve to reveal that "natural religion" was believed to be embedded in the human heart, and they show that humans and their qualities were the focus and starting point, not revelation.

A few decades after the reports about Chinese religion, Europe began to learn about the great religious systems of India. These systems became known in Europe when an Arabian translation of one of the ancient writings of the Brahmins, the *Upanishads,* was translated into Latin by a Frenchman.[12] In certain circles, this book aroused great admiration. Many who read the book were surprised by the great wisdom imparted by Indian hermits thousands of years ago.

Through closer contact with the East, western scholars gradually obtained a wealth of Indian, Chinese, and Japanese literature. The acquisition and study of this literature marked a new epoch in the science of religion in the West because reference to non-Christian religions no longer implied just the ancient religions of Greece and Rome but also the systems that were understood through interaction with and study of Hindus and Buddhists, Muslims, and adherents of so-called primitive religions.

The study of these religions revealed unexpected things. At first scholars were inclined to regard them as a simple conglomeration of superstitious

---

p. 75. The original Latin text reads: "Certe talis nostrarum rerun mihi videtur esse conditio, gliscentibus in immensum corruptelis, ut propemodum necessarium videatur Missionarios Sinensium ad nos mitti, qui Theologiae natrualis, usum praxinque nos doceant, quemadmodum nos illis mittimus qui Theologiam eos doceant revelatam." Liebniz, *Preface,* § X, p. 91.

12. Ed. note: Bavinck is referring to Anquetil-Duperron's Latin translation of the *Upanishads,* which was completed in 1796 and published in 1801-1802 under the title *Oupnek'hat, id est, Secretum tegendum: opus ipsa in India rarissimum, continens antiquam et arcanam, seu theologicam et philosophicam, doctrinam, e' quatuor sacris Indorum libris, Rak Beid, Djedjr Beid, Sam Beid, Athrban Beid, excerptam: ad verbum, e Persico idiomate, Samskreticis vocabulis intermixto, in Latinum conversum: dissertationibus et annotationibus, difficiliora explanantibus, illustratum* and published by Argentorati: Typis et impensis fratrum Levrault; Parisiis: Apud eosd. Bibliopolas. The Arabian translation that Bavinck refers to is a Persian translation of the *Upanishads* that Anquetil-Duperron used.

thoughts and customs, but closer study revealed that these religions were intricate systems in which great and comprehensive concepts of humans, the world, and God were articulated in various ways. Thus, the study of other religions led to several remarkable discoveries that forced scholars to face the question as to what value could be attached to these religious systems.

Understandably, this question was of uttermost importance to the work of missionaries. Missionaries needed to determine whether they should call on Hindus and Buddhists to convert from their "vain way of life" or whether they should emphasize the beautiful elements in these religions and augment them in a Christian sense. The central questions for missions, in this regard, were: Are these religions backsliding from God and revolting against God, or are they to be regarded as imperfect yet earnest attempts to find God? Do these strange religions provide points of contact from which one can start teaching the gospel, or ought the adherents of these religions be called to forswear their old religion? The answers to these questions were essential to everyday practice of mission work and required clear answers.

In the 1900s many missionaries confronted with these questions failed to see the importance of seeking out answers and often worked solely upon the basis of their personal impressions. Some missionaries had nothing favorable to say concerning other religions and described them as Satan's work. Others, however, were struck by the piety, self-surrender, and faithfulness of adherents of other religions. The phenomenon of a Buddhist praying to a Buddha or Bodhisattva or a Hindu praying to a god with great devotion caused many missionaries to ponder whether or not they were actually praying to the God of Christianity even if they prayed to an imperfect and wrong conception of God.[13] Furthermore, they wondered, would God not accept such prayer?

Therefore, for many missionaries the personal experience of interacting with adherents of other religions affected their assessment of these religions. Of course, their reactions differed according to the people groups and religions they encountered. Missionaries who worked in the midst of appalling moral perversion — particularly within certain tribal religions — were less inclined to believe that there could be elements of truth in non-Christian reli-

13. Ed. note: This sentence was rewritten to reflect a concern that the original might not accurately reflect the practices of Buddhist and Hindu believers and give unnecessary offense. Bavinck's original reads: "The view of a Buddhist or Hindu, praying to their god with great devotion, caused many a missionary to ponder whether or not such a person really meant the very God, how imperfect and wrong his conception of god might be in many respects, and whether or not God would accept such prayer."

gions than missionaries whose work brought them into contact with religions that had more refined theological and ethical systems. Given the divergence of missionary experience, it is difficult to summarize their perspectives into a common point of view.

International missionary conferences were dedicated to the dialogue between varying perspectives on non-Christian religions. At these conferences missionaries from all over the world as well as members of the new churches were able to discuss differing points of view and exchange their experiences.

These exchanges between missionaries began to occur already at the first World Missionary Conference, held in Edinburgh in 1910. When one reads the records of this conference, one is struck by the positive reports on other religions from some of the missionaries. For example, a missionary working among a particular tribe stated he had found real "God-seekers" among them;[14] a missionary from China commented on the many points where Buddhism touches Christianity;[15] another missionary pronounced one form of Japanese Buddhism "wonderfully like Christianity";[16] and a missionary from India thought that "a sympathetic mind will find very much in Hindu religious ideas which anticipates fuller expression in Christianity."[17] On the other hand, some missionaries presented much less favorable judgments on other religions and consequently did not want to identify "elements of truth" in other religious systems.

As a whole, the delegates at the Edinburgh Conference were inclined to recognize a true search for God in non-Christian religions, but their final conclusions were formulated carefully with the concerns of each particular missionary's perspective in mind. However, it was regrettable that the overarching approach to the issue of the non-Christian religions was based solely on the experience of missionaries. Sadly, at Edinburgh no serious attempt was made to explore the issues biblically and theologically.

At the International Missionary Council held in Jerusalem,[18] the approach to non-Christian religions remained rooted in the experience of missionaries. For example, a report on Hinduism addressed the question of whether or not there is a gulf between Christianity and Hinduism. The

14. World Missionary Conference, *Report of Commission IV: The Missionary Message in Relation to Non-Christian Religions* (New York: Fleming H. Revell, 1910), p. 28.

15. World Missionary Conference, *The Missionary Message,* pp. 56-58.

16. World Missionary Conference, *The Missionary Message,* p. 99.

17. World Missionary Conference, *The Missionary Message,* p. 187.

18. Ed. note: Bavinck is referring to the conference in Jerusalem convened by the International Missionary Council from 24 March to 8 April 1928.

question was answered by referring to the experience of Hindu converts who understood their conversions as a forswearing of their previous beliefs while others found their new religion "scarcely wetting [their] feet."[19] Similarly, with regard to Confucianism one of the reporters stated "that the Confucian literature can nobly supplement the Old Testament in leading its students to Christ and helping them to interpret Him according to their racial genius, as Plato did for the Graeco-Roman world."[20] Furthermore, some of the attendees indicated that they were convinced that Buddhism contained elements of truth. One person who lived in China remarked that Buddhist monks "may give to the Christian Church something of the wonderful treasures which Christ as the Eternal Logos has bestowed upon them through Buddhism."[21]

Again, all of these diverse opinions were based on missionaries reflecting on their personal experiences. A theological and biblical approach concerning how to interact with and view other religions was not attempted. Although at one point in the conference's proceedings some expressed their dissatisfaction with using human experience as axiomatic, the concluding statement of the conference remained positively geared towards other religions based on the personal accounts of missionaries. "We welcome every noble quality in non-Christian persons or systems as further proof that the Father, who sent his Son into the world, has nowhere left Himself without witness. Thus, merely to give illustration and making no attempt to estimate the spiritual value of other religions to their adherents, we recognize as part of the one Truth that sense of the Majesty of God and the consequent reverence in worship, which are conspicuous in Islam, the deep sympathy for the world's sorrow and unselfish search for the way of escape, which are the heart of Buddhism."[22] The statement then goes on to sum up several noble elements from different religions.

---

19. "The Christian Life and Message in Relation to Non-Christian Systems of Thought and Life," in *The Jerusalem Meeting of the International Missionary Council March 24–April 8, 1928*, 8 vols. (New York: International Missionary Council, 1928), 1: 42.

20. "The Christian Life and Message," 1: 65.

21. "The Christian Life and Message," 1: 95.

22. "The Christian Life and Message," 1: 410. Ed. note: The full passage continues as follows: ". . . the desire for contact with Ultimate Reality conceived as spiritual, which is prominent in Hinduism; the belief in a moral order of the universe and consequent insistence on moral conduct, which are inculcated by Confucianism; the disinterested pursuit of truth and of human welfare which are often found in those who stand for secular civilization but do not accept Christ as their Lord and Saviour." "The Christian Life and Message," 1: 410-11.

Although the missionary conferences in Edinburgh and Jerusalem relied on personal experiences, it soon became increasingly clear that Christian reflection on non-Christian religions could not be solved through personal accounts given by missionaries because the resulting conclusions were ultimately unsatisfactory. A sufficient answer could only be attained through an earnest study of what the Bible itself teaches concerning other religions. Thus, renewed biblical reflection on other religions and general revelation began to take place.

The impetus for this renewed reflection came from many places, but one of the most significant was Karl Barth's chapter "Religion as Unbelief," in his *Church Dogmatics*. Barth writes: "From the standpoint of revelation religion is clearly seen to be a human attempt to anticipate what God in his revelation wills to do and does do. It is the attempted replacement of the divine work by a human manufacture. The divine reality offered and manifested to us in revelation is replaced by a concept of God arbitrarily and willfully evolved by man."[23]

Barth's statement sparked a debate as to whether he had neglected the idea that God "has nowhere left Himself without witness."[24] Hendrik Kraemer, in particular, dealt with this question in his book *The Christian Message in a Non-Christian World*. While Kraemer admitted that he was indebted to Barth for bringing up the issue, he ultimately stated that Barth "will not and cannot deny *that* God works and has worked in man outside the Biblical sphere of revelation, but *how* this has happened he refuses to discuss" (emphasis original). Furthermore, Kraemer goes on: "This self-willed refusal to move further will in the long run appear to be untenable."[25] Later Kraemer reveals his desire to discuss that which Barth refused to address. He writes: "General revelation can henceforth only mean that God shines revealingly through the works of His creation (nature), through the thirst and quest for truth and beauty, through conscience and the thirst and quest for goodness, which throbs in man even in his condition of forlorn sinfulness,

23. Karl Barth, *Church Dogmatics: The Doctrine of the Word of God*, I/2, trans. G. T. Thomson and Harold Knight, ed. G. W. Bromiley and T. F. Torrance (Edinburgh: T. & T. Clark, 1956), p. 302.

24. Acts 14:17: "Yet he has not left himself without testimony: He has shown kindness by giving you rain from heaven and crops in their seasons; he provides you with plenty of food and fills your hearts with joy" (Today's New International Version). All subsequent biblical references will be made from the Today's New International Version (TNIV).

25. Hendrik Kraemer, *The Christian Message in a Non-Christian World* (London: Edinburgh House Press, 1938), p. 120.

because God is continuously occupying Himself and wrestling with man, in all ages and with all peoples."[26]

Kraemer's articulation of the issue rejuvenated the discussion of the connection between general revelation and non-Christian religions. Kraemer and Barth agreed on the existence of general revelation but disagreed on the effect that general revelation had on humans. Could general revelation bring about favorable things within human life? In other words, is general revelation the basis of blessings in human life, and are these blessings present in various religions? Are these blessings evident to observers?

Finding adequate answers to these questions was extremely important to understanding the task of Christian mission. In order to engage in the task of mission, missionaries needed a good framework for understanding the religion and people they would be working among.

While important for missionaries, an adequate understanding of general revelation was also extremely important for churches of new Christians who needed to understand their place within non-Christian cultures. Many of these churches readily adopted what they treasured from their previous religious traditions — particularly religious writings. Many came to see their religious writings as valuable books that, although not entirely conforming to the Christian message, contained elements that were acceptable to Christians. In India, China, and Japan some new Christians did not understood their old religions simply as a set of untruths but also the avenue through which God had first spoken to their people. Surely the God who educated the Greek world about Christ through philosophy, as Clement of Alexandria had taught, could have educated their cultures by means of the sacred books of Hinduism, Buddhism, and Islam. And was not Christ the fulfillment of all the beauty and truth within the religions?

Some new converts began to collect diligently the songs, stories, and thoughts from their old religions that displayed similarities with biblical teachings. For example, Hindu mythology describes a primeval age in which a poison appeared over the ocean world. In order to save the world from destruction, the great God Shiva gathered up the world poison into his hands and drank it. In this and other myths, Christians observed that even in the mythology of other religions there was an understanding that salvation could only be accomplished by God. There were many more examples of stories and teachings that shared similarities with the gospel message. Hinduism in southern India had a well-developed theory of grace. This branch

26. Kraemer, *Christian Message*, p. 125.

of Hindu theology taught that humans were incapable of saving themselves. Thus, a strong emphasis was placed on the grace and favor of God as the way of salvation. Similarly, Japanese Buddhism contained a theology of redemption comparable to reformational teachings. Given the similarities, it was difficult not to see the proposition that non-Christian religions were strictly the work of Satan as untenable. To see these religions as only Satanic was to disregard the beautiful and truthful elements found within them.

Therefore, the issue of general revelation again became extremely important. In-depth study of other religions revealed that they could not be easily dismissed but required further investigation in order to understand the spiritual values within their systems of thought. Understanding the complexity of such observations concerning other religions could not be achieved through the stories of missionaries themselves, and therefore theological reflection turned to Scripture to try and understand the phenomena encountered in other religions. Reflection centered around the following four questions:

a. Is there a general revelation of God that reaches and stirs humans?
b. If such a revelation exists, does it bring about blessing and happiness within the culture and practices of people?
c. If it does bring about blessing and happiness, has this also penetrated the religious systems that missionaries encounter in other cultures? In other words, are there any elements of truth in these systems?
d. If there is truth within these systems, can these elements be used as stepping-stones or points of contact to preach the gospel?

It is beyond the scope of this essay to deal with all of these questions in detail. However, we must make a few preliminary remarks of general concern.

First, when considering other religions, we should always take into account that all peoples have kept some vague remembered past of a Paradise, be it ever so distorted. Within many tribal religions, there are myths that recall a glorious primeval age in which there was peace between the gods and men. In these myths, this blissful period ended by means of some type of blunder or accident, but, in general, these accounts acquit humanity of guilt. However, even though human action is rarely considered the cause of paradise lost, these myths reveal that there is some kind of universal memory that relates to that which is recorded in Genesis 1–3. Therefore, it is important to note that when considering non-Christian religions one must not only deal with the issue of general revelation but also with the memory of God's revelation within humanity.

Second, when considering other religions one must not exclude the possibility that they may have been affected by a certain influx of special revelation. The church fathers taught about the possibility of Greek philosophy being influenced by Israel's prophets and incorporating these prophetic teachings into their philosophy. It is not important to assess the accuracy of such a claim for our purposes here, but it is important to note that such a possibility does exist. The gospel was brought to India many centuries ago, and there are legends that tell of the apostle Thomas preaching in India. Even if this legend is discarded due to its improbability, it is still based on the fact that there is a record of churches in India as early as the fourth century. Did these early believers influence the development of Hinduism? In his essay on Bhakti-Marga in the *Encyclopedia of Religion and Ethics,* the English scholar Grierson presents the possibility that the strong emphasis put on grace and bhakti or "abandon" in Hinduism could be based on Hinduism's interaction with early Christian churches in India.[27] Other experts on Hindu religion also leave room for the possibility that the teaching of the early church had some impact on the development of Hinduism.

Similar observations can be made about China. Through many years of contact with and study of Chinese Buddhism, Norwegian missionary Karl Ludvig Reichelt concluded that it was strongly influenced by Nestorianism. Reichelt points out many conceptions that may have been derived from the Nestorians,[28] and from China it is possible that the Nestorian influence traveled to Japan. Even though the connection is difficult to prove, it is important to allow for the possibility to have occurred. Allowing for possible influence from Christianity means that one must allow for the possibility that non-Christian religions were not void of special revelation but that special revelation may have influenced these other religions as they developed.[29]

Third, when dealing with the issue of general revelation and non-Christian religions it is necessary to distinguish between these religions as systems of thought and the personal religious experience and searching of each religion's adherents. In the *Institutes* Calvin writes: "As experience

27. George A. Grierson, "Bhakti-Marga," in *Encyclopedia of Religion and Ethics,* vol. 2, ed. James Hastings (Edinburgh: T. & T. Clark, 1909), pp. 539-51.

28. Karl Ludvig Reichelt, *Religion in Chinese Garment,* trans. Joseph Tetlie (London: Lutterworth, 1951), pp. 124, 129, 130, 170.

29. Ed. note: For a brief and accessible article on Nestorian Christianity in China, with more recent bibliography, see Glen L. Thompson, "Christ on the Silk Road: The Evidences of Nestorian Christianity in Ancient China," *Touchstone Magazine* 20, no. 3 (April 2007): 23-28. Available at http://touchstonemag.com/archives/print.php?id=20-03-030-f.

shows, God has sown a seed of religion in all men. But scarcely one man in a hundred is met with who fosters it, once received, in his heart, and none in whom it ripens — much less shows fruit in season [cf. Ps. 1:3]."[30] Already in Calvin there is an acknowledgment that each individual believer within a religious system is different. Among Hindus, Buddhists, and Muslims there are people who earnestly seek God, but there are also others who have no interest in religion. No one can adequately judge the hearts of individuals, and no one can anticipate the results that the long-suffering goodness of God, through the Spirit, will have on the heart of a particular individual. Therefore, examination of revelation in other religions must be restricted to the religious systems themselves and not focus on the systems' particular adherents.

Now turning back to the four questions formulated above, it is difficult to deny the existence of general revelation. Scripture itself is very clear concerning general revelation. As the psalmist writes: "The heavens declare the glory of God; the skies proclaim the work of his hands" (Ps. 19:1). Similarly, Paul writes: "Since what may be known about God is plain to them, because God has made it plain to them. For since the creation of the world God's invisible qualities — his eternal power and divine nature — have been clearly seen, being understood from what has been made, so that people are without excuse" (Rom. 1:19-20). Paul clearly teaches the existence of general revelation. But, does this revelation also reach humans? Do humans actually perceive it? Does it stir them? The statements of Paul seem to answer these questions affirmatively; somehow this revelation acts upon humans. Furthermore, universal human reflection on and belief in God, gods, or spirits seems to provide a cogent demonstration that humans have always been touched, in some measure, by God's revelation.

The second question is more intricate: Has this general revelation brought about blessings in people's lives? Here a cautious affirmative can be made, for one can observe that there is some effect of general revelation on the human conscience. Paul teaches this when he says that gentiles although having no law still "do by nature things required by the law" (Rom. 2:14). Thus, although people's response to general revelation usually leads them to create idols as they suppress the truth of God, the presence of general revelation is still a blessing. In other words, even though, as Calvin writes, "man's nature . . . is a perpetual factory of idols,"[31] at least in idol worship there is some awareness of divine powers, a measure of reverence and awe, and a de-

---

30. Calvin, *Institutes,* 1.4.1.
31. Calvin, *Institutes,* 1.11.8.

sire for worship. This awareness of the divine and the desire for worship is confused and directed towards the wrong object, yet, the worship of these things protects life to some extent, and so, in a sense, is a blessing. This is even clearer when contrasted to the secularization taking place in the West, where the culture is becoming increasingly godless. As T. S. Eliot reflects: "men have left God not for other gods, they say, but for no God: and this has never happened before."[32] In the modern world, people's spiritual condition is worse than those within the non-Christian religions.

However, admitting this should still be done with the awareness that backsliding from the living God and turning towards created idols leaves humans in a state where they desperately need the gospel. Paul truthfully described the Ephesians pre-conversion as "having no hope and without God in the world" even though they had a religion of their own (Eph. 2:12). This is because the power of Satan, "the ruler of the kingdom of the air, the spirit who is now at work in those who are disobedient" (Eph. 2:2), is present and apparent in other religions. In all of the beauty, devotion, and philosophical contemplation of other religious systems, there remains a horrible void within them, for they search but repress God himself, the living God who came into the mire of this world in Jesus Christ.

Because of this void, it is extremely difficult to discuss truth within these religious systems. Of course, as already mentioned, teachings about the existence of a divine power are an element of truth, but the divine power before whom they kneel is thoroughly different from the God and Father of our Lord Jesus Christ. One may be thankful that other religions believe in some god, but the gods that are created often fill Christians with horror. Thus, when claiming that there is truth within other religions, it all depends on what is meant by an "element of truth." If understood in a vague and general sense, there are certainly elements of truth in non-Christian religions. However, if truth is understood more specifically with a reference to ultimate truth, then to claim that non-Christian religions contain elements of truth would not be tenable. All the essential Christian beliefs like God, creation, man, sin, salvation, law of life, and the conclusion of the world are present within other religions but they are all applied and believed in a fundamentally different sense. The more one explores other religions, the more one becomes aware that there exists a great void between non-Christian religions and Christianity.

32. T. S. Eliot, "Choruses from 'The Rock,'" in *The Complete Poems and Plays: 1909-1950* (New York: Harcourt, Brace & World, 1952), p. 108.

Both the vague and specific understandings of elements of truth in non-Christian religions must serve as the framework for understanding missions. First, it is possible to use these elements as stepping-stones or points of contact in mission. Missionaries often use vernacular words for God, sin, and salvation in order to teach the gospel message. This itself is a point of contact because people all over the world have reflected on these things and have developed concepts of them. However, even in using the vernacular words for these concepts, the concepts themselves must be altered. In obedience to the gospel, missionaries must work to fill the old concepts with new meanings that can only be derived from the gospel itself, not the culture around them. Therefore, although there are rich words, ideas, and parables present in other religions to use to aid in teaching the gospel, these do not provide a full picture of the truth. These words, ideas, and parables must receive new content when the message of Christ is communicated and takes root. To not give these ideas new content would be to sink into syncretism. Thus, on the one hand, missionaries must be constantly aware of the danger of syncretism, but, on the other hand, they must freely use helpful words and concepts within other religions and adapt them for the task of spreading the gospel in service to Jesus Christ. This can be done because all human need, expressed in various ways and religious systems, is fulfilled in Christ. This missiological framework is challenging, but it is also the enthralling and wonderful experience of the missionaries teaching the gospel.

2 Proclaiming Christ to the Nations

Missiology is the newest and least known among theological science's illustrious disciplines. Anyone who passes through its gates immediately feels like a traveler who has entered a previously unknown land, a territory that not only has not been mapped, but one whose borders have not even been clearly defined.

Reasons for this unfamiliarity are not difficult to comprehend. Missions[1] always bring us into contact with what lies at quite some distance away. That which is closer dominates our thoughts and captures our interest more powerfully, as goes without saying. The small, frivolous concerns and struggles closest to us make a stronger claim on our attention than the enormous conflicts that at the moment are being waged on the mission field.

Along with that, the concept of missions still remains too laden with ro-

1. Ed. note: The Dutch word *zending* has, with a few exceptions, been translated in the plural as "missions." When used in the singular, as in the second sentence of the following paragraph, it should be understood as referring to evangelistic "missions" and not in the way it is used in much contemporary literature to refer to the comprehensive "mission of God."

Ed. note: This essay was Bavinck's inaugural lecture in 1939 as Extraordinary Professor of Mission Studies at the Kampen Theological School of the Dutch Reformed Church *(GKN)* and to the same post at the Vrije Universiteit, Amsterdam. He delivered the address at Kampen on October 12 and at the Vrije Universiteit on October 13. Bavinck incorporated many citations from English works that he then translated, often very loosely, into Dutch. Our translation protocol was to preserve as much of the original text of Bavinck's work as possible in the body of the lecture and put the fuller text of the original in footnotes.

mantic associations in the hearts of many people. Use of the word "mission" itself evokes stirring fantasies of missionaries proclaiming the gospel in the face of the greatest dangers, including addressing it to voracious cannibals. But what this all has to do with science, or how one would ever be able to construct a missiology based on such unsettling prospects, necessarily seems to present us with an insuperable problem.

What also captures our attention is that mission work today is beginning to display entirely different features. That tens of millions of people in China, Japan, India, and the Dutch East Indies exist in spiritual turmoil and crises that we can scarcely imagine is not adequately understood. People also realize too little that the Christian mission enters that tumultuous, seething world with the message of Jesus Christ as the only Savior. It addresses people thoroughly saturated with western science and gripped by modern thoughtforms. These people encounter fascist and communist ideas. They deal with the deepest skepticism. All of this is hardly romantic in the usual sense of the term, but it is certainly grippingly serious. When we realize the degree to which the future of Asia depends on the response that the people of Asia[2] will give to the gospel, the situation becomes even more urgent.

Seen in that light, it is entirely understandable and not at all strange that room be made in the theological disciplines for explaining the work of mission. Conflict on the distant battlefront requires that the church in the homeland learn to think and pray empathetically. That kind of missiology, while belonging to the cluster of theological sciences that make the church their object of investigation, is at the same time closely tied to dogmatics and elenctics[3] — at least to the extent that it shares responsibility for comprehending more fully the phenomenon of false religion as it interfaces with missionary methodology. This is a subject demanding our attention.

My pleasure on this solemn occasion when I begin my work at this school[4] is to introduce you to one of the most central issues in missiology. For a few moments, I want to investigate with you the extremely weighty

2. Ed. note: Bavinck has "East"; for our translation decision, see the Preface.

3. Ed. note: The notion of "elenctics" is a key part of Bavinck's theology of missions. He defines it as "the science which is concerned with the conviction of sin. In a special sense then it is the science which unmasks to heathendom all false religions as sin against God, and it calls heathendom to a knowledge of the only true God" (J. H. Bavinck, *An Introduction to the Science of Missions*, trans. David Hugh Freeman [Philadelphia: Presbyterian and Reformed, 1960], p. 222).

4. Ed. note: The reference is to both the Kampen Theological Seminary (12 October 1939) and the Vrije Universiteit, Amsterdam (13 October 1939).

question of how in our day we should preach on the mission fields of Asia the message that Jesus is the Christ.

In considering our question, we have the significant advantage of being able to investigate how those who first brought the gospel, namely the apostles and their helpers, wrestled with the same difficulty placed before us here. As long as these apostles of the Lord labored within the borders of Palestine, they moved in circles where the name "Christ" still had concrete, transparent content. To be sure, the term "Christ" or "Messiah" was loaded with all kinds of national and political expectations and misperceptions. But that did not detract from the fact that it was meaningful in the conflict that these first missionaries had to wage. The word "Christ" evoked associations in the hearts of their listeners. Like waving a magic wand, it created interest. It emphasized what was on the minds of thousands. When by appealing to the writings of the Old Testament it could be demonstrated that Jesus, the prophet of Galilee, actually was the Christ, such a claim would — it might be reasonably expected — make a deep impression. Anyone who said that Jesus, the One who had worn the crown of thorns, is the Christ would immediately stir up all sorts of thoughts and expectations that the people of Israel had harbored for centuries.

The situation was completely different when these men crossed the boundaries of Israel's world and began to penetrate the fashionable but fickle circles of Hellenistic culture more widely. In the first place, an appeal to the Old Testament lost much of its force in those circles. As long as the books of the Old Testament possessed no authority for them, what force did it have to tell the sophisticated thinkers of Athens that various predictions had been made in the Old Testament concerning the Christ and that those prophecies had been fulfilled in Jesus? From the outset, the apostles felt that proof from the old covenant's canon must seem useless and that an entirely different approach needed to be introduced to awaken consciences. In the second place, in such circles the name "Christ" lost the immediate clarity essential for initial preaching. It made no sense to demonstrate emphatically to such people that Jesus is the Christ when they had no clue what that name connoted. What was needed first was a lengthy explanation of the full content of the Christ-concept before they could begin making plain that this content is realized in Jesus. Small wonder, then, that when the first ambassadors of King Jesus walked the roads of the Roman Empire, they soon realized that they would have to apply an entirely different strategy. To be sure, Paul could employ the old approach when in Thessalonica, where he stood among well-schooled Israelites and on three successive Sabbaths made broad appeals to the Old Testament, explaining that Jesus is the Christ, the long-promised Messiah (Acts 17:2-3). But as soon as that same apostle stood on the Areopagus or before a pagan governor, he laid aside those weapons and reached for others. For us, who face the same issues in our severely tested days, it is highly instructive to review how these apostles called by God found their way by the leading of the Holy Spirit.

In this connection, I need to indicate clearly that in the New Testament we possess no more than sporadic material related to the apostles' preaching to the pagans. Just a few examples of such preaching have been communicated to us, and where they have, they are very short and abbreviated. We will have to draw our conclusions, therefore, from just a few givens. By the nature of the case, that requires that we exercise great care. It strikes me, however, that we have a solid basis for saying that these first preachers of the gospel accented three specific ideas inherent in the rich content of the name "Christ."

First, strong emphasis is frequently placed on the fact that Jesus is *Judge of the World*. Even before mention is made of the Savior's redemptive work, and even before the cross is identified in its central significance for the coming of God's kingdom, the appearance of Jesus is earnestly and forcefully presented as the arrival of the world's Judge. When, in the home of Cornelius, Peter suddenly found himself before a circle of deeply interested but very ignorant listeners from an unbelieving background, he began by telling them something about the life and ministry of Jesus while he was on earth. But then the apostle continued in this way: "And he commanded us to preach to the people and to testify that he is the one whom God has appointed as Judge of the living and the dead" (Acts 10:42). In Athens years later, Paul had the opportunity to respond concerning his own faith. He began with an introduction about the nature of religion, but then he continued: "God, then having overlooked the times of ignorance, now proclaims to all people everywhere that they must repent, for he has determined a day on which he will righteously judge the earth through a man whom he has appointed" [Acts 17:30-31].[5] Similarly here, not a word initially appears about atonement through the suffering and death of the Savior. Full emphasis is given to pointing to the Day of Judgment that God will bring about. And yet again, years later when Paul was summoned to appear before the pro-consul Felix and his wife Drusilla in Caesarea in order to explain the Christian faith,

---

5. Ed. note: Textual references in square brackets [ ] have been added by the translator/editor.

he summarized his initial presentation in three points: righteousness, self-control, and the judgment to come (Acts 24:25). Very noteworthy in each of the foregoing instances is that the concept of Judge of the World was the first one preached.

In the second place, we note in quick succession that in non-Christian settings the apostles preached prominently that Jesus is the *Lord (Kurios Iēsous)*. This appears already in Peter's preaching at Cornelius's house: "He is the Lord of all" (Acts 10:36). We also find that this is a frequently repeated refrain in Paul's preaching as seen in his letters, "No one can say that Jesus is Lord, except through the Holy Spirit" (1 Cor. 12:3). In a world that increasingly accorded divine homage to the lord who was the emperor of Rome, the witness that there is only one Lord, Jesus Christ, through whom all things came into being (1 Cor. 8:6), made a deeply powerful impression. When in his letters Paul talks about the way of salvation, he almost never uses the name "Christ" as a predicate. He does not say that Jesus is the Christ. Over and over again he employs the name "Christ" as a proper name, "Jesus Christ," and follows it with the predicate that he "is Lord!" This emphasis resounds in the Apostles' Creed as well: "I believe in Jesus Christ, our Lord."

The third emphasis that strikes us from the earliest apostolic preaching in a non-Christian context is that Jesus as Savior *(Soter)* is frequently prominent. When Paul had to summarize the essence of the gospel in a few words for the Philippian jailer, he put it this way: "Believe in the Lord Jesus Christ and you will be saved." Jesus is the *Soter*. I need not go very deeply into the fact that in those days the name *"Soter"* was readily understood and existential. From the time of Caesar Augustus's reign, the honorary title of *Soter* belonged to the usual epitaphs accorded the imperial leader. By repeatedly preaching that Jesus is the Savior in the fullest sense of that word, the apostles connected his person and work with the numerous salvation expectations harbored in the Hellenistic world.

It seems to us from these considerations that as soon as the apostles had to bring the gospel to the non-Christian world, they could not base their approach on the name "Christ" because its content was not readily understood. They struggled with how to communicate clearly and relevantly in the language of their day what Jesus had done and would do. That they laid such a heavy emphasis on the coming judgment in this context is certainly connected with the dynamic display of Roman imperial power concerning right and wrong. Only the realization of the coming of the wrath of God *(dies irae)* was, by way of contrast, capable of awakening listeners' consciences. What we noted above about the relatively lighter apostolic emphasis on the cross of

Christ deserves clarification here. Admittedly and obviously, Paul's testimony in his first letter to the Corinthians is that he was resolved to know nothing except Jesus Christ and him crucified (1 Cor. 2:2). What is certainly worth noting in this regard, however, is that in the context of this passage the cross of Christ is emphasized as a sign of the secret, completely otherworldly, and spiritual character of the preaching of the gospel. None of the powers of this world acknowledged or recognized him; rather, they crucified him. The cross is our humanity's judgment on Jesus. The other dimension of the cross is the judgment that the Son of Man will one day exercise on humanity. So understood, the words of Paul elicit the same response that we have to the so-called *Acts of Apollonius,* an account of one of the earliest martyrs of the faith. When a judge asked Apollonius about the substance of his faith, he said: "It is what our Savior, Jesus Christ, born in Judea, righteous in every respect and filled with divine wisdom, has taught us in complete love." Then he continued like this: "Now he has been persecuted and killed by ignorant men, just as one of the Greeks had already predicted, saying that the righteous one would be flogged and killed." From these words we see clearly that these first believers, whenever they had to testify to their faith before the unbelieving authorities in power, often portrayed the cross as a frightening symbol of our sinful ignorance incapable of embracing God's highest wisdom.[6]

Precisely here we find ourselves squarely facing the problem of missiology. Missiology in the first instance is not preoccupied with the question of what the truth is, but with the secondary question of how we are to present that truth about Christ. How are we to speak the truth about Christ in such a way that the gospel is comprehensible to its hearers? I might indicate in this connection that evangelization[7] struggles with the same complexities. For, in the western world today, unchristian opinions and tendencies are certainly beginning to be seen in more audacious and flagrant forms, with the result that the difference between missions and evangelism is shriveling. In both terms, at issue is the demand to preach Christ relevantly and compellingly to people who do not know the one who is the Light of our

---

6. Adolf Harnack, *The Mission and Expansion of Christianity: In the First Three Centuries,* trans. and ed. James Moffatt, 2 vols., 2nd exp. and rev. ed. (New York: G. P. Putnam's Sons; London: Williams & Norgate, 1908), 1: 474.

7. Ed. note: It is apparent here that Bavinck considers "missions" *(zending)* to be identical to "evangelization"; i.e., bringing the gospel to those who do not know it. Only the context differs: "missions" takes place in lands that have been relatively untouched by the gospel; "evangelization" occurs in those nations of the western world that have been significantly shaped by the gospel.

light and the Life in our lives. The way of posing the issue in missiology is not the same as it is for dogmatic theology. For missiology, it is not about summarizing synthetically the truth of Scripture as that is mirrored in the church's confession. Nor is it about apologetics, although missiology must often sharply and clearly expose the errors of false religion and ward off all the attacks concentrated against the gospel. But all of this is simply provisional and not yet its actual task. The essential task of missiology is missional [Dutch: *missionair*].[8] As soon as the church moves from a defensive posture concerning unbelief and superstition and assumes the offensive position of positively proclaiming the gospel, it unavoidably faces the weighty issue of the form in which the gospel must be rendered.

When we move from the world of Paul and his fellow workers to the world in which God has called us to work, it seems like a huge step. And in a chronological sense, it is a huge step. But as soon as we look more deeply, it quickly becomes obvious that every reason exists to draw parallels. For in the first place, humanity is always the same. The people with whom we are engaged are sinners too and can be upheld in no other way than by Jesus Christ. In the second place, the message is the same: believe in the Lord Jesus Christ and you will be saved. In the midst of the crashing surf of the ages, this truth stands like a solid rock. In the third place must be cited the very striking similarity that exists, both in an internal and an external sense, between the problems faced by ancient, Hellenistic culture and those faced today. Even the imperial ideal of ancient Rome to establish the *pax Romana*, a peaceable kingdom under the sway of a divine emperor's scepter, is starting to look like present-day Japan's convulsive efforts to establish an imperial order in East Asia.[9] Finally, and in the fourth place, what was required of the first missionaries is asked of us as well, as Paul so profoundly put it: "To the Jew I became a Jew; I became all things to all men that I might save some" (1 Cor. 9:20-22).

Yet, we would certainly be wrong if we were to conclude from the points made above that it is enough for us offhandedly to imitate the missionary methods of the first evangelists — as though we would be able to stand on the Areopagus of modern nations with the same arguments used by the first

8. Ed. note: The translator and editor were unable to find a better translation for the Dutch word *missionair*; it is necessary to note that this should not be confused with the common use of the word "missional" in contemporary missiological and ecclesiological discussions. The most important difference is that Bavinck uses *missionair* as an adjective to describe the specifically *evangelistic* task and not to the broader notion of a *missio Dei*.

9. Ed. note: Bavinck, recall, gave this address in October 1939.

missionaries. Effective evangelistic preaching simply requires us to take the object of our work with completely serious thought and effort. At the most recently held World Missionary Conference in Tambaram,[10] this requirement was formulated in this way:

> It is inadequate to express Christian truth in words and concepts satisfactory only to western theologians. Rather, the gospel must be proclaimed in terms and expressions that make its summons intelligible in the context of life as actually lived. That can only happen when one has first fundamentally and seriously steeped oneself in the religious life of those to whom one goes. Only then will ways be found to approach them.

The Tambaram Conference articulated this calling in a manner similar to Abraham Kuyper's explanation given decades earlier in what follows:

> In missions, it is not enough for you simply to profess Christ, to learn the language of an unfamiliar people, and to dedicate yourself personally to preaching the gospel in that strange tongue; what is even more essential than daily bread in this regard is that you possess a living rapport with the religious thought-world of the people that you would like to convert, and ultimately that you discover that point of connection that makes you one with them.[11]

Within the brief confines of this address, it would take us too far afield to delve more broadly and deeply into the spirituality typical of Asia. For that reason, I will limit myself to a few summary observations. Two major, spiritual streams can be distinguished on the oriental mission field, it seems to me — at least as long as for the moment we leave Islam aside as an entirely unique phenomenon. The two are cosmism and humanism.[12]

---

10. Ed. note: The third missionary conference, convened by the International Missionary Council, which met at Tambaram, near Madras, India, in 1938. The first conference was held in Edinburgh (1910), the second in Jerusalem (1928).

11. Martin Schlunk, *Das Wunder der Kirche unter den Völkern der Erde: Bericht über die Weltmissions-konferenz in Tambaram (südindien) 1938* (Stuttgart and Basel: Evang. Missions, 1939), pp. 83-84. A. Kuyper, *Encyclopaedie der Heilige Godgeleerdheid*, 3 vols. (Amsterdam: J. A. Wormser, 1894), 3: 448-49.

12. Ed. note: After initially translating Bavinck's term *kosmisme* as "naturalism," we decided to use the English neologism "cosmism," which includes the connotation of "cosmic order" in a way that "naturalism" does not. The term points to the approach used by the Leiden University Norwegian phenomenologist of religion, W. Brede Kristensen (1867-1953), who considered the "direct, intuitive apprehension by the Ancients of Cosmos and Nature

Cosmism has been identified by all sorts of names. Professor Kraemer calls it "the naturalistic apperception of life and the world that focuses on self-realization."[13] It can emerge in various contexts. Sometimes it appears in magical form, but it can also appear in world-denying mysticism. It can be strongly materialistic, but it can just as well see the whole material world as *maya,* as empty illusion. Despite these various forms, in its deepest essence all cosmism is the same. It rests on the foundation that God and the world can be covered by one term, namely the word "cosmos," or "the All." Each person is one, small spark in the great fire of the totality who yearns to be separate from the larger surrounding world but in reality is nothing more than a ripple on the mighty ocean. Salvation is release into the Totality. A consequence of this naturalistic perception of life and the world is that cosmism gives little weight to the specifically human. The human is certainly recognized, but it is in every way tied to the natural. Humanity certainly possesses specific capabilities, but those powers upon closer examination prove to be nothing other than a concentration of what is found in the macrocosm, the wider world.

By its very nature, cosmism cannot provide a fully developed ethical component or sense of "good" and "evil." Humanity possesses various capabilities that need to balance one another. The darker inclinations of the heart must be balanced with the quiet, rational, self-controlling ones. Sin is seen as nothing more than unevenness, when the balance tilts too far to one side. Thus, the antithesis between good and evil can be compared with the contrast between light and darkness in the cosmos. Both exist and both

---

as a spiritual, divine reality" as one of the common elements of religions in the Ancient Near East; see his *The Meaning of Religion: Lectures in the Phenomenology of Religion,* trans. John B. Carman (The Hague: Martinus Nijhoff, 1960), pp. xviii, xxii. Hendrik Kraemer, who was a student of Kristensen and his "hand-picked successor at Leiden," wrote the "Introduction" to this work. (See Richard J. Plantinga, "W. B. Kristensen and the Study of Religion," *Numen* 36, no. 2 [1989]: 175.) "Materially, Kristensen divided phenomenology of religion into three areas: religious ideas concerning the world (cosmology), religious ideas about humanity (anthropology), and the practice of worship (cultus)" (Plantinga, "W. B. Kristensen," note 29; cf. Kristensen, *Meaning,* pp. 23, 27-496). Kristensen taught at Leiden for thirty-six years; Kraemer, Gerardus Vander Leeuw, and C. J. Bleeker also taught there. It can hardly be accidental that two of Kristensen's divisions in the phenomenology of religion (cosmology and anthropology) mirror Bavinck's division of "cosmism" and "humanism."

13. Ed. note: Bavinck gives no citation here; the reference, however, is clearly to Dutch missiologist Hendrik Kraemer (1888-1965). The ideas in the cited passage — though not the exact words — can be found in H. Kraemer, *The Christian Message in a Non-Christian World* (London: Edinburgh House Press, 1938), pp. 142-43, 156.

are necessary to maintain life. A few times a year, it might seem as though either light or darkness will triumph, but such instances never last very long because the cosmos always automatically regains its balance. With humanity it is the same. Sometimes the darker forces of the heart become too highly riled, but the brighter powers of reason soon return and begin working; then the balance that was almost lost is restored. Therefore sin is always something relative; it is a temporary deficit of balance, similar to what occurs in the wider world. In the final instance, the idea of sin belongs to the realm of nonessentials; it is a temporary deviation within a natural process.

In addition to cosmism, we encounter what is called "humanism." Humanism is to be distinguished from cosmism in this respect: it accentuates the specifically human functions and more or less isolates them from the cosmos. It posits a huge distance between the human and the natural. The truly human capacities of intelligence and reason, of will and morality, are clearly exposed and understood as something sui generis or without any discernible parallel in nature. Often one is inclined, in this connection, to associate what is specifically human with the concept "God," that is to say, to regard it as that which is divine in humanity. Such humanism operates everywhere in the world, including in Asia. We encounter a remarkable tendency toward this humanism especially in China, where for many centuries already the status and social dimensions of humanity have been subjects of philosophical reflection. This humanism emerges particularly, as one of the modern Chinese thinkers has put it, in the form of the doctrine "of the absolute mean" or of the "religion of the healthy intellect."[14] Humanism was powerfully operative in the philosophical systems of Greece and Rome as well. As a well-developed system in the modern western world, it is even associated with the church. It appears, as it were, on the rim or edge of the church of Christ. Surrounding the church have always been consequential circles of people who embrace something of the moral ideals of the gospel, but who find the power and capacity for achieving those ideals in some human ability or other. In our own day, this sort of humanism takes on propa-

---

14. Lin Yutang, *My Country and My People* (New York: A John Day Book in association with Reynal & Hitchcock, 1935), p. 100. Ed. note: The "doctrine of the mean" is both an idea and one of the four books of Confucian teaching (*Analects, Mencius, Doctrine of the Mean, Great Learning*). It is also described as "unswerving pivot" or "unwobbling pivot." It may be helpful to compare the concept with the "golden mean" of Aristotle; see his *Nicomachean Ethics*, trans. W. D. Ross (available online for download at http://classics.mit.edu/Aristotle/nicomachean.html).

gandistic power and has a mission to the world's nations. It prefers being regarded as idealistic secularism, or even as healthy neutrality.

In Asian thinking, these two spiritual streams of cosmism and humanism flowed together in a most remarkable way to form a closed totality. That totality makes room for God, but not in the biblical sense of the word. It has a place for the concept of sin, but not as developed in the gospel. It recognizes deliverance, but only in the sense of losing one's individuality and allowing oneself to melt into Being-in-general. For many centuries now, that distinctive way of thinking that we have sketched in just a few lines has inspired the great thinkers of Asia and confronts us as a spiritual force. How will we ever be able to open a breach in that walled-off worldview through which Christ can stride? How will we ever batter down a gate in that wall, in order that Christ who is Savior of the world may enter? How are we to proceed? What ideas must we emphasize so that the souls of Asian people learn how to hear him? Here are the missional issues of our time that press in on us with their full weight.

Naturally, we could do what the first missionaries did, namely place heavy emphasis on Jesus as *Judge of the World*. It strikes me that this note was also sounded at Tambaram. In the report of the fifth sectional, which dealt with the witness of the church to the non-Christian religions, we find these striking words:

> We have the audacity to call people to leave their religions and to bow at the feet of Jesus. We do so because we believe that the salvation that people need can be found only in him. We should desire that he will become for others what he is for us: Judge and Savior, Teacher and Friend, Brother and Lord.[15]

Here as well, the first point of emphasis is on Jesus Christ as Judge.

Several complications present themselves and make life extremely difficult for us on the mission field, however, when we prominently emphasize Jesus Christ as Judge. In the first place, I need to mention the sad situation that we ourselves, whether in our thinking or our living, still wrestle with the problem of being oriented too little to the return of the Lord. Our entire existence is so severely famished, eschatologically speaking, that the doctrine of the last things resonates far too little in our own hearts. At the Tambaram Conference, as Rev. Pos noted in his study of what was discussed there,

---

15. M. Schlunk, "Die Bedeutung der konferenz in Tambaram für die Weltmission," *Neue Allgemeine Missionszeitschrift* 16 (1939): 189.

which is well worth reading, the Lord's return was not treated in any of the sixteen sectionals.[16] That is due to our own inner dereliction, and this sin wreaks its vengeance on the mission field. In our preaching on the coming Day of Judgment, we are limited and weakened by our own unbelief. In the second place, it needs to be mentioned here that the people to whom we preach generally show little approachability on eschatological matters. Since cosmism and humanism, universally considered, are so tied to the cosmos they offer very little possibility for an Asian person, with his placid and tranquil view of life, being moved by urgent preaching about a return on the clouds of heaven. Startled by it, he perhaps might initially smile a little. Professor Chao of Yenching University in Beijing puts it this way:

> When this world must be rolled up as a garment in order to make room for a new heaven and a new earth, the date of such an event is a matter of the highest interest. Imagine that it will occur only after a million years have passed, and it becomes difficult to see why any thinking person should feel very concerned about it. He would much rather focus his attention on the pressing needs that beset us now and test our patience and perseverance to the extreme. That a world of eternal value exists outside our own, we can understand. That this eternal world reaches into our world, we can grasp because the incarnation of Christ teaches us as much. But that our world is beyond hope and that human nature could be so corrupt and incapable of rising above that corruption that it is only in the position of waiting for its inevitable end is an idea incomprehensible to the oriental mind.[17]

For that reason, it is noteworthy that for most of the younger churches on the mission field the book of Revelation written by John is scarcely intelligible. The Javanese person, who by nature is inclined to reflect on the things to come, is in general little inspired or gripped by that book. That the demonic powers of imperialism and fierce nationalism presently bringing Asia to the point of burning restlessness and tension will bring about a profound change in that way of thinking is, at the moment, all still uncertain.

Perhaps the thought occurs to some of you that if it is indeed the case that it seems extremely difficult to make the idea that Jesus will return as the

---

16. A. Pos, "De Internationale Zendingsconferentie van Tambaram," *De Macedoniër* 43 (1939): 99-100.

17. Tzu-Chen Chao, *Christendom* (1939); cited in M. Schlunk, "Die Bedeutung der konferenz in Tambaram," p. 229.

world's judge the point of departure in our preaching, is it not possible to begin by preaching that he is the Guru, the master Teacher? Taking that approach, would we not be able to chisel a road into the massive, rock-solid world of [South and Southeast] Asian thought?[18] The expectation of a guru who reveals the message of life to people is one that lives universally; the concept of the guru is one of the most fruitful images in all [South and Southeast] Asian religions. That is based primarily on the fact that these forms of [South and Southeast] Asian thought, because of their structure and orientation, have paid and continue to pay little attention to *soterology*[19] as far as the Savior is concerned. But they have certainly always paid attention to *soteriology* as far as the doctrine of salvation is concerned. The guru is the man who points the way to becoming one with the divine for the soul seeking salvation. Considered against that background, one might [in such contexts] introduce the gospel in one's initial preaching as a word from the perfect guru, the Maha-Guru Jesus Christ, the Lord. By doing so, however, we place Jesus on a level with all the many gurus known from the days of the ancient Veda poets right up to our own time. This remains true even though his position is at the head of that line. Additionally, theosophy in both its eastern and its western versions has promoted the idea of the guru, and it has accorded Christ a spot in that honorable line of human gurus alongside Krishna and Buddha. All of this certainly makes it very difficult for us who believe in the entirely unique character of the gospel to make our point of departure in preaching Jesus as Guru, the World's Teacher. What is also striking is that new Christians in [South and Southeast] Asian nations universally shrink back from proceeding on the basis of the guru idea. Almost unanimously, they emphasize that Jesus is much more, or said better, is completely other than a guru in the oriental sense of that term. He is at one and the same time both

18. Ed. note: Although JHB uses the word "East" here and further in this chapter, he is speaking in this paragraph of the religions of India and not China, Japan, and Korea. "Guru" is a Sanskrit term, and any ascription of divinity to a guru-figure applies only to India, to South and not East Asia and to the "southeast" nations influenced by Sanskrit, i.e., Sri Lanka, Indonesia, Malaysia, Thailand, Cambodia. Here and further in this chapter, for the sake of accuracy, we will be providing an editorial [South and Southeast Asia] bracket to designate India (South Asia) and those (southeast) nations influenced by Sanskrit, be they Hindu or Buddhist. Unless otherwise indicated by context or note, "Asia" and "Asian" will be used in an inclusive sense to include China, Korea, and Japan.

19. Ed. note: Careful readers might assume that they have here an instance of inadequate proofreading: Is the word used here not correctly spelled as s-o-t-e-r-i-o-l-o-g-y? No; Bavinck deliberately plays on the difference between the rare neologism *soterology* (from Σωτήρ = Savior) and *soteriology* (from σωτηρία = salvation).

the teacher and the teaching, the messenger and the message of preaching, and this makes his position among human teachers entirely exceptional.

It seems to me that we must take a totally different approach if we want to achieve clear results. The name of Christ is laden with a wealth of content so rich that the Heidelberg Catechism unpacks it by pointing to his three offices: prophet, priest, and king. Upon further consideration, each of the three terms encompasses a world of thought. For that reason, we are not finished when we affirm that we must preach Jesus as the Christ. We need to ask ourselves seriously and pointedly to which of these terms we should initially call attention and adopt as our point of departure. And in order to answer that question, it seems necessary to me that we reckon with what Asian Christians[20] themselves say and think. By the goodness of God, we have the advantage that these churches already exist. It is certainly the case that in these churches only a very small beginning has as yet been made in developing indigenous theology. By the nature of the situation, they are still strongly influenced by the mission and the missionaries that preached the gospel to them. Yet, it is slowly becoming possible to investigate how the gospel is being appropriated within these younger churches, to assess which of its ideas they initially embrace, and to consider how it is reflected in their own soul. We are on the safest ground, it seems to me, when our investigation begins there. Two concepts often recur in the explanations given by members of these churches: the idea that Jesus is the *Son of God* and the idea that he is *Lord of all*. Those two extremely important truths that we proclaim in the gospel appear to have especially inspired the thought and life of Asian Christians.

I have already indicated that in many Asian churches only a small beginning has as yet been made in developing indigenous theological studies. However, here and there we encounter typically eastern ways of thinking and speaking. The most striking examples of this are among those without theological training, that is, those who have not been educated by western theologians at one of the various theological seminaries. Precisely such people, who have not received training in dogmatics, can sometimes express the content of the gospel in their own unique way using thought-forms and images borrowed entirely from their own world.

Among such Asian nontheologians, I could cite, for example, Kagawa.[21]

---

20. Ed. note: It seems clear that JHB here is casting his net wider than in the ocean of South and Southeast Asian people and religious traditions, and including those of East Asia, i.e., China, Japan, and Korea.

21. Ed. note: Toyohiko Kagawa (1888-1960) was a Japanese convert to Christ who

He is a person who has done much for the spread of the gospel in the slums of Tokyo. Before I lift a few examples from his writings and those of others, I must warn you that some of them might sound peculiar or heretical to you. A few years ago, when one of the most famous American missionary figures paid a visit to our seminary in Jakarta, one of the first questions that he asked was whether heresy had begun to appear among Javanese Christians. When we quickly responded that that was not at all the case, his laconic comment was, "That's too bad." By this he intended to convey that wherever the preaching of God's Word begins to resonate with the indigenous thought-world and emotional life, wherever it begins to permeate all deliberation, the danger of unorthodox ideas naturally arises. People who have only recently heard the gospel simply cannot be measured by the same standards we are accustomed to use on those whose ancestors have already lived with knowledge of the truth for centuries. This is even truer when the mission bringing them the gospel was itself often lacking some semblance of orthodoxy. A strange, perhaps heretical-sounding expression by an Asian Christian can be the symptom of earnest, independent searching and reflecting. It might be born from a genuine need to understand God's Word and to reflect on it from a person's typically eastern spiritual approach. In that case, it would be entirely wrong if we bluntly and insensitively objected to it. What is most important in such situations is that a genuine desire exists to be led by God's Word and to bow before the majesty of what that Word conveys to us. If that desire is present, I believe that we may endeavor to lead such people further down the road of true knowledge with complete confidence and discernment. And then we can also cherish the expectation that Christ's Spirit will gradually lead the churches of Asia more deeply into the truth of God's Word. At this time, then, I do not want first of all to assess the formulations of these eastern Christians critically or to weigh their orthodoxy for you. I will not trouble you by indicating whether they risk the danger of Patripassianism, Docetism, Nestorianism, or some other -ism. Our only concern this afternoon is to reckon with what grip these people have on the gospel and how they have been captivated by the adoration of Christ. As I have already said, this is our first concern: that they have been deeply and powerfully moved by the thought that Jesus is the Son of God.

In Muslim countries, preaching that Jesus is the Son of God is a stumbling stone. The Qur'an definitely makes room for Jesus as belonging to the

---

sought to apply the teachings of Jesus to society as a pacifist, labor activist, social reformer, and evangelist, working especially in the slums of Tokyo.

line of prophets sent by God, but it objects strenuously to any thought that he might be the Son of God.

The Qur'an says,

> Oh, people of the book, only speak the truth about Allah. The messiah Jesus, the son of Mary, is the messenger of Allah and his word, which he also laid on Mary by his spirit. So believe in Allah and his messenger and do not speak of "three." Allah is but one God. The messiah is never too proud to be but a servant of Allah. (Sura 4:169)

> Truly, they are unbelieving who say, "Look Allah, the Son of Mary is the messiah." The messiah himself has said, "O, children of Israel serve Allah, my lord and your lord. Behold, he who has other gods besides Allah, that person Allah has denied paradise." (Sura 5:76-79)

> No one in heaven or on the earth may approach the All-Merciful in any other way than as a slave. (Sura 19:94)

All of these words from the Qur'an make very clear that preaching Jesus as the Son of the God of Islam is an offense. The concept of the sonship of God is totally in conflict with the true Muslim doctrine of God. No wonder, then, that in strictly Muslim countries precisely that dimension of the gospel arouses the most opposition.

In areas where Hinduism and Buddhism have flourished for centuries, however, the situation is different. It is also different in countries where Islam has penetrated, but where alongside it or subservient to it other religious tendencies also nevertheless exist. There, proclamation of Jesus as the Son of God can sometimes have an unusual impact and stir hearts to faith in him. It is worth indicating in that connection that we ought not to explain the name "Son of God" in a directly Trinitarian sense. Then the emphasis does not fall on the fact that he is one person in the holy, indivisible, threefold being of God. Here the designation "Son of God" has much more of the content that we find in the opening of the letter to the Hebrews: that Son who is the reflection of his glory and the imprint of his being. Jesus is that Word, as John expresses it, who proclaims to the world who God is and what God is. He bears the image of God, so that whoever sees him beholds the Father. That idea is the one that time and again is understood on the Asian mission field and that must be regarded as having the greatest appeal in preaching to Muslims.

For centuries already, [South and Southeast] Asia has lived with the ideas that the divine essence is itself complete rest and peace and that it exists in all things and is the goal of all things. The ancient poets of the Vedas in India and their expositors have always placed their emphasis on the fact that Brahma, the highest being of all, is *ananda* or bliss in the sense of all-encompassing tranquility. The world that we inhabit is the realm of *samsara*, a wearisome treadmill, a frivolous world, an illusory world that in and of itself is thoroughly vacuous. But Brahma is true being and blessedness. While we, poor bunglers here on earth, proceed from one misery to the next, from weakness to weakness, would the blessed Brahma in his exalted peace ever trouble himself with us, ever suffer over our sufferings, ever be anxious about our anxieties? And lo and behold, here suddenly comes the gospel of Jesus and tells us about the eternal love of God. Jesus himself testifies that he is the one in whom God himself draws near to us out of the inscrutable darkness of his own unapproachable being. He makes God transparent, reflects God's light flooding the darkness of this vain world. If that is the case, then God is totally different from what the poets of the Vedas have dreamed up; then he has loving compassion for the condition of his erring children. That is the precious treasure that the souls of [South and Southeast] Asia find in the proclamation that Jesus is the Son of God.

Now I would like to point to a few extremely valuable ideas related to this. In doing so, I would like to turn to the words of those who have witnessed this great Light rising in their own lives.

In the first place, it is noteworthy that enormous emphasis is placed on the fact that the incarnation is more than simply appearing in the flesh. From ancient times, India has known stories, so it is said, about avatars or temporary appearances of the gods. Rama and Krishna, heroes from the Indian epics, are honored as such avatars. They came down to earth because in their day the great balance between naked, demonic power and peaceable, good judgment was in danger of being lost. Avatars always appear at such critical moments in order to restore order. Such an avatar is always human, but not in the ordinary sense of the term. His existence has something surreal about it. At any moment he can pour out the eternal radiance of his divine power, just as Krishna did in opposition to the hero Arjuna when he mounted a chariot. Then the lowliness of his earthly trappings is discarded.

With Jesus it is completely different. His humanity is real. "The man Jesus Christ is capable of being moved by experiencing our weaknesses."[22] Emphasis is gratefully placed on Jesus' thoroughgoing humanity. A Chris-

---

22. Vengal Chakkarai, *Jesus the Avatar* (Madras: Christian Literature Society for India, 1926), p. 138.

tian Hindu, connecting with the idea of his "complete humanity" as the *teleios anthropos* that people the world over recognize, says of him: "Jesus is the true man, the ideal man (the term 'ideal' is to be taken in the Platonic sense of the term)."[23] "He is a man among men, the Son of Man, the original model, the idea that God had in mind when he created us humans, the prototype after whom we have all been made, the everlasting human being."[24] This concept has taken powerful hold particularly in the Chinese church. Chinese philosophy has always thought and talked a great deal about the ideal human, "the most holy, the model for all times," in whom the cosmic principle of *tao* is embodied.[25] So, Jesus is the ideal human, our "perfect guide and our model."[26] That this idea can easily lead to superficial humanism needs no further explanation.

That danger is appreciably tempered, however, by the profound reverence that people feel and profess for Jesus. In his extremely important and valuable missiological study *The Christian Message in a Non-Christian World*, Professor Kraemer has noted that the ancient church did not lay especially heavy emphasis on "the unique attractiveness of Jesus."[27] That is different in Asia today. We hear repeatedly about people who, upon reading the gospel writers, are deeply impressed by the incomparable moral majesty radiating from Jesus. The gospel is certainly one of the most powerfully effective missionary instruments that we possess. Whenever people simply read it calmly and allow it to sink in, things develop within them that they never suspected. Kagawa relates somewhere that he, when he was preoccupied with learning the English language, at one point steeped himself in the Gospel of Luke completely and solely from an academic standpoint. He came to 12:27, where Jesus admonishes listeners to consider the lilies of the field. He was so gripped by this verse in the Gospel that he was beside himself with joy. He puts it this way:

I then came to the profound discovery that the love of God encompasses everything. I was completely captivated by that Christ who gave his life in order to reveal the love of God the Father for the entire human race.[28]

23. Chakkarai, *Jesus the Avatar*, p. 30.
24. Chakkarai, *Jesus the Avatar*, p. 125.
25. Jan Julius Lodewijk Duyvendak, *China tegen de Westerkim*, 2nd ed. (Haarlem: Bohn, 1933), p. 72.
26. Kraemer, *Christian Message*, pp. 185, 381.
27. Kraemer, *Christian Message*, p. 71.
28. Toyohiko Kagawa, *Christ and Japan*, trans. William Axling (New York: Friendship Press, 1934), p. 107.

A highly placed Javanese man, a pious person who had reflected deeply on religious questions, came to the conclusion over and over again in a number of debates with the Christian mission that Islam and Christianity are essentially the same. This continued until one evening, after reading about the sufferings and death of Jesus, he burst into tears and said, "This is completely different! God did this, not man!"[29] Chakkaria, the Hindu author whom we quoted above, says in his small book *Jesus the Avatar* that the thousands of merciful deeds that Jesus did during his travels on earth had a powerful attraction for the people of his day.

> For me this has always been a subject of study from the time that I as a Hindu came to know him. The miraculous fascination he holds, the transcendent mystery of his being that defies all thought, his exaltedness far above us, and at the same time his closeness to us and his dwelling within us, all have increasingly drawn me to him as the years have passed.[30]

Jesus himself says very little about his divine nature, but that is also unnecessary. "God's voice reverberates in our hearts in little whispers that are louder than the thunder on Mt. Sinai."[31]

In the third place, what appears from all this is that the divinity of Jesus Christ is best approached through his humanity. Thus, the first disciples learned to confess that Jesus is the Son of God by witnessing that words of eternal life are found with him. The majesty residing in the person of Christ, the power proceeding from him, the simultaneous fascination as well as hesitation and dread regarding him at work in people's hearts — all this opens eyes to the indisputable fact that he is more than a mere human, but that the fullness of the Godhead resides in him bodily. Sometimes faith dawns ever so slowly in people's hearts. Then these Asian Christians talk first of all about the "intimate fellowship" that exists between Jesus and God. "He is the unspotted mirror, the clear image of God," says Chakkarai. "He is a close friend while at the same time remaining deeply mysterious."[32] Then, suddenly, he makes this connection: "God was in Christ Jesus, and in him we encounter God himself. There can be no doubt that the Christian experience has recognized that in him it stands face to face with *Ishvara* [God][33] in a

29. E. G. van Kekem, "Het evangelie en de Moslim," *De Opwekker* 22 (1937): 385.
30. Chakkarai, *Jesus the Avatar*, p. 22.
31. Chakkarai, *Jesus the Avatar*, p. 28.
32. Chakkarai, *Jesus the Avatar*, pp. 6, 12.
33. Ed. note: The term "Ishvara" is a generic Sanskrit name for God; philosophically, the one Supreme personal power who rules the cosmos.

sense which cannot be true of any prophet or saint."[34] "Jesus is God himself. No one has seen the indescribable being of God, and no one can even bear seeing him. But we do see God in the face of Jesus. The dark curtain that hides God from view is drawn back by Jesus."[35] He then continues by describing the appearance of Jesus adorned with a crown of thorns, filled with indignation toward the scribes and Pharisees, but brimming with radiant love for sinners who bow before him. "He is the projection of the flux of life in this ephemeral world; he is the heart and soul of God."[36] At the conclusion of his work, he testifies: "He who sits on the throne over all has the countenance of Jesus."[37]

We discover the same ideas in Kagawa. He speaks with definite gratitude about "the God of Jesus" not as the Absolute or the Eternal, before whom adherents of pantheism bow in homage, but he points to the fact that Jesus calls himself the revelation of the God of salvation. Then he concludes with these words: "Jesus has fundamentally altered religion. He is God descended to earth. As Jesus, God walks the full range of human experience."[38] Upon hearing testimonies like these, we must always remember the spiritual influences that these men formerly experienced. They speak from the sense of their younger days, when God in himself was seen as unachievable peace, the one who is unaffected by human struggle and drudgery and is inaccessible and

---

34. Chakkarai, *Jesus the Avatar,* pp. 129-30.

35. Chakkarai, *Jesus the Avatar,* pp. 168-74. Ed. note: Bavinck took some liberties with his translation of Chakkarai's words. The actual text, cited by Bavinck in his footnote, reads:

To the ordinary and unsophisticated consciousness there is a black veil God would seem to have cast over His face. But now that Jesus has removed the veil, we behold the face of God Himself.

36. Chakkarai, *Jesus the Avatar,* pp. 168-74. Ed. note: This also appears to be a loose translation of the text, which reads: "Out of the infinite nebulousness emerges the face of Jesus. God is the unmanifested and Jesus is the manifested. He is the projection onto the plane of samsara, of the flux of life, the very heart of God."

37. Chakkarai, *Jesus the Avatar,* p. 222. Ed. note: The original text reads: "He who sits on the throne of the universe has the human face divine of Jesus."

38. Toyohiko Kagawa, *The Religion of Jesus,* trans. Helen F. Topping (Chicago: John C. Winston, 1931), pp. 19, 25, 33, 34. See also L. Bevan Jones, *Christianity Explained to Muslims* (Calcutta: YMCA, 1938), p. 70. Ed. note: Bavinck's own footnote cites this passage from Kagawa:

The definition of religion has been rewritten by Jesus. It is not merely a question of man relying on God; it is also of God coming down to earth and experiencing man's way of living. That is, God, as Jesus, entered into man's experience.

exalted high above any hint of such *samsara*. Considering this background, we understand how these men have come to a totally different understanding of God. The God with the face of Jesus is the God who is moved, the God who stoops to his creatures and lives within complete reach of our troubled lives.

We understand this most clearly when we read what these Asian Christians say about the cross. Each time that I see how hesitantly and tremblingly they approach the mystery of the cross, I am troubled again. In general, with most of the Christians in India we find the inclination to see the cross as a reflex of God's suffering because of the sins of the world. Sadhu Sundar Singh, widely recognized in our own country, says somewhere: "Jesus hung on the cross not just for six hours, but for his entire life. The suffering of Christ was in a special sense God suffering for the sins of the world."[39]

A Christian Hindu wrote a very penetrating and very readable little book that he titled *The Suffering God*. In it he concluded his argument like this:

In the Crucified One, we need to see God himself, who allowed himself to be ridiculed, spit upon, crowned with thorns, and condemned by men to the accursed death of the cross. And he endured all this in return for his redeeming love for humanity. Now, what do we learn about God from this? In the crucified Jesus we see the heart of the Eternal One, who considered no cost too high a price for saving our souls.[40]

And still another Christian Hindu put it this way in his worshipful amazement:

The suffering of Christ is and represents the very suffering of God on the human plane and it is by virtue of this representative character that the Cross bears such an intimate relation to our human life and reaches the very foundations of our being.[41]

39. Sundar Singh, *Das Suchen nach Gott: Gedanken über Hinduismus, Buddhismus, Islam und Christentum*, ed. Friedrich Heiler (Munich: F. Reinhardt, 1925), p. 43.

40. C. S. Paul, *The Suffering God* (Madras: Christian Literature Society for India, 1932), p. 247. Ed. note: Bavinck's own footnote cites this passage from Paul:

In the Crucified One, therefore, we must see God allowing Himself to be despised, spat on, throne-crowned, and finally condemned to the accursed death on the Cross by men, and all these in return for God's redeeming love for mankind. What does this show of God? A mere sympathizer, nay more, a fellow-sufferer for our salvation. The Cross is rightly described as the enacting in time and space of an act that is eternally true of God.

41. Vengal Chakkarai, *The Cross and Indian Thought* (Madras: Christian Literature Society for India, 1932), p. 162.

This moves us to adoration with

> the realization that the exalted Lord of all, who was regarded as everlastingly lifted above all time and all human experience, has descended and walked on this sin-filled earth, and that defying all human comprehension he even suffered on the cross for us mere mortals.[42]

Whenever they reflect more deeply on the cross, these Christians from the younger churches in India often grapple with large, perplexing issues. Usually, they find it in some sense difficult to identify with the strongly juridical doctrine of the atonement as that has been developed, for example, in several of Paul's letters.[43] As a rule, Asians by nature certainly feel more powerfully drawn to John than to Paul. The Gospel of John is frequently praised highly and is regarded as the quintessence of the entire Christian religion.[44] When they talk about the significance and the power of Christ's cross, for them it is often in the form of testing and questioning without seeing very clearly how the suffering of the Messiah is able to achieve the salvation of the world. In this regard, they have raised all sorts of considerations that are of great value to us who preach the gospel in Asia.

In the first place, they are deeply moved by the entirely unique character of Jesus' suffering. Jesus is no martyr in the ordinary sense of the word. A martyr in the ordinary sense endures his suffering without complaint and peacefully and confidently meets his death. The Asian par excellence, who often exhibits self-control under suffering, understands this more clearly than we do. Similarly, martyrs in the cause of Christ were often burned at the stake without complaint or outcry. Measured by that standard, it is thoroughly perplexing that for Jesus in his own suffering things were completely different. He knelt down in Gethsemane and in his deep distress pleaded with the Father to deliver him. Hanging on the cross, he uttered his frightful cry of forsakenness. When we read this, only two explanations are possible. The first is that here Jesus sinks below the level of the ordinary martyr. But that explanation is so absurd that we are compelled to discard it completely. The second possibility is that the suffering of Jesus "constitutes an indescribable terror that is totally beyond our comprehen-

---

42. Chakkarai, *Cross and Indian Thought*, p. 162.

43. Chakkarai, *Cross and Indian Thought*, pp. 182ff.

44. Chakkarai, *Cross and Indian Thought*, p. 19; cf. *Jesus the Avatar*, pp. 105-6; and Aiyadurai Jesudasen Appasamy, *Christianity as Bhakti Mārta: A Study in the Mysticism of the Johannine Writings* (London: Macmillan, 1927).

sion."[45] In that case, an unfathomably deep puzzle is tied to Jesus' suffering. His suffering has to be totally different from all ordinary human suffering. It transcends by a measureless distance all human martyrdom. All this we can only comprehend from afar and only if we believe that he carried on his shoulders the full curse against the world. He must have suffered for all our sakes.[46] This is how an Asian Christian reasons.

Kagawa approaches the cross of Christ from yet another angle. In his short book *The Religion of Jesus,* he expresses it like this:

> According to the laws of nature, a process of deliverance exists by means of sacrifice. When anything unusual happens in the body, say a virus of one sort or another develops, a whole army of white blood cells rushes to do battle in that part of the body. By means of their own death, they save the body. In similar fashion, a divine law exists for healing spiritual disorders. Jesus discovered this law and laid the basis for a religion of deliverance where prayer and meditation are united.[47]

When Kagawa spoke on the subject of the cross at Tambaram in December of last year, many years after he had written his little book on *The Religion of Jesus,* he used the same metaphor, which certainly shows that this imagery

45. Chakkarai, *Jesus the Avatar,* p. 65. Ed. note: Bavinck's own footnote cites this passage from Chakkarai:

> Can it be maintained that only our Lord fell beneath the standard and type of the martyr? This is a thought too absurd to be entertained. Then what is the alternative? It must be that His death had some elements of real horror in it, not visible to the outward eye.

Cf. Godfrey Edward Phillips, *The Gospel in the World: A Restatement of Missionary Principles* (London: Duckworth, 1939), p. 147. Professor Phillips shows where we should place the emphasis in dealing with Hindus: "Jesus so made himself one with humanity, that he took upon himself its collective race karma, and in his suffering worked it out."

46. Chakkarai, *Jesus the Avatar,* p. 65.

47. T. Kagawa, *The Religion of Jesus,* pp. 84-85; see also his address at Tambaram, summarized in *De Opwekker* 24 (1939): 98. Ed. note: Bavinck took some liberties with his translation of Kagawa's words. The actual text, cited by Bavinck in his footnote, reads:

> When something unusual has happened to the body and poison has accumulated in some part of it, hosts of leucocytes assemble to that part and fight, and by their death keep the body healthy. So in the same way there exists a divine law for the cure of spiritual pains. *Jesus discovered this law* and established the religion of redemption in which prayer and meditation are combined into one.

made a powerful impression on him. "Blood dies to heal wounds. It is the same with the love of Christ."[48]

We are dealing here with more than a metaphor used simply for the purposes of clarification. I have often observed that Asian thinking is naturalistic, that is, it is inclined to see in all things, also those pertaining to moral and spiritual matters, a universal cosmic law at work. When it can position the cross at the center of that universal cosmic law, the meaning of the cross becomes not only extraordinarily clear but also much more compelling. Golgotha is not merely an isolated place in this amazing world, but what happened on Golgotha is what happens everywhere in God's entire creation. Deliverance, even life itself, is only possible by going through death, by going through substitutionary suffering and dying. Jesus understood this law, and he lived in harmony with this cosmic law. Along this line of thinking, Kagawa emphasizes time and again that also in our lives deliverance is only possible to the extent that we have understood the same cosmic law of the cross and when we are willing to submit to it. He says:

> For years I have made a study of the problem of evil in creation. That problem has fascinated me from the time I was sixteen years old. When I studied anything from the perspective of the evil at work in it, I inevitably found that one force exists that strives to triumph and drives evil from it. I have seen that force working in the locations where I have devoted my life to the weak and the poor. It is the spirit of the cross.[49]

Here again, the awful events that occurred on Golgotha are seen in the context of a universal reality that can be found everywhere in the cosmos.

It is not unlikely that hearing words like these sounds rather strange to our theological ears. And I will not deny that expressions like the one used by Kagawa when he says, "Jesus discovered the law," are rather dubious. But then I want to add one caveat. When our Savior was questioned on one occasion by several Greeks, people whose thinking was also deeply conditioned by the natural order, and he wished to clarify for them something of his suffering and dying, he himself used the following image: "Unless a grain of wheat falls to the earth and dies, it remains alone. But if it dies, then it brings forth much fruit" (John 12:24). In other words, Jesus here places his own suffering and death in the context of a universal cosmic reality, namely the reality that all life proceeds from death. It does not surprise me in the least that

48. See Kagawa's address at Tambaram, summarized in *De Opwekker* 24 (1939): 98.
49. Kagawa, *Religion of Jesus*, pp. 84-85.

precisely this verse is the one cited so frequently by Asian Christians. It casts undeniable light on what took place on Golgotha.

It is worth noting that many Asian Christians achieve insight into the appalling horror of sin by contemplating the cross. Many Asians still have difficulty with the biblical idea of sin, and it is fairly easy to explain why. The naturalistic approach to life, or cosmism, about which we have already spoken, is hardly in a position to impress people with the fact that sin in all its frightening dimensions is the problem gnawing at the roots of their existence. Kagawa once said, "The Japanese have a strong antipathy against the idea of sin. One of the reasons why Christianity is not wholeheartedly embraced by them is the fact that Christ emphasized sin so repeatedly."[50] We often observed among our Javanese assistants that whenever they wanted to speak about sin, they preferred to begin with Adam. That seems to indicate that they did not experience the reality of sin on a personal level, but that for them it remained a hypothetical construct.

Chakkarai, the Christian Hindu whom I have already quoted more than once, possessed the ability by way of exception to see things on a personal level within the framework of his native worldview, and he once acknowledged the following about himself:

> Whenever the subject of our sin and lost condition was preached with considerable emphasis, it often sparked remarkable conversions in Anglo-Saxon countries. . . . But the Hindu does not readily respond to such an appeal. Better said, it does not have the same effect on him. A Hindu is certainly emotional, but his emotional life cannot be approached in the same way. For myself, I was never moved by the terrible side of sin. And perhaps I am still not moved by it like some European believers in Christ. But only when I came to know Jesus in the beauty of his holy life and in his unfathomable, deeply moving personal character did that genuinely Protestant sense of sin become a reality for me. In a word, what was positive about Christ led me to see the negative nature of sin as being in total contrast with what he was.[51]

---

50. Kagawa, *Christ and Japan*, p. 44.

51. Chakkarai, *Cross and Indian Thought*, pp. 153-54. Ed. note: Bavinck took some liberties with his translation of Chakkarai's words. The actual text, cited by Bavinck in his footnote, reads:

> It was fuller acquaintance with Jesus in the beauty of His holiness and matchless and moving character that has made him (i.e., the present writer) realize the Protestant feeling of sin and its enormities. In one word, it is the positive character of Jesus that

He adds, when I came to know him in his undying love, I began to understand Peter's prayer, "Lord depart from me, for I am a sinful man."[52] Later, in his contemplation on the cross of Christ, he says this:

> The cross reveals human sin in all of its awful seriousness and enormity. That someone like Jesus, the very flower of humanity, was killed is a terrible indictment against the human race. In this we experience the depth of the fall that compels us to confront the lost condition of the world.[53]

Before closing our consideration of Jesus as the Son of God, I need to direct attention to one other point of exceptional importance, namely the realism of Christ's life. In general, Asia has shown a rather substantial disdain for historical facts. Hindus are very perturbed when someone points out to them that the heroes they venerate never lived. They are too deeply affected by the *samsara* characterizing this ephemeral world to think that whether something really happened or not has anything much to do with them.[54] But when they encounter the gospel, they encounter something of unusual value: they are dealing with the historical reality that Jesus actually lived and that he actually died for us. That lays a foundation for their thinking that they never recognized before.

Michihata, a Japanese preacher who for many years had been a priest in a Buddhist monastery, in his book *From Buddha to the Christ* describes the road that he walked before he found Jesus. He describes Buddhism as he experienced it in all its unusual features, and in so doing he gives us deep insight

---

has brought out the negative character of sin as the very opposite of all that He stood for.

On the difficulty that the people of the Dutch East Indies (especially the Batak people [in the north of Sumatra]) have with the concept of sin, see: W. Freytag, *Die Junge Christenheit im Umbruch des Ostens* (Berlin, 1938), p. 87.

52. Chakkarai, *Jesus the Avatar*, p. 76; he also uses this expression: "In one word, Jesus points to the hell and the heaven in us."

53. Chakkarai, *Cross and Indian Thought*, p. 160. Ed. note: Bavinck took some liberties with his translation of Chakkarai's words. The actual text, cited by Bavinck in his footnote, reads:

> That such being as Jesus, the very flower of humanity and the "ideal man," should have been brought to a death of such ignominy is a terrible indictment of the human race. [It] made a revelation of our downfall, bringing before us the vision of a lost world and the glories thereof.

54. Chakkarai, *Cross and Indian Thought*, pp. 166-67.

into what that religion means to its adherents. While he was still training at a Buddhist seminary to become a priest, he was frequently addressed by his teachers on the subject of the Amida Buddha and on the promised holy land that would be reached by those who worshiped this Amida Buddha. Then he adds, "People always spoke about things only as they exist in our imagination, as reflections of our longings."[55] Prayers raised were regarded as psychological means for bringing their own souls to the point of stillness and peace.[56] "In other words," he continues, "neither the Amida Buddha nor paradise had any reality. They were merely projections of our own fantasies, the results of religious art."[57] Concerning Christ he then testifies as follows:

> First and foremost, Jesus Christ is a *real*, historical person, not a figment of the imagination, as is the Amida Buddha. That moved my heart to a passionate desire for *real* salvation through the objectivity of a *real* cross.[58]

It is this realism, running through the entire gospel, that grips the Asian. The gospel does not consist of fairy stories, but it is real. Concerning the struggle between Buddhism and Christianity in Japan, Michihata has this confession to make:

> The real test consists of this: which of the two religions is in a position to quicken life in its followers, and which is not? Annihilation seems to me to be the only possible outcome for Buddhism. I am convinced that some day Japan will become a Christian nation.[59]

---

55. Taisei Michihata, *From Buddha to the Christ: The History of a Spiritual Pilgrimage*, trans. P. A. Smith (Tokyo: Church Publishing Society, 1937), p. 46. Ed. note: Bavinck took some liberties with his translation of Michihata's words. The actual text, cited by Bavinck in his footnote, reads:

> The Pure Land and Paradise were both mentioned in the books we studied, but were invariably spoken of as being simply the reflection of our own desires, devoid of all objective reality.

56. Michihata, *Buddha to the Christ*, p. 47. Ed. note: The full text in Bavinck's footnote reads: "The prayers and incantations are simply ways of worshiping empty space, of tranquilizing one's own spirit, so to speak."

57. Michihata, *Buddha to the Christ*, p. 174. Ed. note: The full text in Bavinck's footnote reads: "Neither Amida nor Paradise has any real existence. They are merely figments of the imagination, products of religious awe, human figures made to dance in the background of the emotions."

58. Michihata, *Buddha to the Christ*, p. 61.

59. Michihata, *Buddha to the Christ*, pp. 61-62. Ed. note: Bavinck took some liberties

This testimony concerning Buddhism is identical to what we find in Professor Kraemer's book on missions.

> A very sharp, defining distinction exists between biblical realism and the two religions offering deliverance in Japan. In the former, God's salvation through the incarnation of Jesus Christ is a real, historical fact because God the Creator and his world, the creation, are objective realities. Amida Buddhism with its promises belongs to the realm of mythology.[60]

With this, I come to the second idea connected to the Christ-concept that is especially compelling for Asia, namely the idea that Jesus is Lord. Because it is not possible for me to develop my thoughts on the matter more broadly, I will limit myself to three observations.

In the first place, it is noteworthy that the idea of Jesus as Lord is a notion that gives enormous peace and security to those who have found him. But finding him is difficult, since a person always wants to be his own lord. Michihata explains that in his own conversion he once fasted for an entire week on a high mountain. By the end of the week, he had achieved complete clarity in his heart. He puts it his way: "On the morning of the eighth day, I arose from my meditation and decided to humble myself before Christ and to entrust myself to his grace, to his power to purify me and to lift me out of all my misery."[61]

I myself have had the great privilege of participating for many years in the work of numerous Bible studies in Java. I often received letters from young people that told me how they found the Lord Jesus there. What always

---

with his translation of Michihata's words. The actual text, cited by Bavinck in his footnote, reads:

> The real test lies in the ability or lack of ability to produce life in its followers. Sad as it is, simple annihilation seems to be the only fate possible for Buddhism. For myself, I am certain that some day Japan will be a Christian nation.

60. Kraemer, *Christian Message*, p. 181. Ed. note: Bavinck took some liberties with his translation of Kraemer's words. The actual text, though not cited by Bavinck in his footnote, reads:

> A very marked and decisive difference between Biblical realism and the two Savior-religions of Honen Shonin and Shinran is that in the first God's act of salvation in the incarnation of Jesus Christ is a real historical act, because God, the Creator, and the world, His creation, are objective realities. Amida and his Vow belong to the realm of mythology.

61. Michihata, *Buddha to the Christ*, p. 163.

struck me in all those letters was their tone of deep trust. [They say . . .] "Now I have turned myself over completely to Jesus as my Lord. Now I belong to him, and I know that he will hold me fast and will guide me through all difficulties in the future." Coming to Christ was time and again described as finally bowing one's head to him after a period of struggle and doubt, with this acknowledgment: "You are my Lord." At such times, it would often become clear to me what the early Christians must have felt when they confessed, "I believe in Jesus Christ, his Son, our Lord!" It might well be possible that in our own day, when the ideology of a *Führer* is rampant across Asia and the West, this neglected article of faith will again become central to all Christian life and thought.

A second observation that I need to make is this: the certainty that Jesus is still with us is a conviction that is deep and powerful in the hearts of Asian Christians. He is present in our entire lives. He is simultaneously a historical and a transcendent reality. He stands at the heart of our world. The Christian Hindu Chakkarai somewhere makes this profession: "In the early days that I came to know the Christian faith, I was deeply moved by the historical appearance of Jesus." Later, he continues,

> After I had already been baptized, Jesus sometimes seemed to me to be a distant dream in Galilee, far removed from my own life with its difficulties. I was no longer satisfied with worshiping a remote Jesus. Then I finally discovered that he is very near me, yes, in my heart. He had always been there from the beginning, but I did not know it.

He expresses this new experience like this: "Jesus Christ is the incarnation of God in the world, and the Holy Spirit is the incarnation of Jesus in our hearts."[62] It is amazing how powerfully the consciousness of Jesus Christ's presence permeates the experience of these young Christians. Sadhu Sundar Singh speaks about an appearance that Christ made to him. Others testify that they, as it were, tasted his presence with them. Jesus is not only a Savior who climbed the hills of Galilee in earlier times and gave his life on the cross, but he is just as real and just as powerful in our own lives, working just as he did in the lives of his own disciples. When I heard and saw all these things, it became clear to me why the ancient Christian church could confess with such joy, "Jesus Christ the One who has died, yes, even more, the One who has risen" (Rom. 8:34).

---

62. Chakkarai, *Jesus the Avatar*, pp. 118-21.

Finally, when Asian people think of Jesus as Lord, they do so in a much broader way than we do, generally speaking. They are not accustomed to thinking about a person on a personal level, that is, by placing the individual at the center of attention. For that reason, personal deliverance often does not receive the most prominent attention in their thought but instead is directed to the redemption of all things. A human being is but a small part of that powerful totality of the cosmos, and in the final instance it is not just about his or her salvation but about the salvation of the world. Such considerations are the ones with which Asian Christianity is predominantly occupied. They have opened people's eyes once more to the letters of Paul, as is the case for example with someone like Chakkarai. While he initially emphasized John almost exclusively, he later became increasingly preoccupied with the preaching of the apostle to the Gentiles. "India needs Paul!" he exclaimed.

> [Paul's preaching] on reconciliation and on the work of Christ as a new creation, or as a new phase of development in the labor pains and groaning of all reality revealed to the children of God, throws a bright light on the modern worldview that regards the world as still incomplete and gradually developing.[63]

Of all Paul's letters, those to the Ephesians and the Colossians speak most powerfully to the Asian mind. The Christ portrayed there as the Savior of the entire cosmos in whom the fullness of the godhead dwells bodily is the One who compels worship in the hearts of many.

We have reached the end of our investigation. We have turned a listening ear to what is expressed from the heart by Christians in Asia. We have seen how they read the gospel and how the light of the gospel is reflected in their thinking and living. We have also seen how they slowly draw near to Christ, and how they test and search in order to appropriate the powerful mysteries of his reconciling work. They are cosmic thinkers, these people of Asia. Concepts like the personal and the individual are more remote ideas for them. They regard the few as interwoven with and closely dependent on the community, and they see the community as intimately bound up with the totality of the entire creation. That is why they often understand the letter to the Colossians better than the letter to the Romans, the Gospel of John better than the Psalms. They have difficulty thinking about religious truths in juridical categories, and they are inclined to look for parallels to the work

---

63. Chakkarai, *Cross and Indian Thought*, p. 19.

of Christ in cosmic laws. However this all might be, this single thing is completely clear, namely that in their hearts exists the genuine desire to find and confess the Christ. Many of them make the pilgrimage to which the literature of the Middle Ages already testified, the pilgrimage from Christ as man to Christ as God.

The dangers threatening these Christians in the younger churches of Asia are not difficult to recognize. That over time tendencies toward Gnosticism, Sabellianism, or Arianism might slip into the Asian churches is certainly a possibility, just as they have unsettled the church in the West during its early centuries. This amplifies more strongly the demand on us to preach the gospel in such a way that in the hour of temptation sufficient resistance will have been provided to all ideas that turn hearts away from the only Savior.

Now that we have reached the end of our investigation, we need to return to the question with which we began: How must we then preach about him? I would like to conclude with a few brief suggestions.

First, it is clear that we ought to preach the whole Christ, in the entire riches of his mediatorial work. We may hold nothing back, and we can hold nothing back. The work of Christ is such a seamless unity that every part of the whole, properly understood, necessarily implies all other parts. One cannot talk about sanctification without immediately bringing justification into the picture, for the one is only intelligible in light of the other. One cannot talk about Jesus as prophet without at the same time honoring him as priest and king. We are not permitted to expunge one word from the Book of God (Rev. 22:19) but are compelled to preach it all. Nonetheless, we must do so in a way that is vital and intelligible in each actual context of Asia.

If you ask me what we must emphasize in order to open a breach in the tightly woven fabric of Asian thought and emotions, I would simply summarize our findings. Begin by calmly telling the story of how Jesus lived and died. Do not begin with the difficult concepts of Christ as God's Son, as the Light of Light, or as God from God, for by doing so you too easily threaten Asian people with tedious speculation that offers no salvation. That Christ is the Son of God is in and of itself worthless unless you first have clearly recounted that Jesus, the Prophet of Nazareth who traveled around doing good work and who gave up his life on the cross, is the Christ. Only within the setting of the gospel of Jesus does the Christ-concept achieve credibility, and it takes on wondrously rich content only when you learn how to express that this Jesus Christ must be called the only begotten Son of God. For then God himself immediately becomes something else; then he is no longer the undefined being-in-general, the a-moral being in all being, but he is as Jesus is, holy and sacrificial love. Then the creation is no longer *maya,* no longer an ephemeral and shimmering shadow, but then it becomes the handiwork of God, the work of his hands that has such great value that God has given his own Son to save it. In short, feel free to make as many connections as you like. But just begin by talking about Jesus as he is depicted for us in the holy gospel of God. Our dogmatic approach, which in our estimation causes us to introduce all sorts of theoretical concepts too quickly, too often gets in the way of announcing this joyful message. Mission work is characterized by saying it all, but measured by the standard of not saying it all at once. Just as in ancient times the Greeks once came with this request, "We would like to see Jesus" (John 12:21), so do the people of Asia today. Whenever we are able to portray him in the fullness of his love and in the grandeur of his redeeming work, it is a major accomplishment.

It has pleased our God to position us at a point in world history when all former values appear to be wavering. Thoughts and customs that have been held unchallenged for centuries now buckle and implode. The lives of millions in Asia as well as the West are being hollowed out daily by the materialism of modern culture. Or, they are swept aside by the wild storms deifying nationalism and rendering morality and justice unrecognizable by such distortions. The world of Asia is being shaken awake from centuries of lethargy, and it feels like it is facing problems for which it is neither morally nor religiously prepared. It is being convulsed and hounded. It is being drugged with slogans and expectations about which no one has the faintest idea what they will yield. But precisely there, in that same Asian world, in the midst of all its turmoil and change, the infant church of Christ is standing and doing battle. Without hesitating, she desires to help and to serve in building people's lives. But she wants to do so as the presence of Christ. The longer time goes by, the more she endeavors to approach the cross of Christ, keeping in view him who gave his life for the salvation of the world. She wants to see and think about all of this in her own unique way, using the gifts of heart and mind that God has given her. She wants to articulate her message clearly for the thousands who will hear it, so that the voice of Jesus is heard.

And here in Holland, we stand behind her. We have our own war to fight against the gods of this age. But that in no way excuses us from supporting the younger churches with our love. That love is expressed in many ways. It is expressed in our gifts for the work of missions, although perhaps we are already too disinclined to regard this as primary and too inclined to let it go. It is expressed in fervent prayer for what is happening there, on that distant field. And it is seen also in this, that we learn to think and to struggle with those who are engaged in such an intense battle. If the chair of missiology that from this time on will be connected with this theological school collaborates in these endeavors, so that all of us and the churches in our homeland continue to support this great work of God in Asia with more love and devotion, then I believe that the establishing of this professorship will prove to be fully justified. Then I will personally be heartily thankful to God for having called me to take on this assignment.

II. Religious Consciousness and Christian Faith

3 Defining Religious Consciousness: The Five Magnetic Points

§1. The Real Question

There are good reasons for considering the question addressed here and paying attention to that cluster of problems with which the Western European world has wrestled so intensely in this postwar era. The question has always interested us whether a definite connection exists between a vague, general religious consciousness that pervades human thought and inquiry like a kind of aura on the one hand and the Christian faith that has played such an enormous role in the history of our part of the world on the other. How should we regard these two major forces: religious consciousness and the Christian faith? Are they partners, related in their deepest essence and flowing into and out of one another? Or, are they actually grim antagonists that cannot tolerate one another? That question has definitely acquired new relevance in the contemporary context.

This is prominently connected to the fact that the problem of religion

---

Ed. note: Because of its length (106 pages in the original), we divided chapter 3 in *Religieus Besef en Christelijk Geloof* into two chapters and gave each new chapter a different, more descriptive title; the original title was "The Nature and Development of Religious Consciousness." The specific term "magnetic points" does not play a significant role in this and the next chapter; it does, however, accurately describe its *content*. The use of the specific term "magnetic points" to describe the *content* of religious consciousness similar to Bavinck's description in this chapter features more prominently in his posthumous volume, *The Church between Temple and Mosque* (Grand Rapids: Eerdmans, n.d.), pp. 32ff.

itself has received new attention in recent decades. At one time during the previous century it seemed as though the culture in our part of the world was increasingly distancing itself from religion and turning to what people considered "pure science." Naturally, in those days there were certainly also religious movements, but it seemed as if the whole direction of cultural development was clearly defined by the tendency to loosen itself from the religious ties of previous generations. Those groups or circles in which strong religious life developed became increasingly isolated and were considered in broader circles as backward and not understanding the heartbeat of history. They were seen as standing on the sidelines, while everything else was moving forward. Not a few were deeply persuaded in those days that the sun of religion was slowly setting and that a new day was dawning, a day in which the old myths and dogmas of religion would no longer be taught, but one when a more discerning and cooler reason would take in hand the reins guiding education. Secularism increased exponentially. In all aspects of life and thought a thoroughgoing worldliness set in. Concepts like "God" and "eternal life" became totally remote. People fixed their attention on what could be seen, on natural laws and mathematical formulas. They concentrated on the persistent abilities of those preoccupied with storming the remaining trenches of the Great Mystery that secularism appeared to have grabbed in its throttling fingers, intent on choking off once and for all everything that passed as religious. "Once one said God when one looked upon distant seas; but now I have taught you to say: overman."[1] This is the way Nietzsche instructed people to understand the course of culture. "Once one said God." But that "once" seemed to be an unendingly long time ago!

We would be guilty of a fatal illusion if we imagined that the course of our culture since the inception of this century has taken a radical change of direction. The process of the *"Entgötterung"* of our worldview (emptying it of any sense of God) and of secularizing life is still going on full force. But it can also definitely be said that the question of religion has been taken up by our generation once again and with irresistible force. The dramatic events of recent decades, particularly the two world wars that rapidly followed one another and were accompanied by the countless problems and concerns flowing from them, insofar as they have brought about any change, have caused people today to lose something of their inner certainty. To be sure, they experience the irresistible push toward objectivity and a godless lifestyle that

1. Ed. note: Bavinck is quoting Friedrich W. Nietzsche, *Thus Spoke Zarathustra: A Book for All and None*, trans. Walter Kaufmann (New York: Penguin Books, 1978), p. 85.

drives our culture, but they are inclined to experience this push as a tragic development that they are incapable of withstanding and of whose force and pain they are fully aware. Here and there is even revealed something of the nostalgia in people's hearts for the old, tried religious truths that increasingly slip away but that they relinquish with such great difficulty. It is just as though all kinds of sentiments are awakened in them that have a typically religious cast. When they realize that they have been caught up in the great and fatal events of history, they experience this as their struggle with the inevitable, with the fate that mercilessly tosses them on paths that they had no voice in choosing. They experience their humanity as something tragic, mysterious, confining, compelling, liberating, and conflicting. They recognize the problem of solitude versus community as a religious problem, as a tension, as insoluble conflict. In short, they feel that their entire lives in all their relationships and circumstances exist in a thoroughly perplexing reality. Emotions are evoked within them that are laden with religious tensions. Even when they push back against the ideas and religious propositions of previous generations, they press on with a keen and brusque bitterness that resonates with them as religious. In whatever form people identify with modern life — as existentialism, as humanism, as neo-vitalism, as the myth of national socialism, or as communistic faith in the future — they trip over the unique reality of religious sentiment that fills and quivers in all of it. Contemporary people certainly understand that they are pressed forward by a totally factual world, but they no longer experience this as a process in which they are willingly involved because it no longer accords with the sentiments of their hearts; much more, they submit to it as a kind of fate, such as they clearly witnessed in the terrible circumstances of those who have died.

In general, therefore, we can say that religious consciousness has made itself master of our generation. This is a religious consciousness that assuredly is thoroughly vague and lacks concreteness, but one that nevertheless reverts to deep undercurrents of human thought and inquiry. Such religious consciousness now finds itself in juxtaposition with that other reality of the Christian faith. Clearly, the discussion that needs to happen between these two is one of the most remarkable topics of contemporary history. That conversation addresses the many questions with which we need to wrestle in shaping the new culture for which we yearn. In most countries of the world, a new lifestyle is growing, one that is striving for a new ordering of social relationships and new forms of society. That striving is substantially carried by religious sensitivities and intuitions that vaguely arise from the mists of contemporary spiritual life. The discussion being held between these sensitivities and the clear, defined content of the Christian faith is in large measure important for the further development of our civilization. This is why thoughtfully investigating the relationships between these two is of such enormous significance.

§2. What Is Religious Consciousness?

We now face the necessity of giving a further account of what we understand by "religious consciousness." We have already seen that this religious consciousness is a rather persistent force that can continue operating even after the connection with a given religion has ceased. In our western world there are countless people who no longer call themselves Christian but who are still definitely sustained by that undefined something that we have designated as religious consciousness.[2] In the same way, in Asia and other parts of the world there are millions that no longer place any emphasis on the name Muslim or Hindu or Buddhist, but who are similarly not yet free from a vague, indefinite religious consciousness. "Religion, as I saw it practiced and accepted even by thinking minds, whether it was in Hinduism or Islam or Christianity," said Nehru, the current president of India, "did not attract me." He certainly believed that something mysterious lies behind our human existence. "What that mysteriousness is I do not know. I do not call it God because God has come to mean much that I do not believe in."[3] Religion as the belief in precise doctrines and propositions has died out, and what has remained is a misty religious awareness. That religious consciousness can at any time take shape in various movements. It can be embodied in existentialism, humanistic activity, socialism, or nationalism; it can color all those movements with a wonderfully bright appeal so that they cease being discerning and factual and exercise a compelling fascination. And while through all of this some sort of religious consciousness remains, it is not yet a religion; it is comparable to the last shimmering of the setting sun which continues for quite awhile, and it still holds its power for a number of generations.

As a rule, we clearly encounter this religious consciousness in the several

2. Ed. note: The current form of this distinction is found in the growing number of people who say, "I am not a *religious* person but I am a *spiritual* person."
3. Jawaharlal Nehru, *The Discovery of India* (New York: The John Day Company, 1946), pp. 14, 16.

religions[4] that have existed among us for many centuries. The relationship of a vague, nebulous religious consciousness and these concrete religions will occupy our attention later. Here we will only make a few provisional remarks on the subject. It is transparently obvious that religious consciousness burns in these religions with a flame that cannot be doused; this is the fascination that all of these religions have for their adherents.

In all these religions we face the fact that in all of them is found a distinct set of ideas that are regarded as revelation; certain ideas and propositions rise above any discussion since they are considered to have come directly from the gods or from godly ancestors. In the large group of religions that we generally designate as primitive religions, we usually find numerous oral traditions and legacies that hark back to ancestors or that were addressed to divine figures who previously lived on earth. These deities have established the order and laid down the rules by which nature and human life are thought to function; therefore that which is regarded as *adat* or divine order is worthy of being honored.

In Hinduism, the distinction has been made from ancient times between *Shruti* — revelation — and *Smriti* — tradition.[5] The Vedas or ancient books of the gods were always regarded as revelation, and as such they were considered to be the norm for life and action. Buddhism recognizes its own canon of sacred writings. The ancient Chinese possessed their books from the great teachers, Kong Fuzi (K'ung Fu-tzu, known in English as "Confucius") and others; these were revered as revelation. Every Muslim believes in the Qur'an as the book given by Allah. Thus, each of these religions recognizes a book or a collection of books, sometimes also only a set of oral traditions that are regarded as revelation. The religion is then accountable to that revelation in its totality of convictions, sentiments, morals, and patterns of behavior that are passed down from generation to generation. By the nature of the case, each of these religions is sometimes a very deficient reflection of what is considered to have been revealed. Sometimes the religion as a complex set of religious ideas and practices is much richer than what is prescribed in the book honored as revelation. For example, the massive phenomenon that we identify as Islam is definitely not explainable as being derived directly from the Qur'an. In the course of the centuries, Islam has

---

4. Ed. note: See note 1 in Chapter 1 for our reluctant use of the term "world religions." Here we are once again retaining Bavinck's own usage.

5. Ed. note: Our editorial protocol is to avoid using the diacritical marks for Sanskrit terms; thus, in addition to *Shruti* for *Śruti* and *Smriti* for *Smṛti*, we use, among other things, *Shiva* for *Śiva*, *Vishnu* for *Viṣṇu* and *Ishvara* for *Īśvara*.

absorbed so many religious tendencies from other peoples and made room in its traditions for so many additional ideas and considerations, that it is impossible to explain this religion solely from the Qur'an. Therefore, a kind of tension always exists between what is regarded as revealed and the realm of religious phenomena requiring accountability.

In fact, what is religion, really? During the last century, we often experienced how totally impossible it is clearly to describe the content of this concept. Religion, said Schleiermacher, is in the deepest sense "a feeling of absolute dependence."[6] But soon it became obvious that this definition was totally unsatisfactory. Religion, said Edward B. Tylor in his pioneering book on *Primitive Culture,* is "the belief in spiritual beings."[7] But this description could not stand up either, since people discovered that in some religions like Buddhism, for example, this belief is not at all central. Religion, said others, is "the fruit of a sense of the holy,"[8] or essentially, "the idea of the Holy."[9] But even this definition seemed too impoverished to explain the confusing complexity of religious phenomena. Time and again, it became apparent that the various religions of the human race are so endlessly diverse, so complex, so rich in ideas and experiences, that it is completely impossible to explain them satisfactorily in just a single word. Now, after many years of work in the science of comparative religions, we realize that we are only at the beginning of a long journey in determining what is most essential about religion.

Meanwhile, one thing is becoming increasingly clear. Despite the variation among the various religions that range widely over what they regard as revelation, they also display unusually remarkable parallels. It appears that humanity always and everywhere has fallen back on definite ideas and presumptions, and that these ideas and presumptions always resurface in surprising ways whenever they may have been temporarily repressed for various reasons. According to Kraemer, something like a "universal religious con-

6. Friedrich Schleiermacher, *The Christian Faith,* ed. H. R. Mackintosh and J. S. Stewart, 2nd ed. (Edinburgh: T. & T. Clark, 1928), §4, pp. 12-18.

7. Edward B. Tylor, *Primitive Culture: Researches into the Development of Mythology, Philosophy, Religion, Language, Art, and Custom,* 2 vols., 4th rev. ed. (London: John Murray, 1903), 1: 424.

8. Nathan Söderblom, *Das Werden des Gottesglaubens: Untersuchungen über die Anfänge der Religion,* trans. Rudolf Stübe (Leipzig: J. C. Hinrich, 1926), p. 179.

9. Rudolf Otto, *The Idea of the Holy: An Inquiry into the Non-Rational Factor in the Idea of the Divine and Its Relation to the Rational,* trans. John W. Harvey (New York: Oxford University Press, 1958), p. 173.

sciousness in man" still exists.[10] This is a universal religious consciousness that remains indestructible in the midst of all disturbing and confusing developments. It is this universal religious consciousness that seems to be the driving force behind all we encounter in the different religions and is what makes the religious issue so intensely interesting as well as difficult.

§3. The Content of Religious Consciousness (a)[11] — Experience of Totality

At this point, we must delve more deeply into the content of religious consciousness. We have already observed that it is vague and ephemeral, but that does not detract from the fact that it must be possible to bring its essential elements to the forefront. We will demonstrate that specifically with respect to five elements that are, in our judgment, embedded in this mysterious larger reality. In order to avoid all misunderstanding, we want to make it perfectly clear here that in this investigation we will, for the time being, leave the biblical revelation outside our consideration. We will limit ourselves, therefore, exclusively to the residue of what has grown out of religious sensitivity outside the realm of biblical revelation.

The first of the five we designate as an experience of totality. This experience I can describe no more clearly than by appealing to what was once told me by someone who had made a trip from Japan to Java. He wrote me how one evening he stood on the deck of the ship and looked down into the ship's hold, where a group of Chinese coolies were lying and sitting as they prepared to go to sleep. The sea was calm, and evening descended quickly on the immense expanse of water. This is what he related to me:

> At that moment, all of a sudden I had the amazing sensation of having left myself. I felt like we were all there as insignificant people packed together on that ship making its lonely way through the gradually darkening evening. Stars began twinkling above us. We could hear the slapping of the waves against the bow of the ship. Suddenly, everything became unreal to me. I considered that for many centuries already people had crossed that

10. Hendrik Kraemer, *The Christian Message in a Non-Christian World* (London: Edinburgh House Press, 1938), p. 112.

11. Ed. note: In order to accent the continuity of content between this subsection and the next four, the letters (a)-(e) for Bavinck's five "magnetic points" of religious consciousness have been added by the editor along with the repetition of the subhead "The Content of Religious Consciousness."

sea on ships, how waves were there then, how stars were present on those evenings, and how human life played itself out so insignificantly in that strange complex of things. I even stopped being an "I" that observed the world and that identified other people as "you." I knew that I had been absorbed into that great totality into which all of us, the coolies lying there below and I standing and peering alone there on the deck, were nothing but tiny little atoms in it all. We were nothing more than inseparable little forms that seem to enjoy an independent existence for only a brief moment, and then all of us would once again be submerged into that endless totality of that great, all-encompassing world. It seemed to me as though I now saw the world for the first time, precisely as I ought to see it and as though I had been delivered from the egocentricity that rendered all else an object over against me. Now I was no more than a little ripple on the wide ocean of totality. I had no sense of self any longer. I only felt the majestic silence of that huge connection that embraces us all. Caught up in that sensation, it all of a sudden seemed that my ordinary life was totally foolish and unreal. Why was I so preoccupied with my own ego, with money and recognition and power and who knows what else? Only one thing seemed genuinely real, and that was the totality that captivated me in an inner, unbreakable embrace. It was as though I now saw life and the world for the first time, as through pure crystal, and as though light flooded in from all sides. My sense of ego, that had always acted like a screen between myself and all-embracing totality, now seemed to be suddenly lifted, and I thought that I was now drawing in the breath of the universal.

In this connection, I also want to call attention to a testimonial provided by William James in his well-known work *The Varieties of Religious Experience:*

> I remember the night, and almost the very spot on the hilltop, where my soul opened out, as it were, into the Infinite, and there was a rushing together of the two worlds, the inner and the outer. It was like deep calling unto deep — the deep that my own struggle had opened up within being answered by the unfathomable deep without, reaching beyond the stars. . . . It was like the effect of some great orchestra when all the separate sounds have melted into one swelling harmony that leaves the listener conscious of nothing save that his soul is being wafted upwards, and almost bursting with its own emotion.[12]

12. William James, *The Varieties of Religious Experience: A Study in Human Nature* (New York: Random House/The Modern Library, 1902), p. 66.

Noteworthy here is that the writer whose testimony James repeats identifies as one of the features of this experience of totality the "indescribable joy" that accompanied it.

It would not be difficult to produce a collection of similar examples from both older and more recent literature describing comparable experiences. Apparently, in some instances people even escape the tensions of ego-awareness and for a brief moment feel the pulse of universality beating within them. Many have experienced this sensation in their lives, and almost unanimously testify to the joy awakened in the depths of their souls. But, instead of searching for a few random testimonies from earlier and later periods and bringing them together, we will attempt to research the various religions in order to see whether this totality-experience is recoverable as an essential element in all of them.

We encounter this most readily when we make our way to India, that ancient land of religious song and philosophical systems. The famous author Betty Heimann has produced a study well worth reading on the uniqueness of Indian thought, in which she has attempted to expose the deepest tendencies in India's feeling about life. She comes to the conclusion that Indian thought has been inspired primarily by the idea that humanity is of equal value with all other aspects of nature and can be understood meaningfully only as a small aspect of the great, cosmic totality. The entire Indian ethic, in her opinion, proceeds from the idea that people need to strive toward "losing the individual." The individual, the sense of ego, the *aham-kara,* the ego shaper as Indian people from antiquity called it, is the veil that covers our eyes and makes it impossible for us to become conscious of the fact that we are no more than a little spark in the eternal fire called *Brahman.* In its deepest sense, the word *"Brahman"* denotes "the world's totality," the universal as one, huge, harmonious connectedness.[13] Indian religious thought and experience, therefore, sees humanity as nothing but a tiny ripple on the eternal immensity of All-that-is; we are blind, and we long with greedy aspiration to become the center of a dream-world. As soon as a person has once grasped that mystery, senses are subdued and one approaches the deepest secrets of existence. India has produced a mixture of religious and philosophical movements, but it is not too bold to say that this idea of the experience of totality has been the most controlling motif driving all thought and inquiry.

In essence, the same features apply to religious life on Java. Getting to

---

13. Betty Heimann, *Studien zur Eigenart Indischen Denkens* (Tübingen: J. C. B. Mohr [Paul Siebeck], 1930), pp. 5, 12, 51ff.

the basis of Javanese thinking is not easy, since it is frequently shrouded in all sorts of complicated and fanciful figures and sayings. At the same time, one of the most dominant elements in the spiritual life of Javanese people has clearly been what one of the most knowledgeable scholars on Java has called "the sense of cosmic commonality." The conviction embedded in this expression is that "everything in the world, including human beings and human life, exists in the closest possible connection with the entire cosmos and is interdependent with everything around it, animate as well as inanimate."[14]

This idea of the inner connectedness of all beings within the eternal interdependence of All-that-is is also present in the deepest assumptions of Chinese wisdom. One of the greatest religious leaders of that ancient people once said this: "The germ of life changes in plants and animals according to the circumstances in which they are found. Humanity also emerges in the course of these changes, and in this cycle it returns from whence it came."[15] J. Witte says the following about Chinese thought in his little book on the religions of East Asian cultures:

> The boundaries between divinity, the gods, people, animals, plants, and all other forms of existence are completely fluid. All beings that exist are only diverse but comparable manifestations and embodiments in their own lives of the eternal laws worked out in the effective rules of nature; humanity too is only an embodiment of natural forces, nothing more.[16]

Throughout all of Chinese thought runs that strand of faith that maintains that each little person is enveloped in the enormous cosmos and can only achieve inner freedom by relinquishing ego-consciousness and allowing oneself to rock with the rhythmic motion of *Dao* [*Tao*], the cosmic principle that permeates all things.

The same thing can undoubtedly be said about Japan. The Japanese appreciation of nature is particularly discriminating. "It is only by humility you may enter into the inner shrine of nature," says a Japanese proverb. You can only penetrate the deepest secrets of nature by humbling yourself, in essence by complete submission of self and the abandonment of the egocentricity that makes us the subject and the cosmos our object. In that

---

14. Theodore Gauthier Th. Pigeaud, *Javaanse Volksvertoningen: Bijdrage Tot de Beschrijving van Land en Volk* (Batavia: Nijhoff, 1938), p. 364.

15. Johannes Witte, *Die Ostasiatischen Kulturreligionen* (Leipzig: Quelle and Mayer, 1922), p. 14.

16. Witte, *Die Ostasiatischen Kulturreligionen*, p. 14.

humility, we are drowned in the silent majesty of the All. Of all the spiritual movements that have been or still are dominant in Japan, none has devoted as much attention to becoming one with nature as so-called Zen Buddhism, which is part of the characteristic phenomena of Japanese culture. It proceeds from the basis of mystical experience, called *"satori"* or enlightenment, which consists of abandoning all inner resistance to nature and inserting oneself into the expanse of cosmic living and being, disengaged from all else. The Swiss psychologist Jung, in the introduction to a small book on Japanese thinkers, makes the observation that *satori* is "an answer of Nature, who has succeeded in conveying her reactions direct to the consciousness."[17] In the literature, the subject is always handled with the use of imagery and poetic license. Whenever anyone asks where the point of entry into higher truth can be found, the mysterious answer of the master teacher sounds something like: "Do you hear the murmuring of the brook? That is the entrance." The meaning intended is that if you hear the murmuring so deeply that all other images fade out and withdraw, or if it is as though the brook's murmuring is occurring deep inside you and you are no longer conscious of yourself, then you have merged with nature and discovered *satori*. Notably, this vibrant sense of nature has been one of the most creative forces in Japanese painting, which is experienced as though the human heart stops beating and a person sinks into the immeasurable immensity of the world around.

But, enough on this topic! It would take us too far afield if we would pursue these religious phenomena to completion. If one were to ask the religious thinkers and the poets of Asia what religion really is, in the deepest sense, they would respond with consistent monotony that it is and can only be one thing: [either] the curtain of self-consciousness is momentarily pushed aside, and a person senses that he is nothing other than nature; or, one stands, not on a platform somewhere in the middle of everything that exists but exists only as a moment in nature; or, the breadth of cosmic life gushes through one who is destined shortly to once again disappear into the Totality. "What is life?" asked one of the ancient Japanese philosophers and answered: "It is like a boat. The emerging dawn discloses it as it makes its way on the sea, quickly rowing away. Then, on the heaving waves no trace can be found that it ever passed that way."

17. Daisetz Teitaro Suzuki, *An Introduction to Zen Buddhism,* with a foreword by C. G. Jung, *The Complete Works of D. T. Suzuki,* ed. Christmas Humphreys (London: Rider and Company for the Buddhist Society, [1949]), p. 20.

Is that really the heart of religious consciousness? It is worth the effort to still turn a listening ear to what the European philosophers have thought and said on the subject of religion.

The first one we consider is Baruch Spinoza, the great thinker of the seventeenth century who tells us that there are various grades and levels of human knowledge. The highest level of knowledge is intuitive science *(scientia intuitiva)*, in which all things are seen as existing in one, huge, eternal connection "in the light of eternity." In that case, we feel that all events that affect us — all suffering, all difficulties — are necessary because they all fit into that large, logical connection with the divine action at work in the entire world as an all-determining, all-sustaining power. From this intuitive knowledge arises the intellectual love of God *(amor Dei intellectualis)* that in the deepest sense is identical with the eternal and endless love with which God loves himself.[18] It is the love of God, working through all creatures and through us, that eventually returns again to itself. The only resistance to it that always stands in our way is our sense of ego that concentrates on ourselves, on our desires, on our emotions, on our delusions that we stand above or alongside everything else; the sense of ego that forgets that we are only little sparks in the eternal fire of divine life and work. Religion is to become conscious of the all-embracing Totality and to submit to it in detachment from everything else.

Schleiermacher expresses himself completely in the same spirit. Particularly in the addresses *On Religion,* he turned his attention extensively to the question of the essence of religion. True religion, he asserted, is "a feeling and taste for the infinite." It is "the immediate unity of intuition and feeling in being one with the infinite." "Everything individual not for itself, but as a part of the whole; everything limited not by its opposition to other things, but as a representation of the infinite taken up in our lives and swaying us — that is religion."[19] What is completely clear is that in all these quotations the

18. Baruch Spinoza, *The Ethics* ([Malibu, CA]: Joseph Simon, 1981), pp. 92-95, 234-35.

19. F. Schleiermacher, *On Religion: Speeches to Its Cultured Despisers,* trans. John Oman (Louisville: Westminster John Knox, 1994 [1958]), Second Speech. Ed. note: Bavinck's quoted material combines a number of phrases, clauses, and sentences from the second speech loosely put together. The following are two of the key passages:

> If man is not one with the Eternal in the unity of intuition and feeling which is immediate, he remains, in the unity of consciousness which is derived, forever apart. (p. 40)

> The Universe is ceaselessly active and at every moment is revealing itself to us. Every form it has produced, everything to which, from the fullness of its life, it has given a

essence of religion is found in the amazing, mysterious experience of becoming one with the All. The boundary of our self-awareness, by which we delude ourselves with the idea that we are little worlds unto ourselves, is wiped away and the eternal absorbs us into itself.

Thus, it is no wonder that the most recent psychological research repeatedly points to the sense of the eternal as one of the constitutive elements of religion. Karl Jaspers in his *Psychologie der Weltanschauungen* points to the fact that in mystical engagement *(Einstellung)* the contrast between self and non-self, between subject and object is relinquished. Mystical experience, for that reason, actually is devoid of content and is a sensation *(Erlebnis)* of being overwhelmed for a time by being submerged in the All.[20] That is the mystical intoxication that spills over all restraints and drags everything with it. Having that intoxicating experience flood over oneself is in one sense the most "illumining resolution" *(leichteste Lösung)* of the unfathomably deep problem of a person's place as an "I" in the midst of the endlessness of all that exists.[21] Obviously, that kind of intoxication occurs only very rarely, and then only for very few people. Nevertheless, it has had an enormous influence on life and thought as far as shaping an attitude toward life is concerned. People know in those moments when they are self-conscious of their own living and working that their lives are but fleeting moments in the totality of existence. That knowledge shapes their sense of the ethical, their treatment of self and of the things around them. That intoxicating experience is crystallized, therefore, in a certain view of what is going on, in a certain way of perceiving the meaning of human existence. Worth noting in this regard is that among many people self-consciousness and self-knowledge is regarded as the sin of all sins. The most profound revelation about life is involuntarily sought, therefore, in a person's loss of any self-knowledge and letting oneself simply be driven along on the waves of the cosmos. The Javanese person puts it well this way: the greatest wisdom in life consists of this, that a person comes to feel like "a piece of driftwood on the swells of the ocean."

---

separate existence, every occurrence scattered from its fertile bosom is an operation of the Universe upon us. Now religion is to take up into our lives and to submit to being swayed by them, each of these influences and their consequent emotions, not by themselves but as part of the Whole, not as limited and in opposition to other things, but as an exhibition of the Infinite in our life. (p. 48)

20. Karl Jaspers, *Psychologie der Weltanschauungen*, 3rd ed. (Berlin: Springer, 1925), p. 85.
21. Jaspers, *Psychologie der Weltanschauungen*, p. 406.

This is the heart of religious experience. A person exists in the world, thinks about the world, tries to understand the world, attempts to subject the world to his or her will, shapes the world to meet his or her needs, and continuously deals with the world. But at a given moment the strange realization falls over this person that all of this is complete foolishness. The person suddenly realizes that he or she is nothing more than an incidental aspect of the world. The love and hatred, the hunger and thirst that pulse through the universe are also present in persons' own lives and bundle themselves together into a self-contained totality; at the same time each of them always exists within that Allness, the All that swirls around them on every side and is continually washing over the dams of their sense of separate ego. That is when they give up on their enclosedness, stop resisting, lose their individual standpoint and allow themselves to be borne along on the currents of the unending. At that same instant knowing and seeking and desiring flow together in them and they become aware of the "totality-meaning of personal life" (*"Totalsinn des persönlichen Lebens"*)[22] and, simultaneously, realize something of the never-ceasing illusion that encloses their lives. The spell of *avidya*, of unknowing, that had imprisoned them all the days of their lives, even loses its determinative and repressive power and they are capable of seeing beyond it and through it. They now exist eye to eye with the immeasurable expanse of the All.

I can put it another way. People always maintain a certain distance from nature, which surrounds them continuously. They hold nature in their hands and bow over it inquisitively as an object outside of themselves. They reach out toward it as something good that they desire but always partially, engaged with only some dimensions of their being. One moment they are only busy thinking, investigating, experimenting; then, they are totally active, doing. And sometimes all the forces within them flow together and they feel what it means to be human. Precisely then, all sense of distance over against the world disappears, and they no longer position themselves outside all other things, as though standing alongside or above them; the objective platform on which they previously stood suddenly disappears and they experience being swallowed up in the everlasting. They know that the eternal law governing all life has coursed through them, that they can only exist meaningfully when they accept that they are only small ripples in the totality of everything, and when they allow themselves to be embraced as a prisoner

---

22. Eduard Spranger, *Lebensformen: Geisteswissenschaftliche Psychologie und Ethik der Persönlichkeit*, 5th ed. (Tübingen: M. Niemeyer, 1925), pp. 236-37.

of that totality and stop resisting it. Then they smile. "Now I know what life is," they confess. Light and darkness, grasping and repelling, sun and earth, rising and falling — all of it is part of me, and I am part of it all. Totality belongs to me, and I belong to totality. The enormity of being in general embraces my small being; the macrocosm stretches over my own, insignificant, transitory, earthly existence.

It should be completely obvious that mysticism's religious view of life yields a clearly defined understanding of the relationship of the individual to the community. In the religious systems that we are used to calling "primitive,"[23] the emphasis is placed entirely on the community at the expense of the individual. Whenever humanity is seen entirely within the context of nature, regarded as simply a dimension of nature, and a specific human being is given very little attention, it is inevitable that individuality disappears into collectivity. The tribe or the clan, the tribal ethic, the connection with the tribe — these determine how one sees all of life. The individual is anonymous and simply follows the course determined by the tribe. When a stranger asks someone his name, he answers by giving the name of the tribe or the caste to which he belongs. He is nothing; he is merely a manifestation of the tribe's life displayed in him; his life has no more significance than a spark running along a fuse. The communal governs everything. Wherever the person is not sharply distinguished from nature and the natural side of his being is the essential and prominent side, the individual person loses a sense of his own meaning; the meaning of the community dominates, and that community, in turn, is seen in its harmonious connection with all of nature surrounding it. Blood cannot be thought of apart from the Soil in which it is found nor the community apart from its cosmic context.[24] The entire thought-world of the so-called "native" people or "primitive" people rests on the subtle connection of these two and is the reason why in that world an individual never jumps out, needing to have his name engraved on the monuments of history. No song is sung whose poet is remembered; no myth is retold whose human source is recalled; no custom is observed that is

23. Ed. note: Current usage replaces the pejorative term "primitive" with the more accurately descriptive term "primal." Alternatively, the same religious phenomenon is also spoken of as "indigenous religion," "native religion," or "First Nation religion." We have retained Bavinck's own usage in this chapter and alert the reader to Bavinck's own frequent qualifier "so-called" along with his "scare quotes" on the term itself. Bavinck frequently pairs "primitieve" with "natuurvolken," placing both within quotation marks (see note 25 below).

24. Ed. note: Bavinck uses the German *Blut* and *Boden* here, the hallmark insignia of the National Socialist Party of Germany (Nazi) and the Third Reich.

honored by the name of one who instituted it. What is a poet except a person who sings what everyone sings? What is the source of mythical accounts except someone who simply recites what lives in the beliefs of all? The few figures who are honored as heroes and worshiped as creators really belong to the realm of the demigods; they have no real place in the ordinary history of daily existence.

Herein lies a definite tension that from time to time is painfully felt. Mystical enlightenment, *satori*, the experience of totality, or whatever it might be called, is always an exceptional individual experience. A person — an individual person — receives it suddenly and is overwhelmed by it as it grips him in the depth of his being. He experiences this himself, personally, and no one else participates in this with him. Naturally, it is also possible that the tribe as a whole undergoes this emotion, as for example through a religious rite involving dance, music, or some other activity. But even in many of these instances, it is still an individual who has a special talent for this, who enjoys the experience and then can later talk about it. He has undergone it as something bestowed on him and on him alone. This is why a mystical experience of totality always is inclined to have some individual at its center. Indian religions have a strong sense of the communal, but at the same time they are religions that cultivate the individual experience of the saving process of becoming one with *Brahman*, the All-in-all. The individual stands in total solitude precisely when experiencing the sensation of melding with totality; no one participates or is capable of participating in it with him. When he returns to the world of ordinary human life after such an affective experience, he keenly feels as though no one understands him, no one empathizes with what he has experienced; he is a stranger among his relatives. Henceforth, he is "a dead man among the living," as the Javanese mystic puts it. Capturing the paradox, this expression is sometimes playfully turned around to say "a man living among the dead." In either case, it expresses something of the loneliness such a person feels. At the instant that he submitted to totality, he stood alone; when he embraced everything within his grasp, he felt released from everything. That is the tragedy of the abandonment that mysticism has experienced throughout the ages.

Reviewing for a moment what we have discovered to this point, it is clear to us that the intuition of totality, the experience of totality, or if one would rather call it the feeling of communion with the cosmic whole, is a typically religious phenomenon. That is to say, as soon as a person has this experience, it is presented in religious garb and experienced as religious ecstasy. Does this mean that totality itself is god, or that god and totality are one and the same? That would be a philosophical conclusion that in many cases is not drawn and sometimes is even fearfully avoided. Sometimes Hindus even openly talk about the All as being *Brahman* and that becoming one with *Brahman* is nothing other than relinquishing all resistance to totality and sensing oneself as an aspect of All-that-is. The ideas of other peoples, however, do not go that far. All that they want to say, and they do so repeatedly, is that the experience of cosmic connectedness has an exceptionally noteworthy religious coloration. It exhibits a religious glow that is comparable to nothing else.

The experience of totality gradually ebbs and the glow of a religious sensation slowly fades. All that remains is a sense of having been abandoned, a sense of loneliness, but at the same time a sense of joy over having seen "the mystery." Frequently, this arouses a longing to experience the sensation again and again. In some contexts, an impressive technique has developed — as was to be expected — for invoking the return of the experience of oneness with everything. Precise breathing exercises, exacting discipline of the imagination, withdrawal of sensations comparable to a turtle pulling in its head and legs, and concentrated meditation — all had to serve the purpose of predisposing the soul to receive this overwhelming experience. But even then, the experience itself was felt as being snatched away suddenly and as the soul being overwhelmed and overpowered. Other times use is made of rhythmic dancing and mournful music that slowly makes the heart ripe for what is considered the holiest and most profound experience. In this connection, one thing never varies: the truth of this unifying experience could never really be communicated with others; it was not transferable; it could not be taught. At most, the guru or master teacher could help his students along the way, point out precautions for them to take and instruct them in the technique for subordinating their senses toward a higher striving; he could do nothing more. Each student had to receive the experience for himself, as a gift. He could approach it attentively according to the methods that had been disclosed to him by his master, but then it had to overcome him and drag him along in the maelstrom of the eternal.

Buddhist literature in particular describes with unbelievably detailed attention the stages on the difficult road of unification. There are nine levels through which the pilgrim needs to rise toward immeasurable light before he reaches the mountaintop of annihilation, the nirvana exalted above all striving. Especially the last five stages are described in indistinct, vague terms since they in fact defy all description. Here people enter into "the sphere of endless space"; then they reach "the sphere of ceaseless spiritual consciousness"; and then they approach "the sphere of Nothingness." Beyond this realm lies "the sphere of exaltedness above boundaries between the conscious and the unconscious." Finally, a person reaches the sphere of the annihilation of the fantasies that exist in the inner life but are now refined away through the glowing breath of total unification with the All-in-all. These enumerate the experiences that the individual person undergoes on his journey from this world of struggle to the domain of eternal light.

Finally, underlying all this is the certainty that people unite in themselves the two amazing dimensions of unimaginable insignificance and matchless greatness; in the experience of the Eternal, one feels like a reed swaying to and fro, insignificant, more insignificant than could have been imagined. A person exists imbedded in the immeasurable connectedness of everything, like a little piece of a twig lying in small hollow in an immense wilderness. When resistance stops, when consciousness of self is overcome, one becomes nothing and feels like sinking away into the measureless depths. But at the same time such a person is great, gloriously great, great beyond describing! and, actually grasping the Eternal that resonates deep within, throwing arms around it, forgetting self completely in its sweet embrace. The inexpressible majesty of the totality is reflected in the stillness of the heart, just like the unbounded enormity of the heavens is reflected in the dewdrop clinging to a flower. A person can encompass these things, inhale the eternal, drawing it into the depths of personal being and drowning in it. One has become a microcosm, the world in miniature, with all the features of the macrocosm converging in oneself. There is no dimension, there is no force, no idea of the whole wide world that does not exist in the one who is nothing and at the same time everything. A person is as fragile as a blade of grass, but at the same time as powerful as a god who is able to endure it all and laboriously scale the mountains of Eternity. The distances outside call to the distances within one's deepest being, and one hears their echo reverberating in the recesses of the heart. Precisely in insignificance one feels greatness. It seems as though everything lies at my very feet, as though I stand at the very heart of it all, as though everything around me bows to me in reverent submission. This religious experience that humbles a person in the depth of his or her being has also exalted him or her high above all else and placed him or her on the throne of the universe. This is what it means to be a person! It means to be so powerless as to feel as though one is being crushed by an enormous rock or as though one is being swept along into nothingness by the waves. And yet, it also means to be so powerful as to experience all things converging and uniting within oneself.

This, then, is the first element that we find in religious consciousness: intuition concerning the totality, the experience of the All. That idea has entranced people through all the centuries of human history and led them to ecstasy. Ordinary human life is always broken, incomplete, insignificant, bungling, and banal. As soon as a person approaches that secret border where he leaves behind his own individuality and allows himself to be engulfed by all that there is, he becomes great. That is where he experiences divine reality, not as something that exists outside himself but as something that throbs deep within. He grovels before the eternal majesty of the Everlasting, but in that groveling he feels caught up into the unfathomable glory of the union that is the deepest meaning of all that exists.

§4. The Content of Religious Consciousness (b) — The Notion of Norm

The idea of the moral norm appears as a remarkably important concept in the history of the human race. Whatever wells up in a person and is born in him in a totally natural way is still not what it ought to be. It can happen that something is certainly present, but that it ought not to be there. Throughout his existence, a person has to deal not only with what happens or what emerges from him, but he also has to consider the norm by which his thoughts and actions will be judged. This idea of the norm also belongs to the content of the religious consciousness that a person carries.

Behind the idea of the norm lie several deeper assumptions that are thoroughly and completely mysterious. In the first place, a certain idea of freedom lies concealed in it, at least the idea that it is possible to make choices. A person does something, but in so doing he has the vague sense that he could have done something else. That element of choice is highly important to him, especially in that he knows he is responsible for what he does. A second assumption accompanying the idea of the norm is that a person is bound by values and standards that he himself has not created but that completely apply to him. The moral norm is an objective standard, and it requires total submission of a person. No less, however, the person is aware of that norm, for it is as though the idea of it is innate. This points to the fact that the notion of norm belongs to the idea of human existence's complete inner immersion into a world of a higher order. The idea of the moral norm indicates that not everything that is, is permissible, and that not everything that occurs, should occur; it indicates that a boundary between the permissible and impermissible exists and that it has been drawn by a power far superior to our own.

What cannot be denied is that this idea of the moral norm has engaged human thought from antiquity. Among most "native"[25] peoples the idea of norm exists in the form of the belief that divine or semi-divine ancestors have instituted laws and ordinances, and that keeping those ordinances is essential for the welfare of the tribal group. The concept of *adat* is usually used in Indonesia for designating such regulations. In and of itself, *adat* means no more than "custom" or "usage." But in more recent times, it has been pointed out that this concept has a much deeper foundation. First of all, it consists of the "divinely established cosmic order and harmony" that inheres in the entire structure of the world itself. Secondly, it designates simultaneously living in agreement with this divine order.[26] Most of the so-called "primitive" peoples[27] have received a deep impression of the orderly structure of all that exists. This totality represents an orderly interaction of light and darkness, heaven and earth, life and death; human life is caught up in that interaction. It is pinched by it, drawn into it. This constitutes the deepest basis for the norms with which a person is involved every moment of their lives and is why the idea of a "moral world-order" is found among all peoples.[28] Everywhere it is closely connected with the knowledge that nature can only continue to exist as long as attention is paid to a definite order. The sun needs to rise and set on its schedule; the moon needs to wax and wane in its time; in short, everything needs to occur in an orderly and regular manner. The order that holds the cosmos *together* and sustains it is reflected in the order to which the tribe and every member of it knows it is tied.

Ancient India knew the idea of *Rita* or the divine order that controls everything.[29] This *Rita* was first of all cosmic order. It regulated times and places, and it controlled the course of nature: birth and death, light and darkness, rain and drought, day and night. Everything in the world had its

25. Ed. note: We have translated Bavinck's "natuurvolken" as "native peoples." He has in mind the same religious phenomena and is likely just reflecting variations in scholarly terminology. "Natuurvolken" is frequently paired with "primitieve"; see note 23 above.

26. Hans Schärer, *Ngaju Religion: The Concept of God among a South Borneo People*, trans. Rodney Needham (The Hague: Martinus Nijhoff, 1963), pp. 39ff.

27. Ed. note: See note 23 above.

28. Konrad Theodor Preuss, *Glauben und Mystik: Im Schatten des höchsten Wesens* (Leipzig: C. L. Hirschfeld, 1926), pp. 52, 53.

29. Ed. note: We are following our editorial practice of not using diacritical marks in Sanskrit words; thus *Rita* instead of *Ṛta*. Cf. note 5 above.

assigned place, happened at its appointed time, and fit into the harmonic totality. That is the *Rita* that embraces everything and that sets everything in the cosmic structure in its place. *Rita* is also reflected in the moral order to which human beings are subject. A person also has his or her place in the totality of things, and he or she is held accountable for maintaining that position as the mainstay of his or her life. Particularly with respect to the extremely important relationship of husband and wife — the relationship always seen as a reflection of that great cosmic marriage between the light of heaven and the darkness of the earth — *Rita* appears with compelling authority. It determines with whom a young man may marry and how that marriage is to be conducted if it is to yield health and not lead to ruin. *Rita* regulates the position of the ruler in society and also the honor that his subjects are obligated to show him. *Rita* ordains society's classes and castes and prescribes for each the rules according to which they are to conduct themselves. Only when each member of human society maintains his or her position and does what is prescribed for him or her in that position, is the community a true reflection of its defined connection with the cosmos; only then can it be expected that the entire community will experience blessing and prosperity. The concept of norm or order, therefore, is first seen with respect to nature; from there it is introduced into the realm of human society.

Connected to all of this is the notion that *dharma*, the duty of each person individually, flows out of *Rita*. The *dharma* of the wife is different from that of the husband, since the wife simply has a different place in the cosmic order. She belongs to the earth, to darkness, to the mystery of coming to life and has her own order. In the world of men, the ruler has a different *dharma* from a Brahmin, the field hand from a soldier, the slave from the free man. Every member of society has his or her own *dharma*. Taken together, all these regulations form the composite whole of the world-order. A country where dharma is respected and followed by every citizen is a land where peace and welfare prevail. But woe to the people that rend the divine world-order! Each rending of that order only invites misfortune, sickness, floods, and misery.

In China, the idea of norm does not differ essentially from how it is understood in India. The concept of *Dao* [*Tao*], which means way or norm or law, is important beyond measure. It controls all Chinese thinking and is first of all a cosmic concept. It rules the course of nature and is the order in all that exists. Summer and winter follow one another on the strength of *Dao* [*Tao*]. Heaven marries the earth and to that marriage of the lustrous heaven and the darkened earth are born trees, plants, animals — in short, all living beings. *Dao* [*Tao*] is the law to which everything is subject and that lives and functions in all. Now, that same *Dao* [*Tao*] is projected in human society as *li*, the moral norm. *Dao* [*Tao*] requires that the ruler will be a ruler, the minister a minister, the man a man, the woman a woman, the child a child, and that each of them conduct themselves in a manner consistent with the position they hold relative to everything else. If people do not chafe against *Dao* [*Tao*], but allow *Dao* [*Tao*] to work itself out in their lives and listen carefully to what divine law whispers in their ears, then an entire people grows strong and great and life becomes rich and meaningful.

These are the ways that the people of Asia have from antiquity mused over the moral order of the world. They always regarded that world-order as closely connected with the order of nature. They saw it reflected in the entire cosmic order, in all its dimensions. The ruler and the tribal chief understood that they were the bearers of that order, the personifications of the moral norm that pointed out the direction that the people had to go. If the ruler was a true ruler and did what his *dharma* dictated he should do, then everything went well and everyone would flourish. The contours of the world-order converged in him. This is why the ruler is a kind of mediator, the bearer of salvation who points out the right paths to take. He stands in a very special place and has an inside connection with the divine world because he himself is part of that world and is always beholden to it. He stands between the people and their gods.

Not infrequently we find it said that the gods communicated the moral laws to the people in very ancient times, dictating them to a king who lived then. Since that time they have been handed down from generation to generation. India elevated these laws and regulations to the level of *Manu*, a name derived from the root word for "man" and signifying "thinking," who is the mythical ruler who established the norms for all successive generations.[30]

In Islam, all law is attributed to Allah who revealed his law to the prophet through Gabriel; in this way the Qur'an came into existence as the Muslim holy book. More recently, the question has been raised in Islamic theology of the foundation on which moral norms actually rest. Has Allah posited them because they are good, or are they good because Allah has commanded them? Is the good something that in a sense extends above Al-

---

30. Ed. note: In various Hindu traditions *Manu* is the mythical progenitor of the human race and its first ruler. Since the late nineteenth century the figure became prominent in theosophy circles inspired by the writings of Helena Petrovna Blavatsky, who believed that each "root race" had its own *Manu;* see H. P. Blavatsky, *The Secret Doctrine: The Synthesis of Science, Religion and Philosophy* (Nabu Press, 2010 [1888]); available online at http://www.theosociety.org/pasadena/sd/sd-hp.htm.

lah, and has Allah done nothing more than give expression in his law to what is good? Or, is Allah so completely almighty that he himself determines what is to be considered as good? These questions have preoccupied Muslim theologians for a very long time. In this connection, yet another issue is raised. Is Allah obligated to punish those who have sinned against his law on the basis of an inescapable obligation, or is he completely free to punish whom he will and to extend forgiveness to whomever he pleases? All of these questions were extremely difficult to fathom. The subject of moral norms is such mysterious territory. That moral norms are immediately connected with Allah is clear to everyone; how that connection is to be explained is very difficult to understand. Often the question arises whether a person possesses the capacity within his or her own reason to understand the difference between good and evil. Can reason really serve as our guide on this matter? Is reason, then, perhaps a gift of God, a light within our hearts? If that is the case, has Allah sent his prophet only because we men and women have simply neglected listening to the voice of our reason? This is the way that many theologians in both earlier and more recent times have been governed by the mysterious issues surrounding the idea of norm; norm is like a stranger in the midst of our human existence.

These last questions posed within the framework of Islamic theology owe a debt of gratitude to the influence of Greek thinking that increasingly began to be felt in Muslim society. Greek thinking had been engaged with the problem of the norm already from early times and had opened new perspectives on the subject that signaled nothing short of a revolution in the history of philosophy. In Greece, earlier than elsewhere in the world, philosophical thinking had wrestled itself free from the bands of mythology and pursued its own, independent course. With noteworthy lack of fear, the old wise men of Athens raised questions that in other countries were at most gingerly suggested but that no one dared to pose openly. At a given time in Greek history, a breakthrough occurred that more or less conveyed skepticism toward all certainties and rendered fluid all social conventions. In opposition to this skepticism, Greek thought became determined to penetrate to the deepest meaning and to establish new certainties in place of the old ways being abandoned. This struggle against gnawing skepticism produced the Greek wisdom that has been so valuable to world history.

In one of Plato's dialogues, the issue of the moral norm comes to expression in a wonderfully beautiful and profound way.[31] The baffling question is

---

31. Plato, *The Republic of Plato,* trans. Allan Bloom (New York: Basic Books, 1968).

raised whether so called moral norms do not rest on egoism, on well-understood self-interest. The masses, of which far and away the greatest percentage is made up of weaklings, cannot endure the fact that people exist who crash all barriers and impose their powerful will on others. The masses fearfully pull back to their borders of propriety, to their moral norms, but all of these so-called norms are nothing more than the collective self-defense of the miserable. Egoism is what lies tucked behind their moral standards. In the discussion that is constructed in posing this issue, Plato attempts to penetrate to fundamentals, to eternal principles of good and evil. He probes increasingly deeper toward the idea that the good consists in the fact that each thing exists in the orderly position designated for it in the cosmic harmony of all things. If each person would develop his or her gifts and capacities properly, then the community would be safe and the well-being of all would be assured. But even within each person individually, everything must accept its proper place. Within every person's breast beat the persistent forces of opposition that are ever ready to promote chaos and disturbance, desires that are capable of dragging people into danger zones and bringing them to their knees. Only if everything is properly ordered deep within a person and in tune with cosmic harmony, only if the reins of reason are firmly gripped and control all of life, is safety guaranteed. That harmony rules — that is the secret of true virtue. That the inner and the outer are in concurrence — that produces good order. Evil is chaos, disjointedness, despair; the good is cosmic order, when everything is where it belongs.

Thinking through the mystery of the good, Plato produces magnificent testimonies that seemingly arise from profound wisdom. The idea of the good is *megiston mathema,* the highest knowledge. It precedes all existence; it assumes first place in the hierarchy of ideas. Things exist only insofar as they participate in the idea of the good. The contrast between good and evil is not contrived by the cunning of the human heart to protect one's own interests, but it dominates everything and is a divine reality. This greatest of all ideas is buried deep within the human soul. It is only brought out in people with the greatest of difficulty, and yet they have always known it because they have carried it within them from the time they have appeared in the world. Anyone who has once seen the idea of the good in its radiance can never again forget it and is exhilarated by it. "Virtue is knowledge," Socrates said. Anyone who has been once bewitched by the idea of the good, having contemplated it, is forever its prisoner.

It is not possible to explore these matters more fully at this point. When we let Greek thought about the idea of the good sink in, it strikes us that in every respect it agrees with what has been expressed about moral norms in China and India. This applies to the thought of Plato, and to an even greater degree to the thought of the later philosophical schools, especially Stoicism. Throughout Asia[32] as well as in Greece, it was understood that the concept of order extends much further than only to human society; it opens cosmic perspectives. We live in an ordered world, a cosmos, and its order will come to expression one way or another in our society. In fact, the concept of order goes even deeper. It applies not only to our social relationships, but it even penetrates to the inner composition of our own being. The finite person, who carries around all sorts of polarities within and who is pulled apart by conflicting thoughts and desires, understands that order must come to our little worlds of our own inner conflicts if we are not to be destroyed completely. The majesty and the cosmic significance of the concept of order is experienced in Asia as well as in Greece. To be human implies dialogue, and it is never a peaceful dialogue with the norm and with obligation about existence, about what there is in us and around us. The norm pops up at the most unexpected moments in our discussions, demanding our respect and our obedience. It is part of us, and it exists unbelievably far above us. It is our possession; we see it; we know it; it is born within us, but it bears the marks of its divine origin and expects to be followed by us. Life is a dialogue between the person and the norm. The meaning of existence is only comprehensible from the perspective of that dialogue.

Clear connections exist, therefore, between Greek and Asian thought. But points of difference exist as well. In Greece, thinking was packaged more loosely with mythology and is more conceptual and matter-of-fact. It is worked out much more from a human perspective. It originates on earth, not in the heavens. Asian intellectuals[33] sometimes surveyed the totality of reality in a vision. Speculatively, they rose far above all the incidentals and intricate connections of ordinary, earthly things, and they reveled in the grandeur of the eternal and the divine. Once they had contemplated all of this, they descended to the earth. In Greece, people proceeded much more from ordinary, everyday life. There the poison of doubt coiled, ready to strike; there strenuous objections were raised. But there the thinking also

32. Ed. note: Bavinck's original text has "Far East"; we have chosen to substitute "Asia" for terms such as "the East," "Far East," "Orient," and "oriental." See the Preface and Chapter 2, note 18.

33. Ed. note: As can be seen in the paragraph that follows, Bavinck seems here to be highlighting the religious traditions of South and Southeast Asia (India, Sri Lanka, Indonesia, Malaysia, Thailand) rather than those of China, Korea, and Japan. See Chapter 2, note 18.

wrestled with all those doubts in the human search for what was enduring, for what is grounded deep within, for what is unshakeable and of unchanging value. From that vantage point someone begins to eye the wider world, the orderly movement of the stars, the harmony binding all aspects of reality in their majestic coherence. Here thinking emerges from below, and it addresses eternal ideas from the level ground of the ordinary in human society.

Taking this methodological approach, Greek thought laid the groundwork for western philosophy. Throughout the generations and right down to the present, European philosophers have stammered around about what Greek intellectuals have said. Greek thought has always had immeasurable influence on philosophical discussions that have been carried on throughout the western world. Europe owes an inexpressible debt to its Greek ancestors.

Western thought has reflected at considerable length on the riddle of the moral norm. Time and again, that problem comes to the forefront. Every time that it did, intellectuals were aware of the impenetrable fog that hangs over the concepts of good and evil. The West is inclined to address the problem from the human side, generally speaking, and less from the cosmic perspective. In western philosophy as a rule, the human being is interpreted less as an aspect of the huge cohesiveness of nature in general, and is seen rather as a being having its own character. The specific human person, distinguished from all other living beings and having his or her singular position in the midst of all other creatures, is what has drawn focused attention in the West, which has been interested in what is specifically human. While a human being may certainly be part of the cosmos, bound by cosmic laws on every side, humanity is never to be completely identified with nature and is never simply absorbed passively by it. We are different; the object-side of our lives, the dimension of our lives that is tied to nature, is not the only dimension or even the most important dimension of our existence. That aspect is subordinate to what really makes us human, namely our subjection to moral norms, our accountability, and our rationality. Thus, the West, despite everything else, has kept more of an eye on the distance between human beings and nature.

In this short review, it is impossible to consider everything that has been stirred up in philosophy concerning the issue of moral norms. When Spinoza wrote about the subject of the good in the fourth book of his ethics, he offered this definition: the good is "that about which we are certain that it is useful for us."[34] He clearly did not mean this in a eudaemonistic sense, as if

---

34. Spinoza, *The Ethics*, p. 168.

the norm is concerned only with temporary pleasure. That is evident from the fact that he calls knowledge of God the highest good.[35] That greatest good means that a man must learn to see the entire world and all that happens in it as a powerful, divine activity, and thus understand that his welfare lies in controlling his passions and in complete submission to God's rational will.

The idea of the moral norm is the central thrust of Kant's philosophy. He feels that the great "thou shalt" is the hinge on which our lives turn, and that it never serves us well when we rationalize away the force of that norm. Somewhere he says what amounts to this:

> A man may do his very best to paint, in one way or another, some deed that he has done as an act of carelessness that he could not entirely avoid. He may portray it as something that simply swept him along in the stream of natural necessity. On those grounds, he may plead that he is guiltless. But he will always know that the advocate who defends him is completely unable to silence the accuser that is in him, as long as he is conscious that when he committed his misdeed he was in full possession of his reason.[36]

That is the mysterious norm within us on which Kant reflects. It is a judge that cannot be bought off. Kant wants to know what it is all about, from

35. Spinoza, *The Ethics*, p. 183.

36. Immanuel Kant, *Critique of Practical Reason and Other Works on the Theory of Ethics*, trans. Thomas Kingsmill Abbott, B.D., Fellow and Tutor of Trinity College, Dublin, 6th revised ed. (London: Longmans, Green and Co., 1909), p. 230. Ed. note: As is evident from his lead-in, Bavinck is intentionally citing this passage from Kant about the conscience rather loosely. Abbott's translation of the full passage from which this is taken reads as follows:

> With this agree perfectly the judicial sentences of that wonderful faculty in us which we call conscience. A man may use as much art as he likes in order to paint to himself an unlawful act that he remembers, as an unintentional error, a mere oversight, such as one can never altogether avoid, and therefore as something in which he was carried away by the stream of physical necessity, and thus to make himself out innocent, yet he finds that the advocate who speaks in his favour can by no means silence the accuser within, if only he is conscious that at the time when he did this wrong he was in his senses, that is, in possession of his freedom; and, nevertheless, he accounts for his error from some bad habits, which by gradual neglect of attention he has allowed to grow upon him to such a degree that he can regard his error as its natural consequence, although this cannot protect him from the blame and reproach which he casts upon himself. This is also the ground of repentance for a long past action at every recollection of it; a painful feeling produced by the moral sentiment, and which is practically void in so far as it cannot serve to undo what has been done.

whence it comes, how we develop awareness of it. Increasingly the idea matures within him that the idea of the "thou shalt" is the huge a-priori of our lives with which we are born, given with life itself, and that we can never expunge it. It inheres in our existence here on earth as our ineradicable possession. Kant understands that this is the gateway to religion. In this way, the moral norm along with the idea of the greatest good as the object and goal of practical reason leads to religion, that is, "to the recognition of all duties as divine commands."[37] Kant, then, too, has seen something of the fact that the idea of the moral norm gives off an aroma of eternity and as an inexplicable reality applies to what goes on in everyday life here on earth.

In our part of the world, these Kantian perspectives continue beating like waves on the shores of philosophical thought. In the exposition of the principles behind the Humanistic Alliance here in the Netherlands, founded in 1946, we read that humanism is to be understood as

> that world and life view that, without being based on the existence of a personal God, is founded on a respect for humanity as that special part of the cosmos that is the bearer of a sense of the normative not subject to personal arbitrariness and as the creator of and participant in spiritual values.

Note well the expression: "a sense of the normative not subject to personal arbitrariness." Is that not saying that human beings understand that their sense of the normative is innate, that it is not their property, that they cannot do with it whatever they please, and that it is greater than they are? And while people will not expressly bring to the foreground the issue of the origin of that sense, does it not also indicate that the norm possesses something of divine majesty?

Life is a dialogue. That dimension becomes visible to us time and again. What exists may not be permissible simply because it exists. The strands that people spin into the webs of their lives are not necessarily permissible. A standard exists that overarches everything, permeates everything, and illuminates everything. A person is in conversation with himself. Or to put it more precisely, a person is constantly in dialogue with the norm within him that yet does not originate from him. He attempts to justify himself and plead his innocence, but there comes a time when he simply has to bow his head to that norm that is obviously more powerful than he. This dialogue is

---

37. Kant, *Critique of Practical Reason*, p. 271.

what, above all, makes him human. It is the nobility and at the same time the deep tragedy of his existence. He can flee nowhere to escape the majesty of that norm, for it follows him wherever he goes.

Is this consciousness of the norm not one of the most essential elements of universal religious consciousness about which we are speaking? It definitely need not always be tied to faith in a personal God. One could say that it is something that a person "bears"; one could say that we are ourselves "the creators of and participants in spiritual values." But even then, we cannot close our eyes to the fact that something very unusual is going on with respect to that norm. I can never do whatever I please with that awareness of the norm, but that awareness of the norm can do whatever it pleases with me. It can bring me to despair. It can cast me down. It can hound me into unmentionable despair and fear. If I ignore awareness of the normative, awareness of the normative never ignores me; it refuses to let me avoid it. It is not the case that I am king and the norm is my servant, but the norm is king and I am the accused and the guilty party. The awareness of the normative always contains something from the realm of the divine. This is why all sorts of attempts to explain it as arising from human conventions, from slowly developing customs, from cutting a deal, and from nurture, all hopelessly fail. The norm not only stands above me in my social relationships and my actual living with other people, but it also judges my most intimate thoughts, the ones no one else sees or knows. Not an inch of my existence falls outside its dominion. The consciousness of the norm is essentially religious, and it always reflects divine realities.

§5. The Content of Religious Consciousness (c) — Connection with a Higher Power

As the third element of that amazing reality that we designated as "religious consciousness," we specify awareness of a connection with a higher power. Here we intentionally use an extremely vague description in order to make it possible to include a wide range of phenomena. A connection! Well, what is a connection? The word denotes nothing more than some sort of vague association. This association can be one of any number of types. It could indicate that the human being has been created by that higher power. But it could also leave open the possibility that the human being descended from that higher power, was born from it, is its relative, and is in a certain sense identified with it. Similarly, the word "higher power" is just as vague. The term really says nothing further about the existence of that higher power. Is it a personal God, a Lord? Or should it be thought of as a mixture of gods and spirits? Or, is the supposition itself still not quite right, and should the higher power be seen as a hazy, impersonal force that is present in the world as a mysterious glow? All kinds of assumptions are possible here and are intentionally kept open as possibilities.

Regarding this connection with a higher power, we now move to a special case. When the English academic Edward B. Tylor published his book *Primitive Culture* in 1871, a book in which he devoted an extensive chapter to the religious assumptions of so-called "primitive peoples,"[38] he weighed the assumption that these peoples were initially impressed with the notion of a human soul. That soul is an invisible, thoroughly mysterious entity that apparently temporarily withdraws during sleep, that in times of illness exhibits the inclination to be distracted, and that in death seems to leave the body permanently. At the same time, these "primitive peoples" would have noticed that in dreams their neighbors and their friends, even their already dead fathers and mothers, could appear and speak with them. Apparently, these "souls" are still quite active, even when the person herself is still sleeping or when she has already departed this life. In this way, the soul became the object on which all attention was focused. Consequently, people developed reverence for the soul. People believed that the souls of the dead still wandered around and were capable of appearing to them in dreams and visions. In short, people began to worship these souls and to fear them. Closely connected with this development is the fact that these people gradually began to think that the entire world around them was populated with "souls" — trees, mountains, waterfalls, etc. This is the animistic worldview that according to Tylor came into existence at the beginning of the history of religion. In their spiritual development, some peoples remain at that level, and they are still captivated by this animistic understanding of life. These, then, are the so-called "primitive peoples." Others have developed further. Out of this huge assembly of "souls" that they suspected existed in nature, a few gradually came to the forefront. These were the ones that eventually became gods or demigods. Among these gods, there were several that soon assumed leadership. This is the process, according to Tylor, by which polytheism and monotheism developed out of the animistic world-and-life view.

Tylor's animistic theory initially captured a great deal of interest and stimulated in broader circles scientific investigation into the essential fea-

38. Ed. note: See note 23 above.

tures of "primitive religion." People wanted to know what motivated these "primitive peoples" in their religious considerations. Initially after the appearance of Tylor's book, many academics were inclined to give credence to his animistic theories. Tylor's thought seemed to explain in a fairly compelling way the riddle of religion among "native peoples."

But gradually all sorts of objections arose. Thus it appeared, for example, that the "primitive person" not only believed in spirits and souls that lived in trees, waterfalls, etc., but very often also was of the opinion that mysterious forces were present in the world around him or her. And these mysterious forces definitely were not souls, but they were impersonal, had no definitely directed will, and were simply only mysterious and frightening. For the "primitive person" the world around him or her is something different than it is for us; it is laden with *mana* and supernatural power in many places. The French scholar Lévy-Bruhl produced an interesting study on the psychology of primitive man, particularly with respect to the ideas and considerations that possessions do not belong to the individual but to the entire tribe; these he called *représentations collectives,* collective notions. Through his research he determined that for primitive humans, objects are different than they are for us; for them everything has its own quality that we can best describe as "mystical." *"Tout ce qui existe a des propriétés mystiques."*[39] In the rain, sun, trees, plants, animals, an unusual stone or unusually shaped hill, in colors, numbers, directions — in short, in everything around us — primitive people sense something mysterious, something that can at times fill them with anxiety and at other times overwhelm them with courage. The reality with which they operate is different from our reality.

Here an entirely new concept developed. It was not the phenomena of "souls" that first impressed "primitive people" and put them on the pathway of religion. It was the mysterious force of *mana* that deeply agitated them. They saw nature around them as a strange and cohesive entity that in each of its parts is filled with unknown and overwhelming forces. The "higher power" to which "primitive peoples" felt drawn was first of all *mana,* therefore, an impersonal, supernatural fear and a terribly unsettling power.

The phenomenon of so-called "primitive religion" appeared to be even more complicated, however. In 1898, the Scotsman Andrew Lang published a study titled *The Making of Religion,* in which he called for paying attention to something that to that point had eluded the academic community. He

---

39. Lucien Lévy-Bruhl, *How Natives Think,* trans. Lilian A. Clare (New York: Washington Square, 1966), p. 27.

pointed to the fact that among many "primitive" peoples is found the very important belief in one high god or Supreme Being, a sort of Super Being. What was then accepted about this Super Being, as a rule, is that it created the world or at least brought order to the world. That Super Being also instituted the ordinances governing the world-order to which human beings are subject. What was impossible to accept is that these high gods were nothing more than the "souls" of deceased ancestors, since the striking fact present in all accounts about the Super Being is that they emphasized that these gods existed before death had entered the world. They existed at the outset of everything else. By one extremely "primitive" tribe in Australia, the Super Being is addressed as *mungan ngaur,* our Father, and is thus apparently regarded as the source of all things.[40] Particularly with the most primitive peoples, Lang claimed, we find the major idea of a supreme being "who is primal, who exercises righteousness, and who loves humankind."[41] But with peoples who are somewhat further developed, we often note that that idea has more or less disappeared. There the high god, the Super Being, has become a *deus otiosus,* a remote god who no longer troubles himself with the world. A motley assortment of spirits and deities has taken his place.

In recent decades, an important contribution toward understanding the religion of indigenous peoples has been the study of their myths and their ritual practices. Through these studies a wealth of significant matters has come to light, providing us with deeper insight into what was actually driving these peoples. The myths provide all sorts of insights into the structure of the tribe, social obligations and relationships, the origin of the human race, the rising and setting of the sun, the succession of the phases of human life — in short, everything occupying people in their daily lives. All of this is traced back to primal history, the time before all time, and invested with its meaning. In those primal times, the great events occurred that determine all of life. In this connection, a myth from the Aztec tribe tells how, in the earliest times, the earth gave birth to the sun from her womb. The moon and the four hundred stars laughed at her and mocked her. But scarcely had the child been born, when it hacked off the head of its sister (the moon) and murdered its four hundred brothers (the stars). That same phenomenon occurs once again every year during the sun's winter solstice. Then the sun is born anew out of the darkness of winter, and it banishes the moon and stars from before its face.

40. Andrew Lang, *The Making of Religion,* 3rd ed. (London: Longmans, Green and Co., 1909), p. 181.
41. Lang, *Making of Religion,* p. 267.

But this only occurs when preceded each year in the month of November by a ritual, enacted in a play, in which the earth and the sun, the moon and the four hundred stars, all appear. That play always concludes with the victory of the sun. If that happens in the rite, then it will also definitely happen in nature and the sun will also truly conquer the powers of darkness. In other words, the people reenact ritually what happened in primal time; they do so before it reoccurs in nature, which conforms to the rite. First, the sun, moon, and stars are dramatically depicted in the rite, represented by various actors. Then the great events portrayed will be completed in nature. Here we find all the essential elements of the myth coming together. First, it is obvious that the rite retells what happened in primal times. Second, the myth is seemingly reenacted every year again in the rite, or as Malinowski has said, it is "reality lived."[42] In the third place, that which happened in primal time is repeated every year again. Primal time determines already what will occur later and gives it its meaning.[43] The year is a shadow of the entirety of world history; each year brings together all the great moments of world history.

Further investigation of the myths of various peoples produces a wealth of new discoveries. It becomes apparent that gods having an ambivalent, dual character frequently appear in the myths. There is a god of the higher world (heaven, the sun) and one of the lower world (earth), and these two are actually one. At the deepest level, they are the same divine being that has two dimensions, a heavenly dimension and an earthly dimension. In the religion of the Ngada people of Central Flores,[44] *Déva* is the eternal creator and heavenly god who plays an important role alongside *Nitu*, the earthly goddess of darkness. Most often they are addressed in combination as *Nitu-Déva*. Together they represent all reality in its various manifestations.[45] The dual character of divinity among the Ngaju-Dayak people in South Borneo is even clearer, as a fascinating study by Schärer establishes.[46] There the god

42. Bronislaw Malinowski, *Myth in Primitive Psychology* (New York: W. W. Norton and Co., 1926), p. 21.

43. Konrad Theodor Preuss, *Der Religiöse Gehalt der Mythen* (Tübingen: J. C. B. Mohr [Paul Siebeck], 1933), pp. 15-16.

44. Ed. note: Flores is one of the Lesser Sunda Islands in the Indonesian archipelago, situated to the northwest of Timor. The Ngada are also called Rokka, or Rokanese; from *Encyclopaedia Britannica* online at http://www.britannica.com/EBchecked/topic/413397/Ngada?anchor=ref124971; accessed 7 July 2011.

45. Jan Van Baal, *Over Wegen en Drijfveren der Religie: Een Godsdienstpsychologische Studie* (Amsterdam: Noord-Hollandsche Uitgevers, 1947), p. 177.

46. Schärer, *Ngaju Religion*.

Mahatala, a heavenly god regarded as closely connected to the rhinoceros bird, and the goddess *Jata,* who belongs to the lower world and is usually connected with the water snake, are worshiped together. Both of them, *Mahatala* and *Jata,* constitute the single, ambivalent divinity present in all phenomena. The duality of the heavenly god and the earthly goddess comes to expression in Dayak society in the whole organization of society, in tribal development, and in the relationships between different classes. The entire social order is a reflection, therefore, of the development of everything and of the two-sided importance of the higher being. Schärer even offers the comment that "the divine world is for this reason a reflection of the human, in that man has elevated himself into the transcendental world and has deified himself, i.e. he has removed the community, its laws, tribal area, life and thought, into an absolute and sacred sphere where it is objectified. The world and society have not emanated from the deities, but the deities and their world are the human world and society pronounced sacred by man himself."[47] With this people group, sociology, cosmology, and theology are all intimately connected. The tribe is ordered, they think, in the same way that the cosmos is ordered. And the ordering of the cosmos along the lines of the duality of heaven and earth is in turn a reflection of the world of divine forces.

Thanks to all of this research, our insight into what people used to call "primitive religion" has changed fundamentally. What Tylor used to designate as animistic, the veneration of spirits and gods, nowhere simply stands in isolation but is everywhere understood as part of a more profound grasp of total reality. This is the veneration of the forces that control all things and of the dual-dimensional divinity that reveals itself to us in everything that exists. Nowhere does fear of or respect for the souls of the dead simply stand by itself; we find everywhere that fear and respect are tied to the dead being related to the higher, divine powers and that the divine beings manifest themselves to us through them. In short, behind all the superstitious customs, myths, and ritual practices of "native peoples," we discover a universal view of the world that sometimes surprises us with its depth and magnitude and always impresses us with how all the phenomena of life are ordered within it.

What should impress us above all else in the study of these religions is that almost universally the boundary between the gods and the cosmos is lit-

---

47. Schärer, *Ngaju Religion,* p. 157. Ed. note: Bavinck's quotation from Schärer only includes the partial first sentence up to the explanatory *id est.*

tle more than a very faint dotted line. In many instances, divinity in its dual aspects is identical to the cosmos. The cosmos itself is pulsating with divine power and merges with the divine. The expression of Paul contains an oppressive truth when he says that the pagan religions all disclose that their adherents "replace the majesty of the immortal God with images made to look like mortal men" (Rom. 1:23). God is identified with the creation; the creation itself is deified, despite the fact that humanity is the crown of creation and that creation culminates in humanity. God shrouds himself, obscures himself, loses himself in the overwhelming multiplicity of his creatures. He no longer stands as the divine "I" over against the insignificant human "you," but has evaporated into the secret power present in all things, the mysterious recesses of this capricious world. Dr. van Baal says the following about religious ritual: "In religious ritual, we encounter the attempt to be absorbed into the totality of cosmic events, to become one with the whole that embraces nature as well as human interaction."[48]

Nowhere is the process of the evaporation of the divine figure more clearly obvious than in India. There we encounter, in the ancient texts of the Vedas, a multiplicity of gods. These gods all manifest an exaggeratedly natural nature, which is to say that in essence they are no different than more or less personifications of natural forces. Deeper reflection also discloses that those natural forces are also found in people, and that the harmonization permeating the entire realm of the gods is reflected as well in each little person. A human being is in a complete sense a microcosm, the world in miniature.[49] This means that each person is the point where all the divine forces are concentrated.

Indian religious thought increasingly developed along these lines toward a conception of divinity in which personal nature became totally obscured behind the idea that everything is embraced by the divine. The idea of *Brahman*[50] has become one of the most characteristic concepts of Indian religion. *Brahman* is the divine, irreducible power that seeps into a sacrificial incantation; it is the power that the priest or *brahmin* has at his disposal and that resides in him. *Brahman* appoints him as head of all things, and all phe-

---

48. Van Baal, *Over Wegen en Drijfveren der Religie*, pp. 164, 165.

49. Ed. note: See Chapter 8 for a fuller exploration of this theme.

50. Ed. note: It is important to distinguish *Brahman,* the genderless Supreme Cosmic Spirit in Hindu Vedānta philosophy, from *Brahma,* the male Hindu god of creation and one of the members of the Hindu "trinity" (Trimurti) along with *Vishnu* and *Shiva.* To avoid further confusion, it must be remembered that the Hindu priestly caste is known by the name *Brahmin.*

nomena in this world are subject to him. The force *Brahman* increasingly became identified with the primal divinity from which all else came forth and which now resides as the mysterious depth of all creatures. It is the life in all living, the power within all powers. It dwells in the spike of rice, in the forest monsters, and in human beings. By virtue of *Brahman,* things are what they are. *Brahman* itself is completely unknowable, undifferentiated, primal unity. The most perceptive thinking can never penetrate *Brahman. Brahman* encompasses the great opposites of life and death, light and darkness, male and female, subject and object. It has poured itself out into the immeasurable variety of earthly things, and yet it always lurks in the background as the silent presence, the unchanging, the unchangeable, the eternal. The most profound wisdom attainable by a human being is when he or she realizes that *Brahman* is not a Someone that stands over against us or a Lord who controls us, but that it is the deepest essence of our own being. *Brahman* is the background from which all things emerge and into which they will again return. The entire drama of earthly life possesses a dimension of tragic illusion for those who have come to understand *Brahman* as that which is great and everlasting and themselves as tiny ripples on the immense ocean of *Brahman.*

In India during earlier as well as more recent times, numerous religious sects arose that definitely emphasized that God is an *Ishvara* or Lord before whom we should bow and to whom we should submit. Within all of these trends, religion became an I-Thou relationship, a connection between the little human being and the immense, eternal God. But all of these religious developments nonetheless display at certain critical times a remarkable hesitancy. Is God really only *Ishvara,* only Lord? Is he not also the deepest being of our own being, the light living within us? Are we not actually identical with him? Is he not the divine power slumbering within us and of which we become conscious in certain ecstatic experiences? And is his lordship really not just a thought-form constructed for thinking about him, since in our limited human way of thinking it is impossible for us to think of him in any other way? India has never been able to make a definitive choice between these two concepts of divine being. Is he the Lord, or is he the mysterious, hidden force within all things that also slumbers within us? India has always wanted to recognize the legitimacy of both positions. For that reason, Indian religion never developed into a real I-Thou relationship, but it always remained bound to the vague sense that the Lord is still something totally different and that he coincides with the darker backdrop of all existence.

All of these matters are completely different in Islam, where the personal nature of God is very strongly accented. He is Allah, the Living One, the Almighty. One only need to leaf through the Qur'an, Islam's holy scriptures, to come under the deep impression of the totally exalted nature of Allah proclaimed there. This strikes one already in the reading of the famous first sura:

> Praise be to God, the Cherisher and Sustainer of the Worlds;
> Most Gracious, Most Merciful; Master of the Day of Judgment.
> Thee do we worship, and Thine aid we seek.
> Show us the straight way, the way of those on whom Thou hast
>   bestowed Thy Grace, Those whose (portion) is not wrath,
>   and who go not astray.[51]

This Allah in no way whatsoever possesses the character of the totality of all things, of the cosmos. He is not the light indwelling all people and all things, not the force concealed in everything. In the most absolute sense, he is a "He," a Lord standing over against us, exalted above us, before whom we must bow. In that regard, Islam assumes a unique position among human religions.

In the religious practices of Islam, Allah's transcendence as well as his greatness and his exaltedness are highly emphasized. One only needs to witness the prayer life of a devout Muslim in order to realize the depth to which he or she feels in his or her own life the enormous distance separating the puny human and the Almighty God. Here we find a concept of God that has not fled into some vague, ephemeral vapor that permeates everything; but here Allah is the complete "I" over against whom all people recognize themselves as lowly servants.

Despite this, in Islam there is little room for a life of personal fellowship with God. Allah is so great and so exalted, and his will is so completely dominating, that very little is left on the human side. Religion is a powerful system of collective service to Allah, a faithful, collective completion of what he has commanded. It is a humble bowing of the self to what he has determined for us. In the expression "Allah is great," all other emphases are fused and all other thoughts die out. Even the sense of personal responsibility toward him and the need for forgiveness and reconciliation, find no possibility of development. The absolute greatness of Allah is so predominantly central that all else fades in comparison. In the course of Islamic history, people have seriously contended many times with the question of whether the human will is still of any significance in contrast with the all-deciding and all-determinative will of Allah. Everything human is regarded as powerless and worthless, and

---

51. Ed. note: Qur'an 1:2-7 (A. Yusuf Ali, *The Holy Quran: Text, Translation and Commentary* [Beirut: Dar Al Arabia, 1968]).

what remains is only the majestic greatness of Allah, who acts according to his inscrutable good pleasure. "Say: truly God leaveth, to stray, whom He will; but He guideth to Himself those who will turn to Him."[52] "Now God leaves straying those whom He pleases and guides whom He pleases."[53] Muslim theology has wrestled with these words of the prophet. Often in the first few centuries of Islam, figures have appeared who took up the plea for the personal responsibility of human beings, for human freedom of the will, for Allah's righteousness. People still had to possess something of determination by a free will; it could not be the case that the foreordination of Allah covered all their thoughts and actions so that their lives simply ticked off like clockwork or according to the lines of a previously written program. In one way or another, people still had to be in a position to take the reins of their own destiny in their own hands. Otherwise, they would not be responsible for their own lives. For centuries, these problems flowed back and forth in Islamic theology without reaching a definitive solution. At the same time, this single point was always at issue in these questions: Is religion a form of dialogue between Allah and human beings, or, must the all-determining will of Allah be considered as the one and only reality? Is religion a dialogue, a responsibility, a prayer, an act of trust; or, is it in the deepest sense nothing more than subjection, submission, identifying oneself with, and sinking into the eternal and incomprehensible will of God?

Human history shows us that the awareness of a connection with a higher power has been present everywhere and among all peoples. In some instances, this higher power was seen in a sense of the clear distinction between good and evil powers, gods and demons juxtaposed to each other. Some scholars took the position that demons appeared earlier than gods in the history of human thought. "Everywhere demons are older than gods," says van der Leeuw.[54] "God . . . is a latecomer in the history of religions."[55] It seems to me that this position cannot stand up against the test of critical thought. But what definitely can be acknowledged is that wherever the names of gods are mentioned, the figures of demons also immediately appear. Clearly and from the earliest times, people have been moved by the phenomenon that our capricious world could not be adequately explained

---

52. Qur'an 13:27.

53. Ed. note: Bavinck quotes Qur'an and references Qur'an 16:95; however, it is actually more likely that he is here referring to the passage found in Qur'an 14:4.

54. G. Van der Leeuw, *Religion in Essence and Manifestation: A Study in Phenomenology*, trans. J. E. Turner (London: Allen & Unwin, 1938), p. 139.

55. Van der Leeuw, *Religion in Essence and Manifestation*, p. 104.

or understood only in terms of the gods, but that other, horrible forces exist and are revealed. The world in which we live is a double-sided world. Something of a divine smile is present over the world, but at the same time the demonic work of mysterious forces aimed at our destruction is also palpable. From moment to moment, the human race lives with the deep mystery of all existence. People feel that they are in God's presence, but at the same time they are aware of the power of demons. Our lives are bound by that mystery.

Thus, we find a universal development in human history of the awareness that this world and all that happens in it is intimately connected to the mysterious, supernatural world of the gods. Something of that mystery, of that divine force, is found in everything that exists. People know in every moment of their existence that they are connected to higher powers that they can never fully understand, before which they tremble with fear, and that nevertheless draw them to themselves with magnetic power.

§6. The Content of Religious Consciousness (d) — The Need for Deliverance

One of the very real constituents of universal religious consciousness is the need for deliverance. I might perhaps just as well say: faith in deliverance, confidence that deliverance is possible. This idea has also experienced an extraordinarily remarkable history.

Clearly, attention here needs to be directed first of all to the evil from which one knows that one needs to be delivered. What is it that one has learned to see as a grievous evil and from which one passionately desires to be delivered? Only when we have first understood evil can we form an image of the kind of deliverance needed.

In one of his books, Dr. Adriani tells us that the population of Central Celebes[56] believes that the "Lord of Creation" had the good intention to breathe into human beings "enduring breath," that is to say, eternal life. But before this could happen, the hostile power of the Night had already given them "short-term breath." And just as the night wind blows for a while and then dies down again, so it is with human life. The breathing of humans is usually broken off by sickness and death. "This is how it came to be that people are subject to death."[57] With the same Toraja tribe of Middle Celebes, the

---

56. Ed. note: Celebes, now known as Sulawesi, is one of the four Indonesian islands comprising the Greater Sunda (the others are Borneo, Java, and Sumatra).

57. Nicolaus Adriani, *Verzamelde Geschriften*, vol. 2 (Haarlem: F. Bohn, 1932), p. 286.

idea can be found of a long liana or tropical vine that provides access to heaven. The idea was that it grew in prehistoric times, in the dim past, somewhere to the north of a great lake. Along that liana, uninterrupted traffic between heaven and earth was possible. It made possible fellowship between heaven and earth, between the gods and human beings. But alas, due to some fatal accident this connection was broken and the liana was severed. Earth was left to its own destiny. At present, only a very small number of priestesses are still in a position to have contact with the heavenly world. To achieve this, their inner beings must leave their bodies and rise to the inner chambers of "the Lord of the Secret Places." There they receive new life-forces, new breath, for the sick whose breath is threatened with impending termination.[58]

Two absolutely important ideas are expressed here concerning the nature of the evil that has preoccupied us human beings. The first is the idea of death. We are people with "short-term breath." We have not been given eternal life, and that makes for life that is broken and filled with misery. Closely connected with this is the idea of evil, the severed liana. People were designed to live in fellowship with the gods, but this contact has been lost in some way or another. Humanity is oriented toward the earth; it has lost its ties to heaven. Is deliverance possible for people? There does exist an extremely vague and limited means of help. There are priestesses capable of traveling to heaven and carrying from there the blessings for which people feel such a deeply rooted need. They are the intermediaries between heaven and earth, therefore, and via their secret arts a beginning of deliverance is truly made possible. But that deliverance is never definitive, and ultimately death will still conquer. It is also never complete, because it applies to people only in limited circumstances and never confers on them total deliverance. We see in the very brief account given here several profound sensitivities that apparently have preoccupied people from earliest times.

The Torajas of Central Celebes recognize, therefore, two aspects of misery: short-term breath and the severed liana. We can ask ourselves whether these two dimensions are experienced universally and in the same way. As far as the first is concerned, namely the horror of death, we find it spread across the entire world. From deep in antiquity, we hear lamenting noises about the transience of human life. In the great Gilgamesh epic passed down to us from ancient Babylon, we confront a moving hymn of death. Gilgamesh has lost his trusted friend Enkidu to death. Then he says:

58. Adriani, *Verzamelde Geschriften*, 2: 287; cf. pp. 120, 121.

My friend Enkidu, whom I love so deeply, who went with me through every danger: the doom of mankind overtook him, for six days and seven nights I wept over him. I did not give him up for burial, until a maggot fell from his nostril. Then I was afraid. . . . I grew fearful of death and so roam the wild, the case of my friend was too much for me to bear, so on a distant road I roam the wild.[59]

Sorrow concerning "the land of no return," the realm of the dead, was one of the very real elements in the religion of ancient peoples.

As soon as we turn our eyes toward ancient Egypt, we see how central were the themes of death, sorrow over death, and deliverance from death. The "eternal home," as the grave was called there, is the great place of rest. At the same time, it marks a new beginning of fellowship with Osiris, when one is taken up into Osiris and becomes a subject in the kingdom of Osiris.[60]

On the one hand, we are struck in all these religious ideas and positions by how death is seen as unconquerable and unavoidable. On the other hand, we are impressed that the idea is found almost everywhere in the world that deliverance from the bands of death must be possible. People frequently connect this idea of deliverance closely with natural phenomena. The course of the sun, that in the evening wearily sinks down into the world's ocean and in the morning rises again in the east with renewed strength, appears to have suggested to many peoples that behind the gateway to death, where the sun enters the land of darkness beneath the earth, is a land where the secret to life is preserved. The possibility of returning to life once again and to be born anew must exist. Sometimes we encounter this idea of deliverance from the power of death tightly tied to the natural succession of seasons of the year. The seed is committed to the earth and dies there in the darkness of death. But it is born again in springtime, when the life-giving sun regains its strength. A subtle interdependence exists between the way in which the seed of all living plants, that all experience the mystery of death and that all undergo a new entry to life, and what happens with human beings. Egyptians thought deeply about this inner connection, and it also comes prominently to the forefront in the Greek myths.

Sometimes we find faith in a drink of immortality that will guarantee people everlasting life, if they can only procure it. With Hindus, we hear

59. A. R. George, *The Babylonian Gilgamesh Epic: Introduction, Critical Edition, and Cuneiform Texts*, 2 vols. (Oxford: Oxford University Press, 2003), 1: 681-82.

60. Chantepie de la Saussaye, *Lehrbuch der Religionsgeschichte*, ed. Alfred Bertholet and Edvard Lehmann, 2 vols., 4th ed. (Tübingen: J. C. B. Mohr [Paul Siebeck], 1925), 2: 476.

about *amrta*[61] that rose to the top when the gods churned the Sea of Milk. The drink of immortality is what safeguards against the power of death. The Greeks also spoke of ambrosia, the nectar of life that is reserved for the gods. In the Gilgamesh epic, there is talk of the herb that grows on the floor of the ocean that, when eaten, "will make the greybeards young men once again." Thus, the riddle of death has been pondered from the earliest times onward, and humans "have been doomed to slavery by their fear of death" (Heb. 2:15).

Not only the misery surrounding "short-term breath," but also the suffering inflicted because of the severed liana can be found among all peoples. That suffering plays an important part in the history of religion as well. When we stop to think about that subject, it seems to us that it comes to expression in two ways, namely in both a collective and an individual form.

First, with many people we discover the idea that at the outset of history a paradise existed on earth. People still lived alongside the gods, and a condition of peace and harmony prevailed. In his six-volume work on *Der Ursprung der Gottesidee*, Father Schmidt points out that this idea of paradise still assumes very lively expression among many so-called "primitive peoples." He says that according to the myths found among the Pygmies and tribes in the American polar regions, in prehistoric times the "Highest Being" or divinity still dwelled among humans. "For all of these peoples, this period was the most beautiful and the best — a true paradise."[62] In summary, he explains, concerning all these people considered to be very "primitive," that "they looked back with a painful nostalgia" on the primal times of the human race when people still lived in unbroken peace.[63] It is well possible that Schmidt colors the myths of these people a little too beautifully. But the fact is that time and again when we come close to native tribes, we are amazed at how deeply rooted within them is the faith that this era of misery and death was preceded by one in which boundless peace and blessing were found in this world.

The same idea also spread more widely and profoundly. India turned it into amusement with the great events of world history, presenting them as progress from one yoga to the other, from one century to the next. Concerning the outset of the world, we find described the *krita-yuga* as an age of peace and blessing. In that *krita-yuga,* all people met their obligations, wor-

---

61. Ed. note: *Amrta* is Sanskrit for "not death."

62. P. Wilhelm Schmidt, *Der Ursprung der Gottesidee: Eine Historisch-Kritische und Positive Studie*, vol. 6: *Endsynthese der Religionen der Urvölker Amerikas, Asiens, Australiens, Afrikas* (Münster: Aschendorffsche, 1935), p. 260.

63. Schmidt, *Der Ursprung der Gottesidee*, 6: 416.

shiped the one God, and were content. In the following yoga, the darkness characterizing our present existence slowly broke out for the first time. Now we live in the *kali-yuga,* the last of the four aeons and an age of godlessness and without moral norms.[64] The only hope left for us is that Vishnu, the preserver of all existence, will return to us in a new incarnation *(avatar),* just as he has promised,[65] and will institute a new period.[66]

From time immemorial, China has also looked back to a primitive era when righteousness ruled in the world. The mythical kings of prehistory are the ones to whom Kong Fuzi (K'ung Fu-tzu), reached back when he wanted to lay out the standards by which people should live. We find a paradise at the dawn of history. The human race fell from that paradise. Something occurred there that we can no longer recover, but through which immorality and chaos broke loose in our world.

In all of these testimonies, misery is regarded as universally experienced by humanity. If deliverance is possible, then that deliverance can happen only in the rescue of humanity as a whole, not of the individual person. This is why the thinking of China is always directed at the renewal of the kingdom, to the building of a new social order in which "the ruler is ruler, the minister is a minister, the father a father, the son a son." Even the New Life Movement of modern China is not based on the deliverance of the individual person, but on the restoration of the kingdom.

It would not be difficult at all to produce an anthology of similar ideas from all parts of the world. That people have carried with them in their religious consciousness the idea that suffering threatens all of humankind is becoming increasingly clear. Their individual need and misery are dimensions of that huge, collective need experienced by the entire human race. Precisely for this reason, people have always posited the image of a savior as a figure who rescues humanity as a whole. In their hunger for deliverance, they understand that they can only become participants in ultimate escape if the entire cosmos participates in it with them.

We would misstate the matter, however, if we conveyed the sense that the world's peoples recognize and confess only a collective sense of deliverance. Consistently breaking through this collective longing is the individ-

64. Ed. note: *Kali-yuga* is another name for *Satya-yuga,* which is the more commonly used term today.

65. *The Bhagavad Gita,* trans. W. J. Johnson, The World's Classics (Oxford: Oxford University Press, 1994), pp. 4, 7, 8, 19.

66. Helmuth von Glasenapp, *Der Hinduismus: Religion und Gesellschaft im Heutigen Indien* (Munich: Kurt Wolff, 1922), p. 231.

ual's search and desire to experience that new life for him or her personally. We saw that Gilgamesh already sought for himself the medicinal herbs that would let him conquer death. Gilgamesh is not alone in that regard. We find accounts of people throughout the ages who eagerly reached out for the deliverance of their own existence.

We look in vain for a people whose emotions have been more completely engaged with individual longing for deliverance than the people of India. In India, much has been continually said about deliverance *(moksha)*, and *moksha* is predominantly considered as the liberation of the individual person. Each person must endeavor, through his or her own conduct, to become a participant in this escape. If one were to pose the question of what it is from which a person must escape, India provides this universal answer: from *samsara*, from "wandering." Naturally, *samsara* has numerous dimensions. It is to be held captive by the senses. It is to fall under the power of the lower emotions time and again. It is to operate in the grip of *avidya,* the immense ignorance that blinds our hearts. At the same time, *samsara* is to be incapable of freeing ourselves from our existence and to be swept along from one birth to the next, returning to the world again and again because we can never imbibe enough of the vain pleasures of this passing world. *Moksha* is always an inner benefit; it is to be set free from all delusion; it is to comprehend the vanity of our existence and to return to *Brahman,* the divine primal force from which all beings are generated and in which they are all able to exist.

When the question arises of how one can obtain this *moksha,* India looked to various paths and opportunities *(margas).* One rises above wandering through mystical experience. It represents the highest knowledge, by which one comprehends all things in their one, all-embracing, divine cohesiveness. It permits one to transcend the individual existence that had previously so closely and tightly restricted one, and it allows one to be absorbed into the totality of all things. This is *moksha,* deliverance from the spell of the senses. But alongside this one are other paths. There is the way of obedient ritual practices, sacrifices, and consecrations. Finally, there is the way of childlike submission to deity, or *bhakti.* Each of these pathways serves the same purpose. One needs, once and for all, to be set free from the restrictive ties of *samsara* and be exalted into the glorious deliverance of being absorbed into divinity.

In Buddhism, this idea of individual salvation was an aggravation. Buddhism is a religion preeminently concerned with deliverance. This is in part connected to the fact that Buddha very consciously turned away from the philosophical speculation that was so eagerly pursued in his day. He concentrated all of his attention on the necessity of deliverance, and he wanted to point the way by which deliverance was attainable. When anyone approached Buddha with metaphysical questions about eternity and the world's infinity, the master offered the following response:

> Suppose a man is struck by a poisoned arrow, and his friends call a doctor to attend him. Would he then say, "Leave the arrow in; do not pull it out before I know exactly who the man is who shot me with it, from what family and caste he comes, what he looks like, whether he is small or large, whether his skin is dark or light, where he lives, and what the precise length is of both the bow and the arrow"? If he asked all those questions, the man would die before he could be healed. This is how it would also be if someone were to make joining a circle of disciples dependent on receiving answers to these profound questions. He would die before the master would be able to provide answers to them.[67]

At a very significant and determinative point in his life, Buddha once saw that human beings are like lotus blossoms. Some of them are totally submerged in the water. Some grow entirely above the water level. Then there are those that just begin to reach the surface of the water and almost start rising above it. Buddha understood that on the first group, which is still entirely imprisoned by their own senses, he would have little impact; they would neither understand him nor even be willing to listen to him. He also saw that the second category of people no longer had any need of him; they have already achieved true deliverance from self and are busy disentangling themselves entirely from the power of the senses. It is the last group, which has just begun reaching the truth but has not yet actually and fully found it, to whom Buddha had something to offer. He was capable of leading them out of all the doubt and confusion that still captivated them and thus of making them participants in deliverance.[68]

That from which people needed to be delivered was, as a rule, described in Buddhism as the enormous suffering inherent in human existence.

> Birth is suffering. Old age is suffering. Sickness is suffering. Death is suffering. Bound to that which people do not want is suffering. Separated

---

67. Hermann Beckh, *Buddhismus* (Leipzig: G. J. Göschen, 1916), 1: 118.

68. J. H. Bavinck, *Christus en de Mystiek van het Oosten* (Kampen: J. H. Kok, [1934]), p. 54. Ed. note: This is a reference to an earlier section of *Christus en de Mystiek van het Oosten* that is not included in this volume.

from that which people love is suffering. Not getting what people long to have is suffering. In short, the five ways of embracing what is experienced by the five senses is suffering. The source of suffering is the desire or thirst *(trsna)* that arises and is pursued time and again, that accompanies the passions, and that extends to everything. Conquering suffering comes by annihilating desire, by complete dispassionateness. The road that leads to the conquest of suffering is the distinguished, eightfold path.

In this short summary, we find the major ideas contained in the Buddha's preaching. Obviously, each of the elements is developed at great length. Desire itself, which leads to repeated rebirth or reincarnation, is an extremely complicated subject. An enormous dimension of uncertainty *(avidya)* plays a role in it. To a great extent, it is determined by self-interest, by the self-preservation that depends on blindness and confusion. This is why following the eightfold path is an exceedingly difficult matter. That path is described with numerous, sometimes psychologically refined descriptions. The ultimate goal is to transcend all blindness caused by the senses, all efforts at self-preservation, all desire for pleasures, all pretenses and thoughts; it is to sink away into oblivion, into nirvana, into that great and glorious light that bathes us. A person needs to walk that difficult eightfold path one step at a time. No one can help him or her in this. The guru or the master can certainly explain that path and point out the dangers to which the person should be attentive, but ultimately every person must walk the path alone. No one can take that over for him or her, although fellowship with others walking the same road can make the trail lighter and easier. But in the deepest sense, each person is on his or her own, a lonely pilgrim on the road to ultimate deliverance.

This raises another, very important question, namely that concerning the nature of deliverance. Is all deliverance in essence self-deliverance, or is deliverance only possible through another, a savior, a god? To that question, human religious consciousness has never provided a clear, satisfactory answer. In times of need such as sickness, danger of death, and war, pagan peoples were always accustomed to make their way to their gods for deliverance. That is what the prophets of Baal did when they called on their god on Mount Carmel: "Oh Baal, answer us!" (1 Kings 18:26). Help was received; people lived by the goodness of their gods. But on the other hand, we see everywhere the idea breaking through that people achieve a degree of control over their gods by making sacrifices and following rituals. They can compel them to do what they want done. An offering became a magically laden activity that exercised real influence on the deity. In general, the idea of salvation by another, the idea that another needed to save us, unnoticeably mutated into the idea of self-salvation or the notion that we must and can save ourselves. This ambivalence in paganism was never completely overcome.

Nor is it transcended in the so-called religions of grace found in India and Japan. In southern India, Hinduism has taken forms that very strongly emphasize the necessity of grace. What have developed there are two schools known as the monkey school and the cat school.[69] The latter taught that people are sustained in the same way that a young kitten is rescued from danger. The mother cat simply picks up the kitten between her teeth and carries it away. A person can contribute nothing to his or her salvation, but deliverance is completely and only the work of the Lord. One finds such forceful expressions time and again in Hindu literature. But even then, the ambivalence remains. For, who is that Lord, that *Ishvara?* Is he not the deepest essence of our own being, the great mystery that lies at the foundation of each one's existence? Is he not the Self in our complicated existence, in contrast with whom the little "selves" of our individual egos sink away in helplessness and powerlessness? Then is deliverance not ultimately the inner liberation in which we participate when the god within ourselves — the One we introduce as the Thou in relation to ourselves — frees us from the limitations of our small, egotistical thinking and searching? Even here there definitely is a subtle, gentle transition from deliverance by another to the ideas and expectations of self-salvation.

As far as Japan is concerned, the thought of deliverance with the help of God alone is closely identified with the figure of Shinran, "the Martin Luther of Buddhism," as someone once designated him.[70] For him the big question is whether people are saved by their own power, thus whether they save themselves *(Jiriki)* or whether they can only be saved by the power of another *(Tariki)*. With respect to this question, Shinran deliberately chose the latter alternative. He trusts completely in the promise that Buddha made, according to tradition, just prior to his entrance into nirvana: "No full salvation will be able to be achieved until one knows that all who call on him can be saved." This promise of Buddha was construed by Shinran as the only basis of our hope. He said:

69. Tasuku Harada, *The Faith of Japan* (New York: Macmillan, 1914), p. 95.
70. Ed. note: Shinran (1173-1263) was a Buddhist monk and reformer who founded the Japanese version of Pure Land Buddhism (Amida; Sanskrit: Amitābha).

> I do not desire to do good works, for there is no better work than the promise of Buddha. Further, no sinful activity makes me fearful, since even the most sinful deed cannot impede Buddha's promise.[71]

One of Shinran's disciples put it this way:

> Just as a large stone loaded onto a ship can make a long journey of ten thousand miles over the water without sinking, so all of our sins, though they be as heavy as a giant block of stone, can be borne to another shore by the great promise made by Buddha.[72]

But even this solid conviction that we can be sustained only through the help of Buddha is still not a total guarantee that all reliance on our own strength has been relinquished. Kraemer points to how easily faith in this promise of Buddha can be turned into a "good work," in fact into the only truly saving good work. In place of the many prescriptions and norms set forth to the contrary, the one prescription then emerges that one must place all one's trust in Buddha. That trust then becomes the all-atoning work, the exclusive work. "In reality the *ta-riki* remains a *ji-riki*," says Kraemer.[73] Deliverance by another is nevertheless, in essence, once again self-deliverance.

It becomes clear, therefore, that while the idea is imposed on us that people are powerless in the face of their desperate need and lack of freedom and that someone else needs to help them, faith in self-deliverance subtly and constantly reappears.

§7. The Content of Religious Consciousness (e) — The Course of Life as a Tension Between Action and Fate[74]

The last element in universal, religious consciousness that we want to disentangle and consider might be called the awareness that human life is only thinkable as a continuous dialogue between action and fate. A person is only master of his or her life up to a certain point. A power exists that repeatedly

---

71. Wilhelm Gündert, *Japanische Religionsgeschichte: Die Religionen der Japaner und Koreaner in geschichtlichem Abriss dargestellt* (Tokyo: Japanisch-Deutsches Kulturinstitut, 1935), p. 93.

72. Harada, *The Faith of Japan*, p. 95.

73. Kraemer, *The Christian Message in a Non-Christian World*, p. 180.

74. Ed. note: The words "as a tension between action and fate" have been added to the subheading by the editor.

reaches into a person's existence, that pushes him or her forward with compelling force, and from whose grip the person finds it impossible to struggle loose. Sometimes people can despair that they can lead their own life. Sometimes they gradually achieve the insight, in the school of life's hard knocks, that it is more appropriate to say that they suffer or undergo events that develop in and around them.

The unique tension between action and fate has been one of the most favorite subjects of religious reflection. Little wonder, then, that from earliest times deep and profound ideas have been expressed on this connection.

For the ancient peoples of the Near East, a powerful awareness existed that the lives of people and nations were interwoven in a very mysterious way with the course of the stars, the orbits of heavenly bodies. The movements of the stars controlled all events on earth, since the gods revealed their will through them, and no man could extricate himself from the fate that they had predetermined. "All that happens is predetermined, so that what happens on earth corresponds to the events depicted by movements in the heavens. A harmony exists between the heavenly and earthly worlds, both in time and in space." This is how F. Jeremias summarized one of the main ideas of ancient Babylonian religion. This astral fatalism that reflects a fate tied to nature is definitely penetrated from time to time by the idea of a "divinely determined fate," that is to say, by the thought that behind the regular movement of the stars that is so determinative of all that occurs here on earth is hidden the will of the gods. This indicates that in the final instance we are dealing with the will of the gods.[75] What is clear is that in all these religions based on astrology, the idea of fate gets preference with unassailable force above that of action. Human life in the first instance is to suffer and to submit to what has been written in the stars. Life is thoroughly bound to nature, engaged in the overall course of cosmic process and therefore in all its dimensions gripped by the irresistible power of fate.

This understanding, which lived with such exceptional strength in Babylonian religion as well as other religions of the Near East, has also made a deep impression on other lands and peoples. For example, it influenced Greek and Roman thought in the Hellenistic world to a powerful extent. In Greek and Roman thinking there were certainly numerous elements that already earlier were in harmony with this idea. The Greeks possessed a boundless zest for life and enormous undertakings, but from the earliest days they were also accustomed to laying emphasis on the fact that ruthless fate is the

---

75. Chantepie de la Saussaye, *Lehrbuch der Religionsgeschichte*, 1: 504, 589.

determining factor in all of human existence. The three *Moirai,* the fates, the shooting stars of the night, are what define the course of human life. What can puny man do against them? With the later tragic poets, this problem of fate became a question with which they wrestled but were never able to fathom. Aeschylus is conscious of the fact that the power of fate, *Anangkè,* necessity, extends even beyond that of Zeus. The power of Zeus resides only in the fact that the reins of world government have been entrusted to him. And Sophocles casts glaring light on the totally tragic nature of human life, which is tiny and powerless in the face of the completely inscrutable will of the gods. What remains for humanity, then, except to bow submissively under the irresistible regime of divine power?

In early German religion, belief in the power of fate was already alive and well. The three Norns[76] spun the web of human life and determined the outcome of human existence, and no one could resist them. Even the gods were subject to the all-controlling power of fate, which ultimately affects everyone and from which no one can struggle free. Odin, a hero among the gods, was himself once affected by fate and swept along into death.

Similar ideas seem to be harbored everywhere in the world. In so-called primitive thought, where people were regarded as totally bound by nature and the specifically and distinctly human still received little attention, the idea of fate was prominent. A human being is not regarded as an individual entity or life as a conversation, but both are simply to experience what all-controlling nature imposed. A human being is caught up in the cosmic drama, just like trees and plants, animals, stars, the winds, the seasons of the year — in short, everything is involved in it. Here there is no discussion of an action on the part of people; the idea of fate is in every respect all-controlling. A man or woman is merely a part of the great totality, and the laws that govern that great totality also grip the man or woman. When Islam penetrated Java with its message of Allah's almighty will and that the only actual standard is that predetermining will, it found well-prepared soil there. The proverb still holds: "Fate is inevitable; what is once determined is unmovable."[77]

---

76. Ed. note: "In Norse mythology, the Norns are the demi-goddesses of destiny. They control the destinies of both gods and men, as well as the unchanging laws of the cosmos. They are represented as three sisters: Urd ('fate'), Verdandi ('necessity') and Skuld ('being')." ("Norns." *Encyclopedia Mythica* from Encyclopedia Mythica Online. http://www.pantheon .org/articles/n/norns.html [accessed 8 July 2011].

77. Klaus Albert Hendrik Hidding, *Gebruiken en Godsdienst der Soendanezen* (Batavia: Kolff, 1935), p. 24.

Even an action, reflecting the active side of human existence, is in one way or another subsumed in fate and considered a dimension of it. A person needs to succumb to the forces and yearning dwelling in him, since he is always simply a football on the world's playing field. Even when he thinks he is independent in what he does, it is the hurricane of fate that drives him along. Schiller expressed this sentiment in well-chosen words when he said: "Fate hath no voice but the heart's impulses."[78]

This is to say that in the desires that well up in the human heart, fate is playing its cruel game. With its hungry list, fate reaches into the deepest stirring of our inner selves in order to carry us along to our destruction. "When the gods want to impose destruction, they first blind us."[79] Whenever a person exposes human life at its deepest level, he or she finds that fate and action coincide, that we undergo what we think we undertake, that we endure what we initiate, that even in the active pursuit of our own existence we are dragged along by the blind power of fate.

Obviously, wherever the overwhelming power of fate and the consequent passivity of life has been deeply felt, even in the earliest of times, numerous attempts have been made to interpret fate from a rational, moral perspective. We have seen that already in ancient Babylon, where human life was considered to be closely tied to astrological phenomena, the parallel awareness that the will of the living gods lay behind those heavenly movements also flourished. In other words, people felt that in the last instance they were not dealing with inevitable fate in the form of some immense "It," but with the "Thou" of deity with whom they could hold a conversation and to whom they could pray.

In Greece, philosophy threw itself at this problem with a high level of passion. It looked for a solution to it especially in the direction of proposing that Fate is really nothing other than the Reason that permeates everything. This is never a blind, completely capricious power, but it is a thoroughly reasonable and anticipatory force that directs everything with perfect wisdom. The Stoic tradition attempted, with convulsive tenacity, to expunge all irrational features from the notion of fate and to propose an idea of fate that was completely rational and purposeful. They accomplished this by regarding

---

78. Friedrich Schiller, "The Piccolimini," in *Schiller's Works*, ed. J. G. Fischer, vol. 2 (Philadelphia: George Barrie, 1883), 3.8 (p. 166).

79. Ed. note: This ancient proverb has been stated and restated in various versions by many literary luminati including Sophocles, Euripides, John Dryden, and Henry Wadsworth Longfellow. The best-known version is likely that of Seneca: "Whom the Gods would destroy they first make mad" (Lucius Annaeus Seneca, *De Tranquillitate Animi*, 17.10).

the cosmos as an immense totality and as one cosmic body in which rational divinity dwelt as the all-ruling soul. Those who are wise, therefore, do not oppose fate, but submit to it in the knowledge that it is good. They regard this totality as having been constructed as a completely purposeful whole into which each thing and even every occurrence fits perfectly. This Stoic construction of fate as World-Reason, so understood, has had a very big influence on later thought. With Spinoza, for example, we find numerous ideas that hark back to it. With Schiller, this idea pulsates in his statement: "The world's history is the world's judgment doom."[80]

Fate is not a blind, irrational accident, but it is the highest expression of reason and simultaneously of perfect justice.

In the history of Islam, this sense of the course of life led to a very serious dogmatic conflict at one point. That conflict in this religion was in a sense imperative; it had to happen, because Islam lays such a heavy accent on the unfathomable will of Allah. Earlier we pointed out the emphatic expression from the Qur'an that Allah "leads into error whomever he pleases."[81] This and similar expressions can be understood in the sense of total fatalism, so that no room is left for human freedom or responsibility. A tradition developed in Islam according to which Allah, immediately after the creation of Adam, extracted all of his descendants out of his body in the form of eternal little creatures and already at that time determined which of them would be saved and which would be lost. Then, at the time of their birth, their entire future fate is impressed upon them by an angel and nothing is in a position to change any of it whatever.[82]

An earnest reaction arose rather quickly against this utterly crass position that allows the human act to be totally submerged in fate. From a pious, believing perspective, it was pointed out with some emphasis that a person is the "creator of his or her own actions," and that on the basis of those deeds he or she would therefore be justly judged by Allah. Furthermore, many places could be cited from the Qur'an to support this conviction. Enormous difficulties arose, however, as soon as one began to reflect more fully on the expression "creator of his or her own actions." Does that not mean that one

---

80. Ed. note: This line comes from the penultimate stanza of Schiller's poem, "Resignation"; the line in German reads: "Die Weltgeschichte is das Weltgericht." The translation is that of the nineteenth-century English politician and man of letters, Lord Edward Bulwer-Lytton (1803-1873), *Schiller and Horace*, trans. Edward Bulwer-Lytton (London: George Routledge & Sons, 1875), p. 203.

81. Ed. note: Qur'an 13:27.

82. Ignaz Goldziher, *Vorlesungen über den Islam* (Heidelberg: C. Winter, 1910), p. 96.

takes over that vast area of human thought and action from the almighty will of Allah? Does that not imply that one proceeds to limit the framework of foreordination on the strength of which Allah has foreordained all things for the purpose of being able to control human power and freedom? And does one not then become guilty of synergism or of recognizing and honoring other capabilities alongside, and in a sense independent from, those of Allah?[83]

Especially when in more recent times the dogmatic school of the Muʿtazili[84] energetically proposed the freedom of the human will by appealing to Allah's justice, this idea met with great resistance in Islamic circles. The Muʿtazili dared to say that Allah of necessity had to condemn the sinner and exonerate the righteous. This use of the verb "had to" with respect to Allah sounded so blasphemous to Muslim ears that it unleashed a storm of protest. In the centuries that followed, the orthodox Muslim endeavored to find a balance between the conviction that Allah's foreordination extends to all things, including human thoughts and actions, and the idea that people's actions are to some extent also their own actions, ones for which they bear responsibility.

To be sure, the relationship between human action and fate has awakened many questions in the human heart. It has been clear for a long time that a mysterious connection must exist between these two and that in a sense our deeds are comprehended in our fate. Not infrequently, people are overcome with the strange feeling that a game is being played with them, as though the deeds and thoughts that are most uniquely their own possessions are really more imposed on them than generated by them. Language itself gives expression to this passivity of our existence in all sorts of expressions: we are loved; we are overcome by hunger and thirst; an idea occurs to us or arises within us. In the capricious game of human living, we often feel less like the actors than like those swept along in the maelstrom. And yet, the irreducible knowledge always remains that our actions are really our actions, that we produce them, and that we are accountable for them.

Puny man attempts in vain to pose his activity strongly against his fate. He does not want to yield to the lot imposed on him; like a prisoner, he shakes his bars. By his own action he wants to break through his destiny. But,

---

83. Duncan B. Macdonald, *Development of Muslim Theology, Jurisprudence and Constitutional Theory* (New York: Charles Scribner's Sons, 1926), p. 136.

84. Ed. note: The Muʿtazili (Persia, eighth-tenth centuries CE) were a distinct school of Islamic thought that emphasized reason and human free will.

for a person to struggle despairingly with the fate that grabs him by the neck is completely tragic. When Ludwig von Beethoven, the great composer, began to become increasingly deaf, he wrote these gripping words:

> This Beethoven is living a most unfortunate life in conflict with nature and the Creator. Many times I cursed the latter for exposing his creatures with the smallest accident, so that in this way often the most beautiful blossom is broken or annihilated.[85]

Sometimes one hears in his sonatas the powerful, irascible resistance to the fate that had befallen him precisely in that part of his being to which he was most sensitive.

Action and fate. Of course no one is in a position to solve the puzzle that the two of them pose. No one can say where activity stops and fate begins, or what an act is able to accomplish with respect to fate. But one thing is sure: a thoroughly inscrutable inner connection of the two has from earliest times been felt to exist as a religious reality. In that dialogue between action and fate, human beings face powers greater than their own, and they perceive that they have encountered the deepest foundations of their existence. How they conduct themselves with respect to this is crucial; they can resist fate, or submit to it. They can endeavor to explain fate as reasonable and wise guidance, or they can lay all emphasis on its capricious, arbitrary, irrational character. But in all of these cases, they feel in the very depths of their being that they are standing on religious ground. They sense that their entire existence here on earth is rooted in the immeasurably deep mystery of an all-embracing connection. In thinking through these issues, they suspect that they are standing directly in front of the throne of God. The way that they feel and respond to the subtle connection between human action and destiny is of determinative significance for their entire existence. All of these matters seem to slumber within human beings as vague suspicions that never entirely leave them.

---

85. Karl Heim, *Glaube und Leben: Gesammelte Aufsätze und Vorträge,* 3rd ed. (Berlin: Furche, 1928), p. 421.

4 Debating Religious Consciousness: Natural Religion?

§8. The Content of Religious Consciousness (A Review)

[In the previous chapter] we have tried to shape for ourselves an image of the content of the religious consciousness that people have exhibited throughout the ages. As we now review the various ideas that we have attempted to uncover, it strikes us that they are all connected and that a demonstrable tie between them exists.

We first looked at the idea of the totality of all things. Already at that point we face the question of individual existence and an all-embracing connection. To what extent can we speak about individuality, and to what degree can one person legitimately depict himself or herself as someone unique, as something novel, as something possessing a level of value in and of him- or herself? We saw that from ancient times people have felt that their existence is connected to the totality of all things, or to the great "It." This they experienced as a religious connection, since the meaning of their existence was at issue here. In one way or another, people suspected that that great, cosmic interconnectedness was of a divine nature and origin. They

---

Ed. note: Because of its length (106 pages in the original), chapter 1 in *Religieus Besef en Christelijke Geloof* has been divided into two, and each new chapter given a different, more descriptive title. The original title was "The Nature and Development of Religious Consciousness." For ease of scholarly comparison with the Dutch original, the numbering of the subheadings continues from chapter 3. The parenthesis in subheading §8 was added by the editor.

also thought that the divine world expressed itself in that interconnectedness and was actually embodied in it. For this reason, this problem thoroughly interested them throughout the ages.

We next turned attention to the fact that people are conscious of dealing with a moral norm. This is a norm that is innate, but it is not generated from within them and they have no determination of it. Life can only be understood as a dialogue between that norm and a person as he or she lives, thinks, searches, aspires, hopes, and complains. This is so because the norm is always present, is always being carried around by the person, and cannot be separated from his or her person. It also became clear to us that human beings experienced this dialogue as a religious reality. They suspected that the divine world placed itself in a relationship with them by means of that norm, and that that connection was of great significance for their entire existence here on earth.

In the third place, we noted that people carry with them faith in their connection with a higher power. They have explained that higher power in various ways. Sometimes they thought of it as a higher Super Being that seems hopelessly far removed on some errand, at other times as revealing itself as a crowd of capricious gods and spirits. Sometimes they were convinced that the divine power coincided with the world-order. In that case, it was identical with the totality of all things and was nothing other than the concealed, ordering principle holding all things together. At other times, it appeared as though that divine force was fused with their own consciousness of the norm, with the "thou shalt" that they forever heard resounding within them. But they always felt that in one way or another their small, fragile lives were related to a higher power, whatever it might be. They understood only vaguely that life is only intelligible, therefore, when it is seen as a dialogue between the small human "I" and the infinite, divine "Thou."

We briefly paused, in the fourth place, to consider the undeniable yearning for deliverance that has captivated people. Something within them always caused them to feel that they were fettered, that in the deepest sense they were not what they were intended to be, that somewhere a spring was broken or a wheel was out of alignment. This unique awareness that somewhere at a deeper level of our existence we had been shortchanged and had suffered irreplaceable damage echoed as a monotonous melody throughout all the centuries of human history. In this regard, it is relevant whether one looks for that great deficit in the community and accordingly dreams of the deliverance of the community, the totality, or whether one thinks primarily of the individual person in his or her individual battle and fear. We are again struck by the fact that people nowhere could come to a clear understanding of what it was from which we needed to be saved. We needed to be saved from death, from transitoriness, from the threat of the curse that hangs over our existence — all of this sounds like the belief we encounter from antiquity. We need to be saved from ignorance, from delusion, from our own errors, from *samsara* or the endless cycle of rebirths, and from never-ending suffering that is grounded in existence itself. We need to be saved from our preoccupation with self, from our own selves, from the idea that we are something alongside and in contrast with the totality of all things. But however people construed and presented it, they were always sure that we desperately needed deliverance and that we operated in the condition of being thoroughly dissatisfied with the lives we receive. How can we be saved? Do we need to struggle free from these bonds by ourselves? Do we need to do that alone, one by one, or do we need to do that collectively through a rebirth of the community? Or, is there someone else who needs to save us, perhaps a god or a Savior? And, is that god really the Other One, or is he perhaps the deepest part of our own being? We ask so many questions; we hear so many diverse answers. But that we eagerly reach out for deliverance is the one condition that is unalterably the case for all of us.

Finally, we briefly paid attention to the tension that exists between a person and his or her destiny, between action and fate. Throughout the centuries, the relationship of those two has been perceived as one of the core issues in religion. Is our own action in fact resistance to our fate? Is that permissible? Can it even happen? Or, is our action itself our fate, is it "the voice of fate"? The religious connection of activity and destiny is one of the fundamental problems that have kept human thought and investigation busy.

When we once again review all of this, we cannot deny that these five dimensions influence one another and are tied to each other. The first one, the idea of the totality of all things, for example, is tightly connected to the third, a connection with a higher power. Is that higher power itself the totality of all things, or at least the hidden backdrop of all things? However that might be, what is clear is that between those two — the idea of meaningful coherence of the cosmic order and the idea that we are engaged with a higher power — a very intimate connection must exist. What is also obvious is that these two dimensions exist in close connection again with the fifth dimension, namely that of the tension between human action and fate. For that tension of activity and destiny is essentially an aspect of the tension between a person as a single individual and the totality of all things in which he or she is caught up, or one might say, between the person and the higher power. This is how people have always felt about matters. We have separated these dimensions from one another and set them alongside each other. But in actuality, they are entirely interwoven and the one is controlled by the other.

The ideas of a norm and of deliverance assume a different dimension. In a certain sense, one can say that they break through the others and open entirely new perspectives. The person is an atom in the universe, caught up in the totality of all things that are disclosed to him or her as a meaningful whole. Therefore the cosmic laws that sustain and rule the totality also pertain to the individual, whom they carry along and circumscribe. This is the individual's fate. But at the same time, we perceive that we are addressed, refuted, and accused by the norm. We understand that we are in dialogue with the norm. And from a sense of brokenness and finiteness with respect to the norm, we grasp for deliverance. Here people understandably stand in a new relationship. Here they are no longer simply an atom, a tiny part of the universal, but they are each a single, free, responsible person that needs to be obedient and is capable of sinning.

One could say, therefore, that these last two dimensions of the norm and of deliverance pivot on a completely different point. They lie on an entirely different level than those of the totality of all things, of a higher power, and of fate, which all operate as completely inexplicable.

Upon deeper examination, could we not also say that the religious consciousness that has inspired people actually has two dimensions? The first aspect is the one of being caught up in the totality of all things, and therefore of being defined in every respect by fatalism, or destiny, or a sovereign necessity. The second aspect, coming from scientific insight, is that we are being addressed by the normative, or that we are under the authority of a moral norm, and that we therefore require deliverance from our brokenness. When we make such a distinction, we can point out that the single characteristic of being connected to a higher power lies on the borderline between the two. For, on the one hand, that higher power is on the side of totality, of which it is the heart and core. Thus, it is also the all-determinative power that possesses unlimited control of our lives. On the other hand, however, that higher power presents itself as our norm, as the mighty "thou shalt," or as the ominous law that is at the same time our only hope for deliverance.

The line of totality and fatalism suggests that people live with a sense of their insignificance, being bound, and lacking any power. A human being is merely a ripple on the ocean of the universe, and the great cosmic forces simply play their capricious game with us. A person is nothing, is merely considered to be a cell in the greater context of all things, has no individual existence, is only a little spark in the raging cosmic fire.

The other line — of the norm and of deliverance — evokes thoughts of freedom, of being distinct from nature, of individuality, of accountability, of guilt, and of hope of being set free. Human beings are unique entities, each very special, and hold their own destinies in their hands. Each one is a sort of micro-god, a god in miniature, possessing his or her own existence, responsibility, and potentials.

At the intersection of these two lines of thought — destiny within a totality and freedom to act and be delivered[1] — lies the awareness of being related to a higher power. That higher power is at the same time the deepest meaning of the whole, the bearer of cosmic laws, the energizer of the norm, the helper toward salvation. That intersection of these two lines is obviously the heart of religious consciousness. Precisely there is where the unfathomable mystery of being human lies. Precisely there we find the essence of all religion.

What becomes clear ultimately is that each of the dimensions of religious consciousness receives its uncommon identity from this heart. When the totality of all things, All-being, is no longer only a vague abstraction, a boundless ocean, or a Brahman, but when it is also thought of as being connected to a god, a Higher Being, a definite Someone, then our relationship to and discussion with the totality of all things is transformed in principle. We can no longer merely talk about our "I" in connection with some vague, undefined "It," but we begin thinking in terms a relationship between an "I" and a divine "Thou." The divinity that dwells in everything, permeates everything, completes everything, unites everything, displays the features of an *Ishvara*, a Lord. My own connection with the totality of all things takes on something of an "I-Thou" relationship.

The same holds true for fate and fatalism. As soon as fate is no longer seen as blind, natural causality, irrational law, complete capriciousness, and fickle accident, but as the governance of a higher being, it is essentially changed. Being subject to fate assumes something of the nature of a dialogue with a Someone, and something like yielding and submission enters the picture. The notion that all-determinative fate is in a sense a Someone arouses heightened resistance. A person does not want to be overpowered by a Someone; I do not want to be limited by a greater and more powerful He. On the other hand, however, something of trust and resignation comes to

---

1. Ed note: The explanatory phrase between the dashes was added by the editor.

expression. In any case, the relationship to one's destiny is transformed as soon as it is seen in relationship with a higher power.

And as far as the idea of norm is concerned, it receives its sanction from the thought of being connected with a higher force as its foundation. Then the norm stops being a totally inexplicable thing that, like a stranger, forcibly intrudes into the territory of empirical reality, but it becomes something understandable, familiar, decked in majesty.

Finally, deliverance takes on greater depth from the knowledge that people deal with a higher power. Even when they believe in auto-salvation, that self-deliverance is nevertheless tinged with different hues when it becomes obvious that it is not our small self that accomplishes this, but that a much greater, divine Self within us and working through us sets us free from our fetters.

The content of religious consciousness in its entirety is illumined by that single aspect of a connection with a higher power. One could say that religion acquires its first feature from that one aspect. Something of a wonderful glow, a warmth, and a sheen then falls on all the other aspects that renews and transforms them. From that one aspect, religion first becomes religion in the true sense of that word. A new horizon comes into view; new perspectives emerge. All human relationships assume something of an I-Thou relationship, and life itself becomes a conversation. And if necessary, it involves verbal battle, struggle, or revolt. But in any case, it is discussion. People understand that they have been positioned opposite a mysterious Opponent, Another, who shields his face but who nevertheless encounters us. We engage him daily; we can never escape his grip. This is the nimbus of the idea of God that pervades the human quest and human thought.

§9. Religious Consciousness and Modern Culture

Before we turn our attention to a deeper examination of the underlying principles of religious consciousness, we first need to ask to what extent that consciousness is still alive in our modern world. When we consider religious consciousness, are we dealing with something that belongs to bygone times, or is it still present everywhere, albeit in different forms? This is a question that is of compelling interest in assessing the future prospects of our culture.

In and of itself, it is highly unlikely that the religious consciousness that has played such a weighty role in human thought and reflection throughout the ages could no longer be found whatsoever in our century. This unlikelihood presses itself upon us particularly because it is becoming increasingly apparent that whatever heights modern life might achieve, human beings have essentially changed very little. When we disregard our electric trams and diesel engines, our radios and vacuum cleaners, modern people are startlingly similar to the people of past centuries. They are just as petty, jealous, egotistical, and proud. They are loved just as they were then. They are just as driven as former generations by concerns like providing life's basic needs, having recreation, finding sexual satisfaction, and dealing with their fear of death. When we read the books of ancient Greece and Rome, or even of ancient China and India, we definitely find our modern technological achievements missing. But in the human portraits sketched in those materials, we generally recognize ourselves rather quickly. Indeed much has changed, but on the deeper levels, much remains the same. And religious consciousness belongs on those deeper levels. Just on that basis, it is not at all difficult to accept that modern people would be affected by religious considerations. That the religious sensitivities in their lives assume different forms is of course possible, but to say that they could be entirely lacking would be untenable.

Naturally, it is another question as to what form these religious sensitivities take in our modern culture. In that regard, we must keep in mind that for many centuries Europe has been under the fairly strong influence of the gospel. Obviously, definite residues of that influence are still visible in our culture. This gives the issue of religious consciousness in our modern culture a rather unique character. On the one hand, religious consciousness in our modern culture has been more or less bent in a distinct direction by Christianity while, on the other hand, it is strongly resistant to that same Christianity. In either case, it betrays the significance that Christianity has had on our culture. I want to make very clear at this point that I am not speaking here about the church, but about modern culture in unchurched circles, where in many respects people have left the church and set themselves against the church. In an overwhelmingly huge proportion of our modern culture, we frequently and often unexpectedly see displayed signs of that ineradicable religious consciousness. We see this in its unwarranted ferocity, its bitterness, its sense of tragedy, its fears, and its expectations. This religious consciousness seems to be so thoroughly human that it is woven into the very fabric of our humanity.

When we now take a look at the several dimensions of religious consciousness one by one, it appears that the connection with the totality of all things has been one of the most crucial elements in the spiritual development of Europe. This is only natural. As soon as Europeans began investigating nature at the close of the Middle Ages and started studying the movements of heavenly bodies, they confronted the overwhelming reality of the whole universe. Perfect order rules that universe, they saw, since supreme laws control it in all its parts. By contrast with that majestic realization, they realized that they were momentary and insignificant little parts of that immense totality to which they were bound.

We hear these ideas powerfully expressed already in Giordano Bruno[2] and other observers of nature who lived in the century prior to the transition to our modern world. Giordano Bruno was deeply impressed with the endless expanse of the universe, in which all contrasts fade, everything exists in perfect harmony, and all things are directed by a supreme reason. On the other hand, it struck him that every single thing nevertheless has its own existence, namely that in every monad and every part of the universe the eternal power and immensity of the totality is reflected. Divinity is present with new, creative force in each monad, thus in every human being. Following this line of thought, he looked for "the reconciliation of the ideas of the universal and the individual."[3] He wanted to see all individual entities as swallowed up in the universal, and he still wanted to think of every separate thing as a being having complete beauty and harmony itself. That this effort at reconciliation was not completely successful for him should not surprise us. What is striking is that for him and many of his contemporaries the idea of the totality of all things was so very prevalent that it became extremely difficult for the individual person to be accorded a meaningful position.

In the subsequent period, the problem of the totality of all things dominated European thought with increasing strength. The idea of mechanistic causality that held such fascination for the seventeenth and eighteenth centuries pushed out all notions of freedom and responsibility. It conceded to individuals no ground whatever that they could call their own. All events, including all human activity, appeared to be entirely squeezed into that great cosmic, mechanistic process. In the immeasurably large world machine, the individual person was no more than a futile little fleck driven along by the mechanized energies to which it was bound and that kept the entire world in motion.

---

2. Ed. note: Giordano Bruno (1548-1600) was a Dominican friar, astronomer, and philosopher, best known for his notion of an infinite universe. He was burned at the stake in 1600 by the Inquisition, most likely because of his pantheism.

3. W. Windelband, *Die Geschichte der Neueren Philosophie: In Ihrem Zusammenhange mit der Allgemeinen Cultur und den Besondern Wissenschaft*, 2 vols., 3rd ed. (Leipzig: Breitkopf & Härtel, 1899), 2: 421.

In Spinoza's philosophy, the notion of the totality of all things, or of the entire universe, had already banished any idea of individuality. This caused someone once jokingly to say that in Spinoza's system there is room for everything except for Spinoza himself. Individual persons, who imagine that they are something and consider themselves to be accountable and to have their own existence, sink entirely into the eternal silence of the one Substance identified as God. In the thought of Spinoza, the term "God" is identical with the totality of all things.

Gradually it became increasingly apparent, therefore, that every avenue of thought necessarily led to the idea of the totality of everything as the only truth, and thus to the idea that individuals and their life are only apparently real. The dams of individual human thought and action all burst under the pressure of the idea of totality.

This held true, first of all, with respect to thought itself. For, what is my own thinking except one, little aspect of that single, overwhelming idea of the rationality or *Logos* of nature? To the extent that I actually think, that is, truly think logically and responsibly, my thinking no longer belongs to me but is embedded in universal thought. Logical thinking equals universal thinking, thinking absent individuality. My thinking is swallowed up in universal thought. It is universal thought that flows through me and takes shape in me. For that reason, every form of rational idealism finds making a place for the individual so exceptionally difficult and is predisposed to dissolving all of life into thinking, the insignificant thinking of the individual into the enormous thinking of World-Reason or God. In idealism, says Reinhold Niebuhr, "the actual self [is] absorbed in the universal," the self of the single individual is absorbed into universal thought.[4]

Secondly, it also held with respect to how nature is seen. In just a few centuries, western European thought has made unbelievable progress in the study of nature. Things that previous generations never even suspected were suddenly opened and laid bare. It is as if the most important realities of nature had been hidden from all previous generations and as though the blinders began to fall off only in the last couple of centuries. The laws that totally govern nature are what first impressed people. Nature is above all else orderly, controlled by law. This by itself raises the issues of natural order and of whether human life itself is not included in that system of laws. Is our physical life regulated by law? Does our spiritual life also proceed, like the ticking

---

4. Reinhold Niebuhr, *The Nature and Destiny of Man: A Christian Interpretation,* 2 vols. (London: James Nisbet and Co., 1945), 1: 80.

of a clock, carried along by mechanistic laws similar to those we see working in nature around us? In other words, is our entire existence, physical as well as psychological, simply nothing more than an extremely little fragment of the one, mechanistic reality that we call nature? The more people are oriented to nature, the more insane it seems to recognize an individual's independent existence. Self-awareness is imaginary, deluded, and foolish. This is the final word uttered by naturalistic thinking.

In the seventeenth and eighteenth centuries, we witness a gradual advance in universalistic thought. The individual receded into the mists of the totality of all things, and was swallowed up in the immensity of the All-in-all. This is not to say that the process was entirely quiet and without disturbance. Especially toward the end of the eighteenth century, fascination with the thought of the totality of everything was increasingly felt to be a serious hindrance. Resistance arose that ultimately led to a completely new orientation of thought. Particularly Kant enjoys the honor of having been the spokesperson of this new orientation. Kant, who was deeply impressed with nature's majesty, was indeed one of the first philosophers of the new era who attempted to shatter the spell of totality thinking. As his point of departure, he adopted the great imperative "thou shalt," the moral norm, "the moral law within me." This became the only point of certainty that he could find in the gigantic struggle against abandoning the individual and bowing down to the universal. In that mysterious "thou shalt" presumably lay true freedom like a precious treasure, however incomprehensible that might appear to rational thought.

The influence of totality thinking remained enormously strong also in the nineteenth century. It was dominant in idealism as well as in its romantic and logical forms. The tremendous development of the natural sciences added their weight to expanding its influence. This development of the natural sciences had a twofold effect on European thought. On the one hand, it constituted solid proof of humanity's unbelievable greatness and capabilities. It underlined humanity's nobility and accorded it a level of glory not reached before. On the other hand, however, it increasingly degraded humanity as time passed. In an expanded universe that had to be measured in thousands of light years, and in the midst of a myriad of suns, humanity did not seem that great at all. Is humanity really nothing more than an accident of nature, a tiny offshoot of the great process of cosmic development and destined to once again disappear? The nineteenth century held both of these elements of naturalistic thinking in relative balance. It was quite simply the century of self-reliant "bourgeois society." For the first time, at the end of this century "a bourgeois culture and society at peace with its own this-worldliness was finally achieved."[5]

During recent decades, the riddle of the totality of everything has once again been on the agenda and has assumed various forms. It naturally appeared first of all in its naturalistic form. What is the human being, actually, in this fabulously huge context of all things? What is its position and its potential? Is a human being really nothing more than a highly developed animal that cunningly represses all sorts of sexual and natural passions and assumes a life not basically suited to him or her? And would our culture not be better off if it rejected this colossal repression and compelled us to be more open about all the vital passions and instincts we harbor? Psychoanalysis opened new doors in this regard. People ventured that a collective subconscious lies hidden beneath our individual lives and that it generates the deepest impulses of human activity. In short, the puzzle of the totality of all things in relation to the individual person became painfully obvious from many angles. The Individualistic School of psychology emphasized that self-delusion or focusing completely on self produces serious conflicts and inhibitions, and it sought remedy in complete objectivity and the restless capitulation to endless human activism. Klages[6] thinks that the solution to this problem needs to be found in the direction of having the spirit — that now routinely acts as the soul's adversary, as the major restraint on spontaneous, instinctive living — itself be propelled and inspired by that same soul.[7] Recent psychological studies in general focus on the intimate relation of the individual person to the totality of all things, to nature, to life generally with its imposed limits and tensions.

What is a human being in the immense cosmic order? As soon as one begins reflecting on the subject, the problem of history emerges. On reflection, how peculiar history seems! Is it a single event alongside unchangeable natural developments? Or is history nothing more than a segment of cosmic self-development, a tiny thread in the overwhelming warp and woof of natural evolution? And in the context of history, what is the significance of the singular, incidental event that can often produce such unexpected developments in the historical process?

---

5. Paul Tillich, *Die religiöse Lage der Gegenwart* (Berlin: Ullstein, 1926), p. 26.

6. Ed. note: Ludwig Klages (1872-1956) was a philosopher, psychologist, and graphologist; his most important work is *Widersacher de Seele (Adversary of the Soul)* (1929).

7. Ed. note: The complications of this sentence may be eased by noting that two distinct words, *Geist* or spirit, and *Seele* or soul, are used to describe two faculties of the human person. The idea is that the human spirit should stop acting as the soul's adversary or inhibitor and in fact be animated by the same instinctive spontaneity found in the soul.

It is especially the social dimension of totality thinking that began to impress itself on modern thought. What is the single individual in the community, in the social order, in the tribe, and in humanity as a whole? Should we see human life as an undivided whole into which all individuals are locked, or should we give definite accent to the single person, to his or her accountability and also his or her human rights? Precisely because such questions reach so deeply into the political and social fabric, answers to them have been regarded as compellingly necessary. National Socialism did not hesitate to resort to using romanticist slogans in exaggerating the importance of the social order, particularly the German race. The individual is nothing; the people are everything. The vitality of the people as a whole is the hidden force that propels the individual. This is why the individual has no real rights over against society and can never oppose it, for as soon as that would happen, he or she would become an impediment to the inevitable development of the entire people. In communism, just as much emphasis is laid on totality thinking and on the masses, albeit in another form and on other principles. Our culture is wrestling with these issues in a life-and-death struggle.

Thus, the problematic questions concerning the totality of all things are still as lively for us today as they have been through the ages. Admittedly, they have lost something of their force, for in European thought something has been broken. Our culture is rapidly being secularized, which is to say that in essence religious issues are losing something of their religious force. We are living in a "godless" universe. The social, political, psychological, and philosophical aspects of the problem are still keenly felt, and we struggle with them. But they no longer grab us by the throat; they no longer grip us at the very depths of our existence. Something irrecoverable has been lost in our thinking. The totality of all things is no longer the divinely ordered cosmos. The universe is no longer a harmony based in God or in a divine power; it has all become more crass, more objective, more hardened, and more bitter. But the basic issue has remained unchanged.

From time to time, the religious tension inherent in the problem does emerge again. We have just recently encountered it in National Socialism, which perplexed us with its totalitarian thought and religious freight. Something similar might return at any time. In other words, deep beneath European culture, religious issues are at stake. The dimensions in which we encounter them are usually of an objective, pragmatic, social, philosophical, and political nature. But the fire of religious intensity has still not entirely died out. At any time, the questions that we face can return with such intensity that they once again become as religiously compelling as they have been throughout the ages. Whether we know it or not, we are still always gripped by the religious problematic of being human.

The problem of the norm has preoccupied European thought during the last century just as much as the problem of the totality of all things. We have already seen how through the influence of Kant it became the center of intense religious struggle during his time and how it has never left us since then. This is self-evident. The naturalistic currents of thought in the previous century turned the norm upside down or flattened it into mere social convention, propriety, or an instrument of self-preservation. In Nietzsche, the idea of the normative was worked out in new ways. He wanted to free it from being enslaved to the old notion of morality and to orient it toward nature, which with unrelenting ruthlessness allows less suitable sorts to die out and thus make room for better and more favorable forms of life. In this way, he tried to make room for the morality of power. "*I teach you the overman. Man is something that shall be overcome.*"[8]

Particularly since the end of the recent war, the question of what is normative has become a burning issue for the entire world. The cruelty and bestiality that emerged in concentration camps and prisons have exposed the terrible dangers threatening our culture. Perhaps more strongly than ever before, the need for unshakeable norms and for moral rights and obligations has been realized. We have brushed with chaos, with total degeneration, and with the destruction of all values. We now have a compelling need for a lively and solid understanding of the normative. The indescribable misery poured out on Europe in the name of "Blood and Fatherland" and in the name of social order has made people extremely wary of all that flows out of the new morality born from totality thinking.

But what is the norm that lives in the human soul and yet is not derived from humanity? On what can one base it? How can one safely posit it? Aalders once called conscience "the border guard"[9] between the relative and the absolute, the temporal and the eternal. One thing needs to be understood, and that is that a person who is in touch with the moral norm within may never manipulate it or subvert it for his or her own purposes. The norm exists within the person, yet the norm stands above the person. The person does not test the norm; rather, the norm tests the person. More precisely, the norm grips the person, accuses the person, and dominates the person. In

8. Friedrich Nietzsche, *Thus Spoke Zarathustra,* trans. Walter Kaufman (New York: Penguin, 1978), p. 12.

9. W. J. Aalders, *Het Geweten* (Groningen-Batavia: J. B. Wolters, 1935), p. 120.

more recent forms of humanism, the question of the norm is engaged as one of the most crucial issues of our entire human existence. Once we let go of the normative, nothing can hold back our modern world in its dizzying journey from an irredeemable plummet into destruction.

What makes this entire problem so exceptionally complicated is the sobering fact that people will maintain the absoluteness of the moral norm at any price, but will consciously hesitate to ground it in divine authority. In his book *Religion Within the Limits of Reason Alone,* Kant defined the concept of religion as "the recognition of all duties as divine commands." In so doing, he recognizes the fact that there are people who first want to know whether something is "a command of God" before they will recognize it as an obligation. Such people need some kind of revealed religion. Others, on the contrary, are satisfied with a "religion of pure reason," which is to say that they hear the voice of moral obligation and bow to it.[10] Many in our time have lost faith in God but nonetheless stubbornly hold onto the unassailability of the moral norm because they are clearly aware that the future of humankind is suspended on that slim thread.

In our century, the need for deliverance has again received new urgency. That is due not in the least to the sense of lost-ness that has begun to overwhelm a great majority of contemporary people. The superficiality and mechanizing of life, the dramatic events of recent decades, and the realization that we are standing at one of the most decisive moments in world history all work together to awaken an intense longing for liberation into a new kind of life that really deserves the name "life." This need for deliverance usually manifests itself in collective terms, and it does not strive so much for individual liberation as for deliverance of society, the group, and humanity generally. Contemporary people have become conscious of the fact that liberation of the individual is scarcely imaginable because we all stand or fall together. For that reason, the desire for deliverance is incarnate in various social developments and movements. National Socialism undoubtedly had a fascination for young people because it presented itself as a saving religion and thus appealed to the deepest tendencies in the human heart. The same can be said for all sorts of other movements that at present are manifest in many countries of the world.

That nationalism and national sentiment from time to time manifest

10. Immanuel Kant, *Religion within the Boundaries of Mere Reason: And Other Writings,* trans. and ed. Allen Wood and George Di Giovanni (Cambridge: Cambridge University Press, 1998), pp. 158, 162.

themselves with religious fervor is also a recognizable phenomenon. We experienced as much during the time of the German occupation. Then, for many, national sentiment took on heightened, religious proportions concerning every deed aimed at meeting the needs of society.

Alongside this emphasis on the collective deliverance that is such a powerful force in current world events, however, there is also a genuine longing for individual salvation living in the heart of each person. "The contemporary person faces the fact of meaninglessness in his or her own life and takes flight from that meaninglessness in fun or in suicide." "The creed propounded in the pub — implicitly — is that of Romans 7:24: 'Who, then, will save me?'"[11] These quotations may be a bit exaggerated, but the fact remains that the impetuous pursuit of pleasure and intoxication found in dancehalls and pubs clearly reveals something of the thirst for deliverance that grips the contemporary person.

At this moment in time, all of this is so poignantly depicted because to an unprecedented degree modern people are struggling with the problem of fate, the enigma of their destiny. They know that they are chained and imprisoned in the jail of those immense, global developments that wash over them and sweep them along on their unfathomable journey. Oswald Spengler, in his book *The Decline of the West,* has become one of the major interpreters of that gnawing sense of fate that grips contemporary people. He has relentlessly attempted to unravel "the problem of world history" and to penetrate to "the music of the spheres," the music of fate, by which all cultures are swept away in a wild dance.[12] Many of his explanations have been refuted by more recent social critics, but no one can deny that he has given expression to the unconscious fears living in many. A definite fatalism exists concerning the world's history; we do not have the control of events in our hands. Certain forces unrelentingly, mercilessly push history toward frightening outcomes. It is foolhardy to think that the road ahead for the human race is a road of steady and continuous progress. We are aware every moment that fate is playing with us and that the most determinative forces in our lives are beyond our control.

In our own country, a few years before the war, Huizinga in his book *In the Shadow of Tomorrow* voiced the deep anxiety that began overwhelming Europe at that time. He said the following about the outlook then:

11. J. Sperna Weiland, "De klerk en de modern mens," *Vox Theologica: Interacademiaal Theologisch Tijdschrift* 18, no. 5 (June 1948): 153.

12. Oswald Spengler, *The Decline of the West: Form and Actuality,* trans. Charles Francis Atkinson, 2 vols. (New York: Alfred A. Knopf, 1946), 1: 160.

... This prospect of a civilization left at the mercy of its own intrinsic dynamism, of a still always increasing domination of nature, of still more complete and immediate publicity, possesses the complexion of a nightmare rather than the promise of a purified and improved culture.[13]

... The world shows the aspect of Spengler's *Civilisation* plus a measure of insanity, humbug and cruelty, coupled with sentimentality, which he (Spengler) did not foresee.[14]

But, however frightening the development of cultural life may be to us, "we know that the world of today cannot turn back."[15] We must go forward, even though we are conscious of the fact that we are racing ahead at a jaw-dropping pace, and no one is capable of blocking or even delaying this process. On the contrary, it does seem as if we are being hounded along on a breathtaking trip without any sense of where we are headed.

It would not be difficult to name a long list of novelists, poets, and philosophers who are gripped deep in their souls by the idea of fate and who have expressed their own fears in their works. In this connection, I only need to mention existentialism as it has developed in recent years. This form of existentialism does not want to think from the perspective of some retreat from reality, from theater box-seats. It does not desire to construct a rational system with a beautiful ending. It wants to think from the perspective of life itself, life with all its fickle, thoroughly irrational directions, instincts, passions, and darkness. It wants to stand squarely in the middle of existential realities and to view life, the world, and the course of events from that vantage point. It makes no attempt to rationalize, gloss over, or speak positively about life's harshness, cruelties, frightening forms of enslavement, or about its bizarre, senseless, sordid, and repulsive aspects. It aims to stand in the midst of human existence, and it wants to grasp that existence in the fullness of its irrational, paradoxical tensions. It does not want to photograph life from a safe distance, but wants to take a raw close-up from close by.

During its short history, this existentialism has already gone through various stages. In the contrasts that Kierkegaard saw between time and eternity, it had a deeply religious character. The existential fear he experienced he regarded as a trembling yearning for God. With Heidegger, it was completely

---

13. J. Huizinga, *In the Shadow of Tomorrow: A Diagnosis of the Spiritual Distemper of Our Time,* trans. J. H. Huizinga (London: William Heinemann, 1936), p. 190.

14. Huizinga, *In the Shadow of Tomorrow,* pp. 197-98.

15. Huizinga, *In the Shadow of Tomorrow,* p. 190.

different. While Heidegger employed the same terminology as Kierkegaard, his words took on a different, more secularized content. This tarnishing culminated with Sartre and his companions. With them, existentialism went in a clearly atheistic and nihilistic direction.[16]

Based on its starting point, existentialism is compelled to pay substantial attention to a person's destiny, to his or her fate. People exist in the world, the totality of all things, and in that world they become aware of their lives for the first time. They are conscious of being "thrust" into that world. Standing in that world, they encounter the fate that entangles them in its fickle irrationality. Remarkably, they cling compulsively to their freedom of choice regarding life in the face of that fate. Inherent in that freedom are their fear and their sense of responsibility. In their human insignificance, they see themselves as in every regard being jolted, assaulted, and hopelessly swept along by the currents of a sinister destiny. Nonetheless, they know that they are free people. This is their revolt, the rebellion of their humanity against the forces that threaten them.

In Kafka's novels, this struggle with a sinister destiny, this battle with fate, is the major, overriding theme.[17]

Thus, it is clear that our modern era clearly recognizes that final feature of religious awareness, namely consciousness of the course or direction of life, even though the course of life is primarily experienced as blind chance and sinister fate. To live, to exist, is to struggle with an invisible partner who possesses overwhelmingly strong power and destiny, who has us in a bear-hug and never lets us go. Is that invisible partner a "Someone," a mysterious god behind all things? Or, is it nothing more than nature itself, the totality of all things, the law governing all things, or inevitable fate? One thing is sure. In the convulsiveness with which our modern era clings to ideas like freedom, the fear of death, and revolution, we see something of a religious content. In many cases, this religious content is expressed in anti-Christian, negative, fierce, bitter terms. But even such determined opposition to religion can be religious; that is to say, it can be an expression of having been confronted with supreme reality and of having entered into dialogue with that reality. Modern life and thought suffer many afflictions: irritability, anxiety, a frightening absence of energizing idealism, an indescribable weariness and

16. S. U. Zuidema, *Nacht zonder dageraad: Naar Aanleiding van het Atheistisch en Nihilistisch Existentialisme van Jean-Paul Sartre* (Franeker: T. Wever, [1948]).

17. C. A. van Peursen, *Riskante Philosophie: Een Karakteristiek van het Hedendaagse Existentiële Denken* (Amsterdam: H. J. Paris, 1948), pp. 70ff.

defeatism. Then, the course of world history rushes over and around us, and who knows where it will carry us?

What is really lacking in our modern culture is the one aspect that we have designated as the core of religious consciousness, namely the awareness of being connected to a higher power. As we saw, that consciousness lies at the intersection of two lines; all other aspects are actually determined by it. Precisely there we find the great religious shortfall[18] of our century. For Nietzsche, the feeling of this great deficit receives especially dramatic accent. "Where is God, he asks, for I want to see him. We have killed him! You and I, we are all his murderer!"[19] He represents Zarathustra as saying, "There is also good taste in piety; it was this that at last said: 'Away with such a God! Better to have no God, better to set up destiny on one's own account, better to be a fool, better to be God oneself!'"[20] With clenched fists he can call on the "unknown God," the "cruel hunter,"[21] to be accountable, and, at other moments, he can lift the heartrending complaint: "You never pray any more, no longer beseech, no longer call out in complete trust. What happens makes no sense anymore; there is no love in what happens to you."[22]

With many in our recent times, this religious shortfall is scarcely considered to be a deficit. Contemporary people are so accustomed to thinking in terms of natural science, to thinking outside and beyond themselves, that even in their most intimate thoughts they almost never consider what is wondrously exalted, holy, and great beyond description — that which previous generations described as God. God is dead; we killed him. A generation has grown up for whom God is not much more than a long-forgotten word in ancient texts; and it feels no sorrow in the least that it has lost track of him. Connection with a higher power has lost any emphasis for people today. And because that connection has disappeared, all the other aspects of religious consciousness have become so confused, sterile, dim, and impover-

18. Ed. note: We have rendered Bavinck's word *manko* (usual spelling *manco* = shortage, defect, want, lack, deformity) with a two-word expression "religious shortfall" (and then as "deficit") to capture the full weight of the existential situation of twentieth-century "modern" people who are torn by the pull of a religious yearning that they refuse to acknowledge as real.

19. J. H. Wilhelmi, *Th. Carlyle und F. Nietzsche: Wie sie Gott suchten, und was für einen Gott sie fanden,* 2nd ed. (Göttingen: Vandenhoeck & Ruprecht, 1900), p. 29.

20. Nietzsche, *Thus Spoke Zarathustra,* Book Four, "Retired" (p. 262).

21. Nietzsche, *Thus Spoke Zarathustra,* Fourth and Last Part, "The Magician" (pp. 252-55).

22. Eberhard Arnold, *Urchristliches und Antichristliches im Friedrich Nietzsche's Werdegang* (Eilenburg: B. Becker, 1910), p. 27.

ished. It no longer has any compelling, formative power. Norms clearly remain, but on what do they rest? The totality of all things remains, but is the universe a meaningful whole, or is it thoroughly irrational in its connectedness and is the position of humanity in this endless interdependence that of one who has lost his or her way? To be sure, life still has a course or direction, but is there nothing more than groping through the thick, thick darkness of inscrutable destiny? Need for deliverance definitely exists, but no one knows how to properly explain what people need saving from or from whence that salvation comes. People express themselves passionately on the subject of a thousand-year kingdom, on peace and future salvation. But at the same time, they mock with their imaginations and break out in sarcastic descriptions of that "brave, new world" — the beautiful new world with its horrible perversity and its cool, calculating, and efficient rationalization of the entire social order from which the last small spark of warmth, spontaneity, and spontaneous vitality has been blown away. Toward what world are we rushing, full speed ahead?

Yet, there is hope. There is hope that in one way or another a way out will yet emerge. There is hope that the regenerative powers within society will finally overcome everything that holds them down. There is still hope that something like liberation will appear. There is hope because we simply will not allow ourselves to be defeated and because there is always something that urges us on with the courage that transcends despair.

For many it is as though something of the old glow of religious faith still shines forth. During the war and times of intense conflict, when basic values were at stake, the singing of a folksong could suddenly become a religious ritual, and a flag could become a religious symbol. Out of the incomprehensible depths of the human heart, at unexpected moments, the warm gulf currents of religious experience could flow again. Then it was as though it was not so cold anymore, as though life still made some sense, as though supreme values remained for which living was still worth the effort. Then, if dying became necessary, it was as though fate was no longer so bizarre or so completely irrational. It was as though life, in its depths, still retained something of a dialogue — a dialogue with whom; with which unknown God?

§10. Natural Religion?

Now the time has come to get a grip on that universal religious consciousness about which we have been talking in an effort to make sense of its essence and origin. What is that "religious consciousness," really? Is it perhaps *religio naturalis*, natural religion, about which so much has been spoken and written in the history of human thought? And is that *religio naturalis* perhaps that *Religio* (with a capital letter) of which all the religions of the nations are merely offshoots? Is it the tree on which all of these grow as branches? We cannot simply set aside all these difficult and fascinating questions. We need to formulate answers for them in one way or another.

There has actually been a great deal of interest in the concept of natural religion. That is especially true of the period in the history of European thought usually designated as the Enlightenment. People often accuse that period of being so caught up with universal ideas that it paid little attention to concrete, historically shaped realities. There may well be some exaggeration latent in that preoccupation but it is not entirely without basis. Enlightenment thinkers enjoyed expressing themselves abstractly with respect to religion as a universal phenomenon, without paying close attention to the forms that religion actually took in the course of history. So, Herbert of Cherbury,[23] for example, attempted to penetrate to the *communes notitiae*, the universal concepts held by all peoples and found in all religious life. He thought he could identify five such elements. In the first place, humans have always known and understood that there are one or more divine beings *(esse supremum aliquid numen)*. Secondly, from the outset, they saw that the highest being needed to be revered. Furthermore, it is readily apparent that the most important part of revering God is being virtuous, expressed in a pious and respectful manner. In the fourth place, people from ancient times onward have felt definite horror and revulsion toward crime, and they understood that it needed to be wiped out with contrition. Finally, people believed instinctively that a reward had to be the consequence of good works.[24] These five universal concepts are rooted in human reason, and they accordingly lie at the foundation of all religions, at least to the extent that these religions are not mired in superstition and folly.

The English philosopher John Locke wrote extensively on the relation-

23. Ed. note: Edward Herbert, 1st Baron Herbert of Cherbury (1583-1648), elder brother of the poet George Herbert, was a British soldier, diplomat, and religious philosopher, one of the founders of English Deism. His five "common notions" were: (1) there is a supreme Deity; (2) this Deity ought to be worshiped; (3) virtue combined with piety is the chief part of divine worship; (4) people should repent of their sins and turn from them; (5) God, in his goodness and justice, will reward and punish human conduct.

24. Baron Edward Herbert of Cherbury, *De Veritate, Prout Distinguitur à Revelatione, à Verisimili, à Possibili, et à Falso,* 3rd ed. (1656), p. 265.

ship between natural religion as grounded in human reason and the so-
called "formed religions," or the various human religions that as a rule appeal to revelation and sometimes hold to all sorts of foolishness. He is of the
opinion that revealed religion should never embrace anything other than
what is consistent with reason. The god of revelation cannot contradict the
god that speaks to us through our reason. To that extent we have a yardstick
for measuring the distance between good and evil. With respect to Christianity, Locke was convinced that to a significant degree it was consistent
with the natural religion of reason. Jesus frequently defended pure, reasonable religion over against the Jews and their endless desire to stray into all
sorts of ceremonies. In other words, Jesus did not set aside the natural religion grounded in human reason, nor did he weigh it down with all kinds of
empty speculation. Rather, he grounded it on a sure foundation. That is why
Christianity is the most acceptable manifestation of natural religion.

Many were in total disagreement with this last opinion. Can one really
say that? In Christianity, are there not quite a number of doctrines that really
have very little to do with natural religion, which always only involves the
three cardinal concepts of God, virtue, and immortality? What is obvious is
that a great deal of discussion is still possible on this subject.

Meanwhile, in the Netherlands, Baruch Spinoza was reaching the same
sort of conclusions along entirely different lines. Spinoza had pledged his
heart to philosophy and therefore did not leave himself a lot of room for religion. True philosophy always concludes in the rational love for God *(amor
Dei intellectualis)* that constitutes a dimension of the eternal love with which
God loves himself.[25] But he understood that not all people are philosophical,
or even capable of being philosophical. For these others, prophets are necessary who speak not from the light of reason but in proposals grounded in
their powers of imagination. In the case of such prophets, it is all about people having to learn to walk in the way of obedience. Theology needs to con-
centrate solely on such teachings as reinforce faith *(fidei dogmata)* and as are
necessary for training in obedience. All the rest is merely ballast. As long as
religion limits itself to that, it will never run the danger of coming into conflict with philosophy.[26]

In the circles of Spinoza and his friends, people began circulating a little
treatise that shed bright light on the whole question of natural religion. This
was a small work by the Muslim philosopher Ibn Tufail (d. 1185 AD in Mo-

---

25. Spinoza, *The Ethics*, p. 238.
26. Baruch Spinoza, *Tractatus Theologo-Politicus* (1674), c. 15.

rocco) titled *Hai ibn Yaqzan.* The title means *"Alive, son of Awake."* The work was translated from Arabic into Latin in 1670, and in 1672 it appeared in the Dutch language, translated by Dr. Bouwmeester of Amsterdam. It had a significant impact on the philosophers of that period.[27]

In this book, Ibn Tufail explains how he was laid in a small trunk in his early youth and entrusted to the waves of the ocean. The little trunk washed up on an uninhabited island, where he was discovered and raised by a gazelle. He received no education whatsoever. All that he came to know, he learned through his own experience and reflection. Then, as a bright twenty-eight-year-old, he first came to the overwhelming thought that this world, with its great variety of plants and animals and with the logical order that governs everything, must be the handiwork of a supreme Maker. In the years that followed, he gradually began to understand this Supreme Being more fully. By his own intuition, he also came to the point of directly contemplating this world in the light of eternity. He learned to understand his own reason as a power related to God and born of God. He also now began to understand that he had to bring the lower, sensual powers of his nature under control, that he had to suppress his passions and his sensitivity to sorrow and grief, and that he had to give free rein to the power of his spirit. Following all of this self-transcending asceticism, he ultimately arrived at the point of penetrating to knowledge of the very being of God.

After Hai ibn Yaqzan had achieved this level of wisdom, a Muslim pilgrim named Asal landed on his island on a given day. He had determined that he would climb to a higher level of insight into the Qur'an and into the tradition of Muslim jurisprudence. As soon as Hai and Asal were able to understand one another, they began to exchange their thoughts extensively and came to the surprising discovery that they were in full agreement with each other. Everything that Asal had appropriated from his long years of studying the Qur'an, the tradition, and theology, Hai had discovered himself through his own quiet musing. They now saw that the Qur'an is in complete agreement with what one could discover for oneself using natural, human reason, provided one had not been misled by any external force. That indicates that

27. Ed. note: Ibn Tufail (c. 1105-1185; known by his Latinized name as Abubacer Aben Tofail) is best known for writing the first philosophical novel, *Hai ibn Yaqzan*/Hayy ibn Yaqdhan (Latin: *Philosophus Autodidactus;* English: *The Improvement of Human Reason: Exhibited in the Life of Hai Ebn Yakdhan*), in the western world. Key themes include a desert island and a feral child coming of age and discovering, without any contact with other human beings, through reasoned inquiry alone, the ultimate truth about the universe. The work is influenced by Avicenna and later influenced John Locke.

prophets are only necessary in this world because all people simply do not have the leisure and persistence to work through with their own reason the multitude of impressions overwhelming them. But revelation is actually no longer necessary for the philosopher, since he is able to discover by himself everything communicated in the books of the prophets.

Completely overwhelmed by this common discovery, the two men decided to go to the populated world in order to preach their faith. They arrived at the world of King Salaman[28] and began teaching enthusiastically that the deepest truth of the Muslim faith is no different than the natural religion contained in the human spirit itself, and that everything else should be regarded as form and packaging. Remarkably, this preaching aroused no enthusiasm at all among the population, and people simply clung to their inherited forms and customs. They tolerated nothing conveyed by this wisdom. Least of all was the king well disposed toward them, and he saw in their arrival danger for the rest of his people. The end of the story, then, is this: Hai and Asal once again separated themselves from the general population and quietly returned to their isolated island, where they had enjoyed so much blessing together.[29] The moral of this writing is understandably this: a natural religion that is rooted in human reason definitely exists. This natural religion agrees entirely with what constitutes the kernel of the Qur'an and Islamic theology. Whoever seriously allows himself or herself to be led by natural reason possesses what is sufficient and discovers by it all that is religiously necessary. If some of the Enlightenment philosophers took the trouble of demonstrating that Christianity is the purest form of natural religion derived via reason, here, clothed in childishly simple language, is the account that gives Islam claim to the title of honor in that regard.

Meanwhile, the entire situation became even more complicated by the fact that during the same century all kinds of writings by Chinese thinkers began penetrating Europe. At that time, Jesuit missionaries were working in China, and these missionaries were men of substantial scientific ability. They caused a burning interest in Chinese religious writings at the time, and they translated a number of those works into Latin. Thus it happened, that about the same time that the little book of Ibn Tufail was making an impression on Europe, various sacred writings from China began to see the light of day in Europe.

28. Ed. note: On a neighboring island.

29. Tjitze J. de Boer, *The History of Philosophy in Islam,* trans. Edward R. Jones (London: Luzac, 1965), pp. 182-84.

The impression made by these books was simply amazing. Here people had religious writings in front of them that were weaned from any dogmatics and from all useless contemplation, but were only directed at time-honored moral prescriptions. This religion was, theologically speaking, the simplest of all religions. It certainly talked about a Supreme Being, but it lacked any discussion of complicated temple ceremonies and such things. There was no talk of difficult doctrinal positions such as a virgin birth, atonement, and so forth, but it definitely promoted obedient living with liveliness and insistence. It also made mention of justice, on the basis of which good is rewarded and evil is punished. Isn't this exactly what people were looking for? Wasn't this natural religion, probably without external packaging? No one less than the renowned philosopher Leibniz spoke enthusiastically about Chinese religion.

> The irresistible grip of moral corruption has, in my opinion, reached the level that it appears very necessary that Chinese missionaries be sent to us, in order that they may teach us about the value and practice of natural theology, just as we send them our missionaries to preach what has been revealed.[30]

Simply stated, we need to be instructed by the Chinese in natural religion, since they appear to be much further developed than we are in it.

This is how people in those days pondered about the relationship between natural religion and the religions that developed historically. Natural religion was actually the norm, the trunk from which the historically developed religions sprouted like branches on a tree. But these branches were laden with all kinds of superstitious ideas and customs. Degeneration, priestly dishonesty, and confusion had all played a huge role in these historical religions. Our task, and the future task, is to penetrate beneath all of that division, corruption, cover-up, and pretense to the heart of natural religion. Voltaire says somewhere, "Remember that from the heights of natural religion, eternal wisdom has been inscribed on the depths of your heart."[31]

Obviously, in all of these explanations, revelation is put in a difficult position. Moreover, what is revelation anyway? People were inclined to see it as

30. Nathan Söderblom, *Das Werden des Gottesglaubens*, p. 301.

31. G. van der Leeuw, "Inzichten betreffende godsdienst en geschiedenis aan het eind der achttiende en het begin der negentiede eeuw," in *Geschiedenis: Een bundel studies, aangeboden aan Prof. Dr W. J. Aalders bij zijn afscheid als hoogleraar aan de Rijksuniversiteit te Groningen, 1942* (Assen: n.p., 1944), p. 132.

an intuitive projection, a predisposition to see in images and symbols what reason much later and with difficulty tracks down. Schiller once pointedly put it like this: "What maturing reason (finally) discovered after thousands of years had already (long) been revealed before to the childlike mind in symbol(s) of beauty and greatness."[32]

That captured it. Revelation is childish preconceptions. Already centuries earlier, prophets intuited things in poetic language what reason would conquer with difficulty only after considerable struggle. But that kind of revelation is certainly entirely different from what Paul once said: "What no eye has seen, what no ear has heard, and what no human heart has considered, God has prepared for those that love him" (1 Cor. 2:9). But that is a long way from what the thinkers and poets of the Age of Enlightenment meant.

With Kant, the entire issue is not all that different. It was certainly true that Kant did not value religious consciousness on the basis of what he called "pure reason" or theoretical thought. He took his starting point more in practical reason, in moral awareness, in the knowledge of the "thou shalt" that addresses us every moment. But having made that observation, we note that the matter is the same in many respects.

For even Kant believed that people can dredge up from the depths of their own beings the great truths of the law, of freedom (his notion of "you are able"), of God, and of justice. That all of this is understood by practical reason, as part of moral consciousness, is completely natural. By the light of practical reason, all of us feel that sin, "the principle of evil," has a powerful hold on us, and we start to learn the importance of striving against that force. Actually, all those filled with that desire should feel compelled to unite as one people of God. In practice, that is impossible, however, since all sorts of walls erected in the name of faith differences cause division. That happens because people place more weight on holy books, prophets, and revelation than on the voice speaking within their deepest beings. Yet, gradually the faith of the church, or faith as proclaimed by the church, will give way to rational religion. Then the kingdom of God will come on this earth. Kant thought he already saw several hopeful signs of this great victory happening.[33]

32. Ed. note: Bavinck provides no reference for the quotation; the passage is from Schiller's lengthy poetic defense of poetry, "Die Künstler" (1789). For a recent study, see Katrin Kohl, "Poets Triumphant: The Contest with Philosophy in Schiller's 'Die Künstler,'" *Publications of the English Goethe Society* 79, no. 1 (March 2010): 28-41. The editor is indebted to Professor Barbara Carvill of Calvin College's German Department for finding the reference and assisting in translation.

33. Kant, *Religion within the Boundaries of Mere Reason*, pp. 122-29.

All of this would be a lot simpler if people simply detached themselves from all useless, dogmatic hair-splitting and simply listened to Jesus as he addresses us in the four Gospels. For Jesus did not preach dogmas; he limited himself to proclaiming a rational, moral religion that we all recognize and are able to embrace.[34]

When one reviews these ideas of Kant, one recognizes that here once again he was reaching back to natural religion, and that here once again the assumption was being made that true Christianity is in full accord with natural religion. Only the speculating and theorizing of precisionist theologians has saddled us with a long list of doctrinal propositions that have nothing to do any longer with natural reason.

The spell of the notion of natural religion was finally broken to some degree by Schleiermacher when a reckoning with world history gradually gained influence. Schleiermacher still preferred reasoning on the basis of rather vague concepts about religion. He defined it successively as "a sense of and yearning for the eternal," "existing and living in and through God," "feeling totally one with nature," a "sense of the universal," and other such expressions. It all remained quite cloudy. Above all, it seemed as though Schleiermacher saw religion in terms of what we identified as the first element in religious consciousness, namely the idea of totality. The universal played an important role in Schleiermacher's thinking.[35]

Although Schleiermacher did not work with a very clear-cut definition of the concept "religion," he strongly resisted the thought of a natural religion. Such a thing simply does not exist, he stated curtly. If one would attempt to construct one, it would have such an indefinite character that one could really not operate with it. Natural religion is found nowhere, and everywhere we only encounter defined, historically developed religions. Humanity is far too discerning by disposition, both in thought and feeling, than to be capable of depending on one, universal, undiscriminating religion. The eternal is reflected in all of our lives in various ways, and we do well to be very attentive to that diversity. There are tribes among whom the divine is only experienced as a mysterious power. There are others that have already understood that there are gods, but who still regard the gods as persons that exist alongside or sometimes over against one another because they have not yet comprehended the unity within the universe. Still others think there is

---

34. Kant, *Religion within the Boundaries of Mere Reason*, pp. 160-64.

35. Friedrich Schleiermacher, *On Religion: Speeches to Its Cultured Despisers*, trans. and ed. Richard Crouter (Cambridge: Cambridge University Press, 1988).

one, high, personal God, but they do not see that God as being in living fellowship with us. And finally, there are people who out of reverence hesitate to apply the idea of personhood to God, since they experience God much more as a mysterious force that breathes in everything that exists and thus also lives and works in ourselves. All of this is religion, a sense of the eternal, but that one sense is differentiated in numerous forms. Wherever that sense is actually found, religion exists, even though the religions do not all have equal value.[36] In his *Christian Faith* Schleiermacher later attempted to demonstrate that Christianity preaches total dependence on the one God and that it, therefore, is at the pinnacle of all religions.[37]

People gradually became more discriminating about this diversity, therefore, and they began to see that it was important not to trivialize the differences between religions or to belabor topics like the corruption of the priestly class. We definitely face very different religious structures, and it makes no sense to want to toss all of them on the same pile. These religious structures have each had their own history. They are all rooted in the profound life-perceptions of their own people and need to be understood in that context. The thinking of the Enlightenment was far too ahistorical and abstract to work effectively in its approach to the religious problem. Schleiermacher was right when he said that something like natural religion does not exist, that we encounter it nowhere, and that we can only construct it in the places where we retreat to do our private, isolated study and reflection. It becomes obvious that it is totally impossible to measure the various living, breathing, historically developed religions on the Procrustean bed of philosophically construed natural religion. We would be well advised to discard once and for all that vague concept of "natural religion" in the sense in which it was understood during the age of the Enlightenment. In reality, we are not dealing with a completely reasonable natural religion in various dilutions and mixtures, but we are dealing with many religions, each of which displays its own character.

With that said, we are not yet finished with the problem. For all of the historically developed religions, however different they may be from one another, nevertheless have remarkable points of comparison. All of them discuss something like a higher power or divinity, or whatever people choose to call it. They all attempt to see the entire world as a meaningful, structured totality or as a universe possessing harmonic interdependence within which

36. Schleiermacher, *On Religion*, Second Speech: On the Essence of Religion, pp. 18-54.
37. Friedrich Schleiermacher, *Christian Faith*, §7-10, 31-52.

human life has purpose and value. All of them manifest a concept of moral norms, of the command "thou shalt." Each one of them also has a concept comparable to our concept of sin. They show an awareness of life's brokenness, misery, and need for deliverance and salvation. Not all of these characteristics are equally clear in all of them, but we nonetheless discover something of them universally. It is certainly the case that people understand very different things by the different terms we meet. The Buddhist concept of nirvana cannot be compared with the idea of Walhalla in Germanic tribal religion. One cannot compare the hideous deities of many tribal faiths with Allah. A huge gulf exists between the Hindu idea of sin tied to *samsara* or ignorance and, for example, the concept of sin that we encounter in the Babylonian psalms. One simply cannot treat all these concepts alike. They are separated from one another by too much to permit that. But one thing is definitely noteworthy, namely that the religious thought of all these sources has apparently been motivated by the same concerns and manifests the same consciousness. That in itself is already hugely surprising. For that matter, the remarkable fact that the Bible has been able to be translated into all the languages of the world speaks volumes. Frequently it was thought to be unthinkably difficult to accomplish this, but ultimately people have been able to discover terms in all the world's languages that are suitable for biblical concepts like God, creation, sin, forgiveness, grace, and redemption.

For this reason, one cannot say that a natural religion exists, or that it once existed, from which all other religions have grown like branches on a single tree. That image, as has become obvious, is simply wrong. But, in addition, something else needs to be said. There seems to be a kind of framework within which human religions need to operate. There appear to be definite points of contact around which all kinds of ideas crystallize. There seem to be quite vague feelings — one might better call them direction signals — that have been actively brooding everywhere. How people have conceptualized those feelings, the content that they have poured into them, the way in which they have understood and explained them, is all as expansively varied between the different religions as the breadth of the heavens. The amazing fact is that we are becoming increasingly aware that all religions belonging to the so-called primitive religions exhibit a range of sensitivities that are at least comparable even though the religions themselves are in principle different.

Perhaps this can be expressed thus: there seem to be definite magnetic points[38] that time and again irresistibly compel human religious thought.

38. Ed. note: See the unnumbered note at the beginning of Chapter 3.

Human beings cannot escape their power but must provide an answer to those basic questions posed to them. They can answer them with foolish myths, with fairy tales, with totally unique thought-forms, but they cannot ignore them. They impose themselves on people, and in one way or another people must come clean about them. People are simply driven to think about a higher power, about gods and ghosts, or about whatever they might call this force. They are driven to believe in some sort of moral code, however foolishly they might subsequently work that code out. They are driven to summarize all of the connections involving personal life and the world as a whole into some sort of meaningful and coherent plan. They are driven to recognize something of their own limitation, brokenness, and thirst for something like deliverance and liberation. They can pursue the most diverse approaches imaginable; they can push God as far away as possible; they can flee from him and to some ephemeral, invisible force; they can think of him as an entire pantheon of contentious gods and goddesses. In short, they go off in all sorts of directions; but one direction they can never escape. They can never escape dealing with those fundamental issues and remaining within that mysterious framework where all the big religious questions are found.

"What lies behind all of this?" we are compelled to ask ourselves. Where does it come from? If there is no such thing as natural religion, what then are we dealing with? That is one of the problems with which the theological thought of our time needs to wrestle, since this specific issue penetrates so deeply into our assessment of the religious question.

The operative thought can be, and in fact often has been, that religion in human life ultimately rests on an a-priori. This is to say, it is based on a tendency or capacity of our reason or it has been inherent in our humanity itself from the very beginning. People simply *must* react religiously to the realities in their personal lives and in the world at large, based on some deep and inner compulsion. Rudolf Otto was one of the first to expose that compulsion. He did so in his book *The Idea of the Holy (Das Heilige)*. The sense of the holy or religious awe Otto regarded as the core religious experience. Otto was of the opinion that this sense of the holy was not predicated on all kinds of experiences that people may have had, but that it points directly back to a religious a-priori inherent in human nature itself. "No such thing as natural religion exists," says Otto. Nor is such a thing possible. It is impossible to explain religion in terms of something else, for "religion is itself present at its commencement."[39] But what definitely exists and must exist is that religious

---

39. Rudolf Otto, *The Idea of the Holy,* p. 132.

a-priori, that origin. Otherwise, the entire phenomenon of religion that has been of such overwhelming importance would simply be unexplainable. The origin, or instinct, or whatever one wants to call it, based on the reality people have witnessed historically, simply must be understood in a religious sense. History "develops our disposition for knowing the holy."[40] People did not come into the world with the idea of the holy clearly and completely formed or as an innate idea. They needed all sorts of experiences in order to come to that idea of the holy. But the fact that those experiences awakened that idea in them is due to that mysterious tendency within that rendered them amenable to an impression of the holy.

There is something in this explanation of Otto that appeals to us. We have concluded that natural religion does not exist. But we noted that there definitely are a framework, direction signals, and magnetic forces. Concerning this subject, one can raise a host of questions. Are we perhaps talking about the same thing as Otto? And in his explanation of a religious a-priori, might we not find the explanation of the fact that religion is such a universal and ineradicable phenomenon? These questions will have to receive our fuller attention shortly.

§11. Religious Consciousness and Psychology

But first, we have to take a minute to address another question, namely whether it might be possible to explain the phenomenon of religion simply along psychological lines. Is religion really something so extraordinary? Is it not perfectly plausible to explain religion as a type of psychological disorder, as a deficit in mature development, as childlike sentimentality? In short, if we came at it from that angle, would we not be able in that case to talk about an a-priori or a tendency or some such thing? Would that not make all of this much simpler to interpret?

It is necessary to get into this because that approach has actually been taken time and again. Most recently, by name, it has been Freud who simply wanted to explain religion in terms of all the machinations going on in the life of the soul. And it can hardly be denied that in this endeavor he has put his finger on all kinds of extremely fascinating phenomena. The thought process of Freud and the psychoanalytic school is sufficiently well known in general that we can confine ourselves to a few general observations. Freud

40. Otto, *The Idea of the Holy*, p. 176.

reduces the entire life of the human soul to desire, to libido, which from the very earliest years of life is a huge reservoir from which all of a person's impulses come to the surface. Already in early childhood, however, restraints come into play. These are connected to the fact that the small child develops in the social context of father and mother and because he or she finds well-being, safety, and harmony in its shelter. It is particularly the father that fosters the impression of strength, protection, authority, and recognition on the young child. But the father also repeatedly intrudes into the child's life with his expectations and restrictions. In a sense, therefore, he stands as the big restraint between the libido and its free expression. In the child's respect for the father figure, the child unconsciously begins to identify with him and to take on that role him- or herself. From this, the ideal of the ego develops in the child's soul, more or less shaped by the father figure. Due to all sorts of disturbances in human life, that father figure can be projected and assume huge dimensions; it can become "god." The concept of God is really nothing more than a projection of the ideal father figure that a child has appropriated in early childhood. All the feelings that the child then had toward the father figure — honor, fear, sorrow, love, etc. — he or she now directs to his or her image of God that was actually shaped in the child's distant past. The idea of God was born out of the erotic experiences of his or her earliest childhood and from the restraints, the repressed thoughts, and the tensions connected with them at that time.[41]

Reading treatments such as this is unsettling and painful. Could it really be true that religion is nothing more than neurotic disturbance and remnants of infancy in the full-grown person? Could it be that God is no more than a powerful projection of an ideal image that has developed with us and before whom we turn either to tremble fearfully or to kneel in adoration? One shudders momentarily when one thinks about this. Rümke says somewhere that it does no good "to hastily discard or ridicule" such psychological explanations;[42] they possess far too many elements of truth. For, it cannot be denied that the image of God in many people often displays signs of neurotic obsession. It is also undeniably the case that all sorts of infantile sentimentality and erotic tensions still play a major role in the religious lives of many people. Religion is an extremely complicated phenomenon. In the course of history, it

---

41. A. Kuypers and J. H. Bavinck, *Inleiding in de Zielkunde,* 2nd ed. (Kampen: J. H. Kok, 1935), pp. 313-31.

42. H. C. Rümke, *Karakter en Aanleg in verband met het ongeloof* (Amsterdam: n.p., 1935), p. 45.

has often been expressed in forms that are intimately tied to sensuality and to sexual lust. But that is not really the point. The question is not whether religion in some or perhaps even in numerous instances exhibits signs of connections with a father figure or a mother figure, or even expresses neurotic or infantile traits and is a warped institution. The question is whether religion is *always* that or whether it is *essentially* that. The question is whether God is the product of our subconscious, a thoroughly false projection of inner experiences that we objectify and, as a deity, has no external reality at all. The question is whether, when faith would be liberated from all those infantile fixations, it would simply disappear, or whether something of it might not still remain. Rümke gives this answer to that question: "Our ties to our father and our mother, instead of fostering our faith, very clearly impede our faith. My experience in numerous psychoanalytic sessions has taught me that the way to faith is opened up when infantile fixations are discarded."[43]

To reach a clearly defined judgment concerning these ideas of Freud is extremely difficult. Van der Leeuw once reproached Freud for directly reducing everything to mechanistic processes. "But Freud scarcely gets around to the soul and to the person."[44] That is probably stated too crassly, but a dimension of truth is undoubtedly contained in it. At least with respect to religion it is obvious that he has not seen it as a large, deep, all-embracing phenomenon in human history with wide ramifications. When one of Freud's friends wrote that the actual source of religion, namely a sense of the eternal and the supernatural, completely eluded him, Freud responded with these remarkable words; "I simply cannot discover within myself this 'oceanic' feeling."[45] He had focused all his attention so resolutely on the erotic and on the conflicts, deformities, compulsions, and tensions associated with it that it became impossible for him to consider a phenomenon like religion in its total scope and value.

With respect to the validity of all these and similar psychological theories explaining religion, we note that their power is hidden in the fact that they prove nothing but only attempt to provide attractive explanations. In our own country, Vestdijk not long ago endeavored to shed light on the problem of religion by means of a psychological approach. He also con-

---

43. H. C. Rümke, *Karakter en Aanleg,* p. 47.

44. G. van der Leeuw, *Psychologie en Wereldbeschouwing* (Gereformeerde Psychologische Studievereeniging, 1941), p. 20.

45. R. Vedder, "Critische beschouwingen naar annleiding van Freud's Totem und Tabu," in *Het Orgaan der Christelijke Vereeniging van Natuur — en Geneeskundigen in Nederland* (1944), p. 1.

nected his insights directly to the experiences of very early childhood, namely to the feeling of security so characteristic of a young child. The child seeks to satisfy "his yearning for love, power, freedom, confidence, knowledge, and insight" through other people, especially father and mother and his own self. From that position, he or she then develops the idea of "the complete person,"[46] the "immortal person."[47] Vestdijk takes the position, like Freud, that a person then projects that ideal image beyond self and fashions it into a god, endowing it with majesty and glory and other qualities.[48] Once again, in Vestdijk's case too, people time and again have the oppressive feeling that he has really not seen religion for what it is. Yet, it is practically impossible to argue against him because he only opposes, presumes, and pontificates. Freud and Vestdijk, along with all the others who approach the religious problem from a psychological perspective, will not and cannot prove that what they say is true. And for those who do not share their interpretation, it is also impossible to disprove their constructions as untrue. We are impotent over against one another. We cannot refute one another because it appears that we have at this point reached the mysterious boundary of scientific knowledge and investigation.

Thus, the persuasive force of a book like Vestdijk's clearly does not lie in the fact that he actually demonstrates and proves something. Its potency lies only in this: perhaps many who read it find there what they themselves already feel, what they already think, and then, on the basis of completely irrational and subconscious factors, are spontaneously affirming it.

We have, therefore, definitely reached a boundary here. To this point, we have been able to write calmly and purely descriptively. We have been able to point to the fact that certain ideas are held universally, that certain sentiments are felt everywhere, that certain ideas have lived in all places. We have frequently been able to point to evidences of this from both antiquity and modern times. But now we can go no further; now we have hit a wall. We have seen religious consciousness as it unmistakably exists and as it has always existed. We have seen how it stamps all of life and how it affects the understanding of life in all its dimensions. But now we have reached a boundary. Where does this religious consciousness originate? From what spring in the depths of the human soul does it burble up?

46. Simon Vestdijk, *De Toekomst der Religie* (Arnhem: Van Loghum Slaterus, 1947), p. 32.

47. Vestdijk, *De Toekomst der Religie*, p. 45.

48. Vestdijk, *De Toekomst der Religie*, chapter 3.

To repeat: we have hit a wall here. The human eye cannot see over it; human thought cannot penetrate it. Here we can only speak from the vantage point of faith; here we can only talk theologically. This is not disappointing — at least it does not have to be. We need to keep a sharp eye on the fact that Otto, Freud, and Vestdijk also speak from the perspective of faith when they talk about these matters. Here our eyesight fails as it squints into the nebulous distance, and there is no one who is able to penetrate that mist by means of his or her own thought or proofs.

This whole subject, in all its dimensions, rests on a mystery. All of our own inner life — our hating and loving, our thinking and dreaming, our searching and our wandering — is rooted in that mystery. Whoever does not feel this or whoever has never felt it has not yet achieved genuine knowledge. We have reached the point of dealing with ultimate assumptions and the most fundamental principles. Here we are overcome with the awareness of how infinitesimal and powerless we really are — an awareness so characteristic of our human existence. We stand momentarily in this thoroughly baffling world, and we have no knowledge of its origin, its destiny, or how it all works.

From this point on, we are only going to be able to speak theologically. That means that we are going to have to listen to God. Only he is able to explain that religious consciousness that we have been reviewing. Only he is able to show us where it comes from and where it will end. Only God can explain for us the matters of sin, distortion, and deterioration. Only reverence for "the wisdom of God" that comes to us in "the foolishness of preaching" gives us answers on these concerns.

5 Religious Consciousness in History

§1. God

Now we approach a different assignment where everything is turned entirely around. To this point, we have been discussing humanity and something inherent in it, carefully observing religious consciousness as that comes to expression in humanity, and ultimately arriving at the question of the origin of that consciousness. Now we come face to face with an entirely different question: Does that religious consciousness have anything at all to do with God? Does it rest in one way or another on revelation, that is, on divine activity or speech? Is it explainable in terms of humanity alone, or is it only understandable when we bring God into the picture?

As a rule, psychological research never deals with this set of questions. Vestdijk's book, for example,[1] never once raised the question about the truthfulness of religion since for his purposes it was entirely unimportant. The psychologist is interested in religious consciousness purely as a human phenomenon, and he or she wants to explain it purely in human terms. But in the long run, that point of view cannot be sustained. We need to know whether that consciousness, which flows through all of world history like a broad river, corresponds at all to any reality or whether it merely rests on some desperate illusion. When in the previous century Tylor attempted to explain the

---

1. Ed. note: The reference, not indicated here by Bavinck, is to S. Vestdijk, *De Toekomst der Religie* (Arnhem, 1947); Bavinck concluded the previous chapter with a brief introduction to Vestdijk and continues it here.

origin of religion in terms of "primitive"[2] ideas about dreams, the soul, or sickness and death, criticism rightly arose from many sides. And the point of the criticism was that, if Tylor were correct, humanity would have been living with a horrible misunderstanding for all those previous centuries. "In the end, religion would be only a dream, systematized and lived, but without foundation in the real."[3] That same objection could be offered against all the psychological theories of the modern era. If they are true, then people for all these centuries would have been drinking themselves drunk on a phantasm, a neurosis, and a frightful misunderstanding. In that case, the noblest expressions of humanity, its deepest longings and hopes, its sense of guilt, its humility, its boundless trust, and its sense of dependence would all be products of fatal error. All of the world's cultures have developed on the basis of a world-and-life view that is religious. According to the position of the well-known American ethnologist Bronislaw Malinowski, this is not the result of some "cultural epiphenomenon," a by-product of culture, but it is the result of a deeply moral and social force that produces "ultimate integration" in a culture, carries it, and binds it together.[4] If the former were the case, then religion would have been born out of an untenable understanding of dreaming or would have developed from some kind of distorted eroticism. Obviously and above all, we need clarity on this point. What is the basis for the origin of religion? Does it lie with humanity or with God? What precisely is religion? Is it an understanding, a way of life, a conviction, an amalgamation of ideas and emotions born out of our humanity? Or, is it in its deepest sense an answer to what God has first spoken and a reaction to what God did first, to some divine action? We are unable to ignore these questions any longer.

In this connection, we need to understand that generally speaking all things related to human life have both a mother and a father. Science, for example, was not simply born out of the human spirit, but it arose from the human spirit because and to the extent that it is situated in the world, endeavors to make sense of the meaningful relationships that exist in the world around a person, and attempts to understand the thought encountered in the world. The fine arts were not born in the human heart unaided. Artists would never take a brush in hand unless they were not continually struck by the beauty of the world around them. Similarly, poets would never feel a sin-

2. Ed. note: See Chapter 3, notes 23 and 25, for comments about the term "primitive."

3. Emile Durkheim, *The Elementary Forms of Religious life*, trans. Karen E. Fields (New York: The Free Press, 1995), pp. 65-66.

4. Bronislaw Malinowski, *The Dynamics of Culture Change* (New Haven: Yale University Press, 1945), p. 48.

gle line of poetry born within them unless they were constantly inspired by what they saw around them, by what they personally experienced, or by the multicolored hues of the world and of life itself. Humanity is certainly rich with unbelievable possibilities, but not for a second should we ever think of humanity as disengaged from the existential relationships in which human beings exist. In and of itself, a person is nothing, but always exists in relationship, and it is out of those relationships that we live, think, and create.

Now the question is, "What about religion?" It arises in the human heart; it is born within a person. But what is behind it? What moves people to respond religiously to reality? Once again, we face the inevitable problem of whether religion has anything at all to do with God. And if it has something to do with God, then God is not only one element in religion, but he is the origin and the deepest basis for religion. Then he is the only meaning for religion.

As soon as we approach the Bible armed with this question, it strikes us as completely self-evident that religion has something to do with God, so that the most compelling emphasis falls on God's revelation, on what God himself says. God speaks, and all human stammering about God is to be understood as nothing other than an answer and a response. God alone always takes the initiative; what a person does, thinks, dreams, or wishes is reverberation. A person never acts simply from self, but exists because God is perpetually involved with him or her and sustains him or her in life. "In him we live and move and have our being" (Acts 17:28).

It requires no further proof that all of this is of supreme importance for understanding religion. One neither can nor may think about humanity apart from what God has said. In many respects, that divine speech is amazingly remarkable. After a brief initial word about the way day and night quietly fade into one another, one of the Psalms says, "There is no speech, there are no words, their voice is not heard; yet their voice goes out over all the earth" (Ps. 19:3-5). And therein is the puzzle — one could almost say, the paradoxical nature of God's speech fully considered. "There is no speech, there are no words . . . and yet their voice goes out." This passage is all about speech without words, witness without words, that makes an impact on people with invisible force and against which they have no defense because it engulfs them all around in its silent majesty. Whenever the Bible delves more deeply into these matters, it sheds fuller light on new dimensions of creation. Take the starry heavens, first of all, whose dark and endless expanse sends shivers up the spine: "When I consider the heavens, the work of your hands, the moon and the stars that you have made, what is man?" (Ps. 8:4-5). Then, again, there are the mountains, those aloof and princely mountains wearing a forested crown topped with sparkling snow: "You, who have established the mountains by your power and girded them with strength" (Ps. 65:7). But most of all, it is the order, the regular order of day and night and the seasons that follow one another, that evokes praise (Ps. 104). Even the animals are subject to that order: "Even the stork in the heavens knows her appointed times" (Jer. 8:7). The entire universe, in which puny humans are caught up, is an incomparably huge system from which the depths of divine thought take shape everywhere.

All of this belongs, more or less, to the area of reflection and contemplation based on the wordless speech of nature's majesty. God stands before us in the totality of the universe.

Alongside it, revelation is spoken about in an entirely different way when we talk about what we usually call God's "general revelation." The Old Testament in general scarcely makes any mention of the conscience, although the concept is not entirely lacking there. In Amos 4:13 we read this remarkable summary of divine work: "For behold, he who forms the mountains creates the wind and makes known his thoughts to man, he turns the dawn into darkness and walks on the heights of the earth." What impresses us here is that suddenly, in the middle of a poetic depiction of natural phenomena, the remarkable clause is inserted: "and makes known his thoughts to man." Obviously what we are talking about here is what we now call a person's self-consciousness or the discerning eye by which the person understands what he or she thinks and does. People have knowledge of themselves, and know that the discerning eye is also a critical eye. People always are simultaneously doers, observers, and judges. They act, but they also know what they are doing and evaluate what they are doing. In the final instance, this reflects something that comes from God. In that ability to see oneself and to be self-critical, something stifling can be found. And this is something that people should want to escape as well as something that should drive them to despair. Something of God also exists in the great mystery of that double effect on our self-consciousness. It is directly connected to God. "He makes known his thoughts to man."

The same motif is also clearly articulated in Psalm 139. There, as well, the Psalmist trembles at knowing that God "searches and knows" us. "You know my thoughts from afar." This knowledge causes worshipful amazement: "Such knowledge is too wonderful for me." Then, all at once the poet becomes indescribably fearful: "Where can I go from your Spirit; where can I flee from your presence?" That same sense of God's presence exists in the depths of our inner lives, in our consciences.

In Elihu's oration in the book of Job, this insight is developed in a particularly beautiful and poetic manner.

For God does speak — now one way, now another —
though no one perceives it.
In a dream, in a vision of the night,
when deep sleep falls on people
as they slumber in their beds,
he may speak in their ears
and terrify them with warnings,
to turn them from wrongdoing
and keep them from pride.

(Job 33:14-17 TNIV)[5]

What is impressive is how vibrant and realistic all of this is. While the word "conscience" is absent here, the conscience itself is reflected in the passage. Already here in the Old Testament, God's personal intervention in the lives of individuals is seen. When the conscience speaks, as in a dream while a person is sleeping on his or her bed, God "opens his or her ears." Very personal, actual encounters with God occur then.

A strong emphasis is often laid on the presence of God in the events of everyday life, in each individual's personal history, and in the history of an entire people. Particularly in the book of Proverbs, numerous examples are provided of the subtle connection that exists between that perplexing reality that we call sin and suffering in life. The Hindu religion has the concept of karma for designating that automatically activated connection between evil and punishment; punishment follows evils with ironclad necessity. In the book of Proverbs as well as elsewhere in the Old Testament, we find a number of passages that have a karma-like sound to them. Here it is as though sin gives birth to suffering totally automatically. In this connection, I think of texts like Proverbs 1:31: "they will eat the fruit of their ways"; 5:22, "The evil deeds of the wicked ensnare them; the cords of their sins hold them fast." I think of words from the prophet Jeremiah as well: "Your wickedness will punish you; your backsliding will rebuke you" (Jer. 2:19). Most often, sin punishes itself, and in some instances it almost seems as though sin is its own punishment.[6] That same law applies with emphasis. "Righteousness exalts a nation, but sin condemns any people" (Prov. 14:34). Here as well, that karma-like, completely mysterious, and totally inscrutable phenomenon that in the long run sin never does anything but drag misery along behind it.

5. Ed. note: All subsequent biblical references will use Today's New International Version (TNIV).

6. See J. H. Bavinck, *Christus en de Mystiek van het Oosten*, pp. 185ff.; *JHBR*, p. 373.

In the prophetic books, the problem of history is tackled from an entirely different angle. There history is seen primarily from the perspective of God's exalted plan for his people and for his church. All the questions become endlessly more complicated because world events are depicted in terms of one, central idea. But even there, the principle of God's presence in all events is maintained with strict attention. In the entire course of life, in destiny, in life's assigned portion, which is so intimately tied to and often coincides with a specific action in one's life, God is always present. This is why, while all sorts of expressions in the Bible may sound like they express the law of karma, they are really always intended theologically. No automatically activated force of righteousness exists, but the constant and living presence of God certainly does. And it is almost palpable and visible in all that happens.

On the basis of all these biblical references, already in antiquity theology formulated the doctrine of general revelation. It was completely justified in doing so, for general revelation is actually clearly taught in Scripture. Theology has certainly often understood it much too abstractly, too often as an impersonal idea. But in the Bible, particularly in the Old Testament, general revelation is intended to be much more personal. God's majesty is certainly revealed throughout the entire world. But in each instance that it is, whenever a given person begins to see that majesty, when his or her eyes are opened to it and he or she is overwhelmed by it, general revelation takes on the character of a very individual intervention. Conscience is definitely a very universal phenomenon, but when a person is addressed by it, that becomes a very individual encounter. "God speaks in one of two ways." In other words, that so-called general revelation is depicted for us in the Bible as a much more personal involvement of God with each person than we in our theology once understood it to be. We will have to rethink our theological concepts repeatedly in order to disentangle them from all their abstract philosophical accretions and to understand them again in terms of biblical reality.

§2. Natural Knowledge of God

In this study, we are not first of all concerned with the works of God, such as his revelation, but with the religious consciousness that comes to expression in human beings. In other words, we do not have to be preoccupied with general revelation in and of itself, but with the effect that it has on people and what results from that general revelation, what it does to people.

The immediate impression we have is that the Bible speaks about this only rarely. In the Old Testament, very little attention is given to the fruit produced by general revelation. In Psalm 147:19, definite emphasis is placed on the fact that the other nations are also subjects of God's activity (see, for example, vv. 7-9), but that God maintains his most intimate involvement with his people Israel. "He has revealed his word to Jacob, his laws and decrees to Israel" (v. 19). This preferred position conferred on Israel is further illumined in Amos 3:2: "You only have I chosen of all the families of the earth." From the outset, therefore, a sharp boundary is drawn between the territory where God gives his special revelation and that where he also definitely speaks in "the voiceless language" of his works.

The situation of the nations is generally portrayed in the Old Testament as being outside the domain of special revelation and as a condition of ignorance, refusal, and foolishness. Naturally, these other nations certainly have their gods, before whom they bow down, and these gods are also certainly called "gods" *(elohim)*. In the first commandment of the Decalogue, the possession of other gods is forbidden in the strongest possible language, but whether or not these gods really exist gets no attention at all. Even more remarkably, even the possibility of having no gods at all, thus of practical atheism, is not recognized as a real possibility. The nations definitely have their gods as well as their folk customs, but these *elohim* are merely *èlilim*, nonentities or idols. Particularly Jeremiah describes them using the term *hèbèl*, which means "vanity, worthlessness, delusion" (cf. 2:5, 10:15, etc.).

Our total impression, therefore, is that the broad and widely defined general revelation of God that is thoroughly intended as God's personal involvement with each person and with every nation individually has virtually no effect whatever. It is smeared over by human willfulness and folly, is completely misinterpreted, and is subjected to resistance and rejection. The result is no less than worship of the *elohim* that are only nonentities and vanities. There are a few places in the Bible that seem to indicate a somewhat different direction, but we do well to reserve consideration of them until later. Here we definitely need to register the observation that the question is nowhere raised of whether the worship of these nonentities by the heathen nations is not intended to be worship of God, the Maker of heaven and earth. Did they not actually intend to serve the only true God, and is the fact that they distorted his image so much not a consequence of their terrible misunderstanding of the voiceless language that he directed to all peoples? In reality, therefore, is theirs not worship of the same God, even though he is seen erroneously and his word is wrongly understood? That question is nowhere posited in this way. Rather, they are "other" gods, and in reality they are no gods at all (Isa. 37:19).

In the New Testament, the whole problem of the other religions is given sharp examination. Noteworthy is that the fact of ignorance is maintained also there. "You worship what you do not know," Jesus says to the Samaritan woman. The same riddle reappears: worshiping, but now knowing (John 4:22). In Lystra, Paul appeals to people to turn from their "vain deceit" to the living God. By "vain deceit" must have been meant the religion in which the people of that city were enslaved. Paul expresses himself most strongly in Ephesians 2:12, where he says about the Ephesians that before their conversion to Christ they were "without hope and without God in the world." The expression "without God" is exceptionally significant. At the time, they certainly had gods, but they did not have God. What they had offered no anchor and also provided no expectation.

Paul goes into this entire question more deeply in his speech on the Areopagus. The entire speech on the Areopagus is filled with difficulties that have kept minds busy from antiquity. These difficulties in part are connected with the fact that this is a missionary address. And in a missionary address things are stated completely differently than in a theological treatment intended for believers. The prophets of the Old Testament in their severe attacks against idolatry always addressed themselves to the people of Israel, the people that despite their knowledge of God were still subject to the charms and fascination of heathen idol worship. In that prophetic venue, only the sharpest condemnation calling for the rejection expressed was appropriate. But when Paul was standing on the Areopagus, matters were completely different. Here he was dealing with the heathen themselves, people who themselves bowed down to idols. Here people needed to be won over to the faith and walls needed to be broken down. That certainly was one of the causes for the more or less mild and friendly character of this address.[7]

The opening of his approach is already remarkable. "I see that in every way you are very religious" (Acts 17:22). Here Paul uses a neutral word: "religious."[8] He does not talk about idolatry or vanity, which would definitely not be appropriate here. But then he goes on to reflect on the altar to "an unknown god," and he continues: "you are ignorant of the very thing you worship — and this is what I am going to proclaim to you. The God who made

---

7. See J. H. Bavinck, *Alzoo wies het Woord* (Baarn: Bosch & Keuning, [1942]), chapter 6.

8. Ed. note: The Greek word is δεισιδαιμονεστέρους.

the world." Further along in his address, he also begins talking about what we have just called general revelation and God's personal involvement with every person. "He marked out their appointed times in history and the boundaries of their lands (God's involvement with history). God did this so that they would seek him and perhaps reach out for him and find him, though he is not far from any one of us." In this, a few very important matters are briefly touched on. When seen from God's side, his general revelation, his personal involvement with every nation and with every person, has a very specific intent, a purposive "so that." The intent is that God, through that language without speech, calls on these nations and individuals to seek him. God's general revelation is thus obviously intended to evoke a word of response from people in order to render people religiously active.

The question of how far that purpose is achieved, once again, lies beyond consideration here. What is present here is that heathendom is equivalent to a "not knowing." "What you worship without knowing it," is therefore a deep, fundamental, and radical ignorance. This is an ignorance that as a rule is cunningly camouflaged, but here is nakedly but unintentionally exposed by the Athenian altar. For, that one altar erected in Athens, dedicated to "an unknown god," is an acknowledgment that the entire heathen system of gods is based on ignorance. "In fact, the Athenians recognize by speaking about this one god that he must exist, and by acknowledging that they did not know him they admit that their entire system is no good."[9] By doing this, Paul puts them in a headlock. In a way, he is saying that the people of Athens, when they bow down to an unknown god, are actually worshiping him who created the heavens and the earth. "For, without knowing that you are doing so, you are worshiping what I preach to you." They definitely worship God, but they do so "not knowing," that is to say, in ignorance. On the other hand, however, this thought is tempered somewhat by the neutral word "what." "What you worship," is how it stands in the text, not "whom you worship." The matter is intentionally stated in this entirely neutral way because this "unknowing" worship of God cannot in the deepest sense be called a worship of God.

Far and away the most important passage for our purposes is the explanation that Paul has given in the first chapter of his letter to the Romans (vv. 18-32). We will first attempt to read these verses calmly, before we turn to an effort to hear what has been said about them in both earlier and more recent times.

---

9. F. W. Grosheide, *Handelingen*, vol. 2 (Amsterdam: Bottenburg, 1948), p. 66.

Verse 18: The wrath of God is being revealed from heaven against all the godlessness and wickedness of human beings who suppress the truth by their wickedness.

"The wrath of God is being revealed." That reflects not only the proclamation of God's wrath in the preaching of the gospel, but points clearly also to what is to be worked out more fully in the following verses (24, 26, 28). Godlessness exists on the religious level. By "wickedness" something more is obviously intended, namely immorality or obscenity in the broadest sense of the term.

"Of human beings." Here not all people are intended, but only those that suppress the truth in unrighteousness.

"The truth." By this is designated the truth that encompasses all truths, that which is the meaning of all truth, that to which all truth is subordinated.

"Suppress." This need not be understood as a conscious action. It can develop in total silence in the human heart. I am inclined to understand this in the sense of repression, as the concept of repression has been developed in recent psychology. As a rule, repression occurs unconsciously, but that makes it no less real.

"By their wickedness." What is striking here is that the godlessness mentioned earlier is no longer identified here. Apparently this is intended in the sense that wickedness and immorality arise as the driving force (consciously or unconsciously) in the process of repressing. Then, the result of this repression is godlessness. But the deepest motive for this godlessness is the grim grip of immorality. The entire process of repressing is governed by motives in the area of morality.

Verse 19: "Since what may be known about God is plain to them, because God has made it plain to them."

"What may be known about God." These words apparently give a further explanation of "the truth" in the fullest sense, as noted above. At the same time, they convey a limitation: not the full depth of the riches of the wisdom and knowledge of God, but only "what may be known about him."

"Made it plain." The word used here (φανερον) means, particularly, "evident" or "transparent." It grips them in their inner lives.

"Because God has made it plain to them." Here we note that the apostle does not use the usual word for revelation (αποκαλυπτειν), but he chooses a word — (φανερον) — that leans more toward the meaning of "showed them," "made it apparent," and "demonstrated" *(manifestatio).*

Verse 20: "For since the creation of the world God's invisible qualities — his eternal power and divine nature — have been clearly seen, being understood from what has been made, so that people are without excuse."

"*God's invisible qualities.*" Intended here are the divine attributes that are not accessible to human eyes. Among these attributes, two are mentioned specifically, namely his eternal power and his divinity. Why only these two mentioned here (and, for example, not his wisdom and his omnipresence) cannot be explored further at this point. What is certainly worth pointing out here as being of interest is that in these two, everlasting power and divinity, the relationship of human beings to God is posited as a relationship of dependence and accountability. People live and exist only by virtue of God's eternal power. People are creatures, as human beings, with respect to the divinity or deity of their Creator. The first term, everlasting power, conveys the sense that in all things God is the only initiator; he completes everything by virtue of his own capability. This applies to the totality of things. The second, his divinity, conveys the "wholly otherness" of God; God belongs to a completely different order than we human beings, he is the "Holy One." At the same time, inherent in this is a reference to the personhood of God; he is a Someone, not a Something. We are related to him in an I-Thou relationship, in a morally accountable relationship.

What is truly remarkable is that the world's religions give evidence of a persistent inclination to accentuate either the one or the other of these two terms. Hinduism and many related religious phenomena are burdened by the unbearable need to construe God as a dynamic force. They regard him as the power, the δύναμις that visibly manifests itself everywhere. He is the great Brahman that drives all things. God is not a "Thou," but an "It." The relationship of human beings to God is not an I-Thou relationship, but an I-It relationship. On the other hand, in various forms of primitive religion, for example even in the Chinese religions,[10] we find the persistent attempt to accentuate the divinity of God, especially his aloofness and remoteness. Here attempts are made to push God endlessly far away and no longer to regard him as the personal God who drives all that happens or as the power behind all powers. The so-called "high gods" that we find in primitive religious systems have withdrawn to remote places, but they are no longer the determining forces behind what actually happens. In other words, various human re-

10. See Nathan Söderblom, *Das Werden des Gottesglaubens* (Leipzig: Hinrichs, 1926), chapter 6.

ligions always vacillate between eternal power and divinity. Either they dissolve God into an impersonal, vague force and thus lose sight of his divinity, or they push God far away and in the practice of daily life rely on other powers that are more concrete and more understandable. In all of this we see the uncertainty of religious consciousness.

"*Since the creation of the world.*" This means universally, in all times and in all places under the sun.

"*From what has been made.*" Here we do not read, "from his creatures." The word "made" that is used here indicates that we are not to think only of nature, but also of God's works in history, in the daily life of the individual person, and of his work in the human conscience.

"*Have been clearly seen, being understood.*" Here a difficulty surfaces in the translation. Some exegetes, for example, simply want to translate these words like this: "have been evident to the *nous,* the spirit, the mind, the thought."[11] The idea conveyed is of conditional understanding. The issue is whether this understanding ever occurs. The seventeenth-century Dutch *Statenvertaling* (States Translation)[12] as well as the new translation of the Netherlands Bible Society[13] follow the original Greek text, where it literally says, "is evident as comprehended by human understanding." Here understanding is not conditional. In terms of the entire context, this seems to me to be the most accurate translation. The apostle's intention certainly seems to be that it really happens. That which cannot be seen is definitely grasped and understood. The apostle wants to show clearly here that it is not only possible, but that it actually happens.

"*So that people are without excuse.*" Here the result, the necessary consequence of the foregoing, is bluntly stated.

Verses 21-23: "For although they knew God, they neither glorified him as God nor gave thanks to him, but their thinking became futile and their foolish hearts were darkened. Although they claimed to be wise, they be-

11. S. Greijdanus, *De Brief van den Apostel Paulus aan de Gemeente Rome,* vol. 1 (Amsterdam: Bottenburg, 1933), p. 110.

12. Ed. note: This is a reference to the Dutch version of the Bible commissioned by the Synod of Dort (1618-1619) and authorized by the Dutch States-General in 1637. It is the Dutch equivalent of the King James or Authorized Version. The *Statenvertaling* was the first official Dutch Bible directly translated from the original Hebrew and Greek.

13. Ed. note: The New Translation *(Nieuwe Vertaling = NV)* of the Dutch Bible prepared by the Nederlands Bijbel Genootschap (Dutch Bible Society) to replace the *Statenvertaling* (see previous note). The *Nieuwe Vertaling* became publicly available in 1951; it was superseded by the New Bible Translation *(Nieuwe Bijbelvertaling = NBV)* in 2004.

came fools and exchanged the glory of the immortal God for images made to look like mortal human beings and birds and animals and reptiles."

"Although they knew God." Here the fact of knowing is posited as a reality. A knowledge of God exists also among those who in the practice of their religion profess not to know him.

"Their thinking became futile." In the *Statenvertaling* this is stated passively, for translated, it reads, "they have become frustrated." Very little emphasis is placed on personal responsibility, but the full accent lies on the fact that in their consideration (negatively understood), they have given up their relationship with the true God. It became dark — once again, a passive expression. Night descended on their thinking.

"The glory of the immortal God." That word "majesty" (δοξα) obviously summarizes the "eternal power and divinity" of verse 20.

"Exchanged." Here an active verb reappears. They have exchanged. Now the image of the immortal God slips through their fingers, and they fill the void that overwhelms their entire being, including their thinking, with all sorts of fantasies. In those fantasies, they drag God down to the creaturely level, pulling him down to the level of mortality.

"Made to look." This is an extraordinarily cautious statement. The text does not read, "They have exchanged the glory for the images of mortal men, etc." But it reads, "images made to look like mortal human beings." Here account is taken of the fact that pagans also feel that the images that they make of their gods are not totally accurate representations of the gods themselves, but are only approximate expressions of the reality of those gods.

In the apostle's continuing account, the following expressions occur:

1. The verb "exchange" is repeated once more. "They exchanged the truth of God for a lie. This replacing (άλλάσσω, equivalent to *eintauschen* in German)[14] or exchanging or substituting is definitely a very real element in the inner workings of heathenism.

2. That a certain kind of knowledge still exists behind paganism is again expressed in verse 32: "although they know God's righteous decree." Behind all the ignorance that is evident in paganism, there nevertheless is

---

14. Büchsel, "άλλάσσω," in *Theological Dictionary of the New Testament* (hereafter *TDNT*), ed. Gerhard Kittel, trans. and ed. Geoffrey W. Bromiley, 10 vols. (Grand Rapids: Eerdmans, 1964), 1: 251-59.

shrouded a definite knowledge not only of God's existence, but especially of our responsibility toward God.

3. Further emphasis is given to the guilt of ignorance. "They did not think it worthwhile to retain the knowledge of God." They did not consider it necessary (δοκιμάζω plus an infinitive is equivalent to *für notwendig erachten* in German)[15] to maintain a recognition of God. This recognition is obviously stronger than knowledge, since it amounts to a practice of worship, obedience, and esteeming him in his majesty.

4. What is unsettling is the threefold repetition of "God gave them over" (vv. 24, 26, 28). In all three instances, it relates to God giving them up to sexual behavior. They have no resistance any longer to sexual behavior that reveals itself in the most perverse forms imaginable. Anyone who has had any practical experience with paganism understands how terrible the scourge of sexuality is in pagan life.

If we are to summarize this entire passage, we come to several conclusions that could lead to even further examination.

In the first place, a great deal of attention is given to divine speaking in this section of the book of Romans. This is the voiceless speaking of God's revelation. This revelation may not be revelation, apocalypse, or "removal of the veil" in the sense that that word has been given with respect to the work of salvation. But it is nevertheless a φανεροσις, a *manifestatio,* a making visible of "invisible" things. That speech is so powerful that no person can shake it off.

In the second place, that revelation of God also remarkably brings about something in a person — no matter how foolish, how unknowing, however much he or she "worships what they do not know" and "reveres what they do not understand" — that allows them to be addressed as a knower, as someone who knows. Their legal standing is that of someone who knows and who understands, that is to say, of someone who knows in the depths of his or her being that he or she is accountable to the "just demands of God."

In the third place, what is outlined here is nonetheless recognized as not being an actual knowledge. It cannot be, for whenever the living reality of God manifests itself and displays its evidence to such a one, two processes begin working. The first is the process of repressing, the second that of replacing. In the first process, the motive of moral unwillingness is the driving force. Apparently, that develops for the most part unconsciously; as a rule, it

15. Gundman, "δοκιμάζω," *TDNT,* 2: 258-59.

completely eludes a person. In the second process, stronger emphasis is laid on human activity — a person represses. He or she attempts to fill their emptiness.

In the fourth place, it cannot be denied that in this entire process something thoroughly tragic happens. "They are given up." "Their hearts became darkened." When this process begins to work, these people simply do not understand it and over against it they are powerless. They are the active agents who, by virtue of their immorality, wring moral norms out of their life on every side and repress and replace the truth. But, these people at the same time are victims who at any given time can no longer resist, who no longer have any anchor, and who "lose themselves." They do something, but something is also done to them, overwhelms them, sweeps them along, washes away all their resistance.

In addition to this extremely important passage in the letter to the Romans, there are a few other passages in the New Testament that treat this subject. We think, first of all, of the well-known prologue to the Gospel of John. "The Light shines in the darkness, and the darkness has not overcome it" (John 1:5). Does the writer have in mind the incarnate Logos, Jesus Christ in his historical appearance, or is he thinking here of the ever-present revelation of the Logos in the world, in human consciousness? The context makes the last possibility the most likely. The darkness referred to here must then be the same darkness that Paul discusses. The shining of the Light of the Logos then refers to that general revelation or *manifestatio* that Paul treated. And that "overcome" (Ubbink translates it as "being swallowed up")[16] must mean: "has not overcome it," or "could not extinguish it." This expression indicates, therefore, that general revelation is very directly related to the Logos or the Word that was from the beginning and that has become flesh in Jesus Christ.

In the same spirit, Paul also says in 1 Corinthians 2:8, "None of the rulers of this age knew (namely, the secret wisdom of God); for had they known, they would not have crucified the Lord of glory." By the "rulers of this age" is definitely meant in the first instance Herod and Pontius Pilate. But the expression is posited far too generally that it should be limited to them only. It refers in general to the political and also the spiritual leaders, who are the pioneers in thinking as well as the bearers of political authority. All of them have not known "the secret wisdom of God." The repressing and the replac-

16. J. Th. Ubbink, *Het Evangelie van Johannes, Serie Tekst en Uitleg* 2 (Groningen: Wolters, 1924), p. 27.

ing talked about in Romans 1 is in principle the same as what is recognized here in the crucifixion of Christ. The crucifixion of Christ is always the point at which people depart from the truth, and that is the tragic mystery for everyone.

§3. Voices from the Ancient Past

It is helpful for us to pay some attention to the way in which these various emphases in the Old and New Testaments have been understood in the course of history. Naturally, our review can only be cursory.

The ancient Christian church was in general inclined to place high value on the positive aspects of Greek philosophy. They did so, as a rule, in connection with the prologue to the Gospel of John, especially the concept of the Logos "that is the Light of the world." Several times, Clement of Alexandria cites the address of Paul on the Areopagus in his occasional pieces, and from it he concludes that the apostle "gave his seal of approval to the fact that the Greeks had excellently explained the matter."[17] But as a rule, speculation on the value of Greek philosophy was strictly limited to the Logos idea. A large mixture of sources could be cited where the significance of the Logos is expressed in strong terms. Here we name just a few:

Justin Martyr often talks about the Logos in his *Apology*. This is what he says: "For not only among the Greeks did reason (Logos) prevail to condemn these things through Socrates, but also among the Barbarians were they condemned by Reason (or the Word, the Logos) Himself, who took shape, and became man and was called Jesus Christ."[18]

In another place, he expresses himself this way: "We have been taught that Christ is the first-born of God, and we have declared above that He is the Word of whom every race of man were partakers; and those who lived reasonably are Christians, even though they have been thought atheists; as, among the Greeks, Socrates and Heraclitus, and men like them."[19] Elsewhere he says: "And those of the Stoic school — since, so far as their moral teaching went, they were admirable, as were also the poets in some particulars, on account of the seed of reason [the Logos] implanted in every race of

---

17. Clement of Alexandria, *The Stromata, or Miscellanies*, 1.19, in *Ante-Nicene Fathers* (hereafter *ANF*), ed. Rev. Alexander Roberts and James Donaldson, 10 vols. (Grand Rapids: Eerdmans, 1975-1978), 2: 321-22.

18. Justin Martyr, *First Apology*, 5, in *ANF*, 1: 164.

19. Justin Martyr, *First Apology*, 46, in *ANF*, 1: 178.

men — were, we know, hated and put to death."[20] Or, "whatever either law-givers or philosophers uttered well, they elaborated by finding and contemplating some part of the Word."[21] And finally, "For all the writers were able to see realities darkly through the sowing of the implanted word that was in them."[22]

Clement of Alexandria expresses himself this way: "Accordingly, before the advent of the Lord, philosophy was necessary to the Greeks for righteousness. And now it becomes conducive to piety; being a kind of preparatory training to those who attain to faith through demonstration. . . . For this was a schoolmaster to bring the 'Hellenic mind,' as the law, the Hebrews, 'to Christ.'"[23]

These few quotations are sufficient to demonstrate the high value that the ancient apologists and church fathers placed on Greek philosophy. They were inwardly convinced that the Logos was at work in the thinkers and poets of antiquity. That the people of their day had not embraced the philosophers' teachings, and had compelled Socrates to drink the cup of poison, for example, was caused by the fact that the common people were driven by demons, in the opinion of the apologists, and resolutely resisted the working of the Logos.

Meanwhile, these developments in theological thought clearly posed serious threats. In the first place, one can register serious objections to expressions like "the seed of the Logos implanted in the entire human race." In it, the Logos is made into a principle that is embedded in human nature and that is one with human nature. It no longer is the divine Word that stands over against humanity or that calls humanity to responsibility, but it is a power implanted in human nature. The "seed of the Logos" lives in philosophers and poets. A person is able, at least in part, to "possess" the Logos. And here the Logos becomes part of a person, something that a person has. By this, the Logos is dragged down to the human level and the human being is at the same time deified, at least in some of his or her capacities.

A second objection must be found in the fact that in these and similar expressions the concept of "Logos" itself is weakened and reduced to reason and the highest wisdom. But the concept Logos as it appears in the Gospel of John has a clear Old Testament background. But here it is increasingly

20. Justin Martyr, *Second Apology,* 8, in *ANF,* 1: 191.
21. Justin Martyr, *Second Apology,* 10, in *ANF,* 1: 191.
22. Justin Martyr, *Second Apology,* 13, in *ANF,* 1: 193.
23. Clement of Alexandria, *The Stromata, or Miscellanies,* 1.5, in *ANF,* 2: 305-7.

pulled into the Greek world of thought and conflated with the universal reason dwelling in all things. Through such expressions as just noted, theological thought turned down a dangerous road.

These discussions that were conducted in the early church have a very relevant sound today. Just as the ancient apologists and church fathers wrestled with the cultural inheritance of Greece and Rome and time and again asked themselves whether the Greek philosophical systems had not revealed the Logos just as well as the Old Testament had, in our day the Christians in the younger churches of India, China, and other countries wrestle with the extremely complex problem of whether eternal truths do not lie hidden in the religious literature in which they have been educated. A. J. Appasamy wrote in 1928, "Most Christians in India have come to acknowledge that the philosophies and religions of India have not been inspired by the powers of darkness, but that through them all can be seen, sometimes clearly but sometimes dimly, the hand of God leading men on."[24] On that basis, he commands Christians there to make use of the writings of Hindu thinkers and poets for their own personal, religious needs. It hardly need surprise us, therefore, that at a conference in Poona, India, in 1942, on the need to develop an indigenous Indian theology, the expectation was expressed that the young church in India could learn much from a careful study of the ancient apologists and early church fathers.[25] Naturally, the questions currently sizzling on all mission fields are in essence the same ones that were struggled with by the early church.

An entirely different emphasis was given in the first centuries by the church father Tertullian. Tertullian regarded Greek philosophy far more skeptically than most of his contemporaries. In the writings of the philosophers he saw very few points of contact for his preaching. But he did expect that such possibilities existed in the simple, uneducated soul. In one of his five books opposing Marcion, he testified that the consciousness of God *(de conscientia dei)* was from the very beginning a gift of the soul, and concerning the soul he also testified that it is the same throughout the entire world. There is not an Egyptian soul or a Syrian soul, etc., but the soul is always and everywhere the same.[26] Therefore, it belongs to the consciousness of all people *(omnium conscientia)* to recognize that a most highly exalted God exists

---

24. A. J. Appasamy, "An Approach to Hindus," *The International Review of Missions* 17 (1928): 473.

25. Johannes Christiaan Hoekendijk, *De Wereldzending in oorlogstijd, 1940-1944* (The Hague: Boekencentrum, 1945), p. 53.

26. Tertullian, *The Five Books against Marcion*, 1.10, in *ANF*, 3: 278.

and that he is great, eternal, and without beginning.[27] All of this lies indisputably in the recesses of the soul. In his own study of the soul, titled *De anima,* he demonstrates that the source of goodness, the highest good *(bonum principale)* that dwells in the soul and is divine and genuine *(illud divinium atque gemanum)* is darkened by sin. But it has not been extinguished. "For that which is derived from God is rather obscured than extinguished" *(obumbratur).* As soon as the soul comes to faith, "renewed in its second birth by water and the power from above, then the veil of its former corruption being taken away, it beholds the light in all its brightness."[28]

Tertullian delves most deeply into these matters in his small work titled "On the Testimony of the Soul" *(De testimonio animae).* There he appeals to the soul this way: "I address thee simple, rude, uncultured, and untaught, such as they have thee who have thee only; that very thing of the road, the street, the work-shop, wholly. I want thine inexperience, since in thy small experience no one feels any confidence."[29] The simple soul sometimes bears witness at the most unexpected times that it believes in the one God. In moments of danger, it says suddenly, "if God wills it!" Then all at once, it is as if Jupiter or Saturn or all the other gods no longer exist, and as if only the one true God to whom the soul calls out in its deepest need exists any longer.[30]

The instruction of heathen priests and the philosophical systems of all the probing thinkers can corrupt a great deal in the human soul, but deep within it still lives that inextinguishable testimony that is once again awakened in times of danger and crisis. "O, noble testimony of the soul by nature Christian *(O testimonium animae naturaliter Christianae)!*"[31] Tertullian himself felt that he may have said too much here. In more than one place in his writings, he points out that it is by nature inaccurate to say: "Thou art not, as I well know, Christian; for a man becomes a Christian, he is not born one."[32] "Men are made, not born, Christians."[33] And, still, Tertullian cannot point out often enough that the soul lives on the rim of truth. That is because it is a student of nature. Its authority is due to the majesty of nature. Nature is the schoolmarm; the school is her student. *(Magistra natura, anima discipula).* "Is it anything very strange, if it knows the God by whom it

27. Tertullian, *The Five Books against Marcion,* 1.3, in *ANF,* 3: 273.
28. Tertullian, *A Treatise on the Soul,* 41, in *ANF,* 3: 220-21.
29. Tertullian, *The Soul's Testimony,* 1, in *ANF,* 3: 175-76.
30. Tertullian, *The Soul's Testimony,* 2, in *ANF,* 3: 176.
31. Tertullian, *Apology,* 17, in *ANF,* 3: 32.
32. Tertullian, *The Soul's Testimony,* 1, in *ANF,* 3: 176.
33. Tertullian, *Apology,* 18, in *ANF,* 3: 32.

was bestowed?"[34] All of this does not lead Tertullian to conclude in praise of the soul. At the conclusion of his book on the testimony of the soul, he breaks out with a serious warning:

> Most justly, then, every soul is a culprit as well as a witness: in the measure that it testifies for truth, the guilt of error lies on it; and on the day of judgment it will stand before the courts of God, without a word to say. Thou proclaimedst God, O soul, but thou didst not seek to know Him: evil spirits were detested by thee, and yet they were the objects of thy adoration; the punishments of hell were foreseen by thee, but no care was taken to avoid them; thou hadst a savour of Christianity, and withal wert the persecutor of Christians.

Here we have in clear outline what people now call the dialectical position of being human.[35]

It occurs to me that in these explanations of Tertullian we find very valuable elements, also for our theological discussions today. He grabs hold of unmistakable realities. It is a fact, to be specific, that throughout the entire world a person in need in perilous circumstances, when his or her life is in danger, suddenly shakes off, as it were, every theory learned about world order. They also shake off all pagan mythology, and with ordinary, childlike simplicity simply call out to God, just like a terrified child simply calls out to his or her mother or father. Even in uttering a curse, such as a person spits out in suddenly difficult circumstances, there is contained something of the *testimonium animae* that they can never quite escape. The blasphemer who unleashes a torrent of cursing when a disaster unexpectedly strikes, in spite of himself or herself, gives evidence that the "testimony of the soul" has not entirely abandoned him or her. Tertullian is absolutely right in pointing to these realities.[36]

But on the other hand, it cannot be denied that Tertullian runs the same risks as Justin and Clement. He may be less fanatical about philosophy, but even he displays a point of contact in his emphasis on the testimony of the soul. With him, the soul is still much too beautiful, much too divine. It produces its own testimony and witness, and that *testimonium* is an aspect of its own identity. In this, the element that a person is addressed as one who knows God (Rom. 1:21) is definitely recognized. But the other element,

---

34. Tertullian, *The Soul's Testimony*, 5, in *ANF*, 3: 178.
35. Tertullian, *The Soul's Testimony*, 6, in *ANF*, 3: 179.
36. Tertullian, *The Soul's Testimony*, 2, in *ANF*, 3: 176.

namely that from the very start he or she represses and replaces far too much, is discounted. That *testimonium* certainly exists, but not as the *testimonium animae*, the witness of the soul. It is the *testimonium* of God that is always thoroughly repressed and replaced by people, but that sometimes and in unexpected circumstances all at once breaks through to an individual. It is not a dimension of the soul, but it comes from the outside, from above. It is not found on the credit side of the human ledger, but on the debit side. This is why that final sentence of the little book *De testimonium animae*, where the soul is portrayed simultaneously as the accused and as a witness, has such profound, tragic, and evangelical force. It is a compelling paraphrase of "so that they are without excuse."

With Augustine, the problem is much more complicated and difficult from the very beginning. This is because Augustine had such a remarkable, inner personal experience. He made his way from Manicheism to neo-Platonism, and from there he was gradually drawn into faith in Christ. The ties to neo-Platonism remained strong for this church father long after his conversion, and the question is whether he ever achieved complete freedom from them.[37] Nourrisson summarizes the various phases of Augustine's spiritual struggle like this:

> Augustine came to the Christian faith because that faith seemed to him to be in the greatest agreement with Plato's philosophy. In a later period, he continued to hold to platonic philosophy because he judged that it was in agreement with the Christian faith. Thereafter, when the Christian faith took complete possession of his soul, he began in the name of Christian philosophy to reject Plato's philosophy, to which he reduced all heathen wisdom.[38]

In one of the first books he wrote after his conversion (in 388-390; his conversion occurred in 387), namely *On True Religion (De vera religione)*, he still speaks in very glowing terms about the Greek philosophers.

> If Plato and the rest of them in whose names men glory, were to come to life again and find the churches full and the temples empty . . . they would perhaps say: That is what we did not dare preach to the people. We pre-

37. Charles Boyer, *Christianisme et Néo-Platonisme dans la Formation de Saint Augustin* (Paris: G. Beauchesne, 1920).

38. [Jean-Felix] Nourrisson, *La Philosophie de Saint Augustin*, 2 vols. (Paris: Didier and Co., 1865), 1: 60.

ferred to yield to popular custom rather than to bring people over to our way of thinking and living.

Then he continues:

> So if these men could live their lives again to-day, they would see by whose authority measures are best taken for man's salvation, and, with the change of a few words and sentiments they would become Christians.[39]

From this it seems that Augustine was of the opinion that only a few things needed to be changed in Plato's philosophy to make it suitable for application to the Christian faith. The sin of Greek philosophers was not that they did not see the truth, but that they did not display more courage for coming to it out of spiritual thirst.

Eight years later, he wrote his *Confessions*. The influence of Platonism is also clearly visible in that work. However, there are visible indications that this great Christian thinker has slowly begun to free himself from its ties. What is striking in this regard is what he writes in the seventh book of his *Confessions*, where he admits that he had begun reading the Holy Scriptures. Then he adds, "I discovered that what I had read about truth there (namely, in the writings of the Greek philosophers), was also being stated here, with an acknowledgement of your grace." Also here, therefore, we still see a recognition that truth can be found in the writings of Greek thinkers. But immediately thereafter, Augustine says that the message of grace, the message contained in the manuscript of our own sin that has been washed away, is absent from those writings. "Those pages (in the Greek philosophical writings) contain not the expression of piety — the tears of confession, Thy sacrifice, a troubled spirit, 'a broken and contrite heart.'"[40] That one emphasis is not present in those works *(hoc illae litterae non habent)*, and that acknowledgment is a major victory. Here for the first time he clearly states that all those writings of the ancient philosophers, whatever beauty they may contain, have no room for the cross because they have not seen sin in all its terrible dimensions.

Augustine was exceptionally sensitive on this one point of humility, lowliness, and a sense of one's sin. In the works of Plato and others, he al-

---

39. Augustine, *Of True Religion,* in *Augustine: Earlier Writings,* ed. John H. S. Burleigh, The Library of Christian Classics, Ichthus ed. (Philadelphia: Westminster, 1943), pp. 229-30.

40. Augustine, *The Confessions,* 7.21, in *Nicene and Post-Nicene Fathers* (hereafter *NPNF*), First Series, ed. Philip Schaff, 14 vols. (Grand Rapids: Eerdmans, 1969-1979), 1: 114-15.

ways felt a sense of pride, that flimsy human pride that is impressed with bigness and is always far too preoccupied with it. In one of his later works, the well-known book titled *The City of God* (*De civitate dei*, written somewhere between 413 and 426), he treats extensively Plato and the veracity of various ideas that are found in Plato's writings. Sometimes Plato comes remarkably close to Christian knowledge. He is especially astonished that Plato, as it were, sensed that single truth expressed when God said, "I am who I am."[41] But in that same book, he also demonstrates extensively and profoundly that the philosophers have never discovered the full truth.

> And some of them, by God's help (*quantum divinitus adjuti sunt*), made great discoveries; but when left to themselves they were betrayed by human infirmity (*quantum autem humanitus impediti sunt*), and fell into mistakes. And this was ordered by divine providence, that their pride might be restrained.[42]

We see the same thing again — the pride that blinds the eyes. Greece sometimes brushes with the truth, but it never has been able to grab her, since deep humility, which is the only road to truth, completely eludes her. In one of his letters, Augustine says that the example of godly humility (*divinae humilitatis exemplum*) that we see in Jesus Christ is lacking in all the ancient philosophers.[43] From this point on, Augustine's eyes were entirely opened to the deficiency of Greek philosophical thought. Small wonder, then, that in his *Retractions* (written in 427, three years before his death in 430) he expressed regret over his earlier, all-too-enthusiastic appreciation for Plato. "I have been rightly displeased, too, with the praise with which I extolled Plato or the Platonists or the Academic philosophers beyond what was proper for such irreligious men, especially those against whose great errors Christian teaching must be defended."[44]

In general, one can say that Augustine was better able to feel with his heart where the limitations of Greek philosophical systems lie, than he was capable of exposing them with his understanding. This is due to the fact that that he never entirely escaped the idea that the soul, with its rational powers, possessed capacities that are almost divine. Whenever Augustine comes to

---

41. Augustine, *The City of God*, 8.11, in *NPNF*, First Series, 2: 151-52.

42. Augustine, *The City of God*, 2.7, in *NPNF*, First Series, 2: 26-27.

43. Augustine, *The Letters*, 118.3, 17, in *NPNF*, First Series, 1: 439, 444-45.

44. Augustine, *The Retractions*, 1.1, 6-11, trans. Sister Mary Inez Bogan (Washington, DC: Catholic University of America Press, 1968).

the point of talking about the soul, he risks the serious danger of falling into that very real Greek error, namely that the soul, particularly in its rational capacities, possesses godlike qualities. In his observations on the power of memory *(memoria),* he mixes various ideas that are not in harmony with Paul's words that we handled above.[45] Nevertheless and without any hesitation, it can be clearly stated that Augustine has performed an invaluable service in demonstrating the wearying struggle of Christian thought with the legacy of the ancient world.

Meanwhile, the problem of religious consciousness remained in unabated strength. It was certainly gnawed at, but never solved. Is religious consciousness a reflection of some other human capacity? Is it an attribute of humanity? Does it belong to the soul, and if so, then to the soul as informed by philosophy, or simply to the uneducated or unknowing soul? Is it closely associated with reason, or with memory, or with the emotions? What is its source? Where does it reside? Is it one of the elements of humanity's nobility? All of these questions continue to be sounded, and they have preoccupied theological thought for many centuries. Naturally, it is impossible to review this process fully. We can only touch on a few of its more significant aspects.

With Thomas Aquinas, the theological reflection of the Middle Ages reached maturity. In *Summa contra Gentiles,* an apologetic and missionary work opposing the non-Christian religions, Thomas goes into great detail on the value that needs to be accorded these religions. He proceeds on the premise that in discussions with Muslims and heathens it is not possible to appeal to the Old and New Testaments for the simple reason that these people do not acknowledge the authority of those writings. One needs to go back even further, therefore, since there is no other way to proceed than on the basis of natural reason *(ratio naturalis),* "to which everyone needs to yield." But with respect to religious matters, natural reason falls too far short or is deficient *(deficiens),* and that fact makes any discussion very difficult.

Thus, we are now compelled to make a distinction between two kinds of truths: those that "totally transcend the capacity of human reason" and those that are within the reach of natural reason. To the first category, Thomas assigns the Trinity and to the latter the fact that there is a God, only one God, etc. In light of these two categories of truths, we need to employ different methods of approach. As far as the latter category is concerned,

---

45. Étienne Gilson, *Introduction a l'étude de Saint Augustin,* 3rd ed. (Paris: Librairie Philosophique J. Vrin, 1931), pp. 134-35. See also J. H. Bavinck, *Christus en de Mystiek van het Oosten* (Kampen: J. H. Kok, 1934), pp. 118ff.; *JHBR,* pp. 314-16.

truths that are within the reach of natural knowledge, we can make decent use of philosophical reason. We are able, by the use of philosophical arguments, to demonstrate the foolishness of their many deities. We are capable, once again, to help them by means of logical arguments to see the nonsense of thinking that God can be represented in the image of a man, a bull, or something else. In short, we have a whole arsenal of arguments at our disposal by which we can gradually compel them to recognize that there can be only one God. But then the time comes when we can proceed no further with natural reason. Then we are compelled to resort to an entirely different approach, namely that of honestly disclosing the mysteries of the faith. Even then, reason can still definitely be helpful, at least insofar as it is able to demonstrate that these mysteries are not in conflict with reason; but further than that it is incapable of going. That is the point at which faith applies, faith that humbly submits to the truth of God.[46]

This line of thought Thomas works out more fully and illustrates in other writings. It occurs in connection with numerous theological subjects: the doctrine of the image of God, his perspective on humanity, teachings that deal with sin, and those that deal with the relationship of nature and grace. The conviction that a person, by the light of his or her natural reason, can come to the knowledge of God belongs to the Roman Catholic Church's treasured beliefs to this very day. The [first] Vatican Council said this: "This same Holy Mother Church holds and teaches that God, the beginning and the end of all things, can be known by the light of natural, human reason, in distinction from all other creatures."[47]

That this entire construct is of utmost importance for the relationship with other religions certainly needs no further proof. In one of Otto Karrer's books, translated into Dutch as *Het Religieuse in de Menschheid en het Christendom* (Bilthoven, 1939) [English equivalent: *Religiosity in Humanity and in Christianity*], an endorsement in J. Lammertse's Foreword reads as follows:

> For, first of all, according to the biblical perspective, there is in truth no one — no people, no human being — that in their religious quest, their believing, or their living is objective apart from Christ. Even further, it is precisely Christ, the incarnate Word, that illumines every person through-

---

46. Thomas Aquinas, *On the Truth of the Catholic Faith: Summa Contra Gentiles, Book One: God*, trans. Anton C. Pegis (Garden City, NY: Image, 1955), pp. 59-61.

47. Henrico Denzinger, *Enchiridion Symbolorum: Definitionum et Declarationum de Rebus Fidei et Morum*, ed. Clemens Bannwart, 11th ed. (Freiburg: Friburgi Brisgoviae and B. Herder, 1910), §1785, p. 474.

out all generations and works in individuals a salvation-producing drive toward God, regardless of whether he illumines and leads them as "the unknown Christ" in a "strange embrace" or as the historically revealed Word of the gospels.[48]

When speaking about grace and salvation, Karrer says, "In this connection, Christianity only had to establish and deepen what generally appears only as a fearful hope. The sure gospel of salvation is God's answer to 'the world's misery.'"[49] Later he says:

Christianity is in the position with respect to the development of the large, human family of recognizing signs of divine leading. This occurs even with respect to the lowest form of religious practice and least flickering faith, where it still sees "the scattered seeds of a divine Logos." Thus, it recognizes in every religious detour the all-embracing divine plan of nurture by which humanity is gradually lifted from levels of religious naiveté to a higher spirituality.[50]

Entirely consistent with this approach, Roman Catholic missions has from the outset taken an entirely different stance toward non-Christian religions and cultures than Protestant mission work has as a rule been able to do. This different stance is, at the deepest level, definitely connected to the entirely different view of the significance and value of religious consciousness as connected to the Christian faith. Roman Catholic missions has, on repeated occasions, given the impression that it is prepared to recognize valuable dimensions to the religious content existing among various peoples and to connect with them. The relationship between universal religious consciousness and the Christian faith is seen more like the relation between an immature boy and a fully mature man. "Outside Christianity," said the Jesuit theologian Henri de Lubac, "not everything is spoiled. But whatever does not remain on a childish level always runs the risk of becoming misguided or falling into futility, no matter how highly it may be exalted."[51] It is not corrupted, not dislocated, but it is definitely childish (enfantin). This is the way in which religious consciousness is presented.

48. Otto Karrer, *Het Religieuse in de menschheid en het Christendom*, Voorwoord van J. Lammertse (Bilthoven: De Gemeenschap, 1939), p. 11.

49. Otto Karrer, *Het Religieuse*, p. 125.

50. Otto Karrer, *Het Religieuse*, p. 162.

51. Henri de Lubac, *Catholicisme: Les aspects sociaux du dogme* (Paris: Les Éditions du Cerf, 1938), p. 166.

§4. The Reformation

On our excursion through history, with seven-league boots, we make a stop at the Reformation. What is of unusually great interest is that the Reformation also paid a great deal of attention to our question, and it reflected on the problem in a profound way. We will limit ourselves especially to a brief review of Calvin's thoughts on the problem that occupies our attention.

Calvin engages the question of religious consciousness in the first book of his famous *Institutes*. There he treats the knowledge of God the Creator, and in that connection he comes particularly to a consideration of the natural knowledge of God. Already in the second chapter of this book, he produces an outline that can serve as an excellent definition of true religion. The pious soul, he says there, "does not dream up for itself any god it pleases," but "is content to hold him to be as he manifests himself." *(Deum non quemlibet sibi somniat, sed talem habere contenta est qualem se manifestat ipse.)* Therefore, "pure and real religion" can be described as "faith so joined with an earnest fear of God" *(fides cum serio Dei timore conjuncta).*[52]

When he comes to the topic of natural knowledge of God, Calvin observes:

> There is within the human mind, and indeed by natural instinct *(naturali instinctu),* an awareness of divinity *(sensus divinitatis).* This we take to be beyond controversy. . . . God himself has implanted in all men a certain understanding *(sui numinis intelligentiam)* of his divine majesty. Ever renewing its memory, he repeatedly sheds fresh drops. Since, therefore, men one and all perceive that there is a God and that he is their Maker, they are all condemned by their own testimony.

A few lines further, he maintains that even those who in many ways can be compared to wild animals "have . . . a deep-seated conviction that there is a God *(semen religionis)*." This is why people would rather worship wood and stone than maintain that they have no God.[53] In further developing this chapter, Calvin repeats once more that "a sense of divinity *(sensus divinitatis)* which can never be effaced is engraved upon men's minds."[54]

---

52. John Calvin, *Institutes of the Christian Religion,* 2 vols., ed. John T. McNeill, trans. Ford Lewis Battles, The Library of Christian Classics, vol. 20 (Louisville: Westminster John Knox, 1960), 1.2.2.

53. Calvin, *Institutes,* 1.3.1.

54. Calvin, *Institutes,* 1.3.3.

In the fourth chapter, Calvin begins talking about corruption. He begins the chapter like this:

> As experience shows *(experientia testatur)*, God has sown a seed of religion in all men *(semen religionis)*. But scarcely one man in a hundred is met with who fosters it, once received, in his heart, and none in whom it ripens — much less shows fruit in season. . . . They do not therefore apprehend God as he offers himself *(qualem pro sua termeritate fabricate sunt)*. . . . Even though they are compelled to recognize some god, they strip him of glory by taking away his power.[55]

After this, Calvin explores what we usually call general revelation. He treats God's majesty as it is expressed in nature and as we meet it in the entire course of life. God

> not only sowed in men's minds that seed of religion *(semen religionis)* of which we have spoken but revealed *(patefecit)* himself in the whole workmanship of the universe *(palam se offert)*. As a consequence, men cannot open their eyes without being compelled to see him.

He points out that already in antiquity some people, laboring under the impression of the rational construction of the world, have been persuaded of a world spirit or a world reason. He then makes the pointed observation that this demonstrates that they have then made a shadowy god *(umbratile numen facere)* "to drive away the true God." Heathenism has really seen the glory of God in the world, but it has never wanted to understand it and has preferred to fantasize that there are other gods or has bowed to an "unknown god." Calvin continues, "It is therefore no wonder that the Holy Spirit rejects as base all cults contrived through the will of men *(cultus omnes tamquam degeneres repudiet)*." This is definitely an entirely different sound than that made by de Lubac, when he says that they are not entirely corrupt, but that they exist on a childish level. Toward the end of his fifth chapter, which began with a beautiful picture of God's great works, Calvin then concludes like this:

> Many lamps shine for us in the workmanship of the universe to show forth the glory of its Author *(frustra nobis in mundi opificio collucent tot accensae lampades)*. . . . Surely they strike some sparks, but before their fuller light shines forth these are smothered.

55. Calvin, *Institutes*, 1.4.1 and 1.4.2.

This indicates, Calvin continues,

> that the invisible divinity is made manifest in such spectacles, but that we have not the eyes to see this unless they be illumined by the inner revelation of God through faith. . . . For at the same time as we have enjoyed a slight taste of the divine from contemplation of the universe, having neglected the true God *(vero Deo praetermisso),* we raise up in his stead dreams and specters of our own brains *(somnia et spectra cerebri).*[56]

We will not track Calvin's thought on the subject any further. As further proof of his position we simply quote a few of his expressions. Elsewhere he talks about the uncontrollable compulsion in the human heart: "how great the lust to fashion constantly new and artificial religions *(novas et factitias religions).*"[57] In another place, he calls the religion of heathen nations "adulterations *(adulterate).*"[58] Concerning human understanding he observes that it is "a perpetual factory of idols *(idolorum fabricam).*" Saturated with pride and audacity, the human spirit "conceives an unreality and an empty appearance as God." Then, human hands depict that fabricated notion of God in wood or stone. "Therefore the mind begets an idol; the hand gives it birth."[59] All of this leads Calvin to say, with great emphasis, that we can never proceed on the basis of general revelation, however brilliantly it may shine.

> Just as old or bleary-eyed men and those with weak vision, if you thrust before them a most beautiful volume, even if they recognize it to be some sort of writing, yet can scarcely construe two words, but with the aid of spectacles will begin to read distinctly, so Scripture, gathering up the otherwise confused knowledge of God in our minds, having dispersed our dullness, clearly shows us the true God.[60]

Small wonder, then, that the sixth chapter of Book I is titled: "Scripture is needed as guide and teacher for anyone who would come to God the Creator."

This is as far as we go in Calvin's *Institutes.* What he writes about these matters in his other works is in complete accord with it. In his commentary on the Gospel of John he says that "such knowledge of God as now remains

56. Calvin, *Institutes,* 1.5, passim.
57. Calvin, *Institutes,* 1.6.3.
58. Calvin, *Institutes,* 1.10.3.
59. Calvin, *Institutes,* 1.11.8.
60. Calvin, *Institutes,* 1.6.1.

in men is nothing else than a frightful source of idolatry and of all superstitions *(horrenda idololatriae et superstitionum scaturigo)*."[61] And in his commentary on the first letter to the Corinthians, he says, "The right order of things was assuredly this, that man, contemplating the wisdom of God in his works, by the light of the understanding *(mens ingenita sibi ingenii luce)* furnished him by nature, might arrive at an acquaintance with him."[62] He then points out that in reality this does not happen: "as the whole world gained nothing in point of instruction from the circumstance, that God had exhibited his wisdom in his creatures, he then resorted to another method for instructing men."[63]

As for Luther, his ideas about religious consciousness are in many respects parallel to those of Calvin.[64] Prominent in his thought is the idea that people are compelled to come to the knowledge that there is a God by virtue of general revelation, that voiceless speaking. People did not stay with that, however, but applied the term "god" to all sorts of created things and thus clouded the majesty of God. For that reason, Luther also called humanity "god's creator" *(fabricator dei)*, who created their gods in their own image. This ignorance and error comes to expression especially in the fact that people now make distorted use of the law implanted in them and fall into works righteousness. Luther prefers to designate heathen religion as the self-justification of sinful people.[65]

What springs immediately into view is that both Luther and Calvin have made a serious attempt to stay as close to Holy Scripture as possible while addressing the incredibly profound problem of natural religious consciousness. Calvin definitely appeals a few times to experience, and says experience teaches in practice that not much actually comes from the seed of religion *(semen religionis)*. But even that insight is obviously made in conjunction with the ongoing instruction of Scripture. Both of these reformers have attempted to do justice to all the elements of the verses from the first chapter of the book of Romans that we have discussed above.

61. John Calvin, *Commentary on the Gospel According to John,* trans. William Pringle, 2 vols., in Calvin's Commentaries, vol. 17 (reprint Grand Rapids: Baker, 2005), 1: 122-26.

62. John Calvin, *Commentary on the Epistles of Paul the Apostle to the Corinthians,* trans. John Pringle, 2 vols., in Calvin's Commentaries, vol. 20 (reprint Grand Rapids: Baker, 2005), 1: 84.

63. John Calvin, *Corinthians,* 1: 84.

64. Walter Holsten, *Christentum und nichtchristliche Religion nach der Auffassung Luthers* (Gütersloh: C. Bertelsmann, 1932).

65. Holsten, *Christentum und nichtchristliche Religion,* p. 148.

This is not the place to take a thorough approach toward these matters. But we do want to make a few remarks here as an introduction to what we will need to discuss more fully in just a moment.

Calvin begins his explanation with the discussion of the seed or germ of religion *(semen religionis)* implanted within human beings. He compares that seed with a "natural instinct" and explains it as "a consciousness of divinity" *(sensus divinitatis)*. Elsewhere he calls it a "concept of the Godhead" *(numinis intelligentia)* that God has embedded in human beings and that is continuously maintained by him, adding to it drip by drip, as it were. Something is therefore present in human beings, in the natural man and woman, something that is responsive to the general revelation they receive. What that "something" is for Calvin remains very vague. Is it an "innate idea"? Sometimes one would be inclined to think that it is, but that would not yet be its explanation. Is it an aptitude of the human heart, a kind of a-priori in people's thought by virtue of which they, in all their thinking, are always compelled to acknowledge God? Or does it reside in their emotional lives, as Schleiermacher later thought? Is it psychologically situated, and can one find traces of it by tracking down the mysterious motions of the soul? A motley array of unsolvable questions arises in this connection. Calvin gives no further explanation of the *semen religionis,* so that it is certainly not possible to know what his thoughts on the matter might be. What is noteworthy is that he gave a great deal of attention to the matter, cites the concept repeatedly, and apparently attached a great deal of significance to it.

Just as noteworthy is the fact that Calvin treats this *semen religionis* before he talks about God's works in the huge, total structure of the universe. Following his treatment in three chapters of the innate knowledge of God, in the fifth chapter he comes to a discussion of God's majesty that shines on us in nature. He introduces this discussion with the little word "besides." This juxtaposition of general revelation in nature and the *semen religionis* alongside humanity's innate "sense of the Godhead" automatically gives rise to this question: "Can one even separate these two from one another, or even distinguish them?" Are the *semen religionis,* the *sensus divinitatis,* and the concept of the Godhead things that can be separated and thought about in isolation from one another? Must they not all rather be seen as a reaction to the shining of God's glory in the world all around? In other words, does all of it not first of all come to expression from the contemplation of nature through and on the basis of the entire complexity of life-experience, life's needs, the norms governing life? Is Calvin guilty of treating humanity first of all as something separate, something self-contained, and only thereupon discussing the world? Does not one need to think about humanity and the universe together from the outset, since people from the very beginning of their existence exist in such intimate connection with the universe that they cannot for a moment be thought of in distinction from it?

Whenever we set the thoughts of the reformers alongside the thought forms developed in the Middle Ages, several noteworthy distinctions strike us. In the first place, we are struck by the fact that while the Middle Ages took its standpoint on reason *(ratio)* within humanity when it came to general revelation, Calvin, although he also placed a great deal of significance on reason, nevertheless expressed preference for vaguer expressions like "consciousness of the Godhead," "concept of the Godhead," and *semen religionis.*

More remarkable and more illuminating still is another distinction. While the thought of the Middle Ages regarded human reason *(ratio)* as lying outside the powerful reach of sin, so that it was always in a position to achieve a certain measure of the knowledge of God, or a natural theology *(theologia naturalis),* for Calvin it was different. He pointed out with emphasis that the *semen religionis* has been corrupted; the *sensus divinitatis* has been distorted; the idea of God has been darkened. The result is that Calvin can maintain the notion of "natural religion" as representing nothing more than befouled religion, bastardized religion, "fabricated idolatry." Religious consciousness is not accorded the level of childish faith; it is not characterized as immature religion. He characterizes it as completely crippled. "The lamps shine futilely." That is the tragic conclusion to which the reformers come. We are unable to see. We cannot read the book of creation unless our vision is sharpened by the glasses of God's Word. In this approach, religious consciousness is relegated to the outer courts of the temple of true religion and an "abominable source of idolatry."

§5. The Problem Becomes Acute in Modernity

Undeniably, the problem of religious consciousness has received more serious attention in modern times. A number of factors have contributed to this development.

In the first place, we note the huge increase in our knowledge of the non-Christian religions. Into the eighteenth century, people knew but little about foreign religions, and in rendering a judgment about heathenism, they as a rule relied entirely on what they knew about the religion of the ancient Greeks and Romans. From about the middle of that century, an entire line of studies appeared about the various peoples of the world, and they shed entirely new light on their religious systems. Through the work of the Jesuits, a number of ancient Chinese writings became known in Europe. Officials of the British East India Company began publishing Indian accounts and religious works in Europe (see authors such as William Jones[66] and H. J. Colebrooke). As a consequence of the many voyages of discovery, the searchlight of scientific interest was also aimed at the world of so-called "primitive" religions. A number of other factors also ensured that the scientific study of religion was appreciably enriched.[67] All of this had very weighty consequences for the assessment of the phenomenon of religion in general. The big push toward the beginning of what is usually called the science of comparative religions began with Friedrich Max Müller.[68] He produced a series of studies that fixed attention on worthwhile elements in Indian religions and on the course of development that we generally observe in religious subjects.

The scientific investigation of the nineteenth century was hypnotized early on by evolutionary theory. Small wonder, then, that people also approached the subject of religion from an evolutionary perspective. We cite a man like Tylor, for example, when he says that a kind of degeneration can also occur with respect to religion. But he is of the opinion that with respect to religion as well as other areas, the principle of "the survival of the fittest" applies; religions have a chance of surviving and spreading to the degree that they address the major problems that people encounter.[69] As a consequence scholars recognized certain grades of difference among the religions as they

---

66. Ed. note: Sir William Jones (1746-1794) was a British Orientalist and jurist who, among other things, translated numerous works from the literature of Asia and published a grammar of the Persian language in 1771 along with essays about Asian poetry. See *The 1911 Classic Encyclopedia* (based on 11th edition of *The Encyclopedia Britannica*, published in 1911); available online at http://www.1911encyclopedia.org/Sir_William_Jones (accessed on 8 September 2011).

67. E. Lehmann, "Zur Geschichte der Religionsgeschichte," 4.1, in Chantepie de la Saussaye, *Lehrbuch der Religionsgeschichte*, ed. Alfred Bertholet and Edvard Lehmann, 2 vols., 4th ed. (Tübingen: J. C. B. Mohr [Paul Siebeck], 1925).

68. Friedrich Max Müller (1823-1900) was a German philologist and Orientalist and a pioneer in the academic study of religions, especially those of India. See Lourens P. van den Bosch, *Friedrich Max Müller: A Life Devoted to the Humanities*, Numen Book Series, 94 (Leiden: E. J. Brill, 2002); and Jon R. Stone, ed., *The Essential Max Müller: On Language, Mythology, and Religion* (New York: Palgrave, 2002).

69. Edward B. Tylor, *Primitive Culture: Researches into the Development of Mythology, Philosophy, Religion, Language, Art, and Custom*, 2 vols., 4th rev. ed. (London: John Murray, 1903), 1: 69.

developed, accounted for by such factors as race, climate, and historical circumstances that could have an influence on the development of a given religion, but at the same time this did not lead them to accept any fundamental differences between the religions. The basic premise on which scholars proceeded was that in the course of history a universal religious consciousness has developed, of which all separate religions are a concrete, historically defined manifestation.

The philosophical systems of the nineteenth century also supported these sentiments. Hegel viewed the entire history of human spiritual development as a process of supreme Reason becoming self-conscious. We see this emerging consciousness in art, where it is still limited to sensual observation and symbolic representation. But in religion the absolute Spirit manifests itself in the form of emotion and representation. From the perspective of humanity, religion can be described as "the knowledge that human beings have of God and of themselves in God."[70] Seen from the perspective of God, it is the absolute Spirit's self-consciousness in human history. God breaks through the limitations of human consciousness, comes to himself, and becomes conscious of himself. In the more "primitive"[71] religions, this still happens in a very vague and undefined way. But in the higher religions, it happens more clearly and directly. Ultimately, Christianity is the most complete religion, for in it the Absolute achieves full self-consciousness and understands itself in its Three-in-Oneness. This highest form of religion actually, by its own momentum, moves into philosophy, where feeling and imagination are replaced by concept and logical thought. Philosophy also has to undergo a long history before it sheds all error and limitation and breaks through to ultimate truth. Hegel is convinced that this breakthrough to the highest truth has been achieved in his own era and specifically in his own system. "A new epoch has sprung into existence in the world."[72]

Windelband somewhere made the accurate observation that the World Spirit that has assumed such an important place for Hegel in the philosophy of history and of religion in the deepest sense is nothing else than "the Spirit of human culture." "Hegel's absolute Spirit is in truth the human spirit."[73]

---

70. Friedrich Überwegs, *Grundriss der Geschichte der Philosophie*, ed. Traugott Konstantin Oesterreich, 4 vols., 11th ed. (Berlin: Ernst Siegfried Mittler and Son, 1916), 4: 87.

71. Ed. note: On Bavinck's use of the term "primitive" see Chapter 3, note 23.

72. W. Windelband, *Die Geschichte der Neueren Philosophie: In Ihrem Zusammenhange mit der Allgemeinen Cultur und den Besondern Wissenschaft*, 2 vols., 3rd ed. (Leipzig: Breitkopf & Härtel, 1899), 2: 337.

73. Windelband, *Die Geschichte der Neueren Philosophie*, 2: 371.

This fact is one that will necessarily be avenged in the history of philosophy, and this has occurred already with Hegel's own disciples; Feuerbach already drew the consequence from Hegel's philosophy that the absolute Spirit that according to Hegel comes to self-consciousness in religion is none other than "the shape of humanity's rationality," the expanse of humanity's collective thought. In religion, that expanse of humanity's collective thought creates a god in its own image and after its own likeness. The image of God that humanity creates in its religion is in essence nothing other than a gigantic projection of humanity itself that clearly bears all the features of humanity. Hegel says that in religion God achieves self-consciousness. Feuerbach says that in religion humanity comes to self-consciousness. Humanity elevates itself in its image of god and kneels down before its own shadow. Humanity idealizes itself and shrouds itself in all sorts of myths and stories. With these consequences, religion was simply brought back down to earth and misled down extremely remarkable psychological and sociological paths. But there was no longer room for God in this kind of religion.

The progress of human science, which here and there in the nineteenth century bordered on delirium induced by intoxication and pride, was furthermore the reason why people began to see religion as a backward phenomenon. Religion is a phase through which humanity had to pass, but which we have long since transcended. We have now entered the period of positive knowledge, where people no longer repeat mystical stories about gods and demigods, but where they listen to the more practical language of objective facts.

All of these factors were not favorable for a calm, objective assessment of the phenomenon of religion, in particular for clearheaded reflection on the question of truth that is so closely tied to religion. People could still make room for a place for human religious consciousness, and they could still study that consciousness historically and psychologically, but they could no longer do theology or talk about revelation. God does not reveal himself in religion, but religion is the place where people reveal themselves, where they lay themselves bare. Religion lies completely on the plane of this development, as reflected in the Higher Education Law of 1876 in the Netherlands, where the theological faculty was changed into the faculty pursuing the science of religion.[74] The nineteenth century still definitely had a place for reli-

74. Ed. note: For more on this law that turned the theology faculties of Dutch universities into departments of religious studies, see H. Bavinck, *Essays on Religion, Science and Society* (Grand Rapids: Baker Academic, 2008), chapter 3, and especially appendix B.

gion, which people still desired to study. But there was no room any longer for the question concerning religious truth.

We need not be surprised that theology itself, under the pressure of these developments, began finding itself reduced to a much lower position. The question of the absoluteness of Christianity now became one of the burning issues. This became a problem with which people struggled as never before. Ernst Troeltsch made a serious attempt from a historical perspective to save something of that absoluteness. He was convinced that the naïve sense of absoluteness held by the simple Christian was blown away by the winds of historical research. This position is impossible to maintain as soon as a person's eyes are opened to the fact that other peoples have had and still have their own religions in which they are just as convinced of their absoluteness. Nor can we proceed on the basis of some standard or other by which we could judge various religions. Where might we find such a standard? The only thing that remains for us to do is to investigate history from the bottom up. Then we will be unable to deny that such standards were born and that truths developed within history itself.[75] Then we will discover that from the colorful array of religious structures that have sprouted in the course of history, only two religious forces have matured that give any indication of the power and prospect of being repeatedly renewed and adapting to various influences.

The first one identified by Troeltsch is the prophetic-Christian faith; the second is the religious power of Asian Buddhism. In our own period of world events, he continued, these two forms of religion are engaged in a mighty struggle — a life-and-death struggle — and we must maintain the conviction that out of that very struggle the standards will arise by which people will be capable of judging between them. Christianity has the unique feature of respecting the human person. It recognizes and defends the human person as a moral and rational being. Asian religion is predisposed to swallowing up all of this in the totality of all things. Christianity has broken fully with natural religion and focuses all of its attention on redemption. In that sense, then, Troeltsch is inclined to see Christianity not only as the high point, but also as the point of convergence where all lines come together. It is the strongest and most perfect revelation of "personal religious consciousness."[76]

75. Ernst Troeltsch, *Die Absolutheit des Christentums und die Religionsgeschichte: Vortrag gehalten auf der Versammlung der Freunde der Christlichen Welt zu Mühlacker am 3. Oktober 1901*, 2nd ed. (Tübingen: J. C. B. Mohr [Paul Siebeck], 1912), p. 58. ET: *The Absoluteness of Christianity and the History of Religions,* trans. David Reid (Richmond, VA: John Knox Press, 1971).

76. Troeltsch, *Die Absolutheit des Christentums und die Religionsgeschichte,* p. 89.

This conflict about the absoluteness of Christianity also had substantial consequences for missions. Was it actually still responsible to call other peoples to faith in Jesus Christ when those other folks had religions that in any case were still valuable although not yet mature? Does it not seem arrogant to think that only Christianity had the right goal and that all other religions were in error?

For Troeltsch, mission work was actually a problematic subject. He thought it was desirable on psychological and cultural grounds, but to him it was only justifiable because through it a kind of spiritual confrontation occurs between the Christian faith and the Asian religions. For him, mission work must not be about converting pagans but about fertilizing their religious life with new ideas. Then, on the basis of such collaboration between peoples, a spiritual communal effort would arise. That would, in turn, seem to be of the greatest value for the future of humanity.[77]

On the mission fields themselves, all these ideas led to enormous problems. In India, syncretistic from antiquity, it aroused the inclination to suck Christianity into its own hazy idea of religious consciousness and to give it a place alongside all the other religious currents that flow together in Indian thought. Any number of leading Indian thinkers seriously attempted to reconcile the gospel of Christ and the ancient sacred writings of India. The best known is definitely the pronouncement of Gandhi against Joseph J. Doke in January 1908, when he said, "Christianity has a place in my own theology. Christ is a radiant revelation of God, but not the only one. I do not place him on a lonely throne."[78]

In the circles of the younger churches, the notion made the rounds that the older religions of Asia (Hinduism, Buddhism, Taoism, and others) should be regarded as the Old Testament of the Asian nations in which the peoples were nurtured unto Christ. And the New Testament would then have to be seen as the entire New Testament in which the old testaments of all religions come together. In the New Testament, Hinduism and Buddhism and other religions come to fulfillment. Not without some preference, therefore, people cited the words of Jesus where he says that he has come not to destroy "the law and the prophets," thus the Old Testament, but to fulfill

---

77. Ernst Troeltsch, "Missionsmotiv, Missionsaufgabe und neuzeitliches Humanitätschristentum," *Zeitschrift für Missionskunde und Religionswissenschaft* 22 (1907): 129-39, 161-66.

78. Romain Rolland, *Vida de Mahatma Gandhi,* 3rd ed. (Leipzig: Rotapfelverlag, 1922), p. 28.

them. In that same way, he is also the fulfillment of the religious searching and thinking of all the world's peoples.

From the side of missions, as well, these ideas found support rather than refutation. J. N. Farquhar wrote his famous essay "The Crown of Hinduism," where he points to the "broken lights" of Hinduism and recommends the gospel as their fulfillment. The title may not have been intended to be taken so seriously, but it nevertheless contributed to increased confusion.[79] Friedrich Heiler published his book *Revelation in the Religions of British India and the Proclamation of the Gospel,* in which he praised highly the "importance and purity of Indian religious ideas."[80] And I could continue in the same vein to quote a series of names and titles that raise the question of faith and religious consciousness and answer it by saying that the religious consciousness found among all people finds its fulfillment in the Christian faith. The Christian faith is the point of the religious consciousness living among all people. When the International Missionary Conference came together in Jerusalem in 1928, the official statement sent out from that conference to the entire world spoke with deep appreciation for "the spiritual value of the non-Christian religions."[81] That appreciation was expressed even more fully in the so-called "layman's report" that in 1932 appeared under the title *Re-Thinking Missions.* In it the purpose of missions was described as "to seek with people of other lands a true knowledge and love of God, expressing in life and word what we have learned through Jesus Christ, and endeavoring to give effect to his spirit in the life of the world."[82] The task of missions is no longer to preach the gospel, but it has become an exchange of spiritual experiences, influencing one another from both sides, and strengthening our spirit of brotherhood.

No wonder that the question of religious consciousness and the Christian faith took on very serious and relevant dimensions. It revolved around the foundation for missions and around the spiritual struggle of that period. Based on all sorts of national considerations, Asia itself began increasingly

---

79. Godfrey Edward Phillips, *The Gospel in the World: A Restatement of Missionary Principles* (London: Duckworth, 1939), p. 81.

80. Friedrich Heiler and J. C. Helders, *De Openbaring in de Godsdiensten van Britsch-Indië en de Christus-verkondiging* (Amsterdam: II. J. Paris, 1931), p. 15.

81. *The Jerusalem Meeting of the International Missionary Council March 24–April 8, 1928,* 8 vols. (London: International Missionary Council, 1928), 1: 348.

82. The Commission of Appraisal, William Ernest Hocking, Chairman, *Re-Thinking Missions: A Layman's Inquiry After One Hundred Years* (New York: Harper and Brothers, 1932), p. 59.

emphasizing its own, prehistorical, cultural legacy. It also seemed increasingly less inclined to listen to the message that missionaries from the West interpreted for them. For the older generations, the problems related to religious consciousness and Christian faith and to Christianity and the other religions were more or less theoretical problems that could be battled out in the isolation of one's study. But in the heat of modern times, they are urgently relevant questions occupying the thought of many millions and are determinative for the future.

§6. Barth and Brunner

A remarkable turn in European theological thought has occurred in recent decades, a turn in which especially Karl Barth and Emil Brunner played a leading role. When we compare a man like Barth with Schleiermacher, Troeltsch, and others, we can only conclude that he "turned the rudder in a radically different direction."[83] He makes a sharp distinction between God and man, between time and eternity. In humanity, there is not one single point of contact with which God in his revelation would be able to connect. No religious sphere exists that has been able to prepare for receiving it, and no religious emotion is present that can be incorporated into faith as a worthwhile component. Within a human being there is absolutely nothing at all on which God can lay his hand of approval; there is only corruption and guilt.

From this standpoint, Barth passes judgment on the enormous complex of phenomena that we call religion. In his *The Doctrine of the Word of God (Die Lehre vom Worte Gottes),* he deals extensively with the problem of religion as it is to be treated theologically. He points out how that problem has repeatedly been handled in a wrong way. Time and again, people have wanted to approach it from the human side. He then concludes: "on the contrary, the question is uninterruptedly theological: what is this thing which from the standpoint of revelation and faith is revealed in the actuality of human life as religion?"[84] Then he proceeds to depict religion as unbelief and apostasy. "It

83. G. C. Van Niftrik, *Een beroerder Israëls: Enkele Hoofdgedachten in de Theologie van Karl Barth* (Nijkerk: Callenbach, 1948), p. 30.

84. Karl Barth, *Church Dogmatics,* I/2: *The Doctrine of the Word of God,* ed. G. W. Bromiley and T. F. Torrance, trans. G. T. Thompson and Harold Knight (Edinburgh: T. & T. Clark, 1956), pp. 296-97. Ed. note: The original Dutch text has only a fragment of this quotation from the *Church Dogmatics.*

is a concern, indeed, we must say that it is the one great concern, of godless man."[85] For this reason, it is also in and of itself "always self-contradictory and impossible."[86] Thus, we are taught to see it in terms of the revelation of Jesus Christ, who rips off all religious masks and exposes religion for what it really is, namely in its flight from God and its never-ending attempt to justify people. In the name of revelation, Barth issues his withering sentence even on mysticism — that often highly esteemed runaway from religion.

The nature of the issue is such that Barth, in tackling this question, repeatedly runs into the difficult problem of general revelation. One of the most pointed definitions of religions goes like this: "From the standpoint of revelation religion is clearly seen to be a human attempt to anticipate what God in His revelation wills to do and does do. It is the attempted replacement of the divine work by a human manufacture."[87] But, is religion not always tied to and a product of general revelation? And is it really appropriate, then, to register such a harsh judgment against it? Barth gives a clear answer to this question in his short book *The Christian Doctrine of Revelation*. There he says,

> I readily admit that the same eternal Word of God that became flesh can also be heard in nature, in history, and in a person's own heart, conscience, and mind. But he or she then goes further and recognizes, to their own shame, that they in fact have not only never heard it, but that they will never be able to hear it. . . . Because they [namely, believers] are brought under judgment by grace, they will come to recognize that there (namely, in creation) they only hear the voices of idols, that is to say, they have heard and will only hear the elements of this world created by God: the voices of the earth and of animal life; the voice of the seemingly endless heavens and out of it the voice of their apparently inevitable destiny; in their own veins, the voices of their own blood, their parents, and their race; and in their own hearts, the voices of geniuses and heroes. All of these voices are clothed in the vestments of divine falsehood and authority. They have listened to all of them and taken them to be divine. But through them all they have not understood the eternal Word of God.[88]

---

85. Karl Barth, *Church Dogmatics,* I/2, pp. 299-300.

86. Karl Barth, *Church Dogmatics,* I/2, p. 314.

87. Karl Barth, *Church Dogmatics,* I/2, p. 302.

88. Karl Barth, *Het Christelijk Openbaringsbegrip,* trans. H. C. Touw (Nijkerk: Callenbach, 1937), pp. 21-22. Ed. note: This is a translation of *Offenbarung, Kirche, Theologie* (München: Chr. Kaiser, 1934); this book has not been translated into English.

General revelation certainly exists, therefore, but it does not speak to people and remains without effect because no instrument for receiving it, no point of contact, is present in them. This is how Johannes Witte, one of Barth's followers, briefly summarized the doctrine of general revelation:

> There is also in reality no divine general revelation to the heathen, in the sense that these people have been able to participate in this revelation as a revelation from God. God has definitely revealed himself in the creation and in the conscience. But these people were in revolt by virtue of their sin and therefore did not recognize God in this revelation.[89]

Kraemer, who otherwise was in many regards subject to Barth's strong influence, is of the opinion that "even in this fallen world God shines through in a broken, troubled way: in reason, in nature and in history." He considers it wrong of Barth to hesitate entering into a discussion of the question of how God has been at work among these people, even though he definitely recognizes that God has been working and continues working among them.[90]

In the meantime, a serious difference of opinion arose between Barth and Brunner over this whole question of general revelation and the capacity of people to receive it. To a modest work that Brunner wrote on the subject, titled *Nature and Grace,* Barth responded with a vigorous *Nein!* In this ongoing conflict, Brunner responded with a second edition of his *Nature and Grace,* where he attempted to give a careful account of just where he and Barth disagreed. He remained of the conviction that even fallen people retained the "capacity for speech"[91] as well as accountability. This has the consequence "that one can generally reason with people about God."[92] And this is the point of contact for preaching about redemption.[93]

We refrain from going into this difference of opinion between Barth and

---

89. Johannes Witte, *Die Christus-Botschaft und die Religionen* (Göttingen: Vandenhoeck & Ruprecht, 1936), p. 40.

90. H. Kraemer, *The Christian Message in a Non-Christian World* (London: Edinburgh House Press, 1938), p. 120.

91. Ed. note: German: *Wortmächtigkeit*. In his English translation of Brunner's *Natur und Gnade: Zum Gespräch mit Karl Barth,* 2nd ed. (Zürich: Zwingli, 1935), Peter Fraenkel translates *Wortmächtigkeit* as "capacity for words," but in his introduction to the volume, John Baillie indicates his preference for "capacity for speech," and we are following Baillie's suggestion. See Emil Brunner and Karl Barth, *Natural Theology: Comprising "Nature and Grace" and "No!,"* trans. Peter Fraenkel (Eugene, OR: Wipf & Stock, 2002).

92. Brunner and Barth, *Natural Theology,* p. 56.

93. Brunner and Barth, *Natural Theology,* pp. 30-31.

Brunner any further. It strikes us as not totally clear what Brunner means by "the capacity for speech" and whether or not with this term he bootlegged into the conversation elements of natural theology *(theologia naturalis)* in an erroneous sense.[94] Brunner himself emphatically denies this and wishes to use the term "natural theology" only to convey that it is an empirical fact that the natural, sinful person operates with some sort of theology. Nevertheless, here and there he does not escape using expressions that can lead to misunderstanding. On the other hand, Barth gets into not a little trouble with respect to his exposition of Romans 1:18. This was demonstrated several years ago by F. W. A. Korff in his interesting study *The Christian Faith and the Non-Christian Religions (Het Christelijk Geloof en de Niet-Christelijke Godsdiensten).*[95] This point was illumined again more recently by G. C. Berkouwer in his *Conflict with Rome,* where he demonstrates that Barth's exegesis of Romans 1 is not very convincing with respect to Rome's position.[96] This very complicated issue with respect to a natural theology, including the importance of religious consciousness, is a burning one in discussions between dialectical theology and Roman Catholic theology. Increasingly, it is becoming apparent that it will be a cardinal subject in the development of both theological and philosophical thought.

The time has come to bring our historical review to a close. There are a number of very complicated questions from everything that we have said to this point; a few things have become clear. The first is certainly that associated with the problem of religious consciousness and the Christian faith. When we attempt to describe what they are, we can formulate them like this:

1. Does general revelation exist? If so, what is that general revelation? What is its content? And how does it reach us?
2. Does this general revelation also impact humanity, or does it simply and entirely pass people by? If it does impact humanity, does it bring about anything at all in people? Or, must we take Calvin's expression in its fullest sense, when he says, "It is in vain that so many burning lamps in the universe shed their light on us"?
3. If that general revelation in fact reaches humanity and does something

94. Brunner, *Natur und Gnade.* See also *Dogmatics,* vol. 1: *The Christian Doctrine of God,* trans. Olive Wyon (London: Lutterworth, 1949), pp. 132-36.

95. F. W. A. Korff, *Het Christelijk Geloof en de Niet-Christelijke Godsdiensten* (Amsterdam: Holland Uitgeversmaatschappi, 1946), pp. 113ff.

96. G. C. Berkouwer, *Conflict with Rome,* trans. David H. Freeman (Philadelphia: Presbyterian and Reformed, 1958), p. 234.

to people, does that mean, then, that some capacity and capability were present in people beforehand? Is that capacity lodged in human reason, and is that reason unaffected by sin? (Rome) Or, is there a religious a-priori or definite openness of the human soul to holiness? Or, are we not better off speaking of a seed of religion *(semen religionis)* and sense of divinity *(sensus divinitatis)?* What should we understand by these terms? Or, is it even more preferable to acknowledge a human capacity for the Word *(Wortmägtichkeit)*, and what do we mean by it? H. Bavinck demonstrates in his *Reformed Dogmatics* that a religion always contains a unique external principle of knowledge *(principium cognoscendi externum)* as well as a unique internal principle of knowledge *(principium cognoscendi internum)* that is responsive to that revelation.[97] But what, then, is that inner principle and what is its importance? In short, what is the foundation within humanity and what is the human instrument through which religion becomes possible?

4. What is the significance of the religion that develops within humanity? Are there dimensions of truth locked in it, or is it nothing more than unbelief, apostasy, or perversion?

5. Following from #4: What is the relationship of special revelation to general revelation and to human religion? Is there continuity? Do they connect with one another? Or, is there only discontinuity between them? In other words, does special revelation only speak a *"Nein!"* against all human religion?

6. Finally: What is the posture of special revelation and the message of Christ with respect to all human religion?

We leave the historical survey with these questions. Anyone who learns from what has been said about these issues in the course of history is deeply impressed by the force with which they have repeatedly pressed on human consciousness. This began already during the time of the early church fathers, flowed like a river through the Middle Ages, and impacted modern history under various names and many directions. The conflict flamed up again on the mission field. The good news came into the world as a message, "but people did not receive it." Yet, everywhere in the world that it found analogies, it engaged other religions that in many respects seemed to be compara-

---

97. Herman Bavinck, *Reformed Dogmatics*, vol. 1: *Prolegomena*, ed. John Bolt, trans. John Vriend (Grand Rapids: Baker Academic, 2003), p. 505.

ble to what the gospel proclaimed. It is alien, yet so trustworthy; it is different, yet so similar.

Is Christ the "desire of the nations" in the sense that so many, on the basis of a mistaken exegesis of Haggai 2:8, have hailed him? Do people turn to him out of the world's deepest desires? Do all the lines of searching and trying that have run their course as unsettled supplications in religious history come together in him? Is his gospel the meaning and fulfillment of the holy scriptures of all the nations — of the philosophy of the Greeks as well as that of India and China and so many other countries? Does that one remarkable text in the prophecy of Malachi apply here: "For my name is great among the peoples, from the rising to the setting of the sun. In every place, incense and pure offerings are lifted to my name, for it is great among the nations, says the Lord of lords" (Mal. 1:11, as translated by Ridderbos).[98] Should that text be understood as also applying to what the heathen offer to their gods, but at the deepest level be taken to mean offerings to the one, true God? And in his overpowering vision, does Isaiah mean that only the veil of great misunderstanding and illusion needs to be removed, when he says this: On Mount Zion a feast will be laid out for all the peoples "and the shroud covering the faces of the nations will be swept aside" (Isa. 25:7)? How must we see that major, deeply affective relationship between the gospel of Christ and the powerful, unquenchable, ineradicable religious consciousness that humanity has maintained throughout the centuries and that still seems so vital and powerful, despite the secularization of our modern culture? Is what Karrer says somewhere about eastern atheism and even, with some reserve, about western atheism true, when he observes that the words of Eckhart can be applied to these deniers of God, namely that there are those who deny God from religious motives, those who "discredit God because they love God"?[99] Then is everything different from what we have always thought? Does Christ stand high above history as the sole answer to all human searching?

---

98. J. Ridderbos, *De Kleine Profeten: Opnieuw uit, den Grondtekst Vertaald en Verklaard*, 3 vols. (Kampen: J. H. Kok, 1932-1935), 3: 202.

99. Otto Karrer, *Het Religieuse*, pp. 144-45.

6 Religious Consciousness and Christian Faith

§1. Back to Romans 1

Armed with the questions that have been raised historically, it is clear that we need to return to Romans 1 and calmly try reading these verses once more. They have been of such determinative significance for our project that we need to internalize their meaning if we hope to achieve any clarity on the subject.

It is beyond debate that Romans 1 teaches the reality of general revelation. "Since what may be known about God is plain to them, because God has made it plain to them" (v. 19). "For although they knew God, they neither glorified him as God nor gave thanks to him" (v. 21). This general revelation may not be explained here, then, in terms of the verb *apokaluptein*, which is equivalent to removing a curtain, but in terms of a verb emphasizing to make more manifest or more evident. This fact is indisputable.

Regarding this self-manifestation of God or this "voiceless speech," three things that can facilitate a deeper understanding need to be said.

In the first place, attention needs to be focused on the fact that this *manifestatio* constitutes the only point of contact in mission work. When Paul had opportunity to say a few words in Lystra, in the press of a crowd, he did not address them on the basis of human religion, but very directly and intentionally on the basis of God's self-disclosure in the world. "God, who made heaven and earth and sea and everything in them . . . has not left himself without testimony: He has shown kindness by giving you rain from heaven and crops in their seasons; he provides you with plenty of food and fills your hearts with joy" (Acts 14:15, 17). The same thing occurs in his speech on the Areopagus, albeit somewhat more defensively. "The God who made the world and everything in it is the Lord of heaven and earth" (Acts 17:24). In his missionary preaching, Paul very definitely does not take his point of departure from human religion, but from the objective work of God and from God's self-manifestation. My own inner conviction is that this is the only truly relevant and effective point of contact. All others are empty and useless. This point of departure is not simply a beginning for the preaching of the gospel, it is the beginning of a new chapter. "In the past God overlooked such ignorance, but now he commands all people everywhere to repent" (Acts 17:30). We are the bearers of the "now" in this text. We stand in that momentous divine "now," the "now" of a new chapter in God's involvement with his world. All missionary proclamation only stands on solid ground when it is done in this conviction: "God has been busy with you already for a very long time, but you have not understood this. Through my preaching, God is coming to you once again in order to call you to conversion."

In the second place, a good purpose is served in remembering that general revelation occurs in the living connection between people and the world around them, in what one could call the symbiotic relationship of people and the world. Older philosophy was once inclined to isolate people too much from the world and to consider humanity in isolation. It regarded humanity as a subject over against the world. And when it made humanity the object of its study, it placed primary emphasis on humanity's observational and thinking relationship to the world. We need to keep in mind that humanity exists in an unbreakable and living relationship with the world and that it can never be isolated from it for even one moment. All human thinking, longing, feeling, hoping, striving, and fearing — in short, all human dispositions — are comprehended in this living relationship that humanity has with the world around it. This is the reason why general revelation needs to be seen only from the perspective of coming to people in and through that inner relationship that they have with the world around them.

This, then, brings us to the third point. General revelation must be seen less as a philosophical instinct lodged in human superiority and more as a force that people encounter in their life-relationships. In other words, it must be understood more existentially. When in the nineteenth century people began studying the so-called "primitive"[1] religions, "savages" were still definitely profiled as "savage philosophers." Now, what is undeniable is

---

1. Ed. note: See Chapter 3, notes 23 and 25, for comments on the term "primitive."

that people who have an inner bond with nature still definitely have an observational, reflective relationship with respect to reality. But one should not give that too high a value. What grips people first of all is much rather the existential necessities of life such as dealing with loneliness and the fear of death. In his book titled *Concerning the Ways and Mainsprings of Religion: A Study in the Psychology of Religion (Over Wegen en Drijfveren der Religie)*, Van Baal places emphasis rather on the dual-dimensional nature of humanity. Human beings are a part of nature and the cosmos, but they are also more than nature and other than nature. That duality raises new problems for people, especially the problem of their loneliness. Religion, even so-called primitive religion, is all about finding fellowship and discovering safety, shelter, and rest.[2]

This is inherent in the fact that people ought not to see general revelation only or even first of all as appealing to human philosophical reflection. Universally considered, that reflection is fairly undeveloped and probably does not play as important a part as it once was given. People are living entities. They live in their connectedness with the world around them. They realize that they are caught up in this connectedness. But at the same time, they are aware of their uniqueness and their individuality. They walk around with a unique sense of royalty, but at the same time they feel like poor souls and beggars sitting at the world's gates. God stands before them in those realities, in those living connections with the world around them, in their neediness, their recklessness, their abundance, their anxiety. God manifests himself there. If only people could shed their self-awareness, their individuality, their sense of royalty; if only they could simply dissolve into the world around them like plants and animals do, without norms or morals! But they cannot. They are human. They exist with the indescribable greatness as well as the pathetic woefulness that that term covers. That is where God meets them. The meeting point of general revelation and the human being is not isolated, and it is not even first of all found in his or her capacity thoughtfully to contemplate the vastness of all that exists. It lies first of all simply in the problems inherent in being human, that is, in being a fallen human being.

God meets people in that reality. "What may be known about God is plain to them," that is, presents itself as evident to them. What can be known about God is then described more fully as his "eternal power and divine na-

---

2. Jan van Baal, *Over Wegen en Drijfveren der Religie: Een Godsdienstpsychologische Studie* (Amsterdam: N. V. Noord-Hollandsche, 1947), pp. 238ff.

ture." We need to go into those two words more deeply, since they seem to be of central significance for us.

His "eternal power." Anyone who is even slightly at home in the history of religion knows the fascinating effect that the concept of power has. In all religions, it is all about power: the power for living, and the power against which we struggle. This is because a living person always understands that each thing is more than the thing itself and that it contains an inscrutable element that makes it important. A person walks up a steep incline in the mountains. A stone falls and either hits him or just misses him. In both cases, the stone is obviously more than just a stone. It is at one and the same time a threat, a danger, even death, or it is a relief and deliverance. Lightning strikes her house or just misses it. That lightning is more than a flash of light. It is also a threatening, anxiety-producing danger. The seeds that sowers hold in their hands are more than just kernels of grain. When they are sown, they can either germinate or not germinate. In other words, they are either seeds of promise, possibility, abundance, and life, or they are seeds of disappointment, hunger, and death. In the great interconnectedness of life, each thing has its place and is a bearer of definite powers. A person exists in the intricacy of everything in the world working together, in which each thing always carries some mysterious power. Lévy-Bruhl has attempted to demonstrate in an extensive study *(How Natives Think)* that for the "primitive" person each thing possesses its own mysterious characteristics. It is endlessly more than the thing itself, and contained in it are active supernatural forces that have life-and-death significance.[3] I cannot at this point consider the truth of this claim. But it is certainly the case that for a person, and definitely not just for the "primitive" person, a thing is more than the thing itself. When someone is in a hurry and leaves a place in a car, and then blows a tire, other things go wrong. One ends up hitting a tree alongside the road and becoming very angry. In all this a certain mysterious force is at work, a definite malice and judgment. The thought process deals with things, but in the context of life, we contend with forces. These are powers that work with and for us or that are malicious toward us. But it is always about power, the amazing, mysterious potentials inherent in things on the strength of which those things become threats and dangers or produce anticipation and hope. A person encounters this power simply by virtue of existing in the world.[4]

---

3. Lucien Lévy-Bruhl, *How Natives Think,* trans. Lilian A. Clare (New York: Washington Square, 1966), p. 27.

4. Ed. note: Understanding the human religious impulse in terms of power is the char-

His "divine nature." In the previous chapter, I reminded readers that this term apparently indicated what people at present approvingly call "the Holy" or "the Wholly Other." But I am still of the opinion that here we also find a term that points to the personal nature of God. It designates a *Someone*, a mysterious *Someone*, who meets us in our interaction with the world around us. These words intend to convey, therefore, his divine nature as well as his godlikeness. In their engagement with the world around them, people recognize that they are involved with a wisdom that is infinitely higher than their own wisdom, with a power that is infinitely greater than their own strength, and with a greatness with which their own greatness cannot compare. This *Someone* with whom they are involved can make or break them in every respect. And there is something deep within people — despite all their stubborn attempts to reduce that *Someone* to a force, to *mana*, or to *Brahman* — that persuades them with unmistakable emphasis that it is still really a Someone. People stand in an I-Thou and in a dialogical relationship, and they can only really exist in that relationship. As soon as they let go of it, they die. Though, at most, they can sit musing at a distance, they can no longer really live. All of this is presented to people with overwhelming evidence, and they know that they are accountable to this *Someone*.

These two realities, his everlasting power and his divine nature, *"are made plain to them."* Now comes the second question: *"How* are they made plain to them?" Do people have some kind of sensory organ for receiving them, an auditory antenna in order to hear about them? What foundation for general revelation exists in people? What is the *principium internum* or the inner principle that responds to general revelation? We realize that this is the crux of the matter, the heart of the problem.

In this regard, it strikes us that this foundation or inner *principium* within our humanity is never entirely identified in Scripture. The emphasis falls so heavily on the objective self-manifestation of God that the subjective human organ for responding to it simply eludes us. The text definitely says that since the creation of the world these qualities have been understood from his works. These words can leave the impression that such an organ, namely the understanding, is meant. Is it perhaps the capacity to reason, which, according to some, has not been annihilated by sin but still retains the ability to create a natural theology? Is Rome correct, then, when it points

---

acteristic work of Bavinck's Dutch contemporary and phenomenologist of religion Gerardus van der Leeuw; see Gerardus van der Leeuw, *Religion in Essence and Manifestation: A Study in Phenomenology,* trans. J. E. Turner (London: Allen & Unwin, 1938).

to reason as the great, indestructible source of knowledge concerning divine truth? Is reason the subjective basis for general revelation?

When we think through this matter, we note first of all that the "understanding" as such is not mentioned in the Greek text. In the old *Statenvertaling*[5] we read "were understood and clearly seen" (*"worden verstaan en doorzien"*). Quite literally, what stands there is this: "words, being understood, were clearly seen" (*"worden, verstaan wordende, doorzien"*). And for the phrase "being understood," Paul uses a verb in the Greek text that can mean "being true," "being taken as true," or "were realized." Here it is not so much about all sorts of mechanisms in the understanding that were capable of drawing logical conclusions from created realities, on the basis of which they would decide that God exists. Paul certainly does not mean all of this here. Had he intended to say that and wanted to lay his emphasis on the reflective function of the understanding, he would undoubtedly have expressed himself very differently. Actually, he does not point at all in the direction of the understanding as some superior, noble organ with which people can master the truth. He only wants to say that this eternal power and divinity that presses in on us from every side is being taken to be true, is being consciously understood and clearly seen by us. That last verb, "clearly seen," arouses the suggestion that Paul may have had in mind an almost visionary event. Something stands immediately in front of people, and people suddenly "receive insight" and see it as a powerful reality over against themselves.

Is there, then, no specific organ at all that corresponds to general revelation? Is there only an ordinary understanding on which all the weight rests? Naturally, there has to be a *principium internum* or inner principle. Every child has a father and a mother. If general revelation is the father of religion, there must also be something in the human being that makes it possible for a person to receive that general revelation. But then I have to add immediately that Scripture regards that inner principle as so completely unimportant that it does not even mention it. The Bible does not talk about an auditory antenna or some such thing, but it lays the accent so completely on the objective speaking of God that the subjective is overlooked. I am personally inclined to see this single fact as an extremely important indication that human beings can only really engage in living as a dialogical relationship.

5. Ed. note: The *Statenvertaling* is the authorized version of the Dutch Bible, commissioned by the Synod of Dort (1618-19) and authorized by the States-General of the Kingdom of the Netherlands; it corresponds nicely to the English Authorized or King James Version.

Human beings are always in dialogue. They talk to their cows and their horses, to their sown grain and the rain clouds, to the sun and the ground. Only in this way can they exist as living beings. I do not know what this goes back to or what is hidden behind it. But I am definitely deeply conscious of the fact that people, as those standing in this world and living with an inner connection to that world, can do no other than to speak each and every day with that *Someone* whom they meet on a daily basis. That could well be one of the aspects of that mysterious, inexplicable *semen religionis* about which Calvin speaks.[6] Once again, all of this is totally unimportant when compared with that objective voiceless speech with which God addresses people. It certainly seems that the Bible is so preoccupied with arousing this inner principle because it fears that we will focus all our attention on intentionally resisting it and forgetting God. The eye does not see itself! That is the nature of its existence! Likewise, the inner principle does not see itself either. It is allowed only to see God. I am convinced that it will defy the sharpest thought of ever discovering its true nature.

The only thing that we can still say about this subject is that this inner principle is something that can only be understood in terms of God's initiative. It cannot be credited to human beings or registered as a human virtue, for it exists only because God has called it into existence. It is what Augustine and numerous other Christian thinkers suspect is the deep truth disclosed by that beautiful verse in Psalm 36: "In your light, we see light." God himself needs to open our eyes to enable us to see God.

The result is, therefore, that the eternal power and divinity are understood (meaning "brought to attention") and made clear, surveyed, visually comprehended. Thus, people know. Yes, they know. They are addressed as "knowers." "*For although they knew God . . .*" are words that Barthian theology will never give their full due. People know.

This means at the same time that Calvin's expression about so many lamps burning in futility cannot be taken in an ultimate sense. General revelation does not simply slide past people like a drop of rain does off the waxy leaf of a tree. General revelation achieves something and brings something about. It positions people as those who know. The legal status of people is that of those who know. In all of our considerations about religion, we may never neglect that fact.

---

6. Ed. note: See John Calvin, *Institutes of the Christian Religion*, 2 vols., ed. John T. McNeill, trans. Ford Lewis Battles, The Library of Christian Classics, vol. 20 (Louisville: Westminster John Knox, 1960), 1.3.1.

§2. Suppressing and Exchanging

This puts us right in the middle of an incredible problem, since it cannot be denied that Scripture clearly states that people do not know. "You sacrifice to one you do not know"; "You worship that which you do not know"; the pagans "that did not know God." An overwhelming flood of places in the Bible emphasize this not knowing. This forces the conclusion that the position of human beings is paradoxical. They know, and they do not know. Their legal position is that of knowing, but their actual position is that of not knowing. They proceed as unknowing knowers, as though they "might possibly find him."

In this connection, we need to fix our attention on the two words that we identified earlier and that seem to us to govern this whole problem: "suppressing" and "exchanging." Paul uses them alongside each other: *"human beings who suppress the truth by their wickedness"* and *"they exchanged the truth about God for a lie"* (Rom. 1:18 and 25). These two words deserve our full attention here.

What is that "suppressing"? We have described it as a repressing, and we have registered the suspicion that this can also happen unconsciously. The idea might well be that this suppression occurs so directly, so spontaneously, so simultaneously with the "understanding" and "seeing clearly" that at the precise moment that people see, they already no longer see; at the exact moment that they know, they already no longer know. Psychologically considered, this is in and of itself entirely possible. Psychological research has shown clearly that even in the most basic instances of becoming aware of something, many factors are already involved. Thus, becoming consciously aware of something is sometimes much more than, or sometimes quite different from, that which is strictly picked up by the senses. Our awareness is tied to all kinds of inner emotional and volitional dimensions of our lives. We become aware of that about which we have a deep interest. We see what we want to see. This does not happen in the absolute sense that I am describing here. But the fact remains that the entire life of our becoming aware is much more complex than we often think.[7] In this connection, one could even say that human beings, in being addressed by the world around them, always suppress an instance of their becoming aware as an instance in which God, who is present everywhere and in everything, presents himself and manifests himself to them in a very evident way.

---

7. A. Kuyper and J. H. Bavinck, *Inleiding in de Zielkunde*, 2nd ed. (Kampen: J. H. Kok, 1935), pp. 78ff.

This occurs instantly, so that people actually never arrive at the point of knowing. They see, but they do not see. They never fully see. God definitely reveals himself, but people immediately push it away, repress it, suppress it. They are knowers who do not know, seers who do not see. Their juridical position is different from their actual reality.

Concerning this process of suppression, Paul says that moral, or better said, immoral, factors play a role. People suppress *"by their wickedness."* The preposition "by" here really means "in the sphere of." It occurs with the mysterious, always unstated, often also entirely unconscious motive of moral opposition to God.

One only needs to reflect on these matters in order to see their enormous significance for the entire human condition. It strikes me that we can track this significance in the following three points.

In the first place, we need to keep a sharp eye on the fact that there is something distorted in the human condition. People have been resisting, suppressing. They have done so unconsciously. But they do so all the time, moment by moment, always unaware that they are doing so. But at the same time, there is always a definite unsettledness deep within them as a consequence of that suppression. This amounts to a definite dissatisfaction and tension. As a rule, the engine of this suppressing process runs noiselessly, but not so noiselessly that they never feel it running now and then and thereby realize that something is amiss in their lives. People play hide-and-seek with God. They are honest neither with themselves nor with life. They will never admit this, but it always hangs over them. Nevertheless, there are moments when they vaguely suspect something sour and distorted about their existence. Here it is impossible for me to get into this at any depth, so I will only say this. When people begin to be illumined by the light of the gospel, they sometimes suddenly become aware of the horror of this suppressing process and realize that they have always known but have never wanted to know. It strikes me that a great deal of the unsettledness, the primal fear, and the tension of which people give evidence at various times in their lives is connected with this basic phenomenon at the root of their existence: they do not live honestly in this world.

In the second place, we must not overlook the possibility of a variety of individual differences. There are people who appear to be so completely comfortable with the process of repressing that they take no notice of it. These are people without any possibility of forming some idea of what the little word "god" might mean. For them, God is such a nonentity that they have never even given any thought to it. In a manner of speaking, the force of revelation is like that of a stone dropped in the water. The water hardly ripples, and soon nothing is left or is visible any longer. However, there are other cases where the suppression happens with much more difficulty and sometimes even seems to fail entirely. Here it causes constant unrest. Sometimes it seems as if God's presence can manifest itself so obviously to people that they can no longer escape it and have no chance whatsoever of suppressing it. They are simply overwhelmed by it. Somewhere Calvin says that "there are scarcely one in a hundred found who treasure in their hearts the implanted seed (the *semen religionis*)."[8] It seems to me that with this "one in a hundred" he is thinking of those for whom suppressing only takes place accompanied by a great deal of unsettledness. This is due to no human virtue. It proves nothing about the nobility of human nature. It is only due to God's personal involvement with people and to the overpowering force with which he has clearly made himself known to people. Balaam was not inclined in the least to listen to God, but he was simply overwhelmed by God and could utter not a word against what God commanded. That is certainly an entirely different situation, since it falls in the area of special revelation. But it does provide us with a clear example that helps us see that God is capable of breaking through all impediments, smashing all secret maneuvering of our suppression, and compelling us to bow respectfully. The history of religion as well as missionary experience teaches us that it makes no sense to paint all pagans with the same brush. We will have to observe with great care what has happened in every individual life. We need to be sensitive to the wounds inflicted in each person's struggle against God. Feeble human feet can never kick aside God's presence with us without incurring a penalty. That very painful reality is played out in each human life in its own unique way.

In the third place, I believe that we may never forget that what has been suppressed has, for that very reason, not been completely obliterated. It has not been destroyed or rubbed out, but it has only been suppressed — no more and no less than that. That can only mean that somewhere, deep within the hidden recesses of people's beings, that repressed and suppressed truth is still present. It has never simply disappeared but has always been alive and active. Maybe it sometimes accosts them in a dream and at other times hounds them in their doubts. What, then, is that truth? It can be nothing other than certainty about God, certainty that God exists, certainty that

---

8. Ed. note: Bavinck is likely referring to this quote from Calvin: "But scarcely one man in a hundred is met who fosters it, once received, in his heart." Calvin, *Institutes of the Christian Religion*, 1.4.1.

each thing is more than the thing itself because it is controlled by the hand of God. It is the certainty of God's eternal power and divinity against which a mere mortal can never contend without sooner or later being slain by doing so. It is the certainty, as a piercing knowledge, that people are fallen, that something about them is irreparably broken, and that for all the days of their lives they have been playing a detestable game with God.

Does it lie hidden, then, as an undigested truth deep within a human being? Perhaps someone will say to me, "That is where you will find the truest point of contact, the suppressed truth." Or, maybe one might point out to me, "Here is where we wholeheartedly intrude on the field of psychology." To both of these objections, I would respond with an emphatic "No!" I would do so because that repressed truth is not something inherent in our humanity. It remains despite and completely contrary to the human will. It remains because powerless people, in their terrible immorality, are certainly in a position to resist, to banish, and to throw off the truth of God, but they are never in the position to simply obliterate it. It always lurks as a threat in their lives, and it never leaves them alone. At one point, Karl Barth says about missionary preaching that it is not a repeating but a beginning. "It proceeds as teaching. It occurs as hope against hope. It can only connect with those points that it has to establish itself, not ones that were already present beforehand."[9] I think this is just plain wrong. I am prepared to acknowledge everything else that Barth says about the fallen condition of humanity, but on this one point I stand in clear opposition to him. Barth does not see that human beings, even fallen and sinful human beings, can and may never be thought to exist beyond God's revelation. People are always more than as people they actually are. They are people with a wound that cannot be closed — they suppress. But in the most critical moments of their existence, they feel assailed by what they have with such determined certainty attempted to push away. They are people who have assaulted God, who do so every day anew, and who have some sense of what they are doing — however vague that sense may be. They can never entirely rid themselves of the truth about God that they have suppressed, held back, pushed away, sublimated, or crucified. This is what they fear; it is their tragedy.

This implies that we can never get our arms around that suppressed truth as something that still adorns human beings. It is not inherent in humans, but

---

9. Karl Barth, "Die Theologie und die Mission in der Gegenwart: Vortrag, gehalten an der Brandenburgischen Missionskonferenz in Berlin am 11. April 1932," *Zwischen den Zeiten* 10 (1932): 197.

it exists despite them, is opposed to them, and is their enemy. Missionary proclamation does not proceed as mere teaching, but in the knowledge that God has already been busy with people long before we came to them, and that God already began the discussion with them before we have spoken even one word to them. It also proceeds in the certainty that through preaching, by God's grace, that mishandled truth can be aroused, can be awakened, can grab people by their throats, and can bring them to their knees.

I have the impression that Tertullian puts his finger on one of the most remarkable phenomena in religious studies when he points out that pagans, in their rare moments of existential fear, forget all their own gods and scuttle their cheap myths as they call out to God. In this respect, Tertullian seems to me to be one of the most modern of all the early church fathers. From my perspective, he has the same phenomenon in mind as Heiler does when, in his extensive study on the subject of prayer, he notes that so-called primitive people forget all their spirits and magical techniques in their times of deepest dread and bow down to their high god. "But here in prayer to the Supreme Being is unveiled to us the *personal* prayer of primitive man in all its fervour and passion."[10] At such times, it is as though that repressed and maligned truth begins stirring once more, as though the foundations of the house begin shaking, as though the joists begin creaking, and as though all certainties cave in. Is that the moment that all the gears of the engine of repression seize up, and when *Another,* stronger than individual people, discloses himself in his everlasting power and divinity?

It is completely self-evident that "exchanging" is directly connected to "repressing." The cavity or empty space that occurs as a result of suppressing needs to be filled. It has to be the case that what replaces the [suppressed] truth and sweeps across the entire terrain must be manifest in something resembling eternal power and divinity. People cannot break new ground, but they need to fill the existing emptiness. The human spirit then becomes the factory of idols *(fabrica idolorum),* as Calvin scornfully called it.[11] As a rule, it happens entirely unconsciously, but grows out of an inner loneliness, out of fear, out of one's neediness. People need to know that they exist with connections and that they live in the world as though in a house that suits them and where they feel truly at home. Things are more than the things themselves. But now people no longer realize that there is *Someone* behind all of

---

10. Friedrich Heiler, *Prayer: A Study in the History and Psychology of Religion,* trans. and ed. Samuel McComb with J. Edgar Park (London: Oxford University Press, 1932), p. 50.

11. Ed. note: John Calvin, *Institutes of the Christian Religion,* 1.11.7.

them that gives them meaning; people look for the power, for whatever that more might be, for the mystical in the things themselves. They discover the *mana* or the supernatural in each development.[12] They dream up some god, but then push him away. God is on a trip to a far country, say the myths. Or perhaps they dream up a god, then reduce him to a force pervading everything. Now they can master that mysterious power with their incantations and magic. They desire certainty amid the world's threats. They also do not want to let go of what is normative, because they know that as soon as they do, they will be set hopelessly adrift; they want to cling to what is normative, as it were, with all their tentacles. But those norms now become the customs of their ancestors. They are thought to be interwoven with nature. They are the expression of the meaningful interconnectedness of the totality of all things. People have been preoccupied with filling their emptiness throughout all the centuries of human existence. What a collection of myths people have composed. What a mass of stories about gods and demigods they have brought to light. What an array of philosophical theories they have developed concerning how everything has come into existence. It is all about people filling up their emptiness. Today, people sometimes get the impression that humanity has become dead tired of all these efforts to fill the void, simply leaving the emptiness empty. People are no longer looking for an altar at which to worship. They no longer stretch out their arms longingly toward some god in an effort to find peace. People today have become saturated with all these efforts at replacing and filling back up. It seems as if they feel satisfied with all the empty little niches of their existence. Things are simply things; norms disappear from view. And that great totality of all things and the meaningful cohesiveness of the cosmos is nonsense. Deliverance is found only in becoming intoxicated with life's abundance and frenzy. Or, are even the people of today not totally satisfied with their existence? Like all previous generations, are even they looking for safety, community, and guarantees?

This mysterious process of repressing and exchanging is difficult, in a certain sense even impossible, to explain clearly. If I would have to do so, I would prefer to use the metaphor of the dream. In a dream, this remarkable phenomenon sometimes emerges, namely that objective and completely real things play a part in it. The ticking of an alarm clock, water flowing through a gutter, the light flashing from the headlights of a passing car, the rumbling

---

12. Ed. note: Here we see again an unacknowledged link to van der Leeuw's discussion of *mana* and *tabu*; see van der Leeuw, *Religion in Essence and Manifestation*, pp. 24-28, 43-64, etc.

of a moving train in the distance — in short, all kinds of outside impressions can enter into the consciousness of the dream. Often they assume gigantic proportions in the dream. The monotonous ticking of the alarm clock then becomes the rhythmic marching of passing soldiers. The flowing gutter water then becomes a mighty waterfall in the middle of a forest. The lights of the car become sharp flashes of lightning. In short, each impression that flows in from the outside world is appropriated, but at the same time it is torn from its real context, hugely distorted, and made the heart of an entirely different chain of ideas. This being the case, we find here the two processes of repressing and exchanging in their inner connection. Here the reality is in fact repressed, and yet that repressed reality functions creatively. But what is born out of it is a sheer fantasy, a colorful collection of chaotic images from which the objective elements can only be distinguished with great effort.

With the help of this metaphor, then, I would like to clarify what people do with God's general revelation. That revelation impinges on them and compels them to listen, but it is at the same time pushed down and repressed. And the only aspects of it that remain connected to human consciousness, even while torn from their original context, become the seeds of an entirely different sequence of ideas around which they crystallize. Definite connections exist between general revelation and human religious consciousness, but those connections are extremely complicated because the repressing and replacing actions are inescapably involved in the process.

Simply because the power of repressing and replacing is illustrated so compellingly in the dream, the dream is such an excellent metaphor of all human religion. Calvin talks about "dreamed up gods" with a great deal of emphasis. We are automatically reminded of the words of the prophet Jeremiah here, when he says, "They think the dreams they tell one another will make my people forget my name, just as their fathers forgot my name through Baal worship" (Jer. 23:27). Truly, paganism is a dream, a fearful and unending dream. "Wake up, O sleeper, rise from the dead, and Christ will shine on you" (Eph. 5:14).

In the darkness of human existence, where repressing and replacing focus their empty work day and night, only the proclamation of the gospel of Jesus Christ can bring light. Truth is found in him. This is the complete and living power for people, the power long repressed and rejected. Contained in his words is always something of the "I was always with you, but you were not with me." "I am the Christ whom you have repressed." "I am the one with whom you have struggled and whom you have assaulted." "It is hard for you to kick against the pricks."

§3. Totality and the Kingdom[13]

From the gospel of Jesus Christ, people gain an entirely new vision of the world in which they live and to which they are tied with every fiber of their beings. This is not to say that the gospel of Jesus Christ says something completely different from what general revelation has been saying to them already for a long time in its language without speech. On the contrary, continuity exists between that voiceless language and the gospel; they have an inner connection with each other. There are numerous instances where it is difficult to distinguish whether we are dealing with general or with special revelation. On the mission field, we daily encounter the amazing fact that God, either by means of dreams or by ordinary sight, leads people to the gospel. In such situations, we always ask ourselves whether we are dealing with general revelation or with something more special. This is due to the fact that general revelation itself has a much more personal character than we usually suppose; it more often exhibits the trait of God's self-manifestation than we often think. However that may happen, the gospel of Christ addresses people and rips open their religious consciousness. People want to suppress and push away the gospel in the worst way, just as they repeatedly have done with God. But it can happen that God causes their hearts to submit. Then all the engines of resistance are switched off and people listen. Then the King of Glory makes his entrance, and the everlasting doors of the understanding are thrown open. And this is what we call the new birth.

When that happens to people, a new outlook comes into view, namely that of the kingdom of God about which Jesus begins talking with them. That kingdom of God is a Totality, embracing everything; it is the meaningful coherence that those people [whose souls are overflowing with the results of their suppression and exchange] have been dreaming about for so many centuries. But it is different from what they expected.

What they [in their suppression and exchange] had thought of as the Totality of things was the majestic bond by which all things were connected to one another and in which people also had a place, like that of a little ripple on the ocean of universal Being. For them, that universal Being was God, was divine, was suffused with *Dao* [*Tao*], with cosmic world order itself, with di-

13. Ed. note: In this and the following four subsections of the chapter, Bavinck reintroduces "the five magnetic points" of religious consciousness, though he does not use the term. See the unnumbered note at the beginning of Chapter 3.

vine energy. To exist in meaningful connection with everything meant participating in that divine power and inhaling divine glory and wisdom. In its deepest sense, it was comparable to self-deification.[14] All the religions of the world emphasized that the totality of things needed to be conquered and that people need to deny the urges of their egos and delusions in order to be able to enter the divine state of the All. But the All was an established reality; it existed. People needed to allow themselves to be swallowed up into the endless sea of the Eternal.

Jesus Christ puts these matters in a completely different way. The kingdom of God is not an established reality. On the contrary, this world is filled with shrill dissonance and lies under the curse. It is subject to vanity. The kingdom of God is coming. It breaks through all the hard, obstinate realities of this world. It does not do so from the human side, not as a result of human effort. It does so by grace, as a result of the cross. It is the kingdom that is coming and that is also already present, and it gathers up people into its indescribable rest. People know that their lives receive meaning in that mystery of the kingdom. This is not to say that people cease existing as individual "I's" or as self-conscious beings. They remain individuals and continue to be moral and responsible beings. They are not swallowed up into some ocean, but they willingly, humbly, and obediently join themselves to an all-embracing coherence, the coherence of the new kingdom outside of which is only utter darkness. That kingdom comes by grace, and through grace it draws all dimensions of creation together into one great whole, into a symphony of divine dominion. Within that kingdom, people that believe in Jesus Christ lay down their still wandering ways.

Jesus Christ shows them, furthermore, that that kingdom will one day conquer everything. It will come with a brightness that transcends by far all imaginable glory. God will be all and in all. That is, the suns and the planets, the measureless depths of everything, the seas and mountains and forests, and everything that lives will all be caught up into that wide expanse of the

---

14. Ed. note: Bavinck's thought is very complex and subtle here. It seems counterintuitive for western thinkers to consider any notion of being absorbed into the Great All, the Totality of Being, as a form of deification. Perhaps the best entry point is to consider verse two of the *Mandukya Upanishad,* which identifies the inner essence of a person *(Atman)* with the One Supreme Universal Spirit *(Brahman):*

Brahman is indeed all this.
This Self in us is also Brahman.

Available online at http://www.hinduwebsite.com/mandukya.asp.

kingdom. This is the world's temple about which is written that the sum of God's attire will fill the temple.

Existing within the totality of all things, say the religions of the nations, is to exist in a meaningful, divine connection. "Not at all," says Jesus Christ. To exist in the world is to live under judgment, to stand in condemnation, to exist in relationship with the whole creation that in all its parts groans and yearns for its deliverance. To live within the totality of all things, so people dream, is to participate in the divine powers that flow through all that there is. "Not at all," says Jesus Christ. To live in the world is to participate in un-ending ruin, unless the salvation of Jesus Christ sets people free from the chains of destruction and includes them in the renewal of all things. In other words, that which is the greatest objective in most human religions, namely to allow oneself to melt into the totality of all things and the meaningful co-herence of this world, and thereby to become one with the divine forces that flow through the world, has become something completely different in the gospel of Jesus Christ. Knowing that one is one with the world, or sensing that one is caught up in a powerful connection with this creation, is not the point of departure for people becoming divine, according to the gospel. Rather, it is much more the point of departure for the terrible knowledge that people are dealing with a world that is perishing, for "this world in its present form is passing away" (1 Cor. 7:31). "The world and its desires pass away, but the man who does the will of God lives forever" (1 John 2:17).

People delude others when they say that to stand within the totality of all things is to be swallowed up and to lose all sense of self as one is over-whelmed by the swelling sea of all-that-is. "Not at all," says Jesus Christ. Taking one's stand within the new kingdom definitely does mean dying. But it also means finding oneself anew in the resurrection of the Lord Jesus Christ. This is the ultimate dying and the ultimate rising to a new life. It is what it means that "I no longer live" and that "I live only by the grace of God in Jesus Christ." Taking your stand within the kingdom is living in expecta-tion and with yearning desire; it is living in daily amazement; it is living with eyes set on the dawn of eternal Light.

§4. People and Norms

Human religious consciousness carries with it the certainty that life is tied to norms. Life is a dialogue between law and reality, between natural self-fulfillment and the moral demand for self-restraint. People chafe against the law and they want to be enveloped by it, carried by it. That law is *adat,* say the people of Indonesia. That *adat* is handed down from their ancestors who understood the secrets of the cosmos. That law is *li,* say the Chinese, and *li* flows from *Dao* [*Tao*], that great, cosmic order. That law is *dharma,* say the people of India, and that *dharma* is dependent on the huge cosmic connectedness in which everything exists. People stand over against norms.

In Jesus Christ this is different. That law is God himself: "Be holy, for I am holy." "Be perfect, therefore, as your heavenly Father is perfect." God created human beings in his own image, and in the law he demands that his image be reflected in them. Transgression of the law is not an assault on good order or an agreement, but it is very definitely rebellion against God and an attempt to pry oneself loose from God's grip and to attack the image of God. That law is Jesus Christ, in whom the entire law is fulfilled and who kept every commandment in our place out of the depths of his divine love. The living reality of that Someone, that God, always stands behind the law. Our lives only find fullness and meaning in fellowship with that God, and outside of him safety is nowhere and never found.

§5. Connection with a Higher Power

Included in human religious consciousness is also the dimension of being connected to a higher power. But what have people down through the centuries done with that higher power? They have fled from it, resisted it, lost it in the mists of being in general, diminished it as *mana,* divided it into a motley array of spirits or gods. People understood that their lives were at every moment bound to a higher power, but they have reshaped the higher powers into their own image.

In the gospel of Jesus Christ, that Higher Power draws near to us. It is different from what human hearts ever thought it would be and cannot be described in only one word. It is the father in the parable of the prodigal son. But it is also the master who prepares a feast. It is the king who drives out the rebellious servants and claims his inheritance. We need a Bible filled with history, prophecies, and parables in order to explain how the glory of the one and only God shines in every direction and sparkles in every life that lives in fellowship with him. That Higher Power is the one that came into this world in the form of Jesus Christ and removed the veil over his face so that we might know the Son and the Father. "Whoever has seen me has seen the Father."

§6. Salvation

In every respect, human life is a cry for deliverance. Throughout the ages all nations have retold their history in terms of that cry, and they have endeavored to grasp salvation as a hidden treasure. They looked for salvation from death, from famine, from sickness, from poverty, from dependence, from the chaos threatening the community, from the egocentricity that impeded drowning in the eternal, from the *avidya* or ignorance that obstructed entering nirvana.

Salvation in Jesus Christ is radically and in principle completely different. There is but one thing from which people must be saved, and that is their guilt before him whom they attempt to push away all the time in their pursuit of unrighteousness. It is salvation from enmity and from being lost. That salvation includes all other forms of being made free, like kernels on the ear. It is only imaginable as a whole, with all its dimensions growing from one root. "He who did not spare his own Son, but gave him up for us all — how will he not also, along with him, graciously give us all things?"

§7. A Way of Life

Finally, there is the way of life. Human existence is in fact a wonderful interplay of fate and activity. Fate and activity interact with one another all the time. Fate is the answer to action, just as activity is the response to destiny. Many times the two are so intertwined that they seem to coalesce, and our destiny becomes our action or our activity assumes the character of our destiny.

From antiquity, people have felt the subtle connection between destiny and activity is religious in nature. They have regarded destiny as cosmic law, as karma, as fate, as *Schicksal,* as *takdir.* They have always understood that something mysterious is involved in destiny and that the dialogue between action and fate is embedded in that organic bond that we call religion.

In the gospel, that dialogue between action and destiny is illumined in its inner recesses. Activity receives far more accent in terms of accountability since it is regarded as action toward and with respect to God. And destiny gets a much deeper and more personal emphasis because it is part of a plan. "I, O King, by the grace of God came into this world," begins one of the earliest apologists for the Christian faith in his defense addressed to the emperor. In doing so, he engages one of the deepest certainties involved in that faith.[15] In that inextricable plan of God, too inscrutable for mortal minds, lies the fate of nations and races, but also that of every person separately. "Oh, the depth of the riches of the wisdom and knowledge of God! How unsearchable his judgments, and his paths beyond tracing out" (Rom. 11:33). This is why there are hidden connections between that destiny and the plan of salvation that God has for people. "And we know that in all things God works for the good of those who love him, who have been called according to his purpose" (Rom. 8:28). The lot that is assigned a person is not some dark fate, nor is it cosmic determinism. But in its deepest sense it is the unfolding plan of God. The dialogue that a person experiences between his or her activity and his or her destiny increasingly takes on the character of a dialogue between a child and its father.

§8. Religious Consciousness and Christian Faith

We are approaching the end of our investigation. We need to state the matter once more, conclusively and clearly.

The point of departure for all of our considerations needs to be God's self-disclosure or the general revelation that nonetheless bears the nature of a very personal engagement of God with each person separately. This general revelation is so real, so concrete, so inescapable, and so compelling that no person can escape it. It grips every person and renders him or her someone who knows in "whom the unseen things are revealed." In so doing, it defines the life of every person as a dialogue or a struggle with God. That is at the deepest core of every person's existence.

In reality, this does not produce actual knowledge in people's lives. This is because along with this "understanding" and "seeing clearly," two other processes are at work in the human heart. These are the processes of repressing and replacing. Both of these processes as a general rule occur unconsciously, and they are so irresistible and so immediate that all people are engaged in them at every point in their lives. The engines of repressing and replacing never stop running. This means that the truth of God is suppressed and banished. It is never destroyed, but it has no power over life. Meanwhile, it seems reasonable that both in the repressing and in the replac-

15. Aristides, *Apology*, 1.1, in Helen B. Harris, *The Newly Recovered Apology of Aristides: Its Doctrine and Ethics, with Extracts from the Translation by Prof. J. Rendel Harris* (London: Hodder & Stoughton, 1891), pp. 78-81.

ing individual differences must be taken into account. These processes do not happen everywhere with the same noiselessness or the same degree of completeness.

The outcome of this entire process (understanding and seeing clearly as well as repressing and replacing) is the religious consciousness that from the very beginning is unique to human beings. That religious awareness is not to be construed as an act that flows from human nature. It does not belong to the structure of human nature as such. Rather, it should only be understood as the response or reaction to the voiceless speech of God's self-revelation. However, it needs to be kept in mind that in this reaction the two processes of repressing and replacing are both engaged and both reworked. This religious consciousness reveals itself in human history as the fabrication of idols *(fabrica idolorum)*. It is the mother of all religions, the stem from which all religions sprout.

The religions of the human race may vary in many respects. But they have several striking points in common. It seems as though all religious thought moves within a certain framework and needs to orient itself toward several set points. We have seen that in so doing, it always involves an understanding of everything that exists, the idea of norms, relationship to some higher power, the need for salvation, and a sense of direction in life. Religious consciousness crystallizes around these five, specific points. It does so in frequently new structures.

The gospel of Jesus Christ breaks through human religious consciousness. It may never be put on the same level with the various manifestations of human religious consciousness, as expressed in different religions, since it in fact exists on a different level. No continuity exists between the gospel and human religious consciousness, although definite continuity does exist between the gospel and what lies behind human religious consciousness, namely God's general revelation. These two are definitely intimately related to each other against the background of God's great self-manifestation, which assumes the character of God's personal involvement with each person. This manifestation is expressed in the historical realization of God's plan of salvation that culminates in Jesus Christ. God's general and his special revelation are to be thought of as connected, and they continuously affect one another. Both of them are all about Jesus Christ. The Logos of John 1:14 who became flesh and dwelled among us is the same Logos who "enlightens all people" (John 1:9). But people's religious consciousness — that product of illumination, repression, and replacement — simply stands over against the gospel and is contradicted by the gospel.

Christian faith is the subjective response of the reborn person to the gospel. In a certain sense, it stands with religious consciousness. This is the case to the extent that it is an answer or reaction to divine speaking and acting. At the same time, this determines that Christian faith is always limited and incomplete, always subject to the critique of the gospel itself. It is never a pure and adequate reflection of the gospel's content, for we carry "this treasure in jars of clay" (2 Cor. 4:7). In the Christian's struggles with life, that faith pushes back against the religious consciousness that is still a living and tenacious power even in him or her.

Even in the Christian, something of a pagan still lives and breathes. A pagan is a person who thinks of the totality of all things — the world, the meaningful coherence of everything, human community, the race, and the nation — as one, huge, divine reality, even as the only God. A pagan is a person who regards norms as flowing from and expressing cosmic order, as the law established by All-that-is and pulls every individual life along with it. A pagan is one who dreams up higher powers, gods, and spirits in the images of mortal human beings. A pagan looks for salvation from the human person, either from the collective existence of the community or from the purification of the individual. A pagan thinks about the course of life in terms of destiny and fate; life is swept along by the great cosmic events that simply flow over us. That religious consciousness, with its keenly honed intuitions, with its dark moods, with its defenses and self-reliance and escapism, is also a force with which the Christian struggles daily. It seeps into Christian faith. It infiltrates Christian searching and thinking. It anesthetizes Christian spirituality. The only way that a Christian can triumph over it is to always be exposed to the light of the gospel.

Paul employs this seminal description when speaking of faith's engagement with the struggles of life: "We demolish arguments and every pretension that sets itself up against the knowledge of God, and we take captive every thought to make it obedient to Christ" (2 Cor. 10:5). "Every pretension" refers to the entire apparatus dedicated to the process of repressing, for it is still extremely effective in the Christian's life. "Every thought" mentioned here has reference to the whole mechanism of replacing, whose motors continue whirring in the Christian's experience. This is why the Christian faith needs to push back constantly against religious consciousness and to say "no" to it on a permanent basis. This needs to happen in the experience of every single believer, but also en masse in the church. From its beginning, the church has been burdened by religious consciousness in its disclosure of the Christian faith. Already in antiquity, misguided religious ideas have invaded the church's treasury of the faith, and they have been dragged along through the centuries. This is the dramatic significance of church history. It is the story of relentless decay followed by renewal of the church. It is captured in the terms "formation" and "deformation," and in the never-ending "re-formation" of the church. Christian faith and religious consciousness live together in one house, but they are, or at least they should be, grim enemies of one another. Christian faith is gradually becoming greater faith to the extent that it more fundamentally distances itself from religious consciousness and subjects itself to the gospel.

The missionary calling of the church is to preach the gospel in service to Jesus Christ. That involves speaking an emphatic and convicted "no" to all human religious consciousness — that of the Hindus, the Buddhists, and the Muslims. Those who are sent can say "no" to these religious notions with heartfelt conviction only when they have learned to reject heartily the religious consciousness in their own heart. This also means that they must have said "no" to the Hinduism, Buddhism, and Islam that have attempted to find various flimsy forms in their own hearts. People can really only and genuinely take a stance against spiritual movements that they have encountered, when they have learned first of all to reject them as spiritual temptations in their own experience.

But mission work is far more than simply saying "no." Its heart and core are much more about saying "yes." It is to say "yes" to the voiceless speech of God's self-manifestation in this world that even the pagans "know," even though they do not really know it because they have suppressed and exchanged it. It means saying "yes" to God's personal involvement with every person in the world. "God has not left himself without witness." That is the great and only point of contact that is at the church's disposal in its work on behalf of the gospel. Mission work is to be involved, using weak human muscles — no, using the strong arm of Christ himself — with all the mechanisms of repression's machinery that never shuts down but runs day and night. It is to command them to stop, on the basis of Christ's gospel. It is to say "yes" to that unceasing and inscrutable work of God's mercy that has been active through all generations since the beginning of time. It is never to say "yes" to human effort, but always to say "yes" to God and to his work of mercy. It is to unfurl the gospel to blinded human hearts. It is to bring that always-new revelation of the measureless depth of God's love, seen in the cross of Jesus Christ.

III. Christ and Asian Mysticism

7 God and the World

Theology and Mission

Whenever one is motivated by the desire to preach the gospel of Christ in the world of Asia,[1] one becomes cognizant of all the esoteric speculation concerning divine essence that has persisted there through the centuries; one automatically feels something of what Paul did when he approached Corinth on his second missionary journey. That is when he made that remarkable statement, "When I came to you, I resolved to know nothing except Jesus Christ and him crucified" (1 Cor. 2:1-2). Throughout many centuries, the people of Asia as a whole have contemplated and pondered the secrets of the divine world, and the theories and ideas that have swirled around on this subject are numerous. And in response to all those rarified and profound positions, one is moved initially to present nothing except the foolishness of preaching, by which God is pleased to call people to faith and conversion. One cannot overcome the esoteric speculations by positing still more esoteric and still more unfathomable ideas, but one can only present to these souls the simple, child-like gospel as the response to the basic problems of all of our lives, namely how we sinful and doomed people can by grace be again received by God.

---

1. Ed. note: The original title of the volume from which Chapters 7-11 are taken is "Christ and the Mysticism of the East." Explanation for our editorial change to "Asia" and "Asian" instead of "East" and "Eastern" is given in the Preface. Cf. Chapter 2, note 18.

Ed. note: The numbered chapters 7-11 in this section correspond to chapters 3-7 in the original Dutch edition of *Christus en de Mystiek van het Oosten*.

Frequently, when someone tries to engage you in a profound discussion about the Supreme Being, you have to sweep away the intricate web of ideas and simply tell them about the only thing that is profound and important: reconciliation with God through Jesus Christ our Lord. That is the only demanding and frequently thankless task that we have when we are sent by God to proclaim the way of salvation in the Asian world.

All of this does not exclude, however, the thoroughgoing obligation to give our account of the profound thought concerning life and the world that lies hidden in the gospel. Contact with the people of Asia compels us to familiarize ourselves far more, through serious study, with the important ideas about God revealed to us in Jesus Christ. These force us to confront the deep difference between whatever the people of Asia have said and thought about God and what Christ has revealed to us about God. We need to grasp these differences strongly and clearly if we are not to misguide these people repeatedly. Especially when we address those who have already come to the gospel of Christ and accepted his word, we feel that we need to be intentional and careful in our instruction concerning the differences separating the intricately spun ideas of Asian people and the gospel. We are always profoundly aware that an indigenous Christian theology needs to be developed, both in India and on Java, one that works through struggles with Islamic mysticism and Hinduism. The cultivation of such a theology, to be sure, is a task that will require not just years but centuries. But its seed must be sown already now, so that these kernels can germinate and bear fruit in God's time and with his blessing.

For these reasons, the task that we have in that part of the world is such an important one. The spiritual warfare that engages the gospel in conflicts with Asian worldviews is a battle in which all of Christendom is involved. This is not only the responsibility of the few who labor on the mission field itself, but it is the task of all those who here in the homeland support mission work with their thoughts and prayers. The contemporary period in the history of the Christian church is in every respect one of greatest significance for all sorts of reasons; that is why, for all of us, serious and faithful collaboration in response to Christ's command is crucial.

Are There Essential Differences?

In contact with the people of Asia, a person could hold the short-lived opinion, based on a superficial understanding, that the only thing distinguishing

Asian religious traditions from Christianity is nothing more than a difference in method. Christianity emphasizes faith as the only way to establish contact with God, while the people of Asia testify that approaching God occurs through mystical exercises and its fruit, namely mystical ecstasy. In general, the people of Asia are readily prepared to accord your standpoint a degree of validity. They concede to you that a person also needs faith, particularly in his initial attempts to approach God, but they regard these faith-based encounters as belonging to a lower order that pertains only to those taking the first steps on the path leading to God. Without hesitating, they will also acknowledge that a person can only come to God if, from his side, God is ready by grace to accept such a person. So, they make room for divine grace as the unmistakable precondition for mystical fellowship. Taking this approach, one would almost come to assume that the difference between Christianity and the religions of Asia is little more than a difference in accent, a difference in emphasis on spiritual activities.

One who embraces that delusion for even a short length of time would recognize rather soon that the essential difference had still not been fathomed. The religious quest and reflection that is found among the people of Asia is distinguished from Christianity on a much more fundamental level than first supposed on the basis of initial acquaintance. It is not a difference in method, nor a difference in accent, but it is a much deeper and more principled difference in theology, particularly in the understanding of God. The religions of Asia preach another God than the God that has appeared to us in Jesus Christ. Frequently the words used are similar, but all the concepts are different. The Hindu religion[2] also talks about God, also about submitting to God *(bhakti)*, also about faith, also about the grace of God, also about God's love, also about human sin and insignificance, also about redemption and salvation, but none of these ideas are the same as what Christianity understands by these terms. For that reason, in all of our work with the people of Asia we risk perpetuating a dangerous confusion because we use the same words but mean something completely different by them.

On its own, that is not surprising, and this situation is repeated again and again when the gospel is brought to a new group of people. When Paul announced the message about Jesus Christ in Greece and Rome, he had to use all sorts of terms that had a completely different sound to his listeners

---

2. Ed. note: The original simply has "the East"; the editorial change that specifies Hinduism is an editorial change warranted by the content of the paragraph and is provided for accuracy and clarity.

than what he intended. All sorts of concepts that he employed — words like *grace, sin, redemption, salvation* — were known in the world in which he preached, but they had different content. And we can be sure of this: the preaching of the gospel in the Germanic world occurred in the same way. Christianity is simply something unique and diverges from all human thought. Over and again, whenever it is proclaimed in a different language and to a new people, it must redefine, as it were, all sorts of terms and give them new content. Nowhere in the world is a language found that is completely prepared to fully and purely convey the gospel.

For that reason, it is imperative that we give deeper consideration to the various concepts of God so that we can prevent all misunderstanding and achieve a more accurate judgment about what distinguishes the mysticism of Asia from the Christian faith.

Essence and Attributes

The Personal God and the God within Us

As we have already seen, the Indian world has actually always vacillated between the need to see God as a *Someone* or as a *Something*. It has proceeded on the basis of nature, and has ascribed personhood to the forces of nature; from that moment on the question of the being or essence of God became a major problem in Hindu[3] thinking. Is God actually a *Someone* who stands over against me, who has created me, and who will one day judge me? Or, is he the deepest essence of all things, the mysterious power of life in seminal form, the miraculously overpowering force in all that exists that fulfills and sustains all that is? Should I speak of *Brahma* (the human form of the term) as a God, or should I think about him as *Brahman* (the neutral form), as the huge, hidden essence that silently and mysteriously permeates all things?[4] Is

3. Ed. note: See note 2 above.
4. Ed. note: Bavinck distinguishes *Brahmá* from *Brâhma;* the former a human (personal) form, the latter the neutral (impersonal) force of the universe. The English language distinction is usually between *Brahman* and *Brahma*. *Brahman* refers to the cosmic "soul" of the universe; *Brahma* is the personified creator-god who, along with *Vishnu* (preserver) and *Shiva* (destroyer), forms the "trinity" of Hindu worship. *Brahman* also must not be confused with *Brahmin*, the highest (priestly) caste in Hindu anthropology. Our editorial practice is to avoid using the diacritical marks for Sanskrit terms; thus, in addition to *Brahma* for *Brahmá* and *Brahman* for *Brâhma*, we use *Shiva* for *Śiva*, *Vishnu* for *Viṣṇu*, and *Ishvara* for *Īśvara*. See Chapter 3, note 5.

Vishnu the *Ishvara,* the great Lord,[5] or is he the ground of my own being; is he the being of my being and the soul of my soul? Is *Shiva* the king, or is he my own inner existence? Am I identified with him and fulfilled in him? These are all questions to which the religions of Asia in most instances do not dare give an answer. Admittedly, in the course of history there have certainly been voices raised that have proclaimed emphatically that we should worship God as Lord and that in no case should we ever regard him as identical with ourselves *(Ramanuja).* But in opposition to that position, a whole crowd of thinkers maintained that they had no desire to abandon the typical hesitation and vacillation. Yes, there were even those who emphatically asserted that God must not be seen as Lord over us, but must be felt as the depth of our own beings. *Atman* equals *Brahman.*

This typical wavering has received not a little reinforcing on Java from Islam. Orthodox Islam places great emphasis up-front on God as a king, the Lord of the world. The first chapter of the Qur'an openly states this: "Praise be to Allah, the Lord of the world, the All-compassionate, the All-merciful, the King of the day of judgment." Nevertheless, in Muslim theology the problem of the relationship of God's being to his attributes is addressed very early. In the hands of the Muslim mystics this problem becomes the point of departure for making all sorts of profound distinctions. They talk, for example, about the deepest being of God *(al-Dhāt)* as the absolute unity, the all-embracing, eternal, dim mist *(al Ama).*[6] God is an endless ocean, undivided, unknowable, and indescribable. Contemplating himself first as the *Dhāt* and reflecting on himself, he sees himself as the fullness of all qualities and as the unifier of them all. These attributes are those that, as it were, become specialized, flow out, and are reflected in the creation. A person who seeks God first of all discovers creatures as works of God. Upon deeper reflection, he ascends to God's names as the side of his attributes taking on external expression. Ascending still higher, the mystic himself participates in those attributes, and in his highest ecstasy all divisions fall away for him and he only sees eternal *dhāt,* that which is undivided, unknowable, eternal being as the deepest ground of all existence. He then comes to understand that this *dhāt* is nothing other than the deepest essence of humanity itself and that in the

5. Ed. note: *Ishvara* is more of a philosophical concept in Hinduism, meaning "controller" or the "Supreme Controller" (*The Heart of Hinduism;* see concept of *Ishvara,* available online at http://hinduism.iskcon.com/concepts/107.htm).

6. Ed. note: For a discussion of these two names see Karen Armstrong, *A History of God: The 400-Year Quest of Judaism, Christianity, and Islam* (New York: Random House, 1993), pp. 237ff.

deepest state of enlightenment a person finds that he and God are one and the same.

The distinction between being and attributes is thus one of far-reaching significance. This can best be explained with an example. It is possible to talk about someone in terms of characteristics: large or small, blond or dark-haired, stupid or smart, friendly or unfriendly. All of these qualities are certainly important, but they do not touch what is essential. Even if one of these characteristics were to change, the person would still be human. The characteristics themselves are secondary; they are accidental. This is how the mystic talks about God. You can say about God that he is great, almighty, righteous, etc., but all of these attributes are still secondary and only have incidental value. More important is that God is God; he is the ground, the root of all existence, and all that exists emanates from him; in him is the germ of all things. Therefore, he is the All-embracing, the Eternal, the All-in-All. Only when you see him in this way, do you know him fully and can you, as it were, completely merge with him. He then no longer stands over against you as Lord with all of his attributes, but you then understand that you have emerged from him and that he is in you and you are in him.

According to this way of thinking, we instinctively hesitate to draw conclusions about God's being. Who is God, really? Is he the one standing outside me issuing commands, the Lord? Or is he the Being of my being, the deepest unity of all that exists, the root from which all that is has grown?

The awareness that the consideration of God as the Lord who exists outside us needs to be seen as a relative, temporary truth also developed in Islamic mysticism. Only the mystic has insight into the highest, absolute truth that only God exists and we are all in him. On Java this entire mystical conception of God is most intimately connected to magic. Seen as the highest being, God is the sum of all magical power. Spelling his name, intoning his attributes repetitiously, accords a person magical powers and puts him in the position to deal effectively with life's struggles. Magical power is directionless, rudderless; it is an instrument in the hands of the sorcerer. The sorcerer is the one who has deep insight into the secret forces of nature and who can direct magical power as he chooses. Thus, mysticism unleashes various animistic and dynamistic attitudes and from it develops a fuzzy, yet amazing totality of speculations wherein God's majesty is degraded.

The Christian Alternative

The Christian church in Asia is involved in a life-and-death struggle in opposition to all these ideas. An invaluable privilege in that struggle is that she is able to reach back to what the Christian church in previous centuries and other countries has thought and said about these matters. Why? Because the struggle we have in wrestling with Asian mysticism is comparable in a great many respects to what the church battled earlier. As similar as two drops of water, it is like the Hellenistic mysticism, Gnosticism, and neo-Platonism that as powerful philosophical systems held the early Christian centuries captive. Precisely for that reason, all that the major Christian thinkers of that era said about the being of God is such an exceptional benefit to us. We think here particularly of Augustine, that outstanding Christian theologian, to whom we point because he thought through all these matters so clearly. Augustine experienced the power of false mysticism in his own life. It took him many years to disentangle himself from it, and that is precisely why he is such an outstanding example for all those who still find themselves in the middle of the struggle.

In this connection, we want to focus attention on several points in Augustine's teaching. Whenever Augustine talks about God, he readily refers to him as the Supreme Being. God is the Absolute Being, "above whom nothing exists, outside whom nothing exists, without whom nothing exists."[7] "All that is contained in God is nothing other than Being."[8] Augustine readily proceeds on the basis of the name "Jehovah" as proof that God is Being in the absolute sense.

> The eternal, immutable nature that is God and that is the self-contained ground of his own being is captured in the words that he spoke to Moses: "I am who I am" (Ex. 3:14). This divine nature is something entirely different from created things, for it is true and what exists in the first instance. Furthermore, it is always the same being, and not only is it unchanged, but it can never — in its entirety — be changed.[9]

7. Augustine, *Soliloquies: Augustine's Inner Dialogue,* 1.4, ed. John E. Rotelle, trans. Kim Paffenroth, Augustine Series, vol. 2 (Hyde Park, NY: New City Press, 2000). Ed. note: The translation of this citation and those that follow, unless otherwise indicated, are from the Dutch text. The bibliographic information provided will be to accessible texts.

8. Augustine, *Exposition 2 of Psalm 101,* §10, in *Expositions of the Psalms,* ed. Boniface Ramsey, trans. Maria Boulding, Works of Saint Augustine: A Translation for the 21st Century, part 3, vol. 19 (Brooklyn, NY: New City Press, 2003).

9. Augustine, *Literal Meaning of Genesis,* 5.16, trans. John H. Taylor, Ancient Christian Writers, no. 41-42 (New York: Newman Press).

God is Being in such a manner that, compared with him, created things must be regarded as non-being.[10]

Taken by themselves, these quotations can sound dangerous. They could cause us to think that the great opposition in this world is dominated by that between Being and Non-Being or what is mere shadow. One might even think that also Augustine wants to depict our God as the Being of all being, as the *Dhāt*, the ultimate being without distinguishing characteristics, as an endless sea embracing and sustaining all creatures. Admittedly, there are certainly expressions in Augustine that could cause us to harbor such thoughts, especially when he writes about how all other existence flows out of God's Supreme Being and how God "has to a greater or lesser degree given creatures existence and in so doing has ordained the nature of their existence on varying levels."[11] But to conclude from them that also for Augustine God is the dark mist, the endless sea, the impenetrable depth, the hazy and abstract Being that Indian thinkers consider him to be, would be a serious mistake. For, the eternal being of God is also rich and full with divine virtues for Augustine. It is thoroughly vital and real. Furthermore, all of God's attributes are not merely accidentally impressive qualities that one could just as well set aside as maintain, but they are all so much one with his being that they cannot be detached from him for one moment. All of his qualities are expressive of his Being. "All that God possesses is what he also is!" With a human being one can always make a distinction between his being and his characteristics; his characteristics are somewhat accidental. If a wise person ceases being wise, he is still nevertheless a person. His wisdom, as it were, does not inhere in his person. With God that is completely different. "The attributes of God are truly the being of God himself and they do not differ from his being nor in essence from one another."[12]

By virtue of the idea that with God no separation may be made of his being from his attributes, and that "he is what he possesses," Christian theology is consistent with the Word of God and cuts off all false mysticism at its

10. Augustine, *Exposition of Psalm 34*, §4, in *Expositions of the Psalms*, ed. John E. Rotelle, trans. Maria Boulding, Works of Saint Augustine: A Translation for the 21st Century, part 3, vol. 16 (Brooklyn, NY: New City Press).

11. Augustine, *City of God*, 12.2, trans. Henry Bettenson (Harmondsworth: Penguin, 2004).

12. Augustine, *The Trinity*, 5.1.2, ed. John E. Rotelle, trans. Edmund Hill, Works of Saint Augustine: A Translation for the 21st Century, part 1, vol. 5 (Brooklyn, NY: New City Press, 1991).

root. That is why we can never penetrate unto God's nature beyond his attributes. Asian mysticism has always been inclined to think most deeply about God as a hazy, unfathomable being without names or characteristics. It wants to reach beyond attributes and achieve contemplation of the divine being. As soon as one meets divine being and becomes one with it, all distinctions between good and evil cease and one feels oneself flowing into and being swallowed up by the ocean of what is endless. This is why the mystics in the Asian world are seldom its holy men. The person who dwells close to God, the mystic, is frequently no different from the person who possesses a superabundance of life and who can only give expression to that superabundance by living a more dissolute life than other men. He is the person who differs from other people only in that he possesses more "life," more compulsion to live, more vitality. He also stands above all norms and is a law unto himself, his own norm.

For the Christian, matters are entirely different. God is never nor in any way exalted above all qualities, the abstract Being of all existence, but he is always the Holy One, the righteous God, who considers sin an abomination and who with a holy love wants to preserve the sinner in his reconciliation through Jesus Christ. Whenever we meet God, or by whatever means we meet, he always stands in relationship to us as the Holy One. We cannot rise above that reality, since we can never escape it. There is no way that a human being can rise above God's virtues to a contemplation of his Being and experience himself flowing into Universal Being, for God is what he possesses. Each attribute of God is consistent with his being and is one with it.[13] But if that is the case, as a sinful person I feel that I can in no way have fellowship with God and that I have been cut off from companionship with the Holy One because I will never be able to approach him. That is the terrible reality presented to humanity by the gospel and requiring acknowledgment before it can talk about deliverance.

The Gospel and Magic

Precisely because Christianity never considers God apart from his attributes, it provides powerful weapons against all forms of magic. Magic is always the

---

13. Ed. note: This is the Christian doctrine of divine simplicity: God's essence or being is identical with his attributes. See Herman Bavinck, *Reformed Dogmatics*, vol. 2, ed. John Bolt, trans. John Vriend (Grand Rapids: Baker Academic, 2004), pp. 118ff.

attempt by humans to overpower "the divine," the power that transcends the natural order, and to put it at their service. The Israelites succumbed to magic when they deployed God's holy ark into the battle against the Philistines as a weapon (1 Sam. 4:3). They wanted to control the divine, nature-transcending power, without being controlled by God. They resorted to magic when in later times they began to regard Moses' bronze snake as an object worthy of divine veneration (2 Kings 18:4). They wanted to have divine, supernatural power — magical power — without having anything to do with God. In opposition to all these efforts, God issued his majestic command: this cannot be; this may not be! You cannot appropriate to yourself that which is divine without dealing with God himself, and you can only deal with God himself by humbling yourself before his face. Magic is a-moral; it recognizes neither good nor evil; it is merely nature-transcending. The entire Bible is one, powerful testimony against such magic and against all false mysticism that in a word pursues God without understanding the immeasurable distance separating sinful human beings from the holy God.

The Unfathomable Mystery

That talking about the virtues or attributes of God always confronts a person with major difficulties did not escape the thought of the great Augustine. Actually, we possess no names for God that fully express who he is. The full and endless extent of who God is can never be expressed in our words, which are always thoroughly earthly and limited. In beautiful, paradoxical language, Augustine can sometimes speak of God's virtues. "Thus we should understand God," he says somewhere,

> if we can and as far as we can, to be good without quality, great without quantity, creative without need or necessity, presiding without position, holding all things together without possession, wholly everywhere without place, everlasting without time, without any change in himself making changeable things, and undergoing nothing. Whoever thinks of God like that may not yet be able to discover altogether what he is, but is at least piously on his guard against thinking about him anything that he is not.[14]

Augustine is wrestling here with the struggle that theology always has whenever it talks about God: on the one hand it may not remain silent about God;

---

14. Translation from Augustine, *The Trinity*, 5.1.2.

but on the other hand it can never adequately express in its own language what it would like to say about God.

Christian thinkers of all ages have grappled with these realities. From Scripture, they understand that God must be seen and considered by us as a person, as someone who rules over us as a king, or as someone who provides for all our needs as a father, or as someone with whom we exist at every moment in a moral relationship. At the same time, we understand that God is the fountain of all that exists, the one from whom everything that exists originates, the one without whom and outside of whom nothing can exist. Thus, "we always especially face the problem of doing equal justice to the absoluteness and the personality of God, the incommunicable and the communicable attributes, God's absolute superiority over, and his communion with the world."[15] Small wonder, then, that it is not a simple matter for us to view clearly the relationship of these matters to one another. Rather than succumbing to the vague, mystical meditation on the depths of Being-in-general that has hypnotized Asia to such a powerful degree, we want to stand on the solid, reassuring foundation of Scripture that reflects both sides of this matter.

Immanence

The Divine "Spark"

The problem of God's immanence in the world and his exaltedness above the world is no less a difficult issue than that of the relation of God's being and attributes. In a special way, Asia has been conscious of this immanence and has reflected on it with remarkable eagerness, since it thought it saw in this indwelling a way for us to approach God. If it is true that God is the deepest being in all things and that all things exist in God and, as it were, are borne by him, then he must also dwell in the depths of my own soul. The boundary marker between time and eternity, between creator and creature, must exist somewhere very deep in my inner self. It is here, somewhere in the deepest recesses of my soul, that a point must exist where the divine and the human touch each other, where resting in and through the wholly other is conveyed. And that point is the deepest core of my existence, the pivot on which life turns.

15. From H. Bavinck, *Reformed Dogmatics,* 2: 117.

The frequently repeated summons is therefore sounded in mysticism — and certainly not only in Asia! — "If you want to find God, turn inward, into yourself." If you descend into your own soul, if your spirit's gaze turns from earthly to inner matters, you will discover a great deal in your own heart that confuses and perhaps even bewilders you. But behind the passions of your heart, behind the thoughts and deliberations, behind all the desires and needs, slumbers in the very depths of your being, the precious core of your oneness with God. God is in your own soul; he is the ground of your soul. Discovering your soul means finding him. Put to death, then, your lower "ego" with all of its weak little threads binding you to this world; put to death your lower will by means of your higher will, and whenever you delve to the very depths, you will find God himself as an enduring presence. All the time when in ignorance you bumbled around in a stupor *(avidya)*[16] and thought that you were far removed from the eternal source of God, he was the deepest being of your being, hidden behind the draperies, behind the sheaths *(koshas)* of your life.[17]

Finding comparable expressions in Augustine's works is not at all difficult. That for Augustine God is present in the soul as a teacher who instructs or as a light that shines is beyond all doubt.[18] For that reason, he can say that

16. Ed. note: *Avidya* is the Sanskrit word for ignorance or delusion.

17. Ed. note: Bavinck transliterates the Sanskrit *kosha (kośa;* alt. *kosa)* as *koça.* The term refers to the Vedantic doctrine that considers the human soul *(Atman)* to be surrounded by layers of covering, or "sheaths" (like an onion). In the words of a contemporary:

> We humans are like a lamp that has five lampshades over our light. Each of the lampshades is a different color and density. As the light shines through the lampshades, it is progressively changed in color and nature. It is a bitter-sweet coloring. On the one hand, the shades provide the individualized beauty of each lamp. Yet, the lampshades also obscure the pure light.

The practice of Yoga offers a way "out"; namely, go within:

> The Yoga path of Self-realization is one of progressively moving inward, through each of those lampshades, so as to experience the purity at the eternal center of consciousness, while at the same time allowing that purity to animate through our individuality. These five levels are called *koshas,* which literally means *sheaths.*

The five levels identified by the Yoga Masters are: physical *(annamaya kosha);* energy *(pranamaya kosha);* mental *(manamaya kosha);* wisdom *(vijnanamaya kosha);* and bliss *(anandamaya kosha).* Information taken from: Swami Jnaneshvara Bharati, "Five Sheaths or Koshas of Yoga," online at http://www.swamij.com/koshas.htm.

18. Étienne Gilson, *Christian Philosophy of Saint Augustine,* trans. L. E. M. Lynch (London: V. Gollancz, 1961), pp. 77-78.

"as the soul is the life of the flesh, so God is the blessed life of the human being."[19] Also, God can surely be called "the life of my life" *(vita vitae meae)*.[20] He lives in the very depths of human existence; one can even say concerning him that he "is more intimately present within me than is my inmost self and he exceeds my highest self" *(interior intimo meo et superior summo meo)*.[21] Augustine connects these insights directly with Holy Scripture, particularly with the well-known words of Paul that "in him we live and move and have our being" (Acts 17:28). Augustine reasons that it is because we really live in God and move and have our being in him that we can also remember him *(et ideo reminisce eius potest)*.[22] The expression "remember him" has a very specific meaning here, one entirely different from its normal linguistic meaning. Specifically, it does not simply mean remembering the past, but being self-conscious of what lies very deep within the soul. It does not refer to reaching back in time, but is a return to the basis of the soul. "The soul remembers God in that it turns to the Lord as to the light by which it is touched, even when it turns away from him."[23]

Comparable sayings on the depth of the soul, that is, on the point where the soul is, as it were, anchored in God, can be multiplied in Augustine's writings. This explains how he can always warn with such emphasis, "You err as long as you ramble around to and fro; turn back! But where? To the Lord! He abides with you; so turn back first of all into your own heart. Christ lives in the inmost place of a person."[24] "Turn back into your own self; the truth dwells in the inmost part of a person."[25] Furthermore, Augustine prays to God with these words: "Call me back from my wandering! Let me return to you by your leading."[26] Precisely because he regarded God and the soul as so tightly bound to each other, he could utter the famous words from his *Soliloquy:* "I desire to know God and my own soul. Really, nothing

19. Augustine, *City of God,* 19.26.

20. Augustine, *The Confessions,* 7.1.2, ed. John E. Rotelle, trans. Marcia Boulding, Works of Saint Augustine: A Translation for the 21st Century, part 1, vol. 1 (Hyde Park, NY: New City Press; Pocket Book Edition, 1997).

21. Augustine, *The Confessions,* 3.6.11.

22. Augustine, *The Trinity,* 14.15.21.

23. Augustine, *The Trinity,* 14.16.21.

24. Augustine, *Homilies on the Gospel of John,* 18.10, in *Nicene and Post-Nicene Fathers* (hereafter *NPNF*), First Series, ed. Philip Schaff, 14 vols. (Grand Rapids: Eerdmans, 1969-1979), 7: 121.

25. Augustine, *On True Religion,* 39.72, in *On Christian Belief,* ed. Boniface Ramsey, trans. John E. Rotelle, part 1, vol. 8 (Hyde Park, NY: New City Press, 2005).

26. Augustine, *Soliloquies,* 2.6.9.

more? No, nothing more at all." *(Deum et animam scire cupio. Nihil ne plus? Nihil omnio.)*[27] Throughout all of his writings, the strongest appeal is to turn into oneself, to return to what is regarded as the ground of our being.

In these and similar passages Augustine shows that he is not entirely free from the influences of pagan mysticism, particularly from neo-Platonic mysticism. We find similar testimony on the deepest essence of the soul already in the writings of Plotinus.[28] Just as Augustine succumbed to the charm of these neo-Platonic ideas, so, with a similar line of thought, he in turn also fascinated the many mystics who followed him. Throughout the entire Middle Ages, we hear mention of that secret place within the human soul where the temporal is grounded in the eternal, where a human being is as it were immersed in an inner intimacy with God. People give that mysterious point several names: they characterize it as "the hidden depths of the spirit" *(abditum mentis);* as "the innermost and highest part of the soul" *(intimum et summum mentis);* as a "little spark"; or as "the ground of the soul." Concerning that inner thirst, people even say — albeit with hesitation — that "it is that element in the soul that is divine." Eckhart goes even farther when he says concerning that yearning: "There is something in the soul that is uncreated and that cannot be created" *(aliquid est in anima quod est increatum en increabile).*[29] Right into modern times, one hears comparable sounds, and in mystical circles there is still always thought and discussion concerning the inner part of the soul where God and the creature meet.

Whenever one lays these expressions and ideas of Augustine and the Christian mystics (insofar as one can still consider someone like Eckhart, for example, as a Christian mystic) side by side with the utterances of Asian mysticism as presented in its most profound writings, one is struck immediately by the substantial agreement. One might even be inclined to say, "Here Asia and the West meet one another in the closest possible way." Is not the Indian *atman* the very depth of the human person and the same as what the Javanese calls *rasha* or "the mystery"? And are not these exactly the same as what the mystics of the West have called "the ground of the soul"? Does there not live, in the consciousness of both Asia and the West, in Christian mystics along with Hindu and Muslim mystics alike, the ineradicable aware-

27. Augustine, *Soliloquies,* 1.2.7.

28. Cf. Joseph Bernhart, *Die Philosophische Mystik des Mittelalters, von ihren antiken Ursprüngen bis zur Renaissance. Mit einer Zeichnung Seuses* (München: E. Reinhardt, 1922), p. 70.

29. Meister Eckhart, *Ausgewählt und übersetzt,* by Josef Bernhart (Kempten-München: n.p., 1914), p. 200.

ness that somewhere, very deep within our most inner being — so far that the scrutiny of our self-consciousness cannot even reach it — there exists a mysterious point where the transition from creature to Creator must be sought? And if there in fact is such a point, must the harmonious admonition not resound from all these religions: "Turn, O man, into yourself if you would reach your deepest self and there stand before the face of God"?

Scriptural Givens

We must try to come to clarity on these matters by going back to what the Bible itself has to teach about them. At the outset, we want to call attention to one thing: whenever Augustine talks about God dwelling in the depths of the soul, about that secret place where God himself carries a person into existence, so to speak, that is something totally different from when the Hindu says the same thing concerning Brahman. That is the case because the God whom Augustine serves is different from Brahman and is also different from the "endless sea of being" *(al-dhāt)* sought by Islamic mysticism. For Augustine, God is always the living God, rich with being, filled with divine virtues, while also being the holy God. When Augustine says that God is present in the soul, he does not mean that our souls bobble on the ocean of infinity, but he is conscious of the fact that against the background of our entire lives, God's voice and his almighty power call us back to himself in the midst of our sinful living. It is not mere ignorance or *avidya* that entangles a person, but it is always the power of the sinful will that causes a person to prefer the darkness of being outside God to his light. In other words, while it might sound as though substantial agreement exists between what Asian mysticism and Christianity say on these matters, materially there is a huge difference between them.

Setting that aside momentarily, we need to admit that formally, at least, substantial similarity exists between them. The question presses itself on us, "How does the matter stand, actually?" Is there such a place in the soul where the temporal is rooted in the eternal, where God and the human person meet one another?

When we look for an answer to that question, we need to accent in the very first place those passages that provide testimony on the matter. Now, there are many places in Scripture that compel us to conclude that the creation does not exist in and of itself but that it is sustained, moment-by-moment, by God. That applies to all creatures, not only to humanity. The Lord is the one who has created all things, but he is also the one who from moment to moment "makes all things alive" (Neh. 9:6). One feels the presence of God in all parts of nature: "When you send your Spirit, they are created, and you renew the face of the ground" (Ps. 104:30). This is why it can be said that all things exist not just from God, but also by God (Rom. 11:36), and that God *"sustain[s] all things by his word of power"* (Heb. 1:3). Not only does every creature owe its origin to God, so too its continuing existence from moment to moment (Rev. 4:11). Since this applies broadly to all creatures, it undoubtedly applies also to the human person of whom it can be said that God upholds him or her from moment to moment by his word of power. Paul certainly expressed this most emphatically in his speech on the Areopagus: "For in him we live and move and have our being" (Acts 17:28). We rest in the hands of God; if the Almighty were to let go of us for even one moment, we at that moment would disappear into oblivion. Only because he upholds us, body and soul, by the word of his power, can we live and think and continue to exist. When the Bible speaks about these matters, it often calls this upholding work of God a creating and a making alive. By this is certainly not meant that God creates the world anew every moment, but that the world once created by his almighty power continues to be upheld, fulfilled, and sustained by him. "His will, his power, his being are immediately present in every creature and every event. All things exist and live together in him."[30]

God's Indwelling in the World

When we set these words of Scripture alongside what we have just examined from the writings of Augustine and other mystics, several things directly catch our attention.

1. In the first place, we need to note that Scripture does not limit God's immanence to the human soul. It is not only in the soul that God dwells as Sustainer; his sustaining presence equally upholds our body. Yes, each living cell, even every atom in the mighty universe, participates in God's sustaining power. Not only the soul that rests in God, but our entire being, body and soul, exists and finds its place only in and through him. Augustine also certainly felt and expressed this, but he did not entirely avoid succumbing to the inclination to limit these matters to the soul. He was unable to extricate himself completely from the truly Greek opposition of flesh and spirit, and in the course of the history of mysticism that emerged in more than one way.

---

30. H. Bavinck, *Reformed Dogmatics,* 2: 610.

The idea of God's immanence, specifically as presented scripturally, presents no danger whatsoever for falling into that mysticism from which the Christian church has suffered so much.

God in the Soul

One could respond to this by acknowledging that God sustains the body as well as the soul, not to mention all creatures and even atoms, but then adding this: It is still the case that atoms know nothing of this divine sustaining; only humans, only the human soul can be conscious of this divine presence. Above all, then, consciousness of God must be an integral part of, must lie embedded in any well-developed human self-consciousness. Someone who comes to self-consciousness must be conscious of existing as a being that rests in God; a being upheld by God from moment to moment; a being in whom God is immanent. From this the common advice then still seems true: "If you want to find God, turn in on yourself, for God dwells in your own soul. Somewhere within your being there is a place where the temporal is anchored in the eternal. Whether you call that place the 'ground of the soul' or 'that secret place,' or whatever you want to call it, it is there and with it is also given the potential for finding God." To continue: "Are you seeking God's presence? God is close. He is closer to you than you are to yourself. In him you live, you move, you exist! To draw near to God, then, is nothing else than to become conscious of being near to God. Then you fall back on the many means that mysticism has employed from ancient times to make yourself conscious of the nearness of God."

It is not easy to respond to all these observations, especially because we sense that, against our will, we are standing here before one of the greatest of all mysteries. Nothing is more difficult for a person to understand than the riddle of God dwelling in the creature, of the presence of eternity in time. In addition, the Bible always speaks of these things with extreme sobriety and care. Thus, only with great reservation and reverence do we endeavor to make a few comments.

Two Sorts of World Order

The greatest difficulty, and one that easily confounds us, is that on this point the metaphysical world order does not coincide with the moral world order. A person rests in God, exists only through God, and God is at every moment present in him. Yet, at the same moment that same person can be very far from God, so far that the distance separates him or her from God. We live in God, we exist by the word of his power, and yet we wander around in the darkness of abandonment. And that estrangement does not only exist in the psychological sense that we are unaware of God's indwelling, but also in the theological sense that God places us outside of his fellowship. We cannot draw near to God because God as the Holy One cannot bear that which is unholy. Yet, in a metaphysical sense, as his creatures, we are always close to God, for if God were to withdraw his hand from us, we would disappear into nothingness. Even with respect to hell, it holds that God is present there, for it is always so that all that is can only exist because it is in God.

There exist two sorts of communion with God, therefore. There is a fellowship with God in a creaturely sense, in a metaphysical sense; in that case we may say that every creature only exists through fellowship with God. The greatest sinner lives in God, moves in God, and has being in God. As soon as he or she would stand outside that fellowship, he or she would no longer exist, would no longer be able to live.

Then, there is also a religious or moral fellowship. By this we understand that a person can stand in God's light and can participate in the blessedness that streams from his face. This last type of fellowship can only be given to a person when he or she is a redeemed creature in Christ, the Savior, and is again received by God.

These two forms of fellowship are always sharply distinguished from one another in Scripture. To put it even more strongly, Scripture only talks about the latter and only points to the former from a distance. The first is certainly important insofar as humanity can only exist thanks to that form of communion. But in no sense whatever is it capable of leading humanity to salvation and blessedness. At most, it can point to that kind of fellowship by sharply illumining the terribleness of sin. For this is the curse of sin, that the person who has life only from God and in God uses that life against God.

What follows from this, then, is that we search the Scriptures in vain for places where humanity is encouraged to become conscious of immanence. The Bible nowhere says, "Turn in on yourself; delve into yourself; approach that place where you rest in the hands of God!" For the Bible, that way to God simply does not exist. To come to God in that way is not only impossible, it is also impermissible. It amounts to a desire to eat of the tree of life after one has sinned. By contrast, the Bible now has no other message than that the angels bar the way to the tree of life with flaming swords in order that a person will not, like a thief, falsely grasp at life. What is also unique is that people in their self-consciousness can never comprehend this. If people were to come to self-consciousness, they would never be aware that they are beings that are sustained by God, but they would feel that they are beings that exist in and of themselves. The sharpest reflection escapes them; their deepest introspection is incapable of reaching that point. The indwelling of God is a mystery in each of our lives; we know of it through God's Word, but in the practice of daily living it simply escapes us.

No Secret Entrance

There are good reasons, therefore, why Christians have not spent a great deal of time on the subject of immanence. It can never serve as a springboard by which a person, with a leap, can grasp eternity. Something prevents us from ever meeting God — and God alone knows what it is — by way of our consciousness of his immanence within us. That approach is simply closed to us. God has simply not willed that we should approach him in this manner for the simple reason that we would then draw near to him in an entirely wrong way. Then, as sinful, unreconciled beings, we would simply slip over immediately from the world to God, from the creature to the Creator. But that route is absolutely and for all time closed; no person can or may take it. There is nowhere a secret entrance deep within our souls that gives us an entry to God or opens the way to salvation. God can certainly come to me; he can certainly call me into existence by his Word; my soul is certainly accessible to him. But I cannot come to God or of myself stand before his face.

The Fellowship of Faith

The Lord Jesus speaks to us a great deal and with more frequency and preference about fellowship with God in that profound and sacred sense whose meaning we understand only through him. Time and again he talks about coming to God by way of faith and conversion, the way opened by God through the great act of his love in the atonement. Concerning that fellowship with the Father the Savior shares amazing things with us, for God is always the God who loves us. The person who accepts the Lord Jesus by way of faith and conversion thereby comes to the Father, and that person will never again be shut out of fellowship with the Father. For this reason Jesus can say, "I am the Way, the Truth and the Life; no one comes to the Father except through me" (John 14:6). Whenever one enters the world of the gospel, one feels from the outset that one has entered a totally different climate and a completely different thought-world than the world of magic and mysticism that exists in Asia. The only gateway about which the Savior speaks is not a secret entrance deep within the soul to which one must try to descend by means of all sorts of religious exercises, but the entrance of honestly approaching God with all one's sin and guilt and of asking him for his grace. That explains why the fellowship with God that one receives through that gateway is not the ecstatic communion of drowning in the eternal, but the peaceful bond of the constant love that binds him to a person and that person to him through Jesus Christ as Savior and King. All who point the religious inquirer to an indwelling God or his immanence as the way to draw near to him and to experience fellowship with him take that person down the wrong track. For the inquirer who wants to descend in this way into the depths of God will meet on this toilsome route those cherubim that block the entrance with flaming swords, and he or she will actually never come to stand before the throne of God. With childlike clarity, Jesus earnestly shows us that no one can enter the kingdom of God aside from conversion and faith, aside from atonement and being born again.

From a purely philosophical perspective, one can say that God is everywhere, that he is present in the soul of everyone, and that he dwells within all people, for we live in him. But, however valuable this insight might be, it offers no possibility of deliverance and points out no way of escape. What does it benefit a person if he or she already knows that the God who brought them into existence is immanent within them, when they realize that they exist far from God with their sinful souls and that outside of God they will be lost? This is why the Lord Jesus never points us in the direction of immanence, but with all the more emphasis he calls us to walk in that inner, very real fellowship with God that he will open for us. "To say that God dwells within the sinner just as surely as he dwells within the saint is fatal for our reliance on moral truths." "God is separated from all that is evil, ugly and false." Those were conclusions reached by a small group of Indians that met with Stanley Jones for a few weeks and engaged in a unique study and in reflecting together somewhere in the solitude of the Himalayas.[31] And are they not extremely valuable for preaching in the Asian world? Whenever we as human beings devote too much of our soul's attention to the indwelling

---

31. E. Stanley Jones, *The Message of Sat Tal Ashram, 1931* (Calcutta: Association Press, 1932), pp. 74, 77.

power of God present in all creatures, all boundaries slowly fade from our view. Then it seems to us as though both good and evil grow and blossom by the power of God and as though God is present in both simultaneously. Here we find subtle divergences; here lie thoroughly mysterious distinctions that elude the sharpest intellect and that confuse the most profound thinker. God is not the All-pervasive Spirit from which all things blossom forth and who is thus the seed of all that exists, but he certainly is present in everything and everything exists only through him. God is in the midst of the world, but he himself is certainly not the world. He dwells in the soul, but he is completely separated from the sin imprisoning the soul. He is closer to us than we can ever dream possible, but eternal distances separate our souls from his light and his blessedness. This is why it is not wholesome to focus the attention of the soul too intently on God's immanence, for this runs the risk for someone that everything flows together and the person is no longer able to distinguish the boundary between *Creator* and *creature.*

Asian thought has paid too much attention to the order or gradations of existence and has alleged that the world must rest in God, that God is in the world, and therefore also in me. The narcosis of this idea has allowed this perspective to delve into the ocean of the eternal where all cosmic boundaries are lost.

Jesus does not deny the first proposition: God certainly lives in all things and a person only lives because upheld by the power of God. But he shakes us out of the stupor this causes. What is important is not that one lives by the power of God but rather how one uses this divine power and what one does with it — that is what life is all about. If one lives the life God has granted set in enmity against God, then that life becomes a curse. "It would be better that you had not been born!" For this reason Jesus fastens our attention so little on the order of existence, knowing that as haughty people we cannot readily endure knowing that God is so very close to us. But with unyielding seriousness, he directs our attention to the moral order and shows us the unbridgeable distance that separates the sinful heart from the holy God. He speaks to us about this distance and he will remove this distance for us. Schweitzer said:

> In Indian religiosity, the divine is presented as pure, spiritual being. It is the ocean in which humanity will be submerged, swimming. But the God of the gospel of Jesus is a living, moral will who desires to grant me a new direction.[32]

32. Albert Schweitzer, *Christianity and the Religions of the World,* trans. Johanna Powers (London: Allen & Unwin, 1923), pp. 46-47.

Creation and Emanation

The Birth of the World

In answer to the question of how the world came into existence, the Hindu[33] world in general has had a strong tendency to believe in a type of emanation that flows from the godhead. In the ancient Vedas, we see this spelled out especially in mythological form. When early Aryan thinkers occupied themselves with the question of the world's origin, their preference was to look for images borrowed from nature. Consequently, they spoke of the world being born from an important divine being. Often this birth was embellished and explained with various stories. So, for example, the one God, *Prajapati*, entered the primal waters that he had previously made and thereafter returned as a "golden germ." From that golden germ the world thereafter developed in all its fullness.[34] Writers also spoke of a "cosmic egg" that came forth from the godhead and from which all else subsequently developed. In the world's birth, love *(kama)* played an especially significant role. This love assures that the godhead enters into the all-embracing world ocean that came into being through it until the earth is born as the miraculous fruit of divine creative energy.[35] But however else the subject might be considered, thinkers always clung to images that depicted the world as being born, proceeding from God, and flowing out of God.

In subsequent days, the mythological representations were transposed into concepts, but they clearly retained the same inclination. The Brahmins maintained that the world is created by God, but the word that they used for "creation," *srishti*, has more the meaning of something set loose by God, something poured out from God, something flowing forth from the fullness

33. Ed. note: The original reads "Eastern"; in keeping with our editorial policy to use "Asia" and "Asian" for Bavinck's "East" and "Eastern" and, where warranted, to specify either geography or religious tradition, we chose "Hindu" for the sake of accuracy and clarity.

34. *The Rig Veda: An Anthology; One Hundred and Eight Hymns, Selected, Translated and Annotated,* 10.121, trans. Wendy Doniger (New York: Penguin Books, 1981).

35. Ed. note: The myth of the cosmic egg has a long and rich history in Hindu thought. It is first present in the *Rig Veda* (10.81-82), and it is found in a more fully developed form in the *Shatapatha Bramana* (11.1.1.6ff.), *Chandogya Upanishad* (3.19), and in the *Markandeya Purana* (vv. 61-67). For more information on this myth see *Classic Hindu Mythology: A Reader in the Sanskrit Purānas,* ed. and trans. Cornelia Dimmit and J. A. B. van Buitenen (Philadelphia: Temple University Press, 1978); "Origins" and Swami Parmeshwaranand, "Cosmogony," in *Encyclopaedic Dictionary of Purānas,* vol. 1 (New Delhi: Sarup & Sons, 2001), pp. 311-20.

of divine being. Thus, it remained a being born, a coming forth from the godhead, similar to how a wave rises on the sea and as a crackling spark rises out of a fire. And precisely because they held so tenaciously to the notion of being born these writers could do no less, in fact were compelled to show that in the deepest sense this world is divine, is a little chunk of God, a wave on the ocean of divinity that is destined eventually to sink back into the godhead. Later philosophical presentations expanded more broadly on these matters and reworked them logically, but essential changes were never made in these fundamental principles.[36] The world came into existence via emanation from the godhead; in the full sense of that term, it has been born out of God.

Islamic mysticism has articulated the same thought in a variety of forms and images. In doing so, it found itself in the favorable position of being able to work various thought forms that blossomed in neo-Platonism and different Gnostic systems and that threatened the Christian church in its early centuries. These often vague and phantasmal representations men connected with speculation on the Logos, the divine Word, as it is called in the first chapter of the Gospel of John. This Logos *(Amr)* or highest form of reason *(akl)* as understood in an Islamic sense is then united with the *"Nur Mohamed"* or divine light that in the prophet Mohammad "became flesh." In this way, the mystics transplanted ideas from the Gospel of John into Islam, understanding them in the Gnostic sense widely understood in the Asian setting. It would take us too far afield to get too deeply into the subject. Suffice it to say that in Islamic mysticism a system was developed that taught that the world flowed from the godhead in a range of intermediate levels, descending from the heights of divine Light.

This entire descent or flowing out *(tanazzul)* is a process of unfolding into endless diversity; it is continuing individualization *(ta'ayyun)*. From the one divine being *(al-Dhāt)*, the enormous diversity of the world developed on successive levels. This is the all-embracing emanation process carried out in creation and that can be consummated first of all in the human being, for the human being turns the process back, as it were, and makes his or her way back to God and is absorbed again into God. That is the return *(tarakki)* that puts an end to emanation. The Logos that assumes such a prominent place

36. For understanding *srishti* see Paul Deussen, *Allgemeine Geschichte der Philosophie: Mit besonderer Berücksichtigung der Religionen 1,2 Die Philosophie der Upanishads* (Leipzig: Brockhaus, 1919), p. 176; and Hermann Oldenberg, *Die Weltanschauung der Brāhmanatexte* (Göttingen: Vandenhoeck & Ruprecht, 1919), pp. 168-69.

in this flowing forth is in fact nothing other than the summation of divine ideas, which are designed to bring the world into existence.[37]

Creation

In contrast with all this speculation about the emanation of the world, the gospel steadfastly holds to the idea of creation. Understood in a proper sense, certainly even we can speak of "the birth of the heavens and the earth" (Gen. 2:4). Or, we can think of the Spirit "brooding" on the face of the waters, imagery reminding us of a hen brooding on an egg (the world) (Gen. 1:2). By faith we can understand that the visible things "have come into being" from the invisible and even that all things are "from" God (Heb. 11:3; Rom. 11:36).

But these expressions may not sidetrack us for one moment. They were never intended to convey that the world emanates from God, like a brook flows from a spring or as a spark flits from a fire. The world is not a small part of God's being that, as it were, in one moment emerges from God and slowly makes its long way back into God. If that were the case, we would have to conclude that the cosmos itself is divine and that God himself encounters us in nature, in fact, in everything and everywhere. Then, truly everything is God *(panta theos)* and every distinction between Creator and creation becomes wiped out. Against this deification of the world that also includes deification of humanity the gospel warns repeatedly and emphatically. A person may be "descended from God" (Acts 17:28) and may be regarded as related to God as to a Father (Mal. 2:10), but he or she always remains on this side of the deep divide separating creature from the Creator.

To see these matters in a proper light is of utmost importance because every misunderstanding results in terrible catastrophe. As soon as we say that everything flows out of God and that the world therefore possesses a divine nature, we immediately involve God in sin. Then there is only one subject who acts, thinks, lives, and unfolds in the diversity of all things — namely God. Then it is the divine within me, God himself, that thinks, that sins, and that eventually returns to his own self. Then sin itself becomes a phenomenon that has its origin in God. Precisely for these reasons, we need to maintain the boundary between us so emphatically. To be sure, the crea-

---

37. This doctrine of descent and return corresponds to the system of Plotinus: *dhat* = the one *(monē)*; *tanazzul* = emanation *(prohodos)*; *tarakki* = return *(epistophē)*.

ture has been created by God and in a certain sense is "out of" God, but an essential distinction nonetheless remains between God and the world, between God and humanity. That distinction can be described in no better way than to set forth that the creation is a new subject that has come into existence by God alone but that is something completely separate and unique. When I sin, it is not God that sins because I am a new subject. My life is not God's life, and my destiny is not God's destiny. I certainly owe my life, my strength, my all to God, but I am still not a little part of God, a spark of the divine. I am a new subject with my own will and my own accountability. I can use the strength and the life that God has given me either to honor him or to oppose him.

All of this is what Christian theology intends when in contrast with the doctrine of emanation it posits the conviction that the world has been created "out of nothing."[38] To think that all puzzles have been solved by this would be foolhardy, for the concept of creation is extremely difficult to comprehend. Rather, as Scripture itself tells us, we here once again are on the terrain of faith (Heb. 11:3), where all of our thinking must recognize its own weakness. But this one thing is incontrovertible: the world is something distinctive and is not God, even though everything has been made by God and in one sense has been born out of him. It has its own existence and is a rich and beautiful totality that exhibits the mind of God, but it may still never be identified with God. Only by maintaining the distinction between the creature and the Creator in this clear manner can the Christian continue believing that God is the immutable One who is exalted above all changes. He or she can also continue to believe that God is the holy God who cannot and will not abide evil and who may not be identified with evil in any way whatsoever.

The Son and the World

Belief in the Trinity has been of inestimable value in explaining all these matters. Scripture clearly teaches us that the Logos, the divine Word, is the mediator of creation. "Without him is nothing made that has been made" (John 1:3). But this Logos is not some sort of intermediary being between God and the world, not the first step in the descent downwards, but he is God himself; he is the one in whom God himself speaks from eternity. One might say about him that he has emanated from God, flowed forth from

38. H. Bavinck, *Reformed Dogmatics,* 2: 416ff.

him, since in every way he is God; he is the "express image of God's very being" (Heb. 1:3). In him, the Father expresses all his thoughts about the creation, all his plans regarding each, separate creature. All God's thoughts are comprehended in the Logos, and in him God expresses himself. For this reason, the Logos is also the Son, who in every regard is one with the Father. Precisely because Christian theology kept in mind such a glorious image of generation and emanation, it could also maintain such a clear distinction between creation and Creator. The Son was born, emanated, and is therefore God himself and is himself holy, perfect, almighty, eternal, immutable — in short, he is one with God; he is very God. The world has been created and certainly bears evidences of God, but it is finite, bound by time and changeable.[39] It is also the place where sin displays its devastating effects. The more deeply one ponders the birth and the glory of the Son, the more clearly one understands the indescribable separation between him and us. He stands on one side of the boundary, we on the other. He is the perfect and complete expression of God's being; while we are definitely God's image-bearers, we are finite image-bearers and because of sin we have lost much of the luster of that image.

Islamic mysticism certainly talks about *Amr,* about a divine word that has emanated from God, and it believes that this world flowed out of this *Amr.* It sees all things on the same line, all the result of one process. But Christian faith feels the difference profoundly and comprehensively. Consequently, it always sees God as the All-Holy One, who is exalted far above all sin.

Considered purely philosophically, withstanding Asian thought will always prove difficult. Distinguishing the immanence of Brahman in the world from what the Bible teaches concerning God's immanence is very difficult. Creation and emanation appear to lie so close to one another that it is extremely difficult to distinguish them sharply. But it is of greatest importance that we understand these matters correctly. Nothing less than God's

---

39. Ed. note: With respect to generation, emanation, and creation, Herman Bavinck says the following in *Reformed Dogmatics:*

> Christian theology knows both emanation and creation, a twofold communication of God — one within and the other outside the divine being; one to the Son who was in the beginning with God and was himself God, and another to creatures who originated in time; one from the being and another by the will of God. The former is called generation; the latter, creation. By generation, from all eternity, the full image of God is communicated to the Son; by creation only a weak and pale image of God is communicated to the creature. (2: 420)

holiness is at stake. Does one consider sin as one expression of God himself, or does one maintain as great a distance as possible between God and evil? Is it one and the same being of God expressed in the murderer as well as the saint so that it embraces all things alike? Or, is God the fullness of holiness and majesty that is far removed from ungodliness and falsehood, and does he banish from his presence all that forsake him in pride and sinful self-service? These are the questions involved in the struggle between the gospel and the religions of Asia.

Jesus, the image of God in whom God reveals himself to the world, stands in the middle of this fight. Whoever sees him sees the Father as he is. Whoever sees him leaves the vague and confused ideas about God and turns to the living, true God who is both just and merciful. As has been true throughout the centuries, so will it be true for Asia: anyone who does what is true, who genuinely seeks the truth with his or her whole soul, will come into the Light and will be set free by the Light of Jesus Christ.

8 Microcosm and Macrocosm

Humanity as a Microcosm

Throughout its history there is one idea upon which the people of Asia agreed, namely the unity of microcosm and macrocosm, or the small and large worlds. Each human person is a small and self-contained world within itself, possessing all the powers and components of the large world all around it; the human person is like the focal point on which all the rays of the cosmos converge. The beauty of this idea has not only inspired poets, it has also strongly influenced religious life in all sorts of ways. What is essential, therefore, is that we give an account of the scope of this concept and investigate the extent to which we can agree with this identification of a smaller and larger world.

A powerful harmony between the human person and the world was already felt in the texts of the ancient Vedas. Already then, the forces of nature were regarded as gods and worshiped as deities. People realized that human beings as creatures of nature preeminently possessed within themselves these various powers and that they therefore shared in divine life. The wind is present in human breath, fire in one's mind or in the warmth of one's body, sun and moon in one's eyes; in short, everything that we find in the world at large, we find in miniature form in the human person. This identity was so compelling that people were inclined to regard the larger world as an incredibly huge Person, a Giant, an enormous *Purusha*,[1] and thus to think of

1. Ed. note: The Hindu idea of *Purusha* (Sanskrit *puruṣa* = "man, Cosmic man") comes

the individual person as a faithful but small copy of this cosmic giant. Along these lines, people found an extremely close connection between these two worlds. The more they were steeped in the idea that behind all the dimensions of one's humanity lived a kind of ego, a deeper being, the more persuaded people were that a spiritual Ego, a spiritual force, had to exist and that it embraced all things. In that setting, faith in Brahman was born as faith in a world-soul that determines the life of the world and that rules within all the phenomena of nature. That divine Brahman as the heart of all things corresponds with the human atman or the deepest human self that encompasses all dimensions of human life. This is how the precise comparison between larger and smaller worlds was developed.

When one once started down this road, a broad panoply of conceptually refined options lay ahead. One could attempt to draw out the comparison between the smaller and larger worlds to great lengths and in many directions; poetically, one could extend the lines extremely far. The more fully developed the depiction of the All-in-all, the stronger became the compulsion to depict humanity as a microcosm. Then thinkers embraced the idea that all that exists consists of, or rather is centered around, a midpoint, a high mountain, the large cosmic mountain called *Maha-Meru*.[2] People thought this *Maha-Meru* existed somewhere in the Himalayas and considered it to be the dwelling place of the gods. Surrounding the cosmic mountain is the round disk of the earth, and around it swirls the world-ocean from which the earth has come into being. This is approximately the way they thought about the structure of the larger world. What a splendid opportunity exists here for the reflective mind to make comparisons! The *Maha-Meru* can be found in the human person. One sees the spinal column in the human body as the great center point that holds everything else together. If one wants to probe more deeply, spiritually speaking, one can regard the *atman* itself, the deepest ego, as the world-mountain around which all else is clustered. One can divide the body into different areas arranged around the midpoint. Bodily fluids were seen as manifestations of the world-ocean. Thus, one could discover everything reflected back in the smaller world, and the parallelism was filled out in every respect.

---

from the Vedic tradition where *Purusha* is described as a primeval giant that is sacrificed by the gods and from whose body the world and the *varnas* (castes) are built.

2. Ed. note: *Mahu-meru* ("The Great Mountain") is also a stratovolcano located in East Java, Indonesia; the current name is Semeru, or Mount Semeru (Indonesian: *Gunung Semeru*).

The Holy Number

In this entire fantasy about the connection between a larger and a smaller world, several magical numbers play a major role. The numbers four and five, in particular, assume an especially important place. One finds four wind-territories associated with the *Meru*. One finds four elements in the larger cosmos: earth, water, fire, and air; and when one includes ether, there are five. The four or five sense-organs of the microcosm are controlled by these four or five elements. Thus, the sense of smell corresponds to earth, the tongue to water, the eye to fire, skin to air or wind, and the ear to ether. The different sense-organs in turn are connected to the passions that stir the human soul, while further analogies exist between the passions and the different colors. Thus, the entire macrocosm is a wondrously constituted whole consisting of fours and fives, and these in turn control something in the human microcosm that harmonizes with them. To be sure, even the planetary world is understood within this theory. The planet Jupiter is thought to correspond with the East, Mars with the South, Venus with the West, Saturn with the North, and Mercury with the zenith. In the animal kingdom, the eagle is associated with the East, the lion with the South, the snake with the West, and the elephant with the North. In short, there is no hesitation whatsoever in drawing these principles to their most extreme consequences once they have been embraced, even when these consequences strike us as completely meaningless and useless. Particularly in later Hinduism and in Mahayana and Tantric Buddhism, these speculations assume totally fantastic proportions.[3]

Microcosm in Islam

As we have already noted more than once, Islam — especially Islamic mysticism — appropriated a whole body of important philosophical ideas from neo-Platonism that in no small measure also stimulate the mind to draw analogies. Articulated by no one less than its greatest thinker, Plotinus (d. 270 BC), neo-Platonism taught that the world has emanated from God as pure Being and as the highest monad or unity. This supreme "One" is at the same time the highest good, even greater than good. He is so filled with be-

3. Compare R. Heine, "Geldern, Weltbild und Bauform in Süd Ost Asien," in *Wiener Beiträge zur Kunst- und Kulturgesch. Asiens* (1930).

ing, that it overflows, as it were, and his fullness is poured out. From that Oneness there flows in the first place World-Reason. In it are contained all the ideas and plans concerning all beings. The soul developed from World-Reason, and all emanations of the material world, in the final analysis, come from the soul. The material is really only darkness or nothingness, since in being so far removed from the One or from God, it possesses nothing of the divine within it. The human soul is actually imprisoned under the dominion of matter, and it can only escape through a long and difficult process of purification (catharsis). By taking flight into its thoughts, the soul can thereby climb to knowledge of the eternal ideas comprehended in the realm of reason. But it can transcend even that, for through mystical contemplation it can even become united with the One, with the divine from which everything has come into being. For this reason, one can say that the human being, in this highest manifestation, can be considered a microcosm of the macrocosm that it reflects. Then a person is one with Being itself, with the One, and shares in everything that has flowed from the One. He or she embraces Creator and creature alike, possesses all capacities and circumstances, all elements that play a part in the entire cosmos. That is what is so unique and so noble about the human mystic.

All these ideas have made no small contribution to the development of mystical theology in Islam. In all sorts of ways, they were connected with material in the Qur'an and in sacred tradition. People showed partiality for appealing to the tradition *(hadith)* that God created Adam in his own image. The thought that a human being bears the divine image stimulated fanciful notions in several ways. This made it possible to hold that in Adam all reality was reflected, with the result that all the powers of the cosmos were joined in him. And at the same time, since Adam was one with Allah, with God himself, he stood all the closer to the Creator. He spanned time and eternity, bore both God and the world, was rightly the perfected human in whom all powers belonging to the whole were concentrated. What was true of Adam is true of all prophets, who must always be venerated as perfected people. But this is even more true with respect to the great mystics, who have traversed the remaining distance on the mystical road to salvation and who therefore may be regarded as *wali,* as people "close" to God and as "friends" of Allah. This is how the idea of a microcosm also penetrated the world of Islam.

This entire doctrine of the microcosm that is found in the perfected human being received powerful development in the thought of the Spanish theologian Ibn al Arabi (b. 1165 AD) and especially in his student Abd al-

Karīm ibn Ibrāhīm al-Jīlī (1366-1424), the Sufi author of *The Perfect Man (Al-Insānu l-Kamīl)*.[4] It outlines for us a complete description of this "perfected human person" or this mystic who has risen to unity with the highest Being *(dhāt)*.[5]

In principle, the ideas developed in this book agreed closely with the philosophical principles of Plotinus. Abd al-Karīm also states that the Supreme Being is Oneness in the most complete sense of that term *(dhāt)*. The world in all its fullness and on its various levels flows from that Supreme Being. The lowest level that flows from God is the material world or matter, for it is actually nothingness or that which is formless and without essence and that in and of itself has no value. Humanity is tied to the material, but a person can loosen his or her ties to it by means of mystical practices. Such a person can become contemplative of divine thought and can even allow him- or herself to sink into the endless sea of eternal being. At the highest level, he or she can legitimately be called a "perfected person" in whom the duality of Lord (God) and servant (creature) is transcended and in whom all things are comprehended. That person then becomes a pure, true reflection of all that exists with respect to both God and the world. All aspects and phenomena of this Being are then reflected in such a person.

The Perfected Person

That Islamic mysticism reaches such conclusions concerning the existence of the "perfected human being" is not at all surprising. The idea that forms the basis for this notion was universally present in the Orient during mysticism's zenith. It can be found in the secret doctrines of Kabbalistic thought,[6] in the Manichaeism against which Augustine contended so fiercely, in Philo, and in neo-Platonic philosophy. At certain times, a given idea can infect the very air, as it were, so that the same noises are heard in all sorts of places and

4. Ed. note: Bavinck gives *Humanity, Perfected in the Knowledge of the First and Last Things* as the full title of this work.

5. Ed. note: It is important to distinguish here the Sanskrit (Hindu) term *dhatu* = the root of a word; from the Arabic *dhāt* – essence or nature. Thus, in Arabic, the essence or nature of something is called *dhāt al-Shay*, and the essence of God is called *al-Dhāt*. Cf. Shukri B. Abed, *Aristotelian Logic and the Arabic Language in Alfārāabi* (Albany: State University of New York Press, 1991), pp. 62, 68. Abū Naṣr al-Fārābī (c. 872-951) was one of the greatest scientists and philosophers of the Islamic world in his day.

6. On the Kabbala see J. van Nes, *Het Jodendom* (Kampen: J. H. Kok, 1933), pp. 437ff.

schools of thought. Such was the case with respect to this belief in the "perfected person." The perfected person is someone who is god-like, who possesses divine powers, and who carries the "Being" within himself as a mystery and embraces within himself all emanations that flow from divine being. This person is in union with both God and the world and as such is a seedbed for all things.

Obviously, the entire doctrine of the perfected person as a microcosm was readily embraced on Java.[7] It constituted one of many points at which the new religion displayed similarity to the manner of speaking of the old. Hinduism, Buddhism, and Islam form a brotherhood in this regard. A Javanese person, armed with new names and terminology, could continue philosophizing about a smaller and a larger world, and he or she could talk about a perfected or true human being *(manusia sejati)* in whom the idea of the microcosm is most purely realized.

Thus, religious thinking became stuffed with an array of symbols and meanings from two worlds. The combination of Indian and Islamic mysticism helped the Javanese people to advance down the road of mystical meditation with respect to the unity of microcosm and macrocosm. Such meditation found room for all kinds of emphases. In it one encounters the distinction between the being and the attributes of God that Islamic theology had developed. There one meets World-Reason, the Logos, and the *'Aql*[8] or the *Nur Mohamed* — all the first emanation flowing from the highest Being.

In it one finds many other symbols, such as the tree of life and the white pearl or prototypical jewel from which the world came forth. There one hears about the *Kaaba*[9] and about the temple in Jerusalem as designated holy places in the microcosm. In summary, a large variety of images and expressions serve to show the marvelous character of the smaller world and its intimate harmony with the larger world. By no means were all of these em-

---

7. Ed. note: It is worth reminding the reader that the first two chapters of *Christus en de Mystiek van het Oosten* were titled "The Arrival of Hinduism on Java" and "The Progress of Islam on Java." Bavinck uses his own extensive knowledge of Indonesian religious traditions as the springboard for a broader discussion.

8. Ed note: The Arabic word *'Aql* means intellect or reason; it is the usual translation of the Greek word *nous*.

9. Ed note: *Kaaba* is the Arabic term for cube and designates the cube-like black stone in the Masjid al-Haram Mosque in Mecca. It is the most sacred site in the world for Muslims; when devout Muslims pray the five daily prayers they face Mecca; pilgrimage *(Hajj)* to the site is one of the five pillars of Islam.

phases always understood in the same sense, and often they were in conflict with one another. But the leading idea of all these reflections has always been that the microcosm reflects the macrocosm and that both of them, therefore, are united as the one and the many, subject and object, Lord and servant, spirit and matter.

Islamic mysticism on Java, containing all these ideas, is capable of being portrayed in a schematic drawing.

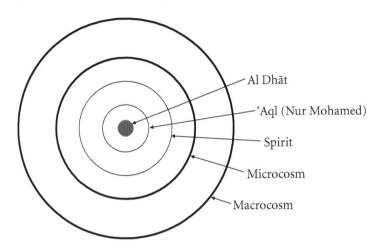

Such a schematic representation is called a *da'ira* in Arabic or a *daerah* in Javanese and is an attempt to represent with a few strokes of the pen the mystery of the All-in-all. It depicts the larger world as a large circle in which God *(dhāt)* is the center. In between the outer circle as the circumference and the center are a series of smaller circles that symbolize various stages of emanation. Thus one finds, for example, the *Nur Mohammed* or World-Reason and the soul and its capacities included in the entire scheme. The perfected person is capable of being clearly depicted as a little circle that encompasses all the elements of the macrocosm and whose center coincides with being itself *(dhāt)*. Larger and smaller worlds are thus concentric circles with an identical center point but with a different circumference. This is the secret or mystery of the perfected human being, presented schematically.

Whenever we take time to inquire, prior to looking at these ideas individually, and consider what the consequences of this model have been for the oriental world, I believe that we may point to several phenomena.

The Meaning of History

First of all, I would like to state here that damage is done to history by putting equal emphasis on the smaller and the larger worlds. History becomes symbolical. In one way or another, people attempt to understand everything that happens in the larger world symbolically, as a reflection of inner phenomena. The historical figures of a given era become larger than life and signify various powers or passions of the human soul. In this way far too much is lost for an understanding of history's process. People take from events only that which fits into a symbolical framework. This serves them no useful purpose for reflecting on problems or learning to submit to reality. Time and again in studying Javanese history, we have been impressed by this pull to treat people symbolically and to explain all of history as an emblematic depiction of inner realities, and we have noted how great has been the damage to useful, truly faithful objectivity.[10] Most importantly, people do not regard history as a whole, but they repeatedly extract a given moment from it and twist that moment as long as it takes to subvert it to completely symbolical ends.

One finds these phenomena represented most forcefully in the puppetry of *wayang*.[11] *Wayang* always depicts the wars that the ancient Aryans had to conduct after their invasion of northern India. Thus it is a drama about warfare, and in the wars a few heroic figures come to the fore. But in the *wayang* all these heroes become symbols larger than life. The entire *wayang* is a skillful embellishment of the inner warfare that each person has to wage en route to perfection.

There is obviously a good element in all of this. A powerful dimension of symbolism actually exists within history. Those of us who know biblical history, including the history of Israel, understand that in the circumstances faced by these people God has portrayed very significant and valuable ideas applicable to the lives of all the saints. We have been so entrusted with that kind of symbolical exposition that, without any hesitation whatever, we understand in their typological, representational significance such events as the Israelites' slavery in Egypt, their journey through the desert, their arrival in Canaan, and so many more things. But that approach may never cause us to

---

10. Compare William Huibert Rassers, *De Pandji-roman* (Antwerp: D. de Vos-van Kleef, 1922), chapter 5. Ed. note: A review of this work can be found online at http://onlinelibrary.wiley.com/doi/10.1525/aa.1926.28.1.02a00160/pdf.

11. Ed. note: *Wayang* is a Javanese word for shadow and is applied to a form of puppetry that utilizes light and shadow to great effect.

overlook the fact that we are dealing with the symbolic side of the matter. The events represented have an importance in their own right; they are dimensions of God's counsel in the unfolding of major historical events. The symbolical is certainly a dimension of historical events that is permissible in some instances, but it is never the only dimension. It must be immediately amplified and corrected with an entirely different interpretation of history that creates room for the wise counsel and plan of God involving all world events.

There is, however, a second and much more serious objection to this identification of the macrocosm and microcosm. Throughout Asia, this identification has significantly increased the appeal of magic. We need to think of ourselves as having achieved the status of a "perfected person," that is to say, of a person who has covered the long distance of mystical practice and arrived at ecstatic union with the One or with deepest Being. Such an individual realizes that he has achieved union with God and feels that the very center of his own being coincides with the center of the macrocosm. In this state, all that exists lies at his feet, as it were; the person has in a certain sense become the center of all that exists. Creator and creature are truly united in this person. Small wonder, then, that all the powers of the universe are subject to him. The winds and all the elements of nature obey his will; he understands all mysteries. Concerning such a person one can say, according to the treasured Javanese saying, that he knows all things "before he is even told of them" and that everything "that this person sees at that instant exists, and all that this person imagines at that moment comes into being." This person becomes a participant in the creative power of Allah, and he can even create since he is one with the ground of all being. Not surprisingly, such a man is regarded as having mystically become one with Allah and is venerated as a holy man and a miracle worker. The ordinary villager has high regard for the magician, whose grave enjoys idolatrous worship even after his death. All these things depend on their closest connection with each other.

There is more! The perfected human being — or the one so regarded — stands at the center of everything, which is why the totality of all things lives along with his or her destiny. In Javanese literature, these ideas often take on a beautiful, poetic expression. Whenever the heroes that are lauded in Javanese songs venture out, it is as though the flowers emit their fragrances and as though all nature welcomes them. Whenever they find themselves on a pathway threatened by danger, it begins raining gently, the mischief-making birds begin their squawking, and the whole natural world sings a song of sadness and fear. When Arjuna[12] follows his ascetic practices on the heights of the Himalayas, it seems as though "the mountain is a holy man, clothed with the clouds and wearing a huge breadfruit tree as a cap." Then nature takes the form of a hermit. In this way all that exists lives along with the person in joy or in sorrow, in prosperity and in adversity. So do all the struggles of a hero, and it seems as if all the powers of the larger world move in synchronization with the emotional waves flooding over a person who as a microcosm feels his or her oneness with the world.

These things all come to strongest expression in the *wayang*. The destiny of heroes is depicted in the dramas of the *wayang*. Whenever one of the heroes finds himself in dire need, what repeatedly happens is that the entire world-order is disturbed. All the powers of nature suddenly become aroused; a shock pierces the world. These plays are called the *gara-gara*,[13] and they certainly give very strong expression to the notion of the unity of smaller and larger worlds. This is especially the case when the smaller world is actually self-conscious of its unity with divinity. Clearly, here we are not dealing with mere poetic exaggeration — as we find in Dutch poetic expressions such as "the dunes shriek together" when something terrible has just occurred. There is a worldview hidden behind all this preoccupation with the shaking of nature surrounding the hero. Against this background, one discovers — not always consciously but certainly always presumptively — the complete correspondence between the smaller and larger worlds. As soon as people achieve union with God and arrive at the very center of all that exists, all things lie at their feet; the entire world lives along with them and is related to them. "Perfected persons" are the center of the cosmos, and it is as though they draw all the powers of nature along with them.

One need know only a little about Asia to understand how eagerly all these emphases are embraced in Asian emotional life. The people of Asia ea-

---

12. Ed. note: Arjuna is one of the heroes of the Hindu epics; reluctant to go into battle to kill members of his own family, he is persuaded by his charioteer, Lord Krishna, to change his mind. Their dialogue about courage, a warrior's duty, the nature of human life and the soul, and the role of gods forms the subject of the *Bhagavad Gita*.

13. K. G. P. A. A. Mangkoenagoro, "Over de wayang koelit in het algemeen en over de daarin voorkomende symbolische en mystieke elementen," *Djawa* 7 (1933): 12ff. Ed note: René T. A. Lysloff understands *gara-gara* in this way: "Brought about through a crisis in the narrative, gara-gara represents an upheaval of the wayang cosmos — a retreat into complete chaos that spreads from the world of mortals to the realm of the gods and culminates in the liminal domain of the clowns" ("A Wrinkle in Time: The Shadow Puppet Theatre of Banyumas," *Asian Theatre Journal* 10, no. 1 [Spring 1993]: 49-50). The editor acknowledges his debt to CTS graduate student Amos Oei for this reference.

gerly listen to explanations of magical objects and supernatural persons blessed with magical powers. They yearn for the supernatural to a much greater degree than we with our often far more pragmatic intellect can imagine. This is why the idea of a "perfected person" who stands at the very center of the cosmos assumes such a large place in religious thought and emotions.

What is remarkable in this connection is that the gospel is gladly read in the same mode. When one reads the gospel with a person from Java, the Javanese repeatedly finds traces that are reminders of the "perfected person." Jesus always knows things before they are told to him; all that he intends is realized and what he wills happens. He is that person who knows that he is united with God and who regards all the powers of creation as subject to him. He can calm the winds as though being amazed that they themselves do not comprehend that they must serve him. He is able to cast out demons and cause amazing things to happen that are beyond human comprehension. When he was born, a special star shone and the angels sang. The entire cosmos momentarily caught its breath at the majesty of his appearance. And one sees the bond between him and the cosmos most clearly in the history of his suffering. Then the cosmos trembled, the sun hid, the stones cried out, and the earth shook. All these phenomena automatically remind people of what was said would happen in the case of the "perfected person." He is the center of creation; in connection with his every emotion and each event in his life, all things trembled to their very foundations. This is how all the events in the gospels can be connected with the typically mystical ideas that have circulated from ancient times.

The Place of the Human Person in Creation

Keeping an eye on the enormous interest in all these matters, we need to consider how we ought to think about this close connection between microcosm and macrocosm. First of all, let us acknowledge that Asian people in general have seen the delicate strands that connect humanity and the world to one another more precisely than we have. For that reason, we can learn all sorts of things on these matters from them. However, of greater importance for our investigation is that we can also better comprehend many things in the Bible that point us to the unity of microcosm and macrocosm.

We can point directly to the intimate connection that the Bible depicts between the major events in individual human life and those of the world in general. When humanity still existed in a pure and sinless state before God, the world around Adam and Eve simply sang one hymn of praise to God. Perfect harmony existed between the smaller and the larger worlds. But when humans succumbed to the power of sin, they dragged the entire creation down with them in their fall. The world was cursed, and this against its will. This curse gripped the entire creation to such an extent that from that moment on we can say that it has been "subject to vanity." Harmony still remains, but now it is maintained at a horrible cost. Not a single thing in all creation has kept its designated place, because humanity has lost its intended position. The entire world order is shattered, because humanity has broken it.

With respect to Christ, we see this intimate connection once again portrayed in exalted features. In fact, throughout the gospel we can read that all things hold their breath when he enters the world. The powers of nature instantly gather around him as his servants. When he was crucified at the hands of sinful men, immediately it was as though a shiver of dismay quivered through all levels of the cosmos. But, it was also as though new life flowed into the world through him. No one has depicted this more profoundly than Paul in the eighth chapter of his letter to the Romans. As he tells it, the entire creation is subject to vanity and the power of destruction; but he goes on to describe how, since Christ's coming, a new expectation permeates the entire creation. Creation now harbors the hope that it will be delivered from subjection to destruction. Paul even sees the creation as caught in labor pains and straining its neck in looking for the joyous morning of its delivery. That description is certainly the most glorious one ever written on the bond between microcosm and macrocosm. In the monotonous sound of the waves washing on the shore, in the moaning of the trees, in the harsh autumn wind that bends and breaks, in the rustling of the reeds, in the rejoicing of a spring morning, yes, in all the forces of nature something exists of being borne along by the human condition. There is also something of hope in Christ, so that it seems that all things are reaching out to him. In him, God reconciles all things to himself, all things on earth and all things in heaven (Col. 1:20). Furthermore, by all things we need to clearly understand all strata of creation, all forces, and all dimensions of all of creation. At the conclusion of world history and of human history, Scripture depicts "the restoration of all things" and the rebirth of the world. It is, therefore, not too much to say that the entire Scripture is filled with references to the delicate and intimate bond between the smaller and larger worlds, between microcosm and macrocosm, between humanity and nature.

What must be added immediately in this regard is that this bond has a totally different character in the Bible than it does in the world of Asian thought which sees the bond of microcosm and macrocosm as a *magical* connection. Happenings in the life of a person automatically, with magical necessity, involve happenings in all creation. This can best be compared to a magnet. When I move a magnet, I automatically move the iron clinging to it. The one necessarily follows the other. Similarly, in the world a mysterious magnetism binds the person to the world, particularly to the perfected person. What happens to the one happens by magical necessity to the other; the one pulls the other along behind it. The perfected person is ruler of the cosmic forces, since he or she is the center of all that exists. When he bends, everything else bends with him; if she is joyful, all else rejoices with her. A mysterious magnetism that permeates the world and holds everything together is the wonderful, magical power that is the basis of so many stories.

By contrast, it must be emphasized that the Scriptures see this connection between the smaller and larger worlds in an entirely different light. Scripture describes the close connection between the individual human being and cosmos *theologically,* from the perspective of God and not as a magical connection. It is, therefore, a connection that depends on a divine plan, on divine will. God has bound together the lot of the human being and the world most intimately. This is why the fall of creation did not follow the fall into sin of human beings automatically or by magical compulsion, but because this was separately foreordained by God. "Therefore, the ground is cursed because of you!" This is the divine word or command that stands between the two and ties them to one another. The same applies everywhere that a close connection of the smaller and larger worlds becomes apparent. The star of the wise men at the time of the Lord's birth did not move by magical necessity, but it was determined by God that the heavens would share in the human joy at that event. The miracles at the time of the Savior's suffering and death did not happen automatically because of his suffering, but they happened by divine command. Even when that is not expressly stated, the entire thought-world of Scripture makes it clear that it always sees this connection as having been established by God's decree. God is always the One who joins the two together and who protects this cosmic coherence. When we properly understand this, we will easily be able to tend to ourselves in the face of all those seeming dangers that are improperly so identified by a magical view of things.

But having noted the foregoing, we may nonetheless at the same time recognize that in biblical thought humanity and the world are closely connected. For this reason, many comparisons are possible on a wide range of matters. To a certain extent, one can see the forces and movements of nature as symbols of inner, spiritual realities. Remarkably, almost all the phenomena in the world can be so understood. Blossom, bud, and fruit are natural things that are easily understood in a spiritual sense! Concepts such as light, dusk, and darkness are borrowed from the world outside us, but they have found a place in our inner lives. Dark times may occur in our souls, and when our souls walk with God, it is as though the entire world is flooded with sunlight. Winter and summer, cold and warmth, ebb and flow all are found in the macrocosm; but how meaningful these terms are when applied to the microcosm! It certainly seems as though every chord played on cosmic strings resonates with the delicate strumming within us. How amazing that you can find yourself in the world and that you can appropriate both the delight and the pain of the world internally. Does not all poetry and ultimately all art in the broadest sense of the term symbolically connect all dimensions of reality with the whole? The death of a grain of wheat in the earth can serve as a symbol of Christ's death; nature speaks the same language as human experience. This is also the reason that the Bible is so full of marvelous comparisons and why the Savior can explain almost everything about the kingdom of heaven with natural images. Yes, sometimes it is even as though he intentionally emphasizes the symbolical character of natural occurrences. When he calls himself "the true vine," it is as though he wants to make clear to us that the vine has been created in order to be an image of the inner fellowship between Christ and his followers, and thus as if the vine is only a shadow of spiritual things. The Bible expresses itself so obviously on these matters that they need not be intentionally explained. Who is surprised when he or she reads testimonies in the Psalms that the mountains dance and shout for joy, that the fields rejoice, and that the deep calls to the deep? For the soul that sees the world in the light of this binding activity of God, all things speak — even "the flowers with one language" — because all things have been created by God.

Even the Christian, therefore, recognizes the harmony of the inner bond that so powerfully holds the smaller and larger worlds together. Thus, for us the macrocosm can be a book in which our entire inner life is beautifully described, but then with everything reflecting the glory of God.

These ideas are significant in more than one respect. They are important not only for the life of poetry where they shape a poetic view of reality, but they can also be valuable for us in a philosophical sense. This is certainly not the place to spell this out in full detail, but several observations deserve mention at this point.

Science and Its Object

Scientific investigation busies itself with the phenomena of the macrocosm in the broad sense of the term. When we leave theology and philosophy aside for the time being, since they are accorded an entirely special status, we can divide the various sciences into four separate groups.

1. In the first place, there are the natural sciences. They examine the order of nature and the forces and phenomena found there.
2. The second group of sciences is concerned with process. In the world around us, there exists constant process. That process emerges already in nature, in the history of the earth's development, and also in the history of nature's development. But that process is found to an even stronger degree in human life. The history of peoples and races is one approach that in many instances reveals surprising changes, but that must never be understood in circular fashion. World history often seems to repeat itself, as the expression *"l'histoire se répète toujours"* goes, but upon closer examination there appears to be no real repetition. A plan is unfolding in history in which a definite line and growth can be traced.
3. In the third place, we can distinguish the sciences that deal with norms. All of life is governed by a vast array of norms: norms for truth, for morality, for law, and also norms for beauty.
4. In the fourth place, we can also designate those sciences that are strongly oriented to practice. Here the point of application is prominent. Within this last group we recognize, for example, technology as the application of natural sciences and also therapeutic occupations based on the medical sciences. Similarly, in the field of the more spiritual sciences we also find transition to practical applications.

When we place these four groups of sciences alongside each other for a moment, we clearly see that they certainly can be distinguished from one another but that they can never be separated from one another. They are entangled with one another in every respect; some of them are almost impossible to categorize. Furthermore, the relationship of each of the four to God clearly bears a unique character. Concerning the first group that examines nature as an orderly totality, God is approached as Creator and Maintainer of the world's order. Concerning the second group that is oriented to unrepeatable process found in world history and human history, God is approached as the World Ruler, who guides the unfolding of events. Concerning the third group of sciences that track the norms that secure all of life, God is seen as the great Lawgiver, as the Norm for truth, goodness, and glory. In the fourth group of sciences, we discover God as the Almighty, the all-wise One, who "has given the world to the children of men" and who has endowed humans with a reflection of some of his power. In each of these four areas of science, therefore, God is considered in a unique way. Thus, the direction of all thought leads to him.

These are the sciences involved with the macrocosm. But they are at the same time sciences involved with the microcosm. For, what is remarkable about human beings is that these several lines of investigation converge in them. A human person is always also a natural being who is subject to the laws of nature. As such, the person is in a relationship with God that is a relationship of dependence upon the Creator and Maintainer of all things. The person is also a historical being, a part of history, and a subject of history; and the individual life of every single human being completes a history that in many respects recalls the history of the entire world. In that regard, a human being deals with God as the World Ruler, the great Mover and Guide of all events in history. In the third place, a human being's existence is pervaded by norms. A person carries norms within with his or her awareness of good and evil, truth and falsehood, justice and injustice, usefulness and uselessness, beauty and ugliness. Because this is so, a person has a moral relationship with God. God is a person's ultimate Norm, the Lawgiver. In the final place, a person is also an active being who is called by the cultural mandate to be active and to control. Here a person encounters God as the Almighty, from whom all power and wisdom are derived and who ultimately is the only Master. This is human life, life in microcosm, life connected to God by all sorts of threads. Thus, human beings are connected to God in a living, multi-sided relationship that is so precise and so profound that we can never completely comprehend it. In all these matters, people are a mirror image of the cosmos. It is as though the entire cosmos is found in them in concentrated form. It is as though the rich life of the whole cosmos converges in them. Human beings' lives are so full and multidimensional that they can never comprehend their life in their own self-consciousness. That is the riddle of being human.

According to the most profound thought of Scripture, the highest dimension of one's humanity is that the person in all of these matters is the image-bearer of God. The person has been created in the image and likeness of the Eternal King. This likeness is displayed in many ways, both in body and in soul. This likeness to the Creator is replicated in the creature. Each person stands in the fullest, closest connection with the creation, and at the same time displays a likeness to him from whom the entire creation has come into being. The position of the human being in the macrocosm is therefore certainly a very special one, and oriental thinking has been correct in laying such emphasis on it.

The Great Boundary

In two respects, the thought of Asia misconstrues the status of humanity. First of all, it has not sufficiently appreciated that humanity exists and always remains on the creaturely level. The human person is never the same as God; human being never coincides with divine being. That is the reason why we need to depict humanity and the world, macrocosm and microcosm, as concentric circles, as long as we understand that God himself is not comprehended in such a circle. God is not a part of the macrocosm and cannot even be portrayed as the central point of the circles. Nor is God a dimension of the microcosm, not even the central part of it. The greatest mistake of Asian thinking has been that it wanted to picture God and the world, also God and humanity, on the same level; and, in doing so it has made God part of the world and pulled him down to the level of a creature. If one wants to portray this in a *daerah* or symbolical sketch, one can depict the human being as the central point of the macrocosm. But then one needs to sketch God above the drawing, since he is not a part of the creation. He is the Maker and King who sustains all things and who also then maintains a very intimate relationship with each creature.

This also defines our relationship to the "perfected person." By a "perfected person" Asian thought understands the mystic, that person who by all sorts of methods has arrived at unity or fusion with the All-in-One, with God. According to a favorite expression, in such a person the servant has become Lord; therefore the servant is no longer a servant, but he or she has become Lord of all. All powers of the cosmos lie at such a person's feet; he is master of the world, the ruler of all powers contained in all things. Christianity knows no comparable "perfected person," but one should rather think of the Lord that appeared in the form of a servant, namely Jesus Christ. But even he is completely different from the "perfected person" of whom Asia dreams, for he is not the mystic who through an array of spiritual exercises achieved unity with the Lord. But from the very beginning, he is the Lord who came to earth in the form of a servant, but he took an entirely unique and incomparable position there.

346

Magic and Faith

Scripture recognizes no perfected people among us. It certainly does recognize people who through faith in Jesus Christ have become one with the Father and are those who have been reconciled to the Father. These people who have been reconciled to the Father and who have been made one with God stand at the center of creation, as it were; all authority of the cosmos is subject to them. They can say to the mountains: "Be lifted up and thrown into the depths of the sea." Nothing will be impossible for them. But this power is in no respect whatsoever comparable to magical power. The believer who lives in close fellowship with his or her Father is not a person who has been made divine, one who is filled with magical power, but he or she is powerful through faith. Scripture regards these matters theologically, not magically. It is the living God who does great things in response to the prayers of his children. When Elijah said that it would not rain for many months, he was not a sorcerer, not a perfected human being, but simply a believer who knew what he had received from God. When David slung a stone at the giant, he did not use some magical, charmed weapon, but he rested on faith. The Christian is lord of all things through faith. He stands close to the heart of all reality, close to the King of all, and through the power of that King, by faith, he can do all things.

An extremely fine line, but at the same time an extremely important one, exists between magic and faith. Magic searches for communion with the primal, magical power asleep in everything; faith seeks fellowship with God. Magic recognizes only the directionless, rudderless God of magical power; faith recognizes the living God who hears prayer and who can deliver those people who call on him. God is always present in faith, and God can only be approached through sorrow and conversion, also through faith and trust.

The history of religion shows us that people always exhibit the inclination to follow magic. It is so bewitching to strive for amazing magical powers and to deify one's own self! This is so because via magic you are ultimately able to maintain yourself; you can stand by your own power; you allow yourself to drown in the Unending, but you do so in order that, enriched by magical powers, you may find yourself once again. The people of Asia have sought that route with total effort, and have often dreamed that they have found it. How much more difficult, by contrast, is the way of faith! Faith allows no self-maintenance; it demands a dying of self and a complete turning of self over to God. You can never appear before that God with your pride; you can only approach him as a humble sinner. You feel that you stay a sinner even later, for

347

your entire life. You never become powerful, but you are only powerful in him; his strength is made complete in your weakness. This is why living by faith is miles away from what Asian thought glorifies as "the perfected person." The way of magic is a road that does not acknowledge guilt, is without remorse, and is bereft of humbling oneself. It is the deification of the human person; but in doing so, it admits that it does not know God. For it, God is the sum total of all magical power and that mysterious force from which all that exists has been born and which even today still slumbers in everything.

A favorite image exists that first appeared in the *Vedas* but then also found its way to Java. In it God is compared to the warmth in wood. When a person rubs two pieces of wood together, or when one rapidly turns one piece of wood in a hole in another piece, first smoke and then eventually fire appears. Ancient Indians said that the warm glow lived in the wood from the beginning. By turning the wood, one has only awakened warmth from its slumber and made it active. People thought that this is the way it is with God. God slumbers in everything as a hidden glow, as buried magical power. The mystic is the one who activates that power by means of his monotone chanting and his magical incantations, by rubbing them round and round, as it were; he activates this power and in doing so receives power over it.[14] Precisely in that illustration, one sees so clearly that in this mystically magical religion no room exists for a living relationship with God. That hidden, mysterious energy is always all that exists, slumbering and needing to be awakened; and in the hands of the sorcerer, that energy becomes a weapon. Christians can never go down that road. It is not a possibility for us; it is also not permissible for them. The microcosm can only be restored to the proper relationship with the macrocosm and properly accept its place at the center of reality when it becomes one with the Creator of the macrocosm through the atonement of Jesus Christ.

Jesus as the "Perfect Human Being"

Strictly speaking, we would only be able to assign the title of the "perfect human being" to the man Jesus Christ. In him, servant and Lord, creature and

---

14. Compare Paul Deussen, *Philosophie der Upanishads,* 4th ed. (Leipzig: Brockhaus, 1920), p. 150; ET: *The Philosophy of the Upanishads* (Edinburgh: T. & T. Clark, 1906). Ed. note: Bavinck does not specify the edition he cites. Also compare the ancient Javanese poem *Arjuna Wiwaha,* published by R. Ng. Poerbatjaraka (The Hague: Martinus Nijhoff, 1926), stanzas 6 and 9.

Creator, have become one. At one and the same time, he is positioned at the center of all that exists and all power over all that exists lies at his feet. But when we assign him that title, it must be pointed out in the first place that the Lord that appears in him is not the summation of all magical power; rather, he is the Holy King, the living God. Moreover, it needs to be pointed out that Christ alone is such, and that in this regard no one will ever be like him. He has come from above and therefore is above all things. He is both true man and true God, and as such he is exalted far above all creatures. To be sure, he is the Word who has become flesh. Therefore, any thought that we might be able to become little "christs," or that in any sense we could achieve unity with God, must once and for all be rejected.

This is noteworthy as well: that while Jesus Christ at the time of his humiliation definitely shows us the unity of his human and divine natures, he simultaneously stands before us as the Perfecter of our faith (Heb. 12:1-2). Even he does his miracles by faith. He receives them in faith, from the Father, and he rejoices when the Father always hears him (John 11:41-42). He empties himself, makes himself nothing, and takes the form of a servant (Phil. 2:7). This is why he does his work by faith and why he is so completely different from what people expect.

In the entire area of the relationship of the smaller and the larger worlds, many questions remain. That we are spurred by the people of Asia to think about these matters and to search for the precise representation of them is a good thing. In all of its inner coherence, creation is much more complicated than we could have imagined, and many connections remain within it that we still do not understand. But one thing is certain for us: all these connections within creation do not rest on some mysterious, magical magnetism, but they are dependent on God's holy, divine will, and thus all things have their existence only in him. When we understand this, we will become much smaller in our own eyes on the one hand. But on the other hand, we Christians will feel called in this century to display the power of the faith that is not magical, but before which all the powers of the entire creation bow, because God is with us in the person of our Lord Jesus Christ.

9 The World-Order

Cosmos and Chaos

The world in which we live is in its entirety a wondrously colorful array of forces and phenomena. We live amid an overwhelming plethora of creatures and events, the underlying coherence of which we often cannot comprehend, much less even survey. In the entire sweep of things, we become confused in our thinking and we are unable to draw the lines that would be able to clarify the order in the whole.

Nevertheless, buried deep in every human heart from the beginning of time lies the certainty that we exist in the middle of a cosmos, not a chaos. We sense that it is possible for the world to be so rich in phenomena because an immense and powerful order exists that ties it all together. We trust that all the vast diversity encompassed by the world is the expression of a wise, profound mind, a Logos present in creation, who causes all dimensions and all forces of all that exists to concur and cooperate in achieving one huge, glorious purpose. This is why all human thought from the very beginning has been focused on understanding the world-order that we all instinctively believe exists. We do so in order that we may no longer be perplexed by the diversity of phenomena, but may learn to see the mighty harmony holding together all that exists. All our scientific endeavor that investigates the various dimensions of reality is one great attempt to expose this world-order and to comprehend its meaning.

When we reflect on this world-order, it becomes apparent immediately that it can be considered in one of two ways. First of all, by the world-order we can understand that each group of creatures has its own, unique place in the cosmic house. Every being that exists has been assigned its own position in the whole by the great and wise Creator, and all groups of creatures collectively form that tremendous totality whose architectonic lines we are hardly capable of discovering. A human being has a different position in the overarching global project than an angel, an animal a different position from a plant, the earth another position than the sun that illumines it. A living cell has a different position than inorganic matter. A man has a different position than a woman, the sea a different position than the land. In the wise plan of the Creator, each thing and every being is assigned its unique position, where it can flourish according to its own nature and where it can contribute toward the development of the whole. This is the secret of the cosmic positioning that is of such great value for understanding the coherence of the world-order.

In the second place, by the world-order we can understand the law that regulates all that happens in this world and thus governs each process and leads it to its appointed end. Every creature has its place in the world structure. But every event also has its place in the cumulative world process or the totality of world history, a history that has unfolded through the ages and works itself out toward the goal intended by God. A connection exists between all events, therefore; one thing leads to another, so that the future is in seminal form buried in the present.

Thus, the world-order can be approached in two ways: we can see it as the orderliness of existence or as the orderliness of events. We can see the Logos inherent in the clustering of creatures, or we can encounter the same Logos in the laws investigated in the unfolding of history. In both respects, for us the world is not a chaotic totality of phenomena that accidentally converge, but it is a whole ordered by the divine Logos that from every angle reveals to us divine wisdom and power.

When we reflect on these matters, we are not surprised that both Asia and the West have been preoccupied with this order. They have certainly approached the subject in different ways, and this has produced different principles. In the West, more emphasis has been placed in recent centuries on the technological, analytical models and approaches. In Asia, more emphasis has been accorded to combining emotional fluctuation and a poetic vision in which the mind bows to life's riddles. Asia and the West have approached the reality of a world-order from different directions, therefore, and it is undeniable that the poetic approach of the Orient often strikes us as childish and naïve. But Asia and the West, while differing in their methods of working and thinking, find one another in the common striving to uncover something of the major cosmic mysteries.

The Great Design

World-Order in Asia

When we attempt to get a bird's-eye view of what Far Asia thinks about cosmic order, we encounter first of all the concept of *Rita*.[1] The ancient Aryans, who established themselves in the floodplain of the Indus River, believed in a world-order or *Rita* that determined the course of events and also governed human obligations. This *Rita* is not so much a *someone* as a *something*. It is an ordering principle that dwells in all things and that, for that reason, needs to be reverenced by a person if he or she does not want to make a mistake on any given occasion. The gods *Mitra*[2] and *Varuna*[3] were above all the custodians of *Rita*. They were the ones who maintained order and who therefore punished every transgression against good order. All things were subject to this *Rita,* all the heavenly bodies as well as all things on earth, and at the same time it was the principle of justice that was so prominent in the lives of people. By virtue of *Rita,* one had to meet one's obligations, keep one's promises, and pay one's debts. Thus, a world-order exists that has power equally in all spheres of reality. In some respects, the

1. Ed. note: *Rita (Rta)* is a Sanskrit term that denotes the principle of natural order governing the universe. According to Raimundo Panikkar, "*Rta* is the ultimate foundation of everything; it is 'the supreme,' although this is not to be understood in a static sense. . . . It is the expression of the primordial dynamism that is inherent in everything" (*The Vedic Experience: Mantramañjar* (*an Anthology of the Vedas for Modern Man and Celebration* [Bangalore: Motilal Banarsidass, 2001], pp. 350-51). We follow here our editorial practice of not including Sanskrit diacritical marks; see Chapter 3, note 5.

2. Ed. note: *Mitra* is an Indo-Iranian common noun possibly meaning "covenant, treaty, agreement, promise." It came to denote different religious entities: in Sanskrit, *Mitrá (Mitráḥ)* is a deity who appears frequently in the *Rigveda;* in the Zoroastrian sacred scripture of the *Avesta* as the god *Mithra;* and in the Greco-Roman world as Μιθρας *(Mithras),* the principal figure of Mithraism. See Roger Beck, "Mithraism, *Encyclopaedia Iranica,* online edition, 20 July 2002, available at http://www.iranica.com/articles/mithraism.

3. Ed. note: *Varuna (Vāruṇā)* is the Indo-Iranian name for the other half of the dual deity *Mitrā Vāruṇā,* who governs the cosmic world order *(Rita; Ṛta). Varuna* is the "wise one" who is "Lord of the waters." See F. B. J. Kuiper, "Ahura," *Encyclopaedia Iranica,* online edition, 15 December 1984.

concept of *Rita* is comparable to the idea of the Logos that we meet in the ancient Greek philosopher Heraclitus (c. 535–c. 475 BC).[4] For Heraclitus, this world is permeated with divine order, and this same order regulates human laws and obligations.

Tied to the idea of *Rita* are several very important principles that perhaps would have come to much more substantial development if a number of other factors in the religion of the *Vedas* had not taken a different direction. *Mitra* and *Varuna* receded increasingly to the background, and we see that particularly *Indra*[5] came to the foreground as the great god of war from whom people sought help under the pressures of the regular warfare entangling them. And centuries later, when the Aryans enjoyed uncontested control of the Indus and Ganges valleys that they had conquered, the Brahmins introduced yet another concept that was just as dominant, gradually attracted all the attention, and pushed all other ideas into the shadows. From that point on, people focused attention on Brahman,[6] the divine primordial principle from which all things flowed and that penetrated this world like a knife in a sheath or like fire in a piece of burning wood.[7] The ancient Brahmins speculated about this wondrous Brahman that possessed exceptional magical properties, and they looked for a connection between Brahman and Atman, between the deepest essence of the world and the deepest essence of the human soul.

In the same Brahmin era in which these ideas were developed, people became increasingly involved with questions about the structure of the cosmos. Cosmology became a favorite field of investigation, and with fervent devotion people sought the architectonic lines of the macrocosm in order to be able to discern from it the structure of the microcosm. For from the outset, it was uncontested that the smaller and the larger worlds, the human being and all existence, completely conform to one another.

---

4. Heraclitus of Ephesus was a pre-Socratic Greek philosopher, most famous for a saying attributed to him: "everything flows" (Τα Πάντα ρεῖ; *ta panta rhei*). He also held the idea that all things come to pass in accordance with a common "*Logos.*" See Hermann Diels, *Die Fragmente der Vorsokratiker*, 6th ed., rev. Walther Kranz (Berlin, 1952), B1, B2.

5. Ed. note: In Hindu mythology *Indra* is the King of the gods, Lord of heaven, the god of war, storms, and rainfall. See Benjamin Slade, "Indra the Storm-God: Images, Information and Worship/*puja*"; online at http://www.jnanam.net/indra/.

6. Ed. note: An important distinction must be remembered here between *Brahman* = the creative power of the universe, and *Brahmin* = the highest (priestly) caste in the Hindu hierarchy of human orders.

7. *The Upanishads*, trans. Friedrich Max Miller (Oxford: Clarendon, 1879-1884), Brihadaranyaka-Upanishad 1.4.7.

In all the pondering over these matters, the concept of *dharma*[8] assumed a significant place. Buddhism in particular talked a great deal about dharma and with the help of this idea wanted to make life understandable. By the word "dharma" one must understand the following: that which maintains existence, law, and obligation. It is a word that is very difficult to translate, because it increasingly connected two ideas that we generally attempt to keep separate. It can be regarded simultaneously either as the natural law or highest order that governs all natural phenomena, or as the moral law that functions as a yardstick for measuring a person's life and thought.[9] In a certain sense, all people have their own dharma, that is to say, their own position in the all-encompassing house of the universe. In harmony with this position people also have their obligations.[10] The knight *(Kshatriya)* has a different place in the world-order than the priest (Brahmin), and for that reason he also has a different dharma and a different set of obligations and regulations. When the knight follows ascetic practices, he does so in a completely differently way than the Brahmin does. By means of his established and mystical practices, the Brahmin endeavors to achieve perfect insight and deliverance *(moksha)*[11] from the circularity of existence. By his asceticism, the knight aims at nothing less than receiving supernatural, magical powers that he needs in his battles against giants and enemies. Each of them lives in harmony with his dharma, therefore, in harmony with the position he has in the world-order. Seeing the larger picture, one can say that the entire world is governed by a dharma that assigns each thing its place and that covers all events as a powerful law.

For Indian intellectuals, it was of extremely great interest to investigate more thoroughly this world-order in all its particularities. For example,

8. Ed. note: *Dharma* is a Sanskrit term and, in the context of the Hindu religious tradition, refers to one's religious obligation, an obligation placed upon each person by his or her station in life. To achieve personal salvation (liberation) one must live according to one's *dharma*. In Buddhism and Jainism, *dharma* also refers to the teachings of each religion's founders respectively.

9. Compare Dr. H. Beck, *Buddhismus: Buddha und seine Lehre*, vol. 1 (Leipzig: Göschen, 1916), p. 20, footnote. Also Hermann Oldenberg, *Die Weltanschauung der Brāhmana Texte* (Göttingen: Vandenhoeck & Ruprecht, 1919), pp. 188ff.

10. Ed note: The Hindu caste system is fourfold: *Brahmins* (teachers, scholars, and priests); the *Kshatriyas* (kings, warriors, and administrators); the *Vaishyas* (agriculturists and traders), and *Shudras* (service providers, laborers).

11. Ed. note: *Moksha* is a Sanskrit term that refers to the liberation from *Samsara* *(Saṅsāra* or *Saṃsāra),* the endlessly repeated cycle of life, death, reincarnation that is the cause of suffering in this world.

when one had gained insight into the place of each thing in the totality of the cosmos, one could also investigate their analogies and conclude from this how each thing needed to be treated. Once one understood, for example, that the position of a king in a kingdom corresponds with that of Vishnu among the gods, it is fairly easy to derive from this all sorts of standards pertinent for one's conduct with the king. If one can draw the dotted lines between phenomena in the cosmos, one can compare one area with another and from that comparison deduce valuable conclusions. This is how the need for a widely developed classification was born. It is precisely this desire for classifying that we encounter in various forms, especially on Java.

Classification

When we use the word "classification" here, we approach a concept that has recently attracted the attention of many researchers in the field of Asian religion.[12] By it they have understood that system according to which many peoples cluster the various phenomena in the world and think about how they are related. "Primitive classification" belongs, they think, primarily to a totemistic milieu, that is to say, to a society that places heavy emphasis on tribal divisions, where the various elements or clans of the tribe are thought to be closely tied to specific kinds of animals, trees, or other objects. Should a certain clan within a tribe feel closely connected to the horse, for example, the horse becomes the totem of that clan and is considered to be a holy animal by the members of that clan; they even call themselves the horse clan and feel one with the horse. Then it seems as though any difference is no longer felt and as though one only feels the union of the clan with its totem. Other clans will regard the deer, crocodile, or other animals as their totem. In this way, the animal world is divided in close conjunction with human tribal divisions. In the same way, one can arrange all sorts of other phenomena in harmony with existing divisions and thus develop a scheme that encompasses all areas of life.

We will not evaluate here whether or not there are good reasons to propose the prevalence of totemistic notions on Java in earlier times. What is

---

12. On these classifications, compare E. Durkheim and M. Mauss, *Primitive Classification*, trans. Rodney Needham (Chicago: University of Chicago Press, 1963); Emile Durkheim, *The Elementary Forms of Religious Life*, trans. Karen E. Fields (New York: Free Press, 1995); F. D. E. van Ossenbruggen, *De Oorsprong van het Javaansche Begrip Montjâ-pat, in Verband met Primitieve Classificaties* (Amsterdam: Müller, 1917).

certain is that the Javanese people have had a very strong inclination from early days to arrange the various phenomena of the cosmos into families and thus to make connections that are able to make the whole comprehensible. We have already had more than one opportunity to point out this typical need to classify, and it seems to us that within this framework the numbers four and five play a large role:

- The compass has four points, and the layout of villages that together form a city is arranged accordingly. Of course, the points of the compass are of great interest in many instances. In building a palace or a temple, one must pay careful attention to directional orientation.
- The Javanese week is divided into five days which are seen to exist in the same sort of relation.[13]
- In subdividing a kingdom, one must also consider the cosmic order,[14] since everything must be in agreement with world-order.
- There are four castes in Hindu society; as we have shown, this division is not accidental.
- The world is constituted by four elements: water, fire, air, and earth.
- There are four primary colors that affect human beings.
- There are four (or five) human senses: hearing, seeing, smelling, tasting, and touching.
- There are four phases of the moon: new moon, half moon, full moon, waning moon.
- There are five heroes in the *wayang* (the *Pandawas*), and they represent cosmic order.
- There were four initial great Caliphs venerated in Islam.

13. Ed. note: For a helpful discussion of the Javanese calendar see John Crawford, *History of the Indian Archipelago Containing an Account of the Manners, Arts, Languages, Religions, Institutions, and Commerce of Its Inhabitants,* 3 vols. (Edinburgh: Archibald Constable & Co., 1820), 1: 285-306. According to Crawford, "the Javanese have a native week besides the usual week of seven days borrowed first from the Hindus and then from the Arabs. The original Javanese week, like that of the Mexicans, consists of five days, and its principal use, like that of the same people, is to determine the markets or fairs held in the principal villages or districts. This arbitrary period has probably no better foundation than the relation of the numbers to that of the fingers of the hand. The names of the days of the week are as follow: *Lăggi, Pahing, Pon, Wagi, Kliwon.* . . . It is highly probable, that, like the week of the continental nations in Asia and Europe, the days were named after the national gods" (pp. 289-90). (Available online at http://books.google.com.)

14. Willem Huibert Rassers, *De Pandji-roman* (Antwerpen: D. de Vos-van Kleef, 1922), pp. 132ff.

- There are four passions that drive human life.
- There are five stipulated times of prayer in Islam.
- There are four postures that the pious Muslim uses in his ritual prayers (the *salát*).
- There are four levels on the way toward mystical fulfillment through which the devout person must pass.

In this way, the number four could be found back in every area of the entire creation. It certainly seemed as though the entire larger world consisted of one tribe, or one large family, where the separate groups constituted various subdivisions. People felt the connection of all things so closely, so intimately, that they identified the various subsets of four with each other and thus juxtaposed the strangest sorts of things with one another or connected them with each other. This was the mysterious world-order that people could not comprehend logically, of course, but which, in childish delusion, they thought they saw.

The Male and Female Principles

Straight through the configurations into fours and fives runs a major, important, twofold division. Everywhere in the cosmos one can find both the male and the female principles. That this distinction has fueled the imagination and generated all sorts of representations is understandable. One can regard the heavens as the male principle and the earth as the female force that conceives and gives birth! In the ancient myths about the birth of the earth, divinity was portrayed as the male principle that entered the primal waters and caused the world to be born. The spirit *(purusha)* is the male principle in human beings that gives form and exerts controls, while the body *(prakrti)* is the female force that conceives and complies. To demonstrate that this twofold division is universally applicable does not take much effort, since the male and female principles can be found everywhere. It is incorporated into stories about the gods and spills over into widely shared fairy tales that talk about gods and goddesses and all their troubles.

Seen from this perspective, it is obvious that all that happens in the world can be compared to a marriage. Always and everywhere, it is the male force that unites with the female to give form, to create, to make fruitful, and to rule. Always and repeatedly, it is the heavens that come to the earth, the light that floods the darkness, and the spirit that gives shape to the material.

All world events are one huge marriage of the forces that determine everything. And once people see matters this way, they obviously show an intense interest in the phenomena associated with them. The numerous occurrences of immoral practices in religious life that function as symbols of the divine order are consequences of this construal of things.

With the investigation of these ideas, one is often automatically reminded of what is thought and taught in another country of Asia, namely China. Already in very ancient times, Chinese religious feelings emphasized that the male and the female principles are two cosmic forces from which the world is born. These two principles were called *Yin* and *Yang*, and people endeavored to understand all events in nature in terms of them. Heaven and earth come together in such matters as growth and fruitfulness in nature and as the seasons of the year. Sometimes the one principle is more dominant, then the other. But in general, as far as one can determine, one finds these two fundamental principles back in all that has been made. According to Chinese thought, the remarkable thing in this world is not so much the existence of these two forces of *Yin* and *Yang*, but the fact that they come together. The two principles continually seek out one another, approach each other, pair up with each other, and need each other. That wonderful coming together on which all birth depends is called *Dao (Tao)*, which literally means "the way." *Dao (Tao)* is the order that controls the movements of *Yin* and *Yang*; it is the eternal law that determines that the two major forces search each other out in every part of reality and unite with one another. In the profound philosophy of the major thinker Laozi, who lived in the sixth century BC, the idea is more fully developed that *Dao (Tao)*, or the world-order, is also the basic principle from which *Yin* and *Yang* have developed. For this reason, *Dao (Tao)* is the great divine reality that we reverently need to seek and follow.

Yin-Yang Symbol

Thus, one can see many connections in cosmic events, paying attention to the fourfold division that cuts through all aspects of reality. And, within the framework of this fourfold division one can still keep an eye on the great contrast between the male and female. The nature of the case is that the cosmos, within which such contrasting forces dwell, is a dramatic production depicting continual conflict. In that conflict, the plot is always about conquering the female, as it always has been in ancient tribal life. Thus, one can interpret the sun shining on the earth as the attempt to make her fruitful, to assure that she produces abundantly. But one can also see the storm and the earthquake as attempts to destroy the harvest! Then the battle begins between the light and the destructive forces of nature, those giants that bring destruction. In that battle, the issue is possession of the fruit-bearing earth. Everywhere in the course of world events, war rages; but this warfare is regarded as necessary and is seen within the framework that people have developed. And when people see cosmic phenomena as powerful projections of what afflicts developments within the tribe, such as wars and other tribal events, it is not difficult to make endless associations. Even within the smallest microcosm, within a human being, the battle exists between the spiritual principle and the brute forces of those human passions that seek to imprison life.

To summarize, clearly all thought and speculation in Javanese religious feelings and ideas fall back on a defined model of reality. People keep that model in front of them. They comprehend all that occurs in both the macrocosm and the microcosm in terms of that model. They are of the opinion that they have penetrated the meaning of the world-order via that model.

Practical Consequences

In more than one respect, these things were all of very great significance. In the first place, from this model that had been created it became clear how the state needed to be ordered. In the organization of the state, in the relationship of monarch and subjects, one had to be able to see the great cosmic forces reflected in some way. The entire administrative structure had a model at its disposal for doing so. The sovereign needed to be enthroned in the midst of the people, for he was the embodiment of divine power, mysterious, reverenced as holy, and the bearer of cosmic order. He was the one who protected the people from disasters, and he made sure that all things in nature happened in good order. The number four was again especially important in how the court officials were divided, for the entire organization of the kingdom had to reflect the cosmic order.

The *keraton*,[15] or palace of the prince, was laid out accordingly. It was built as a microcosm or model of all reality. Not only the *keraton*, however, but also the temples and *candis*[16] were regarded as little worlds in themselves. All Javanese architecture — in fact, all Asian architecture — is one powerful attempt to repeat the structure of all that exists in the small representation of a house or a temple. In these buildings, the key elements of the Javanese worldview are always present: they always reflect the *Meru*, the high mountain on which the gods dwell and that stands at the center of the world; they always take into account the four directions of the compass; they always depict the various spheres of the cosmos. Architecture equals cosmology; the edifice represents the cosmos. And it is in a building that heaven and earth also come together. It is as though all the forces within creation are concentrated in it.

Furthermore, all literature rests on this cosmology. Almost all the various Javanese tales go back to the same model. In all of them, some hero is described for us, some leader who wants to marry a princess. Enemies appear who are often giants and wild powers that stand in the hero's way. A battle ensues, then a victory, and in the end the hero always achieves what he has desired. Most of the stories are developed along that model, and the model is always the great cosmic drama.

But this approach comes to the fore with special force in the *wayang* or puppet show. Every *wayang* drama *(wayang-lakon)* is a symbolical reenactment of events in the world. In every *wayang* plot there is a hero who is on the side of the gods, a battle against enemies and giants, and a victory. The same basic motifs recur in all of them. I once asked a Javanese person, upon watching a *wayang* performance, "What is the symbolism of all of this? What is the meaning of the giant, for example, who does battle with the hero?" Smiling, he looked at me and then said:

> You may understand by all this whatever you like. If by the giant you want to understand Russian communism, then you may do so. If by it you want to understand the volcano Merapi that devastates and covers the earth, then you may do so. If by it you want to understand some human passion that impedes and triumphs over the spirit, then you may do so. You may

15. Ed. note: For the meaning of "keraton" as "royal palace" and "court," see Indonesian-English Dictionary at http://www.eudict.com.

16. Ed. note: *Candi* are Hindu and Buddhist temples or sanctuaries in Indonesia, most of which were built from the eighth to the fifteenth centuries. The most famous is the Borobudur Stupa in Central Java.

understand by it anything you like, just as long as it is applicable to the great scheme of all things.

There one has the distinctive viewpoint at the basis of the Javanese play. All the great cosmic phenomena, all elements of the world-order, one can find back in the history of the *wayang*.

But this cosmology is reflected not only in architecture and literature, it is consistent also with psychology. The human soul is likewise a reflection of cosmic events. There as well, the hero consists of the divine that dwells in the inmost part of the inner self. Giants that the hero wants to resist and restrain lurk there too, as the passions that oppress the soul. The Javanese person recognizes four of them, and he describes them in vivid color.[17] The first of these is the giant *Amarah* (from the Arabic), based on Sura 12:53 of the Qur'an.[18] The word means "self-directed"; *Amarah* always incites evil and is pictured by the color red. Powerful and dangerous, it rankles the soul to anger and jealousy. Then there is "Greed," in Javanese called *loammah*, and it is borrowed from Sura 75:2.[19] Its literal meaning is "self-reproaching," and it is portrayed as the black giant intent on devouring everything within its grasp. *Sawiah*, "Sensual Lust," is refined and polished; it operates subtly and traps the soul in the snares of fleshly desire.

---

17. Ed. note: Though Bavinck mentions four, there are a total of five "passions" or needs of the human soul (the Javanese and Indonesian word for these is *nafsu*). The first four, with their Arabic-appropriated names, are *Amarah* (the impulse of anger), *Wamah* (bodily needs such as eating and other material needs), *Sawiah* (the sexual drive), and *Loamah* (animal side and drive to communicate). The fifth *(Mutmainah)* is given directly by Allah and has no negative character; it returns to Allah at death. The goal of Ramadan fasting is to control the first four so they do not destroy *Mutmainah*. See Jörgen Hellman, "Creating Religious Bodies: Fasting Rituals in West Java," in *The Body in Asia,* ed. Bryan S. Turner and Zheng Yangwen, Asia and Pacific Studies: Past and Present, vol. 3 (New York and Oxford: Berghahn Books, 2009), p. 68. Available online at http://www.berghahnbooks.com/title.php?rowtag =TurnerBody#toc. Key pages from this volume are available from http://books.google.com. I am indebted to CTS Ph.D. student Amos Oei from Indonesia for his help in tracing this material and reference.

18. Ed. note: The Quranic verse in English, with the key word highlighted in transliteration: 12:53 "Nor do I absolve my own self (of blame): the (human) soul is certainly prone to evil, unless my Lord do bestow His Mercy: but surely my Lord is Oft-forgiving, Most Merciful." *(Wama obarri-o nafsee inna alnnafsa laammaratun bialssoo-i illa ma rahima rabbee inna rabbee ghafoorun raheemun.)*

19. Ed. note: The Quranic verse in English, with the key word highlighted in transliteration: And I do call to witness the self-reproaching spirit: (Eschew Evil). *(Wala oqsimu bialnnafsi allawwamati.)*

Finally, there is *Mutmainah*, taken from Sura 89:27; it produces peace.[20] It is "Desire for the Good," and it aspires to good works and is also one of the human passions. These four forces wage their battle in the soul, and this whole conflict is once again a miniature reflection of the cosmic fight. The person is fortunate in whom the evil giants are conquered and in whom the deepest, divine seed is able to triumph!

Undeniably, all these models encountered in Javanese thought strike us as rather naïve. We would say that they present things far too simplistically and much too childishly. But we should never forget one thing: buried in all of this is a powerful dimension of culture. Culture is the organic unity of all aspects of life. The Javanese people are a nation that sees a few immense, general principles that order the world and that reappear in every area of thought and activity: in politics as well as natural science, in architecture as well as in psychology, in religion as well as in literature. And it may well be the case that with the Javanese people of our day, all these matters are found in a rigid and often tangled form. But major ideas lie behind all of this, and they in particular deserve our close attention. Culture can only be won over by culture, not by overwhelming people with the fragmented science that we so frequently want to offer oriental peoples. It is my firm belief that we can be a great blessing to the Asian world only when we are able to provide an alternative model to the fundamental framework out of which they have lived, one that just as completely encompasses all of life and thought as theirs does. This is why one of the greatest issues facing missions in our time is this: Are the Christian churches of our day capable of providing a worldview that is just as fruitful and effective in providing direction for Asian life as their ancient model has been? Mission is much more that simply bringing a few souls into contact with the gospel. It is both an enormous, inner struggle against an entire worldview and an attempt to give birth to a view of all things based on a new set of principles.

The Thought of Augustine

To attempt to find in the short confines of this chapter something that we could posit as an alternative to the major cosmic scheme of Asia would be

---

20. Ed. note: The Quranic verse in English, with the key word highlighted in transliteration: 89:27 "To the righteous soul will be said: "O (thou) soul, in (complete) rest and satisfaction! *(Yā ayyatuhā alnnafsu almutma-innatu.)*

foolish. Such matters are far too complicated for that and by their very nature cannot be easily developed; they need to grow slowly. Nevertheless, we offer a few comments that seem to us to be important. The towering figure of the Christian thinker Augustine comes to mind once again. In his own day and in his own way, he fought the good fight and sought to articulate the broad contours of the world-order. In this regard, Augustine is also highly valuable to us because he wrestled with neo-Platonic philosophy, which in many respects bears a striking resemblance to what is taught these days on Java.

When we review what Augustine said about the world-order, we are clear from the outset that he erected an entire system on the basis of several *theological* principles. That is probably the greatest difference that you could think of. Asia proceeds from the cosmos. It has contemplated and conceptually arranged the cosmos. It has situated the gods within that structure it has perceived. Augustine began from the totally opposite direction. He proceeded from God and from what he found Scripture to say about God. He is not cosmological but theological in how he proceeds to order things. He looked for evidences of God in the cosmos. Thus, God stood at the center, and God was not for a moment identified with the world. In thinking about these matters, Augustine regarded the Trinitarian God as the great mystery from which all things must be seen. The divine Trinity is reflected in all parts of the totality, and its image appears in humanity as well. The holy number three can be found everywhere, and whoever has seen that number there has, as it were, approached God himself. The cosmic number is four, referring to what is extensive and expansive, determined by the four directions. The divine number is three, and insofar as every creature exhibits traces of God, that number can be found. Augustine wanted to understand all that exists from this perspective on the huge cosmic order. He wanted to address the cosmic order on the basis of it.

In speaking about the Trinitarian God, Augustine took great care to guard against many dangers that trip up human thought on the subject. Thus, he remained alert so as to never give the impression that behind the three persons of the divine being a hidden divinity itself lies, vague and undefined. He wanted to warn emphatically against seeing the three persons as arising from some darker divinity that exists behind them and emerges from those darker depths. For then there would always actually be four: the darker deity behind all else and the three persons as the form its external appearance takes. But this is certainly not how things are! "God *is* the Trinity." "The divine being is none other than the Trinity." "The Trinity is the one Lord, our God, of whom it is said: 'Hear, O Israel, the Lord your God is one Lord.'"[21]

But when Augustine thinks about the one God, he encounters the splendor of the Trinity everywhere. The images and ideas with which Augustine explains the Trinity to us are amazing. In God he sees first of all the unending fullness of *Being*. God is always Jehovah, absolute Being, who is the source of all that exists. At the same time, he is the fullness of *Knowledge*, for he knows himself fully and he knows all things as his creatures. He does not know them because they exist, but because he has known them. In the third place, God is the fullness of *Willing*. His willing is in complete harmony with his being; he wills what he is, and his will is in no respect whatsoever determined by anything outside himself. Furthermore, all that he wills, he can accomplish, for he is also the almighty God. Thus, his Being, his Knowing, and his Willing are bound together in deep harmony: he knows who he is and he wills what he is.[22]

Because God is all of this simultaneously, and is so perfectly, he can also be called "the *cause* of all being, the *truth* of all thinking, and the *order* of all living" *(causa subsistendi et ratio intelligendi et ordo vivendi)*. For this reason, we may also address him as "the *principle* of nature, the *truth* of doctrine, and the *blessedness* of life." He is similarly "our principle, our light, and our good" *(principium nostrum, lumen nostrum, bonum nostrum)* because he is ever "the cause by which all things are established, the light by which the truth is known, and the source from which blessedness is imbibed."[23]

One can think of each of these great attributes of God as divisible further. When God is regarded as the highest Being, being in the perfect sense of the word, what follows from this is that one must at the same time worship him as the greatest Truth, the greatest Good, and the highest Beauty.[24]

In the most profound and beautiful way, Augustine connects all of this to the triune God. The eternal Father causes the Son to be born from him. For Augustine that is the same thing as saying: the Speaker speaks the Word. The Son is also the Word, that is to say, he is the perfect expression of the being of the Father. He is the image of the Father. In him the Father himself speaks, and in him the Father sees his own image reflected. Because Being and

21. On this compare Dr. Michael Schmaus, *Die psychologische Trinitätslehre des heiligen Augustinus* (Münster: n.p., 1927), p. 102, where the sources cited above are also found.

22. Schmaus, *Die psychologische Trinitätslehre*, § 5 passim.

23. Martin Grabmann, *Die Grundgedanken des heiligen Augustinus über Seele und Gott*, 2nd ed. (Köln: Bachem, 1929), pp. 104-5.

24. Schmaus, *Die psychologische Trinitätslehre*, p. 94.

Knowing coincide in God, and because God knows himself perfectly, the Son is also one with the Father. Nothing exists in the Father that does not exist in the Son; nothing exists in the Speaker that does not exist in the Word.[25] And just as the Son proceeds from the Father, so the Holy Spirit proceeds from the Father and the Son as the Holy Love with which the Father loves the Son and with which the Son loves the Father. "The Father rejoices with a holy joy when he considers in his full being the Son born from him." "He loves his Son, because he is fully like him." "When the love with which the Father loves the Son and the Son loves the Father, when the oneness of the two is displayed in an indescribable way, then what more can be desired than that he who is the Spirit is in a special sense called Love and is bound to both alike?"[26]

When Augustine regards the person of the Holy Spirit primarily as Love, he appeals to several places in the Bible. He supports his reasoning specifically on the basis of 1 John 4:7 and following. There we read, "Beloved! Let us love one another, for love is from God. He who does not love does not know God, for God is love." In the first sentence is stated that love is *from* God, and in the second that it even is God. Thus, God is from God. How could that be anything else than the Holy Ghost that always proceeds from the Father and the Son and who himself is God? Support for this idea he sees in Romans 5:5, where it is said that "God's love is poured into our hearts by the Holy Spirit." There, as well, love is seen as a gift from God, particularly as a gift of the Spirit, who himself is love.[27]

We leave aside the question as to how far all these ideas of Augustine can be legitimately accepted. In any case, what is clear is the striking way in which Augustine sheds light on the divine Trinity. The Father is he who from eternity brings forth the Son as the perfect expression of his being; and it is the Father and the Son together who love one another perfectly. Knowing in God coincides with being and willing; that is the love that coincides with both his being and his knowing.

Signs of the Trinity

Whenever Augustine investigated these subjects, it struck him that all of creation bears the signs *(vestigia)* of this three-in-oneness. How could it be oth-

25. Schmaus, *Die psychologische Trinitätslehre*, pp. 348ff.
26. Schmaus, *Die psychologische Trinitätslehre*, pp. 382-83.
27. Schmaus, *Die psychologische Trinitätslehre*, p. 383.

erwise? The world has come into existence from God, and it must in every respect bear reminders of God! These reminders can be found in all parts of creation. Once again in this connection, Augustine works in a profound and lucid way. He shows that three things can be distinguished concerning every creature, not in the sense that one creature bears more the image of the Father and another that of the Son or the Spirit, but in the sense that each creature combines the three within itself.

In the first place, each creature has a being. It is something; it exists; it has received its existence from God as the source of its being. Not every creature has that existence in the same measure or in the same form, but all alike exist in one way or another. That existence Augustine calls "unity" *(unitas)* or "manner" *(modus).*

In the second place, each creature possesses a uniqueness that it displays in a definite form *(species).* Each creature has its special characteristics. It displays its own character and so carries within itself what is its own, individual possession and keeps it distinct from all other creatures.

In the third place, each creature has a place in the great, divine order *(ordo)* that includes everything. By virtue of that divine order, each creature has its assigned position in the totality, its own purpose in God's great plan. As long as a subject or another creature is out of the place it belongs by virtue of the divine order, it is unsettled and is filled with a longing "to find its place and come to its order" *(locorum atque ordinis appetitus).* But as soon as it finds its balance or place in the divine order, it is at rest *(tranquillitas)* and peace. Also, within each creature separately, the various components are in orderly relationship with one another. On the human face, for example, the position of the nose, the eyes, the mouth, and the ears is consistent with the order that reflects the special purpose assigned to each of them.[28]

In this fashion, Augustine shows that each creature possesses a definite threefold character and that this has its basis in the divine Trinity, which it reflects. What is self-evident is that not every creature exhibits this threefold character in the same way or to the same degree. One is simply higher in rank and is vested with a more important place in the cosmic order than another. Each thing has its own cosmic position. The lowliest creature that can be imagined is the unformed matter of which Genesis 1:2 speaks. "Being" is present there, to be sure, but it has precious little form and defined specifica-

28. Schmaus, *Die psychologische Trinitätslehre,* pp. 192ff. Compare also Konrad Scipio, *Des Aurelius Augustinus Metaphysik: Im Rahmen seiner Lehre vom Übel* (Leipzig: Breitkopf & Härtel, 1886), pp. 47ff.

tion, and here order is entirely undeveloped. Ascending higher, one reaches the level of ordered matter that bears the seed of life, namely plants and animals. At the pinnacle of all creatures one finds human beings, fashioned in the image of God. This is why they bear the image of the Trinity in the clearest way, and in them this threefold character shines forth most beautifully, above all in the soul.

Many expressions of this threefold character can be found in the human soul. One notes in the first place that the threefold features of being, knowing, and willing are expressed in the soul. "We are, we also know that we are, and we love that being and that knowing" *(Nam et sumus et nos esse novimus et id esse ac nos se diligimus)*. We exist, we are aware that we exist, and we want to be preserved in that existence. That is the triunity of human life.[29]

This threefold feature in essence agrees with another, namely that of the spirit, self-consciousness, and love *(mens, notitia, amor)*. The human soul is of a spiritual nature; in its self-consciousness it knows itself and also loves itself.

On this threefold feature, in turn, rests yet another: memory, insight, and will *(memoria, intelligentia, voluntas)*. By means of memory, people hold onto their identity, as it were, and also hold onto all that they have previously experienced. It is even true that by means of memory people hold onto God, for they remember that God is the ground of their being. The concept of memory has very special significance in the writings of Augustine.[30] Through insight — *intelligentia* designates approximately what we used to call intuition[31] — people understand themselves with that deep self-awareness that recalls so clearly what God possesses perfectly. And through the will people love themselves and also demonstrate that love in their actions.

In this vein, one could continue delving into many such threefold clusters in the works of Augustine, for it is remarkable how consistently this major thinker sees everything in the light of the Trinity. He searched everywhere for the sacred image of God, and he knew how to find it everywhere. We need not agree with him on every point in order to understand how exceptionally valuable these thoughts have been for understanding the cosmic order. In grappling with Asia, we can gain a great deal from many of these concisely formulated distinctions. In order to visualize the subject, we provide a simple chart summarizing the various threefold constellations.[32]

29. Schmaus, *Die psychologische Trinitätslehre*, pp. 230ff.
30. See p. 315 in Chapter 7 above.
31. Schmaus, *Die psychologische Trinitätslehre*, pp. 266ff.
32. One finds a similar scheme in Scipio, *Des Aurelius Augustinus Metaphysik*, pp. 66-67.

GOD	Father	Son	Holy Spirit
	(Supreme) Being	Knowing	Willing
	Cause of all being	Truth of all being	Order of all living
	Principle of nature	Truth of doctrine	Blessedness of life
	Speaker	Word	Love
CREATURES	Being *(esse)*	Form *(species)*	Order *(ordo)*
HUMAN BEINGS	Being	Knowing	Willing
	Spirit	Self-consciousness	Love
	Memory	Insight	Will

Cosmic Numbers

When one proceeds on the basis of the undoubtedly correct idea that the entire creation discloses signs of the triune God, it is not difficult to find it in many areas. In doing so, one naturally may not always be warranted in connecting the first element of a threefold configuration with the Father, the second with the Son, or the third with the Holy Spirit. The various components are not always so easily connected with the divine Trinity. But we should always be alert to the fact that we find threefold configurations everywhere, especially with respect to spiritual life, and that these configurations must each be thought of as a unity.

- When speaking about the image of God in which Adam was created, one can distinguish within it knowledge, righteousness, and holiness (on the basis of Eph. 4:24 and Col. 3:10).
- The Christian's spiritual calling can be divided into the roles of prophet, priest, and king.
- These three roles can be shown to have been fulfilled in Christ and united in him. Jesus explains God to us as a prophet (John 1:18); he reconciles us to God as a priest (2 Cor. 5:19); and transforms us into his image as a king.
- The Christian life can be characterized in terms of faith, hope, and love. (1 Cor. 13:13).

- There is a close connection between justification, sanctification, and glorification.
- The church of the New Testament recognizes three offices in its organizational life.

Thus, the threefold distinction can be found in all dimensions of spiritual life. And in each of the examples, what is remarkable is that on the deepest level the three are in essence one. Always, again and again, the unity consists of a triad.

In the realm of ordinary life and of world affairs, one can draw the same conclusions. With the bread I eat, the clothing I wear, the furniture I use — whenever I look closely — a threefold configuration emerges. There is the basic material investigated; there is the form given this basic material; and there is the distribution of the resulting product to those who need it. Connected with this threefold division are the various functions within human society and the various social classes. The concepts of price and value assigned to everything can also be seen on the basis of this model.

One could delve more deeply into every field of endeavor in tracking down examples of threefold configuration. In connection with the state, the sciences, society, the church, art, and literature, one observes the *vestigial trinitatis,* the signs of the Trinity.

This entire idea becomes even more beautiful when one's eyes are opened to the fact that the Bible also recognizes the cosmic number four that is accorded such a prominent place in Asia. It is found back in the four living creatures that John saw as representatives of the cosmos (Rev. 4:6). The four rivers that flow out of Paradise (Gen. 2:10 and following) probably already indicate the cosmic diversity that can be seen especially in the four directions. When the Savior comes to earth, four evangelists recorded his history in their books.

Everywhere, then, where the divine approaches cosmic life and becomes involved with it, the Bible reflects both numbers, and by extension assigns preeminence to the holy numbers seven (3 + 4) and twelve (3 × 4). Perhaps it is good, therefore, that both of these numbers play such an important role in all of recorded history. In seven days, God created the heavens and the earth in all of their fullness and diversity. And the rhythms of this great event God carries over into our lives with a week consisting of seven days. The division of the people of Israel into twelve tribes is a representation of the fullness of the people whom God has called, just as the twelve apostles later were called to bring the message of the gospel to all creatures. Thus with just a few numbers, God can communicate great things to the human race, and in the symbolism of these numbers he unveils something of the enormous mysteries of his own being.

The Great Distinction

God and the Cosmos

When one sets alongside each other the great models of Asian and Christian thought, one is struck initially by their remarkable similarity. Both of them, Indian and Christian, recognize the great cosmic order that holds all things together and assigns each individual thing its special, cosmic place. Indian thought has also understood that this world does not possess a chaotic nature in any way whatsoever, but that in all its connections it displays a majestic order. Both proceed on the basis that a few major features characterize the whole cosmos and that they cut through all its spheres and compel us to focus on the same numerical relationships. And both understand that these numbers, therefore, take on special significance. Both also explain that the cosmic order is not only of interest to us as an object, but that it also has great value for us as a gauge for our living. From this cosmic order flows the designed place that every creature has in the divine plan and thus the calling that it must fulfill. The agricultural worker has a different cosmic position than the educated person, also a different calling and a different pressure from the moral law binding on all humans. In a certain sense, each person has his or her own dharma, and one person cannot intrude on that of another. When a soldier and a tax collector come to John, he has a unique word for each of them (Luke 3:12-14).

More significant for us than their agreement is the great difference between these two systems. In part, that difference depends on a different way of thinking. The Javanese way of classifying things often strikes us as being childish because it frequently employs so little logical thought and ends in confusion. Furthermore, Javanese thought does not always readily understand that because a given phenomenon usefully serves as a symbol for something else in an entirely different area, it is not for that reason the same thing. But all of this does not yet touch the heart of the matter and might better be left aside at this point.

Dominating everything else is the contrast that we find concerning the number component in the two systems. Asian thinking operates with one number, the cosmic number par excellence. It addresses God from within the cosmos and as it were sees God as coinciding with the cosmos. God is the mysterious order that carries the cosmos. This is why Asian thought can understand all cosmic phenomena and divine life from four angles. Christian thought always works with two components. It sees God and the world as separate from one another but still having an enduring connection. Augustine addressed the cosmic order first of all from the perspective of the Trinity, and he saw evidences of the Trinity everywhere. So construed, one can say that this world consists of a threefold dimension imprinted on the four dimensions of reality, the image of the Trinitarian God imposed on the cosmos. In this connection, it is not first of all about the numbers themselves. We should pay attention to them in order that we not misuse the numbers by looking everywhere for evidences of threes and fours. The bigger principle is what is at stake here, and that is all-defining. Christianity does not locate the divine within the cosmos and does not see God and the world as one, but it distinguishes the two as sharply as possible.

Christianity distinguishes God and the world, and yet it does not situate the two loosely beside each other. But it brings them together on many occasions and in a great many ways. Thus, in Christianity the numbers seven and twelve are holy numbers par excellence. Christianity is theistic through and through. While it does not identify God and the world, it also does not separate them. God is in the world, and the world is in God. From him and through him and unto him are all things. And yet the world has its own existence and may never be worshiped as God himself. Asian thought has the divine merging with cosmic events, but Christian thought is from the outset theological, that is to say, it begins and ends with God. All additional distinctions are founded on this contrast. In Asia, to come to God is more or less identical with coming to oneself and coming to oneness with the cosmos and the world-order. To come to God for Christianity is something totally different: it is to rise far above self and far beyond the world. To come to oneself in the gospel is identical with coming to the awareness that one is distinct from God (Luke 15:17).

Sin and the World-Order

Seen from this perspective, the contrast readily leads to a number of additional differences. One could apply the well-known words of Anselm to the entire Javanese world of thought and feeling: you still have not felt the great significance of your sin *(nondum considerasti quanti ponderis sit peccatum)*.[33] Javanese people easily — all too easily — include sin in the cosmic order and do not feel that they are dealing with something terribly distorting. When the passions of the human soul are identified in the same breath with colors, natural objects, or some other phenomena, you shudder momentarily because this gaping wound in the cosmos is casually wiped away without fathoming its bitter seriousness. People often rashly attempt to include all cosmic phenomena, including sin, in their scheme of cosmic order, and in doing so they actually include it in God as the summation of all that exists. But sin is never an element in the divine world-order; it is always a distortion and displacement of that order. Everything is jolted out of its cosmic position and has become unfaithful to its defined place. Humanity has forsaken its cosmic place, its position in the divine order for the world, and it has usurped God's throne in its terrible attempt to be like God. This forsaking of its cosmic position has brought about God's curse on human life, with the result that all of life reflects this distorted order. It is no longer chaos; it is also no longer order; it is distorted order, the opposite of harmony. Therefore, every remaining attempt to understand cosmic life as a well-ordered whole is doomed to fail.

What also follows from this is that Christianity sees the world's moral order in a completely different way than South and Southeast Asia does. Indian thought has construed the moral order as a natural law, something that simply follows from the nature of things, just as sin itself does. Especially Buddhism has attempted in a major way to see the relationship between sin and punishment as a self-evident, causal necessity. It talks about the various links *(nidana)* in the chain of causal events.[34] In doing so, it identifies the following stages: from erring *(avidya)* proceed the formative powers in the subconscious; from these mysterious powers, consciousness *(vijnana)* comes into existence, and from consciousness awakens the principle of "name and shape" *(namarupa)* that forms the human ego. From it develop the senses, and these senses produce contact with the world. These generate sensation, which in turn produces desire *(trisna)*. From desire comes passionate grasping for the world in an effort to satisfy an inner thirst. This grasping takes on existence in the form of an embodied being, from which

33. Ed. note: Anselm of Canterbury, *Why God Became Man,* 1.20, in *The Major Works,* ed. Brian Davies and Gillian Evans (Oxford: Oxford University Press, 1998).

34. These links between cause and effect in Buddhism are called *pratityasamutpada,* which is literally equivalent to the simultaneous origin of something in connection with something else.

again come birth, aging, and death. Contained in this chain of causes and consequences is a great deal more that is still not entirely clear and that we will not probe further here. The main point for us in this connection is simply this: the entire process is regarded as a process of cause and effect, as inherently a necessarily unfolding law. The entire concept of karma that is so frequently cited in Asian religion is obviously a concept that points to this inherently necessary, consequential process. This is the perspective from which South and Southeast Asia have seen justice in the world. It is like the fruit growing on a tree: good seed produces good fruit; bad seed produces bad fruit. The one innately grows from the other. There is a natural moral law according to which evil on earth wreaks vengeance on itself.

Now, Christianity also certainly speaks of the fruit of sin and it admonishes that a man will reap what he sows. It is actually by divine wisdom that a mysterious connection exists within the cosmos that assures that sin often almost inherently produces punishment. How often does it not seem as though it punishes itself! Punishment often is not imposed on us, but the exact connection between a certain sin of our character and an affliction in life frequently follows much more naturally; amazingly, the latter often seems as if it grows from seed of the former. Nevertheless, we may not regard these things as magical, nor as happening by natural necessity, but rather we should see them theologically, from the perspective of God. All punishment has a divine element; God himself is involved in it. When sin itself appears to mete out punishment, the hand of God is at work. You can never leave the holy and righteous God out of the picture. The one never proceeds from the other by itself. When the one leads to the other, it is by God's hand. This is why in our religious lives, we are never involved with magical, mysterious laws that impinge on us, but we are always and only involved with the living God who is present and rules in the cosmos. But he may never be identified with the cosmic order itself. Only when we see ourselves in contrast with the living God, and when we see his hand as directing punishment, is a true sense of sin awakened within us.

All of this we find portrayed in the Psalms in a very unsettling manner. What resounds there is a deep sense of guilt: against you, and you only, have I sinned. We are not saying that Asia never acknowledges the same. There, as well, one hears the sound of tender and deep sorrow for evil in its songs. There, as well, people implore the God they serve for forgiveness. But it certainly seems time and again that childlike communion with God is smothered by faith in the magical powers present everywhere and by the mysterious laws by which one thing controls another. Then religion dies and philosophical speculation that leaves the heart empty arises. Asia has never been able to separate God from the cosmos. It has always dragged him down, as it were, to the level of cosmic phenomena and the natural order. As soon as one makes God part of the cosmos, there is no longer any room for remorse, for a true sense of guilt, or for pleading for grace.

When Christ extends his hands to the people of Asia, he does so to lead those who are searching in that faraway, extended world out of their cocoon-like searching and reflecting. He wants them to approach that one great God of whom he is the revelation on earth. Whoever sees him, instantly forgets the world with all its powers and its natural order and only sees the incomprehensible and indescribable majesty of the almighty King. Then everything else falls away, including our pride, and we simply become erring, straying children who have wandered far from our Father's home. He wants to lead us, as he also wants to lead the children of Asia, into that living fellowship with God. There we see everything that happens — the growing of the flowers from the ground and the emerging of suffering from sins — as coming from the hand of God the Father. For, he is above all things, and through him all that exists has come into being.

At the same time, he reveals to us how he, by his great suffering and death, restores order within this distorted world and gathers all things unto himself. On that day that he "will restore the kingdom to God the Father, and he will have destroyed all dominion, power, and authority. . . . Then the Son himself will become subject to him who has made all things subject to him, so that God may be all in all" (1 Cor. 15:24, 28).

10 The Mysterious Drama of Human Life

Life's Riddles

When young people begin thinking about life, it has to impress them that this world we call home is an amazing place. Often things happen unexpectedly that offer up no explanation. A child drops something out of his little hands, and it instantly falls to the floor as though some strong, invisible hand quickly pulled it there. The water of a brook hidden in the woods flows downward, bubbling and splashing as it does, apparently drawn there by some strange, unseen hand — one that seems to be present everywhere. But the sun and moon, as well as a thousand twinkling little stars, seem not to be bothered in the least by that hand; they simply move forward in the heavens as though not threatened in the least by any danger. In the evening, a slight haze hangs over the land; when it is seen from afar, it seems to take on all sorts of shapes. But as soon as you get closer, you no longer see it, as though some invisible force hastily pulled it away. The trees rustle and sway, but what is the power that causes this? What is it that moves them? A human being is engrossed in an amazing house of magic, and who can explain its secrets? Why do trees and plants grow? And why does one grow so much faster and so differently than another? Wherever we look in this world we call home, we encounter fleeting phenomena that are inexplicable and that at best we become accustomed to when we see them with new eyes.

Already in fairly early times, western thought found key concepts to unlock these various riddles. Once the concepts were formulated and people began speaking in terms of gravity, electricity, magnetism, or whatever else, it was as though their amazement softened and the mystery became less awesome than before. All these strange, whimsical forces in the world now seemed to be under our control. Even to this day, however, the Asian sees these phenomena differently and in terms of fairy tales, and speaks about all sorts of invisible beings that fill the world. Asians know the history of things in a way that explains why they have to be the way they are, and they try hard to stay on friendly terms with strange forces or avoid their dangerous influences by using cunning deception. Thus, the Asian lives in a world that is a baffling place, and day after day is overcome with amazement at so many puzzling things.

The most mysterious of all is human life itself. Where, really, does a person come from? What is the depth of our being? What will shortly become of us, when our eyes become fixed and strength slips from our limbs? Has a person descended from some other, higher realm simply to wander around until it is possible shortly to return to that higher world? What secrets do we carry around within us, secrets of which even we are not aware and will never be able to resolve? What happens in sleep, and what really is this strange experience that we call dreaming? Does the soul travel outside the body and all around the world, and can it see and hear things that otherwise are hidden from it? How, then, does it all at once return to the body? By what routes does it reenter? What a countless number of questions we have that besiege the heart once people begin thinking about life itself and themselves in particular. No wonder that at such times powerful fantasies take people down secret paths and produce strange explanations that try to make sense of life.

The Important Moments in Life

From cradle to grave, a person's life is threatened by all sorts of dangers. For that reason, the great task of one's life is always to maintain contact with the great forces within the cosmos in order to protect oneself. Already before the birth of a child, all sorts of practices need to be followed scrupulously in order to guarantee that nothing harmful will befall the infant, even before birth. Meals are held and other solemn, symbolic actions are observed that are regarded as necessary to protect life. Once a child has been born, all sorts of new dangers appear from the outset. For example, angry forces threaten precisely such nursing infants, and various magical devices *(sarats)* need to be employed against their evil work. Particularly noteworthy is the fearful *Kuntianak,* the soul of a female who died in childbirth and roams around looking for young children to devour.[1] Thus, during the first forty days of a child's life, the mother must be constantly vigilant, for the dangers that lie in wait on every side are numerous. Fortunately, there are also invisible protectors that carefully guard those lives threatened on so many sides. Of great significance in the life of a young child is the day that it first comes into contact with the all-providing mother earth. In earlier times, solemn contact with the earth was observed with many ceremonies, for from that moment on children deal with the world on their own and take their place in that great cosmic whole with all its strange and powerful forces.

There are significant times throughout a person's entire life when great dangers threaten and when special care must be taken. For example, the occasion of circumcision is significant since that is when a child is received into the larger religious community and requires many solemn rituals in preparation. The person stays awake the night before; the body is carefully prepared ahead of time and holy incantations made to ward off all dangers. In the whole circumcision ceremony itself, numerous steps that accompany inducting a young man into the tribe's mysteries existed for many centuries before the arrival of Islam.

The next important event is marriage, where all sorts of sacred steps need to be remembered and long-established rites that determine how everything should happen must be observed, lest threatening forces steal marital blessing.

All times in life are fraught with danger. In agriculture, the time of the rice harvest is especially important. This explains why there are many accounts of the origin of rice circulating among Javanese people. All these stories come down to one thing: rice is a plant that has a divine beginning. Many festive, symbolical activities seek to ensure that everything related to the crop happens in an orderly, uninterrupted way.

Other significant occasions in life include: building a house, starting a new line of work, and beginning a new task. Whenever a person wants to undertake something in the great, cosmic order, forces always enter that could cause catastrophe and misery. This world simply traffics in situations ex-

---

1. Ed. note: Bavinck spells this as "Koentianak"; alternative spellings are Pontianak, Kuntilanak, Matianak. Whatever the spelling, the creatures are a type of vampire, like the langsuir of Malaysia; they are women who died in childbirth and after resuscitation seek revenge by terrorizing people in the villages with their wailing and shrieking (banshees) and drinking the blood of newborns. See Rosemary Guiley, *The Encyclopedia of Vampires, Werewolves, and Other Monsters* (New York: Checkmark Books, 2004), s.v. "Pontianak"; also see the online *monstropedia* at http://www.monstropedia.org/index.php?title=Pontianak.

tremely susceptible to having the balance between the forces of life and the forces of death disturbed. Thus, extreme caution must be exercised at all times so as not to disturb that balance and to avoid disaster. By exercising his sacred obligations, the prince in particular can collaborate in maintaining cosmic order and thus affect the well-being of his people. So, whenever a people is tested by an epidemic or experiences various terrible catastrophes, it usually indicates that in one way or another the prince has violated the cosmic order and disturbed the balance of the world-order.

Death

The most significant of all events, obviously, is the moment when the soul is separated from life and death gains its great victory. Before it comes to that, people attempt to save life with all the existing means at their disposal. But when they realize that death is stretching out its unrelenting hand, people know enough to relinquish everything with wonderfully strong peace. We all need to die at the moment God has determined in his great plan for the world. This is the defined order *(takdir)* that pleases him. It is of no use to sulk about it; it is much better to be humbly submissive, leaving matters in his hands.

But as soon as the soul leaves the body, a period of deep concern commences for those left behind. They must now meet all sorts of important solemn obligations. They must take care, first of all, to ensure that the deceased can be freed and unimpeded from this world and can enter that great realm of the dead, where they must dwell forever. At the same time, they must take every precaution to prevent the deceased from remaining behind to haunt the present and produce all kinds of calamity instead of entering that far-off land. It is even possible that the soul of the person who died might enter one or another animal or be manifested in some other way to avenge previously unresolved injustices or to cause damage among the living. A particularly great and threatening danger is the possibility that the victorious powers of death, in their overconfidence, will enlist others in an attempt to wreak destruction on those who now live peaceful, undisturbed lives. Relatives need to attend to many worries. And these are even greater when the deceased person died in the strength of his or her younger years and failed to reach old age and depart after a normal lifespan. The many ceremonies observed at the funeral and for some time afterwards indicate the kinds of fear that fill relatives' hearts. For that reason, precise directions must always be remembered. While the corpse is still in the house, it must be laid out with head turned to the west, and when the body is placed on the bier a north-south placement must be observed. People enter the cemetery from the south end, and a westward orientation is again selected for the grave. On the way to the graveyard, people continuously recite a variety of sacred proverbs and especially confessional statements, all sung repetitiously and in monotone. After the burial, a funeral meal is held that, like other sacred meals, has special significance and serves the purpose of strengthening the life-forces of those who remain behind. People believe that the soul of a dead person still lingers in the vicinity where that person lived earlier. Thereafter, however, it gradually withdraws into that mysterious realm of the dead, but even then, it is good to consider the dead from time to time, for they possess great power and hold an important position in the cosmos. It is thus desirable to ask the dead for permission and to honor them in connection with all special occasions.

Death is always a very mysterious event that people regard with timidity. On the one hand, death is the annihilation of life. But, on the other hand, the Javanese people have retained the idea from antiquity that death marks the transition to life on another, higher level. Since death frees one from the curse, it is a deliverance. In the *wayang* stories, one or another divinity or some high-ranking being often meets with a curse from an even more powerful divinity and is thereby changed into a giant or a monster. In those cases, death is always deliverance. As soon as the giant is killed by a mighty hero, the curse is broken and the god is restored to glory. This is how things are everywhere in the world; death is never only destruction, but it is always at the same time a "return home" (in Javanese: *mulih*) to the true, everlasting world. People return once again to true selfhood, to what they are in the depths of their being, because that is their origin. With all the fear of death that fills the hearts of easterner and westerner alike comes the certainty — or at least the presumption — in both places that death can mark the beginning of a much higher life characterized by perfection and eternity. This is why dead people are thought to possess powers that an ordinary person does not. And this is also why it is advisable to visit the graves of especially holy people whenever one wants to share in the blessings emanating from them.[2]

---

2. For additional material on Javanese customs, see C. Snouck Hurgronje, *Verspreide Geschriften van C. Snouck Hurgronje*, 6 vols. (Bonn and Leipzig: K. Schroeder, 1923-1927), 4: 1; K. A. Hidding, *Gebruiken en Godsdienst der Soendaneezen* (Batavia: Kolff, 1935); "Religieuze Waarden in den Volksgodsdienst," *De Opwekker* 77, no. 9 (1932); H. Bergema, "Over de Beteekenis van de Kennis der Javaansche Cultuur voor het Verstaan van de Javaansche Levensvisie," *De Macedoniër* 37 (1935).

Thus, the life of the Javanese people is totally different from ours in every respect. They feel one with the surrounding world to a much greater degree than we do, and know more deeply than we that they are caught up in the overarching order ruling the world. In every aspect of life they expect to encounter all sorts of rules for moderation that are of great self-interest. The examination of those rules does not depend so much on logical reasoning about cause and effect, but involves vaguer suspicions resting on various analogies. We westerners stand over against the world to a much greater degree than they do. We see ourselves as individuals who lead independent lives, and we regard the world around us as territory over which humanity is given control. By contrast, the Javanese regard individual persons more like tiny parts of the huge cosmic order, merely one of millions of other phenomena that are controlled in this world by eternal laws. Resting on this perspective are the many, numerous practices that encircle the lives of easterners as inviolable customs.

This explains why so few things in the life of a Javanese person are of no consequence. We have frequently noted before that in all kinds of activities it makes a difference in what way things are done. It matters what plants grow in a cemetery, what flowers are used in a wedding ceremony, what patterns are worked out in clothing. Each thing has its established, defined place in the cosmic order, and reckoning with that order must be maintained at all times. Even less indifferent is the *place* where various events occur. The whole wide world is not just a huge expanse of space and nothing more. Places exist that for one reason or another are sacred: special forces are at work there, and these places may therefore not be used for just any purpose. If someone wants to build a house, establish a village, or do something else of importance, the obligation always exists to find just the right spot so that nothing harmful threatens those involved. Of no less value is the importance of determining exactly the right *time* to do things, since all times and all days are not equal. Rather, various days and hours are replete with mysterious powers, as it were. There are special "lucky" days among the seven days of the Islamic week as well as the five-day Javanese market week. Thus, it is desirable for matters of especially great concern to find the most opportune day of one week that coincides with the most suitable day of another. But the system of the most auspicious days is more complicated than we can explain in just a few words. Days exist that are most suited for selling; others that lend themselves best to religious instruction. Similarly, all months of the year are not the same. Certain years are even accorded sacred places.

Among the hours of the day, once again, each has its own character and value. Particularly holy activities are preferably held at night. The *wayang* dramas themselves last from evening until sunrise the following day. Even within the play itself, all the events have their established time and sequence. The various struggles in which the hero is involved happen at precise moments, and the hero's inevitable triumph coincides precisely with the moment outside when in nature the sun's first rays strike the earth. Thus, it is a drama involving cosmic forces, and as such it is a representation of the drama in human life that is always determined by the mysterious totality of laws at work.

The *Wayang:* The Great Symbol of Life

With all of its struggle as well as its beauty, the *wayang* is certainly a marvelous symbol of life in more than one respect. It asks us to think of all that accompanies the unfolding of the drama: the nighttime stillness in which it develops as well as the soft and more or less monotone and sometimes powerfully swelling music of the gamelan, an instrument symbolizing the rhythmic occurring of cosmic events. The intricately crafted puppets are dramatically manipulated by the *dalang*, the man directing the drama, and one can observe all the intriguing vicissitudes.[3] The hero of the story often initially finds himself in distressing circumstances, sometimes not even knowing who his parents are. Like people in this world, he is unaware of this *sangkanparan*, the place from which he came and to which he will again return. He enters a huge forest, the symbol of the perplexing variety of things in the world among which he has to choose the proper course of action and becomes entangled in all kinds of conflicts with enemies and giants. In a certain sense, these giants once again symbolize the destructive, disruptive desires within him that could lead to his own undoing. We are carried along in the overwhelming struggle in which goodness and even life itself are at stake and live along with the glory of ultimate triumph. Sometimes the entire *wayang* drama is one beautiful rendering of the struggle a person needs to endure before reaching the divine, making very meaningful the words at the end of the emotional struggle that convey the deeply mystical wisdom concerning the ultimate union of God and a human being.

---

3. Ed. note: Wayang Golek Purwa is the popular Puppet Theater of West Java, the province known in Indonesian as Sunda. The wooden doll puppets are operated from below by rods connected to the hands and a central control rod that runs through the body to the head.

With a strange whimsy, scenes of foolish jesting or of filthy immorality are often presented in the middle of serious drama. That, too, is fully consistent with the cosmic life of which the *wayang* is an interpretation. In Javanese literature, one often finds passages of mystical wisdom strangely intermingled with thoroughly sensuous descriptions of all sorts of unchaste behavior. It is almost as though the poignant contrast is not felt and as though all of this simply exists side by side. Obviously, the *wayang* drama's more profound ideas are simply lost on many observers, as they only gape at all the jokes and the dirty language that are part of the presentation. But for those seeking something more profound, they can always find a great deal of material that stimulates serious reflection. Especially toward the end of the drama, when the outcome is within view, various ideas about the meaning and mysteries of human life come into play.

It is at that point, for example, that the big, perplexing question emerges — "Who am I?" Giants always appear in the *wayang* play, and they represent the human passions that consume the soul.[4] One can see there the self-centeredness, the greed, the immoral lust, and the materialism that still exist in the human soul. The Javanese person sees these forces not in isolation, but as intimately connected with all sorts of cosmic phenomena and forces of nature. Just as life in the cosmos is one big struggle, so too is life in microcosm within the human soul. There, as well, various actors enter the play: the powers of destruction, of error, and of anger; they are sometimes so amazingly strong that the human soul cannot withstand them. But the question comes: "Who are you, then, in that mysterious *wayang* drama going on within your own soul? Are you the *dalang* manipulating the puppets? Do you have control of your own passions, and are you able to direct their role in the play at will? Are you, therefore, the lord of your own soul?" Or, do you often feel more like the football of these forces being kicked around within you but not at all characteristic of your deepest self? The great psychological questions that have always preoccupied western thought — those concerning our power in the life of our own souls — are often approached with great precision in the symbolical language of the *wayang* drama. In the totality of

4. Ed. note: The giants who represent the four passions that consume the human soul — the general, comprehensive Javanese and Indonesian word for these is *nafsu* — are *Amarah* (the impulse of anger), *Wamah* (bodily needs such as eating and other material needs), *Sawiah* (the sexual drive), and *Loamah* (animal side and drive to communicate). A fifth *(Mutmainah)* is given directly by Allah and has no negative character; it returns to Allah at death. The goal of Ramadan fasting is to control the first four so they do not destroy *Mutmainah*. See Chapter 9, note 17.

my own soul's life, are there forces that are not my true self, and if so, what then is my role in the middle of all the wild turmoil they cause?

Thus, all sorts of problems arise in the heart of the person who observes the *wayang* dramatization of human living. Am I merely a *wayang* puppet in the great world-drama; and, throughout my entire life, am I completely in the grip of the great *Dalang*, God, who holds the lives of everyone in his hands? Or is God only the lamp that by its light creates the shadows but who is no further involved in the shifting drama of heroes and giants? Is the depth of my own soul, perhaps, no more than a lamp that causes all the writhing and conflicting forces in my life, but who, for the rest, stands completely above the fray? Am I, then, nothing more than a spectator in the *wayang* drama of my soul's activity, and do I experience my entire life as merely a dream that slips away and in which I myself actually play no role?

When you simply sit and listen to the notes of the gamelan with its exotic, mysterious music, it is as though you are caught up in that world of questions. Then it can happen all of a sudden that the strange feeling overwhelms you that you are only dreaming and that all of human life is only one, big dream about war and tension from which you will awaken shortly. The entire atmosphere of the *wayang* stirs up wondrous thoughts in the human soul and poses for us questions about appearance and reality, shadow and actuality, dreaming and waking. This is precisely what that unique drama that has such a prominent place in Javanese popular culture intends to do.

In recent times, experts have reflected at considerable length on the question of the origin and causes of the *wayang* drama. They see it as a remnant of ancient ancestor worship, in which the ancestors reappear in puppet figures. They have discovered traces in it that remind them of what many peoples in Asia use with the initiation of young men into the secrets of the tribe and their acceptance into the circle of male adulthood. But whatever the explanation, what is clear is that for the contemporary Javanese person it is a representation of various important spiritual issues. In that connection, it is used as a parable for explaining the wonders of life in this world.[5]

---

5. On the origins of *wayang* cf. W. H. Rassers, *Over den Oorsprong van het Javaansche Toneel* (no publisher, 1931); also, K. G. P. A. A. Mangkoenagoro, "Over de wajang koelit in het algemeen en over de daarin voorkomende symbolische en mystieke elementen," *Djawa* 7 (1933): 12ff.

The Christian Attitude Toward Life

Whenever I watched a *wayang* drama or spoke about it, I was always struck by the beautiful and yet thoroughly dangerous power this dramatic art form has in the lives of Javanese people. It was often quite difficult to explain precisely wherein that danger resides. Is it because the *wayang* spoke about the most holy and the most profane subjects in the same breath? Is it because the *wayang* wants to serve as a symbol for the most profound matters but also wants to describe the most mundane things? Is it because in it human moral tension is weakened and everything is jumbled together in the larger context of human existence, then set to lyrics for the wailing notes of the gamelan's rhythmic presentation of a world order involving good as well as evil? Certainly its greatest danger is that it hypnotizes the soul with that amazing view of the world that involves everything.

But all of this is merely an indication of something much deeper, something that penetrates to the foundation. The whole atmosphere of the *wayang* is one that turns everything about life into a dream, and in that dream the stability of life's basic reality is lost and is immersed in one big cosmic game. And if that is where you find yourself, it seems like you are no longer yourself and that you live in a world that is not real, swept along in that huge shadow game of existence. Then all boundaries simply fade into the illusion of everything, and then everything flows together in an amazing conglomeration. You live in a kind of fascination with the development of that shadow drama that presents all cosmic conflicts for your consideration and that — amused — you join; everything is just a game, shadows that flit past you. That mood carries you along, and it is what characterizes Asia's full, fascinating grip on the human soul.

In the final instance, Asia experiences life as a reality to a much lesser degree than we do. It regards a person much more as a tiny speck in this world, one with whom the cosmic powers play their capricious game until the notes of the gamelan fade away and the game is over. In the depths of our being, we are only spectators of the world drama, as many eastern poets have reflected. We are really not players in this game, not partners, but we are only silent spectators, momentarily under the impression that we are being carried along on the stream of life until we awaken from the dream and see our true selves again.

Now, I do not deny that a great deal of truth is contained in that whole eastern view of life. That human life is often comparable to one long stupor is actually the case — a dream that slides across the soul. It is also true that a person is often more of a spectator of his own life than an active participant in it, one actively engaged in everything and giving birth from within to what he does. That we are often tossed along atop the waves of cosmic powers, even without being conscious of this happening, is also often the case. A woman often lives surprisingly outside her true self, and the powers at work in her own soul often express so little of what she herself actually wants or expects. An oppressive degree of illusion and dreaming exists in human life, so much that Jesus could say of the prodigal son after he had plunged into the seething world of his own passions that he first "came to himself" when he sat down with pigs as a destitute vagabond. Then the game was over, the spell was broken, and the soul saw itself for what it really was. There is a great deal more daze in all of our lives than we ourselves probably suspect. Nevertheless, the gospel views human life completely differently from the way that the *wayang* performance does because it sees us as being completely, truly alive and human, even with all our dimness. Even when we fall into a stupor, that condition is not in the first place a fate that befalls us, but it follows from profound choices that we have made earlier. Even the prodigal son sunk into a haziness that was simply a consequence of his running away from his fatherly home in an attempt to find himself through his untamed desires. Sin can definitely be compared to darkness, that is to say, nonreality. But the fact is that such darkness achieves so much power over the human heart because of the terrible reality that a person prefers the darkness to the light.

Although Christianity fully recognizes the fact that human life is often comparable to one big dream and that it is like the football of cosmic powers, it continues warning people with emphatic, terrible seriousness not to succumb to such a trance. In this connection, the admonition is true: "Awake, you who sleep, and arise from the dead and Christ will shine on you!" (Eph. 5:14). Christianity certainly recognizes the state of being in a stupor, but it denies in the strongest possible way that such a state has a claim on human beings. Just the opposite! The truth is that a human being is a great and glorious creature of God, made in his image and intended to live in this great cosmos in fellowship with his Lord, fully conscious of doing so. When a person allows himself to drown in the giddiness of his own passions or of the untamed powers that move the world around him, he is sucked into the vortex of life-destroying forces. Then the gospel comes to him, making a strong appeal to his conscience in order to snatch him from that descent and to open his eyes to the light. Or better, Jesus teaches people who see themselves in such circumstances to call on God with a great longing for his grace and help, so that he might deliver them from the grip of darkness and place them in the kingdom of the Son of his love.

The Alternate View of God

When people take basic stock of these matters, they become convinced that they ultimately rest on a vastly different view of God. The God of Asia is different from the God that has appeared to us in Jesus Christ. In all of their thinking about God, the people of Asia could never escape the supposition that God is identical with the cosmos, that he is the summation of all cosmic forces and cosmic order. If a person once proceeds on that basis, it does not matter any longer whether the world is considered as real or regarded as a great illusion. The terrible consequence is inescapable: In God all contrast between good and evil or between the holy and the profane melts away, washed out in the amazing vagueness of his being. Never again will we stand opposite him as sinners who dare to hope only in his grace. We can still talk about sin, if we mean by it that people often overstep cosmic order and in so doing cause themselves all kinds of harm. But all of this is something completely different from sin. We first experience sin when we see ourselves as straying children, still enough of a child never to be able to forget our Father, but still submerged in the stupor of our own sinful desires that we ourselves first placed on the throne.

A person's life is an amazingly big riddle. Longfellow's powerful expression, "Life is real, life is earnest," may sound very beautiful, but it still does not plumb the depths of life's mystery. In reality, life is often less "real" and is often more of a dream; but it certainly always is "earnest" to the extent that it is less "real." The longer we live under the hypnosis of various powers and regard ourselves as spectators of all that happens alongside us, the more dangerous our situation becomes and the more urgently we need the forceful prodding that awakens us from the surreal *wayang* drama of our thoughts and sets us before what finally is ultimate reality. Not wafted away on the notes of the drama and then sucked into life's immense haze, but awakened and seeing precisely where we stand, is the great calling by which Jesus draws people to himself. We want to lead people to the truth, to the hard and bitter truth that we first confront and learn to recognize before we are able to discover that only that truth is able to make us free.

I do not know what will become of the *wayang* drama, or whether it can maintain its position alongside modern movies.[6] When a strong Christian church emerges on Java, I do not know whether that church will seize on the *wayang* as a means for leading people into the mysteries of its worship. But I certainly do know that if the *wayang* drama ever becomes a bearer of Christian ideas, it will have to be changed fundamentally. It is not about whether various characters will have to be eliminated from the *wayang* or whether various impure elements will have to be banned from it, but it is all about what makes the *wayang* drama a *wayang* — its alien vision of life and the world; this will have to be transformed. Life is something different; the world is something different. God is different and I myself am different from what the *wayang* depicts. Everything is different, and it is not subject to the haziness of being caught up in some ephemeral unity behind it all, because sin really exists and God really exists. And if we are ever going to truly find God, we will have to walk the road of truth that lies before us in Jesus Christ. But how that will have to happen, we are incapable of saying at this time. A great deal of thought and struggle will have to happen in Asia before the church in those countries will find the ways, true to their own style and character, of presenting the joy of salvation expressed in Christian living and that serves God in gratitude.

6. Ed. note: The close connection between the *wayang* tradition and movies was noted very early on by cinematographers. See Hereford Tynes Cowling, "Wayang-Wayang: Filmless 'Movies' of the Orient Called Wayang-Wayang More Than a Thousand Years Old. Moving Pictures Probably the Oldest Form of Theatrical Entertainment," *The American Cinematographer* 3, no. 1 (April 1922): 4-6. A more recent treatment makes a similar point and also claims that the presence of movies, especially drive-in movies, may have been the major contributor to the demise of the Malaysian *Kulit* form of Wayang: Firik Jemadi, "Origins of Film: Wayang Kulit in Malaysia," Parts 1 and 2; available online at http://thoughtsonfilms.wordpress.com/2009/11/30/ origins-of-film-wayang-kulit-in-malaysia-part-1; http://thoughtsonfilms.wordpress.com/ 2009/12/02/origins-of-film-wayang-kulit-in-malaysia-part-2/.

11 The Way of Deliverance

The Gospel in Asia

People of Asia who first come into contact with the gospel message immediately find much that strikes them as true and involuntarily find it attractive. They are even filled with special sympathy, at least upon first contact, for its many compelling features, and these already clearly lay the foundation for deep appreciation.

In the first place, the gospel is presented in the country's own language. The ancient writings of the *Vedas* were given in a language capable of being known to only a few, and for that reason they were regarded as exceptionally sacred. Islam certainly came proclaiming its message to all the people, but it conveyed its doctrine in the Arabic language and demanded knowledge of all kinds of terms and sayings in it. For the ordinary villager, it was and still is exceptionally difficult to comprehend these strange Arabic words and to identify with their religious background. On the other hand, the gospel of Jesus Christ is proclaimed universally in Asia not in some sacred language, but in the language of the people. It is announced in old, reliable terms. For that very reason, it meets with attentive listening from the outset. It makes no distinction between Brahmin and lower castes, between initiated and uninitiated. It recognizes only people in need of deliverance and who must, therefore, be shown the sure way to it. It is convinced that even the intellectually weak and powerless are always capable of understanding the childlike message of grace. It does not exclude even the women and children, because it is good tidings of salvation for them as well. For many people who were previously considered to be stupid and backward, all of this inevitably evokes happiness and sympathy; it simply has to awaken joy in hearts long imprisoned in darkness and despair.

In the words of the gospel message, the Javanese found much that struck them as pleasing. Many terms in the gospel were recognizable and reminded them of ideas in ancient Javanese wisdom. An example is the whole frugal lifestyle of Jesus and his disciples. Jesus was truly a teacher, a guru in the Javanese sense of the term. He was poor among the poor, but without experiencing poverty as a burden. He was little attached to earthly possessions and did not complain that he "had nowhere to lay his head." As a simple wanderer, he traveled around from place to place, and with a total lack of self-interest he devoted himself to the holy task he had come to serve. He demanded from his disciples the same world-renouncing attitude. He would not tolerate them heaping up treasures on earth or scrounging and worrying about tomorrow. He demanded that they live with the same childlike faith from one day to the next, never being fearful in times of want or proud in days of plenty. This world is only a very unimportant and temporary phenomenon through which we must travel as pilgrims on our way to the higher world. We are wise when we do not dwell all that much on this world's beauty and treasures, for the form it takes quickly passes.

No wonder that Jesus, when the devil showed him in a vision all the glories of this world, rejected them with determination. In doing so, he revealed that he was an accomplished guru who had learned that the inner things are hidden riches of eternally more value than the treasures of this earth. The Javanese person found it completely incomprehensible that westerners, who had known the words of Jesus for centuries already, understood and followed him so little.

Once I attended a gathering of Javanese people where all sorts of religious topics were being discussed. One of those present then made this remarkable comment:

> We Javanese never knew the teachings of Jesus (by this he meant the words of the Sermon on the Mount about not gathering treasures on earth and not being anxious about tomorrow), but we have always unconsciously lived by them and embraced them, as it were, in our hearts. Westerners have known them for centuries already, but they have never understood or applied them.

This man felt drawn to Jesus from the beginning and saw him as a guru who explicitly taught what he and others had already long believed.

Other ideas in the gospel also strike Javanese as highly reliable. For example, there is the fact that Jesus often fasted or that he spent entire nights in prayer. In the entire Asian world, fasting is a very familiar phenomenon that serves the purpose of lessening the grip of earthly existence and strengthening the soul in its attempts to appropriate heavenly realities. When the gospel sometimes describes how Jesus occasionally spent the entire night praying on the mountain, the Javanese are reminded of much that lives in their own religious accounts and they feel that Jesus is an authentic guru.

They also find it completely understandable, then, that Jesus possesses remarkable powers. A Javanese has several stereotypical requirements for the qualities of an authentic guru: He may "not be stained by sin," "he knows things before they are told to him," "everything that he suggests actually exists, and everything he wills actually occurs." Remarkably, each of these descriptions is also applicable to Jesus, and it obviously follows that Javanese people believe they see in Jesus the confirmation of their own ideals. That the saliva of Jesus seems to heal the blind (Mark 8:23; John 9:6) the Javanese sees as very ordinary. The same is true about making the dumb speak, or that magical power seems to radiate from the tips of his fingers that can heal the deaf (Mark 7:33). Even the fact that the hem of Jesus' garment is laden with magical power (Luke 8:44) is entirely consistent with Javanese notions of the magically empowered guru to whom all the powers of the cosmos are subject.

Furthermore, the entire method of instruction that we meet in Jesus is familiar to the Javanese. Frequently, Jesus resorts to the use of parables, just like Javanese teachers do when they clarify their ideas by employing all sorts of parables and symbols. Jesus often utters short, pithy proverbs that summarize his intent, just as we so frequently find that Javanese literature does in describing the great truths of religion — often in a paradoxical way. Also the tone of Jesus' lengthy discourses that we find in the Gospel of John and the frequently repetitious references to major mystical truths resonate as completely plausible to eastern ears. And the big concepts of light, life, living water, and darkness treated there recall the many wise teachings that Javanese teachers imparted on these subjects. So, both in form as well as content, the gospel contains an enormous amount that both attracts and fascinates the Javanese person.

In some respects, the Javanese are not surprised either that Jesus got so little hearing in his own time and was even killed at the hands of angry men. Javanese mysticism also talks about their mystical teachers who were killed because their teachings were not understood, or perhaps because they spoke too candidly about great mysteries; after their deaths, these were people who came to be thought of as completely innocent because their blood was white, a symbol of innocence. In this, there is nothing that Javanese people find inconceivable.

Most of all, however, the Javanese and other Asian people are moved by the words of Jesus which say that a man must not only forsake his father and mother, but that he must also hate his own life and lose it. "Whoever loses his own soul will find it!" To Javanese eyes that is a proverb laden with mystical truth. It encompasses in just a few words the complete mystery about how a person leaves this world of vanity and folly and enters the real world of "light without any shadow." Already from very ancient times, the Javanese person understood that there is only one way of participating in deliverance and that that is the way of death. Only the person who dies to self, who loses himself completely and entirely, who "is dead in the midst of life," can receive the highest of all blessings. This is why it is so easy for the Javanese to understand what is meant when the gospel speaks about "taking up one's cross and denying oneself." This is why they agree so completely that a person must put to death "his sufferings here on earth," must crucify his flesh until it is no longer he that lives, but Christ that lives within him. A Javanese person immediately sees that losing oneself and putting oneself to death is a process, which is why such words in the mouths of Jesus and Paul are completely intelligible to him.

Losing Oneself

A Javanese person who is so open to all the teachings that point him in the direction of dying to himself has a tradition behind him that is centuries old.

The ancient Brahmin texts already contain the idea that the great *Atman* is only knowable to those who have freed themselves from sensuous desires and completely lose themselves. In mystical contemplation, all the voices of our own ego fall silent, and the saving secrets of such contemplation can only be revealed to those who are no longer tied to any earthly desire. When all the tension of self-preservation and pursuing riches ceases, it becomes possible for the soul to be overwhelmed by the indescribable majesty of *Brahman. Atman* can only be awakened in the person who has been delivered from the limitations of egotistical living and selfishness. The path to life in the fullest sense of the word runs straight through death. Only the one who dies to self can again find himself on a higher level. This is why only the *sannyasin*[1] who denies himself can experience the highest joy.

Throughout all of Indian religion from the most ancient of times one hears the earnest admonition: "Die and become!" That mystical doctrine is also propagated in the more recent schools of Hinduism, and its serious pursuit is advanced in all sorts of ways. People naturally differ with respect to the question of to what extent they may still participate in the life of this world. There are those who in the most rigorous sense think that one must completely break all ties with what is earthly and devote oneself entirely to mystical practices. There are also those who defend the idea that the saved may certainly still live in the world, but in such a way that they have shed all earthly desire. Such a person can be compared to a turtle that pulls in his head and feet and remains motionless when any danger threatens him. He certainly is still alive then, eats and drinks, works and rests, but he does so as though he is a sleepwalker who is completely oblivious and has not the least interest in what is going on around him. Such a person is thoroughly "estranged from the world," and life slides alongside him the way water flows past a lotus pad without disturbing it *(Shaiva Siddhanta).*[2] Others believe that people existing in a state of deliverance still participate in the daily life of this world to some extent and may certainly even promote their own affairs, but that in all of this they must only serve God and thus must dedicate all they possess to the divinity (the *Vishnu* orientation). Differences in accent are possible, therefore, but all eastern teachings on salvation concur on one thing: they direct a person to sink away from self, to disengage from all lively interest in ordinary and earthly matters, and to withdraw inwardly.

All these ideas agree in more than one sense with what Islamic Sufi mystics taught their followers. While the Sufis also taught the beauty of a life of withdrawal from the world, they held up to people the unquestioning compliance of Abraham, the trustfulness of Isaac, the virtue of Job, the wanderings of Jesus, and the poverty of Mohammed.[3] Islamic mysticism testifies in

---

1. Ed. note: *Sannyāsa* is the Sanskrit word for "renunciation" or "abandonment." *Sannyasa* is the highest life-stage in Hinduism in which one dedicates one's life wholly to spiritual pursuits and renounces all worldly thoughts and desires. Someone who attains this is known as a *Sannyasin.*

2. Ed. note: *Shaiva Siddhanta* is one of the major schools of Indian Shaivism (devotion to *Shiva*) and is concentrated among the Tamil of Southern India and Sri Lanka. Shaivism is one of the four major sects of Hinduism.

3. Other prophets set forth as examples of this set of virtues include Zechariah, John the Baptist, and Moses.

tender descriptions to the beauty of a life in the process of losing itself. The ceaseless love for Allah that fills the true and enlightened pilgrim so looses him from himself and from all other things that he totally forgets self. Such mystical ecstasy of union with God can best be compared to drunkenness wherein a person becomes intoxicated with delight whenever the greatness of Allah is contemplated from afar and is permitted to approach him. Such a person no longer thinks about self; then exits self *(faná)* and drowns in the blessedness of communion with God. *Faná* is nothing less than the self-realization that one does not exist and that nothing exists besides God alone.[4] Therefore, a person must escape his own soul *(nafs)* and put his soul to death. When Abu Said was once asked, "What is sin and what is the greatest sin?" he gave this answer: "Sin is 'you' and the greatest sin is 'you' whenever you do not know this!"[5] He meant that sin is when you feel yourself, see yourself, search for yourself, and love yourself. "To be a Sufi is to cease being concerned; and there is no greater concern for you than your own self, for whenever you are busy with yourself, you remain far from God."[6] "Hell is where you are, and paradise is where you are not."[7] As long as a person still feels as a self, even when standing on the holiest of spots, he would still be unable to find God. Only when he totally forgets himself and enters the intoxicated state of being drunk on Allah, can he enjoy the exalted blessedness that is beyond description.

This is the direction in which the ancient thinkers of India as well as the Islamic mystics pointed the Javanese people in their search for salvation by putting self to death; it was the only path by which people could enter the gates of mystical enlightenment. And this doctrine that flowed into Java from several directions agreed amazingly well with the earlier experiences of Indonesian people.

With most Indonesian peoples, and particularly on Java, it is self-evident that life is concealed in death and that life comes forth from death.[8] The Javanese person feels that our normal, ordinary consciousness, which is informed by our self-consciousness, limits and walls us in on all sides. First of all, whenever we sink into the stupor of no longer being self-aware, we are amenable to impressions from that higher, everlasting world that completely

4. Reynold Alleyne Nicholson, *Studies in Islamic Mysticism* (Cambridge: Cambridge University Press, 1921), p. 50.

5. Nicholson, *Islamic Mysticism*, p. 53.

6. Nicholson, *Islamic Mysticism*, p. 49.

7. Nicholson, *Islamic Mysticism*, p. 64.

8. Douwe A. Rinks, *De Heiligen van Java* (Batavia: Albrecht, 1910), p. 41.

surrounds us. Found among all the peoples of India is the amazing presumption that in ecstatic stupor, other forces take possession of us and fill us with magical capabilities that greatly surpass ordinary human capacities. In our own, tiny self-consciousness and its egocentricity, we are no-account bunglers; but as soon as we transcend ourselves by means of music, dance, or drama and reach another level of consciousness or trance, we immediately become beings of a completely different sort. Then we are able to see faces, utter amazing prophecies, become invulnerable, no longer feel any pain when someone stabs or pricks us — in short, we have crossed over to another kind of existence. The ties that fetter us to the external *(lahir)* and temporal are, as it were, loosened, and the inner *(batin)* and magical *(gaib)* forces sweep us along in their powerful flow. People like this are to be greatly reverenced and respected. Immense magical power radiates from them and can bring healing to those who are living in need or facing difficulty. On the island of Bali, the custom still persists that on certain occasions small girls are allowed to fall asleep, and then, while sleeping, are carried into a dance to the sound of music so that they might be possessed by divine forces while engaged in their sleepwalking dance. This need to transcend self and cross the boundaries of limited consciousness presents the major obstacle to achieving this highest kind of mystical deliverance.

All such ideas have lived in Asia from ancient times to the present. A person can become a participant in the mysterious forces of life. She can climb to a higher, different world, one without limitations and filled with magical powers. She can do so only when she does not shrink from death, when she offers no objection to it, when she totally and completely loses herself and rises above her own senses. In death there is life; in the trance there is transport to a higher order; in spiritual intoxication, the highest wisdom is to be found. Even in an ordinary play, in a drama, the Javanese person attempts to rise above self to be released from the chains of confining self-consciousness and to become inebriated with ecstasy. The idea that it is possible in this way to acquire elevated capabilities and more profound enlightenment has produced the strongest possible fascination in the religious life and aspirations of many East Asian peoples.[9]

9. For more on this, see Klaus Albert Hibbing, *Gebruiken end Godsdienst der Soendanezen* (Batavia: Kolff, 1935).

The Gospel and Self-Denial

All the foregoing ideas easily lead one to connect with those expressions in the gospel that talk about losing oneself and crucifying the flesh. The gospel also recognizes that in death there is life and, in so doing, does it not completely agree with what Asia has understood for so long? Mystical experiences similar to those that Paul had, when he was caught up into paradise and heard unspeakable things (2 Cor. 12:4), are alluring to the people of Asia as an ideal expression of transcending all things, worth coveting, and they strive for similar, wonderful experiences themselves. At the same time, they are aware of the fact that all of this is only possible when they have completely let go of all worldly concerns and have allowed other powers to take possession of their souls.

When Javanese people read the gospel attentively, they read it very differently from the way we do. They encounter all sorts of phenomena and ideas that are recognizable to them, and they search for words that concur with their own insights. They are readily inclined to think: "Jesus is one of us," and they quickly acknowledge that he meets the highest ideals of a mystic. Notably, Sufism has always spoken appreciatively about Jesus and has never hesitated to designate him as a pure Sufi, an *Imâm-i-Aschin* or mentor of those on the mystical pilgrimage. Thus, it is very easy to incorporate the entire gospel into the spiritual fabric of Asian people and to interpret it in a sense that is fully applicable to Asian ideas. No wonder, then, that people from all backgrounds praise Jesus' religion as one of humanity's highest forms of spiritual instruction. They accord Jesus a position among the great masters that people want to follow on the road to salvation, and they do so in the conviction that they understand his will accurately.

The great Indian teacher of the nineteenth century, Ramakrishna Paramahamsa (b. 1834), who exercised a huge influence on many disciples, was a true Hindu who desired to achieve deliverance in an Indian manner. That did not prevent him from living as a follower of Islam for quite some time; and when he once saw Jesus in a vision, for three days afterwards, he could think about nothing other than Jesus' love. From that time on, he taught that the different religions are nothing else than different ways leading to the same end. His great student Vivekananda (b. 1862) followed him down that path and taught that all religions are true and good; for that reason, he said, everyone needs to stay with their own religion.[10]

---

10. J. N. Farquhar, *Modern Religious Movements in India* (New York: Macmillan, 1915), pp. 193ff., 203.

Frequently, Asian people even accord Jesus first place in the ranks of the great human teachers. In a book titled *Positive Religion,* one of the leading Hindus of our day writes:

> For Christianity, the ideal life is the life of its great and perfect example, Jesus Christ, for he refined and honored the ideal life in a way that our world had never before considered. The world certainly knew, even prior to the time of Jesus, that it is a noble thing to work for the salvation of others and to sacrifice oneself in this cause. But it had scarcely any understanding of the actual significance of this ideal for this life. The great Buddhist Arhat spent his life in solitary reflection on compassion and gentleness. He even considered self-sacrifice to be necessary, but to be actively busy for others for one's entire life was not the Buddhist ideal. The Hindu gave food to strangers, animals, and the masses; he cast butter into the fire; but he would never have touched a suffering pariah or a leper. Only the white Christian offers his life in personal service to black lepers. He (that is, Christ) has bestowed knowledge and freedom on all people, without distinctions based on class or race.[11]

We might gratefully affirm such a beautiful testimonial, and it might even fill us with joy; but it may never blind us to the fact that a huge part of the world of Asia, while readily according the person of Jesus a position of honor, nevertheless interprets him in an Asian spirit and finds Asian ideas in him.

On Java, just as everywhere in Asia during our day, the conviction is gaining ground that the gospel of Jesus Christ lays out treasures of religious wisdom that to a great extent are worthy of consideration. Many people there will only make room for him in their life and thought when he is seen as the great mystic who in an exemplary way lost himself; for then he elevated *fâna* to its highest expression and united the greatest magical powers in his own person.

Difficulties Related to Preaching

What is difficult about all of this is that one often feels almost paralyzed in preaching the gospel of grace in such a context. Whenever you emphasize

---

11. Ed. note: Bavinck's own note indicates that the author of this quotation is J. C. Ghose, president of the Theistic Society of Calcutta; it is taken from Jogendra Chunder Ghose, *Positive Religion* (München: Verlag Ernst Reinhardt, 1925). Bavinck indicates as his source, Hilko Wiardo Schomerus, *Indien und Christentum,* 3 vols. (Halle-Saale: Buchhandlung des Waisenhauses, 1931-1933), 1: 14-15.

that Christianity is totally unique, you will often be met with a smile from your attentive listener who lets you know that he thinks he understands Christianity much better than you do. You are told that you stare yourself blind on the external form of religion *(saréngat)*, and that from that perspective all religions indeed do diverge, but that you have not yet considered their deeper unity in the realm of the mystical. Then what often happens to you on the mission field is that you are schooled about mysticism and in return met with an almost haughty disdain, since so little of the essence of true religion has gotten through to you. Then the really big question hits you all the harder: What is the relationship of Christianity to the other religions? Is the gospel comparable, for example, to the *Bhagavad Gita* or other major products of eastern religious life? Is there a noticeable transfer from the mystical feelings and thoughts of South and Southeast Asia to the mysteries of faith in Jesus Christ? And if none of that is the case, how is it that at first glance so amazingly much similarity exists between the Asian ideal of life and the ideas of self-denial, taking up one's cross, and losing one's own soul that assume such a prominent position also in the gospel?

What is remarkable in this regard is that Christians in the countries of Asia often have a great deal of difficulty in coming to clarity on these questions. There are those who want nothing more, insofar as is possible, than to acknowledge the goodness in Asian religions into which they were born. These people, therefore, emphasize the points of agreement between the gospel and the religious feelings of Hinduism and Islam. There are also those that find it extremely difficult to gauge the mutual relationship and therefore prefer not to talk about it. And finally, there are many that emphatically contend that Christianity is radically unique and differs absolutely from all Asian religious thinking and searching. Sadhu Sundar Singh, who is widely known in the Netherlands,[12] incorporates a great deal that is typically Indian into his summaries of ideas contained in the gospel. But with extraordinary precision, he still perceives an enormous difference between Hinduism and Christianity. He says this about his earlier situation:

> At one time I thought myself to be righteous, since I did my best to be consistent with the Hindu religion. I was satisfied with myself, even though my soul was not at peace. Through Jesus Christ, I first became conscious of my own corrupt condition, both in my outward and my in-

---

12. Ed. note: Bavinck wrote "in our own country."

ner lives. I saw that I was a great sinner and that I needed to receive salvation from Jesus Christ.[13]

The aristocratic Christian woman Ramabhai was even so deeply convinced of the radical difference between the gospel and all forms of Indian religion that she endeavored to make her own translation of the Bible. In it, to a much greater degree than is usually the case, she avoided using even once all specifically religious terms borrowed from Hinduism, so that in no instance whatever could the impression possibly be given that the basis for Christianity is the same as what Asian wise men teach.[14]

The Japanese Christian Kokichi Kurosaki had earnestly sought contentment in strict Confucianism and Buddhism's mysticism of eternity.[15] Once he found Christ, he understood that all this mystical striving to save himself was nothing more than one large source of guilt. As a fallen person, he was attempting to break down by force the gateway to lost paradise, while that gate can only be unlocked when God himself wants to be reconciled with us.[16]

---

13. Cited by Fr. Heiler, *Christlicher Glaube und Indisches Geistesleben: Rabindranath Tagore, Mahatma Gandhi, Brahmabandhav Upadhyaya, Sadhu Sundar Singh* (München: Ernst Reinhardt, 1926), p. 84.

14. Rudolf Otto, *Die Gnadenreligion Indiens und das Christentum: Vergleich und Unterscheidung* (Gotha: L. Klotz, 1930), pp. 44, 45.

15. Ed. note: "Mysticism of eternity" is our rendition of a single, capitalized word in the original that seems to serve as a technical term for Bavinck: "Oneindigheidsmystiek." Quite likely the reference is to the Tibetan Buddhist notion of the awakened mind *(Mahamudra)*, whose ultimate nature is known as *bodhicitta*. According to the Tibetan Buddhist lama and *Dzogchen* master, Tulku Chökyi Nyima Rinpoche (b. 1951), this is the Buddha's teaching on the ultimate nature of the Awakened Mind:

> What is ultimate bodhicitta? It is truly free from all mental constructs, like space; it cannot be indicated by any analogy whatsoever. It falls into no extreme or category; it is beyond mental constructs. It is the unity of emptiness and compassion; it is empty like space. Yet it is loving and compassionate, open and clear. That is ultimate bodhicitta. . . . According to Mahamudra, the essence is non-arising, its expression is unceasing, and its manifestation is the unity of these two. According to Dzogchen, the essence is empty, the nature is cognizant or luminous and the compassion is the unity of these two.

(Chökyi Nyima Rinpoche, *Union of Mahamudra and Dzogchen: A Commentary on the Quintessence of Spiritual Practice, the Direct Instructions of the Great Compassionate One* [Berkeley, CA: North Atlantic Books, 2004], pp. 188-89.)

16. According to Martin Schlunk, *Von den Höhen des Oelberges: Bericht der deutschen Abordnung über die Missionstagung in Jerusalem* (Stuttgart: Evang. Missionsverlag; Berlin: Furche-Verlag, 1928), p. 95.

Thus it is not difficult at all to collect testimonies from many Asian Christians that help us see with great clarity that a deep chasm exists between the gospel and eastern wisdom, however close the apparent agreement may seem to be in many respects. If we do not wish to mislead others and ourselves, we need to reckon more deeply and seriously with this essential difference.

Mysticism and Ethics

It is obvious to us that several points can be made to demonstrate clearly that there is a big difference between the Christian teaching about life and that of Asian mysticism. As our point of departure, we need to emphasize that the Asian world generally feels too little the distance between Creator and creature and therefore identifies the cosmic with the divine. God is the sum total of everything or the great totality that holds all of it together and encompasses all parts as members sharing in the great, divine order. To draw near to God, therefore, is to come to a consciousness of one's union with the cosmos and of rising into the eternal. What is obvious about wanting to rise into divine fullness is that it necessarily requires a total annihilation of the idea of the individual. As long as a person still considers self as an "I," in distinction from the great cosmic "I" that he or she encounters in the world, that person still remains in a relationship of duality. As soon as a person loses self, that is to say all self-consciousness, and extinguishes all ego-consciousness, he or she becomes susceptible to the overwhelming sensation of becoming one with the All. At that point all boundaries fall away and all contrasts are replaced because the individual person falls away, and what remains is only the universal experience of the All-in-all, the divine entirety into which the "I" flows.

To the extent that mysticism deals with the annihilation of any sense of ego it can be called moral and be seen as conveying a set of ethical regulations for living. These regulations, then, are oriented to the destruction of all feelings of ego. Forget yourself! Let all the "I" within you die out; behave as though you are dreaming; lose yourself. That implies also that you desire not a single thing, that you are bound by nothing whatever, and that you also are not imprisoned by the powers of your own passions. For as long as you are so tied down, you still exist as an "I." Seek the stupor in which all distinctions are replaced, in which all contours fade out, in which you no longer have a sense of "I" and "not me" or of me and you, but in which everything melts into an undefined, filmy unity. Hate no one, but also love no one. Do not be hotheaded with anyone, but also never be misled by sentimental sympathy into an attachment to anyone. The great Islamic saint Rabi'a, a woman who seemed to be filled with love for Allah, said of herself, "I have ceased to exist and have transcended myself." She admonished a friend who still desired to have children with these words, "I never would have thought that you still had room in your heart for any other love than for love for God."[17] Among Islamic mystics, Rabi'a is considered to be one of the most exemplary, and among her words are amazingly many that bear a striking resemblance to biblical expressions. Yet, time and again it is obvious that she proceeds from totally different premises. Hovering over all Asian mysticism as its highest, recognizable ideal is that a person no longer feels a distinction between me and you, not even with respect to God, and that all contrast therefore disappears. That is the drunkenness of mysticism to which people aspire with great longing.

The ethics of mysticism has a completely unique character from the ground up. In the first place, it is thoroughly *psychological*. This is to say that from the outset it is oriented toward achieving a special psychological character. It is flight from ego-tension, from the inhibiting attempt to give in to *"das Leiden am Ich."*[18] For this reason, all conduct of the mystic is characterized by a heartfelt aspiration to the narcosis of mystical ecstasy. No greater joy is thinkable than to be lifted completely above oneself and to be elevated to the heights of divine light.

In the second place, connected to this psychological point of departure is that *sinning* is experienced simply as a psychological phenomenon. Sin does not produce any essential change in the relationship between God and a person. God is not predisposed toward a person any differently because a person has sinned; but the person does sense something different. For by sinning a person pushes God over the horizon of his or her life, since the person has limited his or her consciousness by conceding to a clear expression of ego feeling. Rabindranath Tagore puts it like this:

17. Cf. the biography of Rabi'a by Margaret Smith, *Rabi'a the Mystic and Her Fellow Saints in Islam: Being the Life and Teachings of Rabi'a al-'Adawiyya Al-Qaysiyya of Basra, Together with Some Account of the Place of the Women Saints in Islam* (Cambridge: Cambridge University Press, 1928). The words cited are taken from G. Simon, *Die Auseinandersetzun des Christentums mit der ausserchristlichen Mystik* (Gütersloh: Bertelsmann, 1930), pp. 58, 60.

18. Barend Martinus Schuurman, *Mystik und Glaube im Zusammenhang mit der Mission auf Java* (The Hague: Martinus Nijhoff, 1933), p. 67.

When a person sins, he becomes party to the temporal in opposition to the eternal. Sin is the triumph over his soul by his ego. Sin darkens truth and it clouds a clear view of consciousness. In sin we long for pleasures, not because in themselves they are worth craving, but because the red lights of our passions make them seem so.[19]

The only change that sin imposes on our lives is that it changes our souls. The more often we give in to our sinful inclinations, the more we become confused in the labyrinth of our own ego sensations and the further removed we become from that little light that always still burns most deeply within us. To that extent, a law of retribution exists, since the inner consequence of all our actions is that our soul over time becomes increasingly bound to sin. The only consequence of sin, therefore, is a psychological effect. As far as sin is concerned, it has nothing to do with God and us (Heb. 2:17), but it only changes something in the person. The concept of karma also needs to be interpreted psychologically and is explained as the sediment of our previous actions and thoughts that the soul carries with it after death. Due to causality in the world order, these require that a new birth must follow.

A consequence of the foregoing, in the third place, is that *deliverance* is also experienced as a psychological process. Through a life of self-denial and asceticism, in his or her subconscious a person destroys the residue of previous sins and desires. She works from the outside to the inside, suffocating in her subconscious the remnants of earlier passions. He does this until he has overcome the instinctive, formative powers *(samskára)* dwelling in his subconscious — those secret shapers — and he has escaped the grip of *avidya*.[20] Only then is a person free and able by means of mystical practices to climb to higher ground, where there is no longer any place for passion. The life of self-denial is thus an essential preparation that is required because our earlier sinful life still has a powerful influence deep within our subconscious. With us it is like unplowed ground in which all kinds of weed seeds lie hidden. Only when they have been removed can the soul come into the full light of divine fellowship. This is the reason why the ethic of mysticism is often so unusually powerful, demanding of a person total subjugation of all psychic powers, the full force of world renunciation, and conquest of the body. But all of these requirements of mysticism are not regarded as attempts to gain God's favor or to earn God's grace, but only and entirely as positioning one's own soul for

19. Rabindranath Tagore, *Sadhana: The Realization of Life* (New York: Macmillan, 1913).
20. Hermann Beckh, *Buddhismus (Buddha und seine Lehre)*, 2 vols. (Berlin and Leipzig: G. J. Göschen, 1916), 2: 104ff.

being absorbed into divine enlightenment. Clouds exist that conceal divine light and cause us not to be able to see God, but those are not clouds that surround his throne; they exist within our own souls. The eye of our soul is unclean and needs to be purified. The mists of ignorance in which our souls are trapped need to be whisked away. As soon as that happens, we will notice that the radiance of God's glory shines on us unobstructed.

Now a person can confidently accept — and this is often the case in Asia — that God helps people in sweeping away these clouds. God is the one who will work with the soul to free a person from ignorance. Thus, it is not the person that delivers him- or herself, but it is God who works in us to deliver us from our own ignorance. This makes it possible to talk about God's love and God's grace, but then it is always the case that deliverance is something that happens within our deepest selves. Deliverance is a psychological process that takes place within our own hearts.

In the fourth place, the preparatory practices of asceticism and world flight are intimately involved and need to occur, culminating in actual mystical concentration and contemplation. A mystical *technique* of a very refined nature exists. Asceticism certainly is essential, but it is not enough. At a specified time, a person must sit quietly, turn the senses inward, calm the forces of the heart, and by means of carefully controlled breathing bring the soul to a typically detached state in which all sharp distinctions abate. In that state, the soul needs to direct all its inner energy on the divine, only true realities, and allow the experiences that come to it from that mysterious realm of unseen phenomena to flow over it. Only then can it achieve contemplation of the eternal that lies so amazingly close to us and yet has remained hidden from us for so long.

In the fifth and final place, it seems that mystics, having come thus far, rise above all moral standards. They no longer need to deal with good and evil, but can now even participate in all sorts of things that we can still identify but that no longer apply to them because they themselves are no longer involved with them. Their "I" is no longer engaged. Such people can be immoral, but that does them no damage. They are acting like a sleepwalker, as though in a dream that does not touch the inner person. Only their "flesh" does wrong, but that results in no change in their inner condition. All mystics can readily transition from a very strict legalism to an equally logical *antinomianism* in disdaining all moral norms. That happens because all moral norms in mysticism are either considered to be regulations for good social order or accessories of mystical preparatory practices. In both cases, those who have once arrived at mystical perfection are elevated above norms. Such people exist in human society like a god who has himself become a norm; in their inner self they have become so detached from everything that they may simply do anything without running any risk of being tarnished. At the deepest level, therefore, mystics are free from all moral constraint because they have truly become one with God, and God is exalted above all moral norms. He is the primal basis of everything, good as well as evil. God is the bearer of all existence. He is the one from whom everything has sprung and therefore has nothing more to do with moral norms. Whoever enters the sphere of the divine has arrived in the kingdom without contrast of good and evil and enters the depths where all dissonance flows into a higher harmony. This is what one tries to describe as the a-moral nature of mysticism.[21]

Christianity

The foregoing sketch of the main features of Asian mysticism gives no consideration whatever to the different nuances that one can undoubtedly find. Javanese mysticism has a different tint from the Hindu version, which again is different from the Islamic variety. No attention is given here to those finer distinctions, since we only wanted to look for some main lines along which most of the Asian emphases concur.

When we place the Christian ideas concerning deliverance and fellowship with God next to these others, the first thing that strikes us is that a great deal of agreement actually exists between them. Christian mysticism today recognizes various levels, as it did in the Middle Ages, and these bear a striking resemblance to the gradations that Asian mysticism describes. It also recognizes the way of purification *(via purgativa)* that requires nothing less than putting to death the self, or mortification *(mortificatio),* and annihilation *(annihilation).* It also talks at length about the secrets of meditation, and it can so happen that in the middle of meditating the soul sometimes suddenly enters the wonderful state of contemplation. In contemplation, the soul no longer thinks about self, but it only and exclusively hears the divine word. Christian mysticism even testifies to an experience that far transcends contemplation when it says that the soul no longer hears, sees, thinks about, or feels the self but is

21. Cf. Otto, *Indiens Gnadereligion,* p. 61; Schomerus, *Indien und das Christentum,* 1: 40; Willem Jan Aalders, *Mystiek: Haar Vormen, Wezen, Waarde* (Den Haag and Groningen: J. B. Wolters, 1928), p. 443.

caught up in the exalted ecstasy of beholding God. Then the soul enters the unique state of sleeplessness and is no longer clearly self-conscious. Then it experiences what the writer expressed in the perplexing words of Song of Solomon 5:2, "I sleep, but my heart is awake." All these descriptions of the Christian mystical life offer many parallels with phenomena in Asia.[22]

What impresses us most powerfully is the agreement we see when we pay attention to the frequent admonitions to self-denial and self-renunciation. The gospel intentionally talks about the "I" that needs to be put to death and needs to be crucified. It directs us to a way of living where the soul needs to be set free from all desires that shackle it to this world. The gospel certainly never includes the command that a person may no longer love; rather, the command to love is always glorified as the highest command of all. We need to love our fellow humans with a pure, Christian love that totally and completely ignores self. But that Christian love is never a desire and aspiration based on the will itself, but it is an aspiration concerning the neighbor based on the fact that the neighbor is also created in God's image. All love, therefore, has within it something of love for God and has its explanation and defense in that love for God (cf. James 3:9). Thus, Christian ethics formally has a great deal that agrees with eastern ethics, at least to the extent that it demands dying to self. But materially it goes much further, since it does not regard dying to self as an end in itself, but only as a means to the end that the love of God may come to expression in us.

The Christian Religion and Asian Mysticism

Whenever we attempt to characterize Christianity and to distinguish it from all non-Christian religions, we often do so in the following terms: in Christianity God is the one who delivers people; in all pagan religions a person is the one who delivers himself or herself. Undoubtedly, a great deal of truth is conveyed by this, although this proposition cannot be applied to Asian religions without a degree of reservation. In these religions, abundant discussion of God's grace always occurs as the only possibility for deliverance. For example, the Bhakti religion that we considered above[23] is one example of honoring the divine favor that people have wanted to maintain apart from

22. Cf. Fr. Heiler, *Der Katholizismus: Seine Idee und seine Erscheinung* (München: E. Reinhardt, 1923), p. 498; Aalders, *Mystiek,* pp. 204ff.

23. Ed. note: See p. 305 above.

any merit on their part. Stated already in the *Upanishads,* we find that people can only participate in bliss on the basis of God's election: "Only the person whom God chooses is the person who understands him; he reveals himself to that person."[24]

Asia has certainly been completely open to the fact that people can never come to God by their own striving and searching. They always need the divine assistance that embraces them and qualifies them to inherit the light. This is why, in conversations with people from Asia, you are always struck by the fact that they are fully conscious of divine help and of the deliverance that God wants to bestow.

Despite all of this, there is one all-determining *difference* that cuts so deep that all the words of these Asian religions, even though they sound so much like many Christian terms, have an entirely different meaning. That difference can be captured in one sentence: *Deliverance in the gospel is never only, and never only in the first instance, a psychological process, but it is a thoroughgoing change in the relationship between God and a person consisting of reconciliation and justification.*

That major difference in the concept of deliverance rests on an equally deep difference in the conception of sin. In Christianity, sin is never only — or even in the first instance — a dislocation of our inner self or a disorganization of our soul's powers, but above all else it is a rending of our relationship with God and of becoming God's enemy.

That difference, again, indicates a difference in theology. In the gospel, God is never Universal-Being or the summation of everything cosmic, but he is the holy God exalted far above all else who created people in his own image. Therefore, he requires this of people: "Be holy, for I am holy!"

The people of Asia feel very strongly that sin is a power that binds and imprisons us. But they understand far too little that it is an assault on the holy being of God and therefore subject to God's curse.

They have felt that our souls are so twisted that people often do not even know themselves but are controlled by their personal desires and thus go through life enslaved. They have understood far too little that all the power of sin proceeds from the curse that God has permitted to fall on the sinner. They have understood far too little that the first thing required of us is to ask God for grace. How do I find the gracious God? That is the fundamental question, which precedes by a long way the question of how my soul can be restored from the inside. How can I once again enter his fellowship?

24. *Katha Upanishad,* 2, 23.

The people of Asia have felt with unusually refined sensitivity that in this world there is a power of *avidya* or of ignorance and of the lie that envelops all people. But they have understood far too little that people have willed that ignorance on themselves and still cling to it with every fiber of their being because they live with the illusion that "to be like God" is an ideal not to be relinquished at any cost. They have comprehended far too little that God is not the impersonal, ever-shining source of light, but that he is holy anger against evil, a burning fire, a living God. With profound depth and insight, they have realized that there is an "I-delusion" *(ahamkara)* by which people dream that they are the center of their own little world. And they have longed passionately for a solution to their separation from God and yearned for becoming one with God *(advaita)*. But they have perceived too little that between creature and Creator there is always a line of demarcation that ensures that a person can never be absorbed into God. They have realized too little that God is not the depth of a person's being or the *atman* that slumbers in the hidden background of the soul. They have not adequately perceived that God is the Wholly Other who always dwells with me, who is always behind and before and beside me, who always sees and judges me, and before whom my soul shudders and trembles in fear whenever it considers its sins. That Other One is neither I myself nor the depths of my own being, but he is my King and my God in whose hands I am being held, from whom I live, and against whom I sin day after day.

Only when we who were enemies become reconciled through the death of Jesus Christ may we expect that we, being reconciled, shall also be preserved through his life (Rom. 5:10). The people of Asia, for all the strength of their searching and thinking, while yearning for the latter have never seen that the former is the first requisite.

The ancient Javanese poem called the *"Arjuna Wiwaha"* describes the fasting of Arjuna in pursuit of acquiring supernatural power. When Arjuna achieved higher, mystical enlightenment, divinity itself approached him in the form of a hunter. Initially Arjuna did not recognize this divinity, but when it disclosed itself to him, he fell at its feet and implored it. The words with which Arjuna addresses the divinity are exceptionally characteristic of Javanese religion. They read like this:

Just as fire appears from the wood, just as butter emerges from the milk, so you are seen wherever people are present who speak what is good. You are present in all things, the kernel of the highest truth that is so difficult to achieve. You are the one who maintains your presence in being as well as in non-being, in the greatest as well as in the smallest, in the wicked as well as in the pure. Like moonlight shimmering on the face of pots filled with water, so one finds the moon in the pot containing pure water.[25]

The last image is typical of Javanese religion. The moon is reflected only in pure water; likewise divinity is reflected only in the soul that has abandoned self and no longer considers or seeks itself, one that has divested itself of self. From that image it becomes very clear that deliverance is an inner clarification; it is a purification of the soul. Just as obvious is that God himself simply waits peacefully and radiantly until a person has purified himself or herself. The moonbeams are not interested in whether or not they are reflected in the water. They merely shine. They are totally indifferent to whether or not their shining is able to become one with the water. In this same way, in the depths of his being God is indifferent to whether or not he can shine in our souls.

Asian religion in general has too little understanding that a personal relationship exists between God and people, not just from the side of people, but also from God's side. God is not the exalted rest that exists far above all searching, the ocean into which all rivers of fervent desire gradually flow. But he is the Father who creates, leads, judges, punishes, searches out, loves, saves, and bestows blessing. The relationship of people to God is presented to us in the gospel as a personal relationship, like the connection of king and subject, judge and guilty party, father and child. He is always in an I-thou relationship, one of a covenantal nature.

This is the way one could continue to outline the profound difference between Christianity and Asian mysticism. But all further distinctions flow from the one that maintains that God is different. God is certainly immanent in this world, but he is not contaminated by its sin; he is holy, separate, and exalted far above all impurity.[26]

Moral obligation is not a prerequisite or preparation for mystical ecstasy, but it has its basis in being created in the image of God. "Be holy, for I am holy. Be perfect, as your Father in heaven is perfect."

25. "Arjuna Wiwaha," published by R. Ng. Poerbatjaraka (The Hague: Martinus Nijhoff, 1926), stanza 10/1, 2 and stanza 11.
26. Cf. J. H. Bavinck, *Persoonlijkheid en Wereldbeschouwing* (Kampen: J. H. Kok, 1928), chapter 8.

Christ Alone

All the things about which we have been speaking cannot be made intelligible to an Asian person through reason and precise explanation. After a great deal of detailed explanation of the essential differences between the gospel and Asian mysticism, it strikes me that in the end your listener would still probably add, "And yet, they are still the same!" They are two sides of the same coin.

My deep conviction is that there is only one way that we can help the people of Asia feel the difference deeply and essentially, and that is when we present to them the holy image of Jesus Christ. Paul understood this as well when he determined "to know nothing among you except Jesus Christ and him crucified" (1 Cor. 2:2). All mission work, ultimately, is nothing more than to testify in childlikeness and contrary to all rational argumentation, "Come and see" (John 1:47). When the people of Asia learn to see Jesus and to accept him as the revelation of God, as the light of God shining in this world, then all other issues will be resolved in childlike faith. For, if Christ is the revelation of God, then it becomes clear that God can be found only where the posture of the soul is one of dwelling with Christ. God is certainly omnipresent, but he cannot display his power, love, and blessing everywhere. He can display these only where there is openness to him and where there is faith in Jesus Christ. In the way a ship heading through a dark sea only need aim for the light of the lighthouse, knowing that the safety of the harbor lies behind it, so a person traveling through the turmoil of this world only needs to move continually toward Jesus, knowing that behind him lies the safe but still darkened harbor of life with God. In Christ all of our vague, hazy suspicions about the divine nature are tested, for in him God steps forward in the clarity of his full light. Then we no longer need to probe and pursue hunches, but we simply need to hold fast to him. Then it becomes transparent to us that he is not present in everything. He is not found in sin or in lies, but he is present only where we see the features of Christ.

Just as an invisible hand is unnoticed and changes things in an unnoticed way, so all thought takes a different direction. Then, for example, it becomes immediately clear that God is present in all creatures, but that he has fellowship only with the people who are his children and have been taken into his kingdom.

In the face of Jesus Christ people come to the deep, authentic realization that they exist outside the light of God, that their souls are bound in darkness, and that they experience that darkness as the guilt born of their own willfulness. In that recognition of their guilt, people have no ultimate hiding place into which they can retreat. There they have no faith deep within their souls, no matter how deeply they might look, that still constitutes a tiny plot of holy ground where they can achieve union with God. Rather, they experience that their entire lives, their whole personhood in both body and soul, lies under divine judgment.

This is what it means to crucify the self in a Christian sense. It is not falling back on the deepest core of one's being. It is not having the self be caught up unendingly in the endless. It is not having the limited "I" of the self die so that God is allowed to arise in us. Rather, it is much deeper and more penetrating. It is recognizing that no good thing dwells in me, that is, in my flesh. It is giving the self over to God, in grace or in disgrace, not to God as the one dwelling within us, but as the Wholly Other who is exalted above all of his creatures, as the Not-I who relates to me as judge and king. Asian mysticism certainly puts the person to death in his or her ultimate form, but it comforts the person with the message that the core of his or her being is one with God. As long as one believes that, one can never gauge the seriousness of sin. Then sin is never the house in which one dwells, but it is simply the hotel in which one stays when one is far away from and has lost touch with one's true self. But Christ teaches people to see that sin has become the family home, that they live in sin, and that they can never leave it unless they are delivered by God.

Thus, in the light of Jesus Christ everything is different. God is seen differently by us, for we no longer regard him as the fullness of all that exists, the root of the cosmos from which all that it contains emanates and from which both good and evil sprout. He is not the fountain out of which all that exists bubbles up. Rather, he is the perfectly sinless One, who is far removed from unrighteousness and falsehood. And even I myself become different. I am no longer merely a tiny spark in the eternal fire of divinity or a ripple on the ocean of deity. I am different from God. I am a being distinct from God. I am a sinful, puny creature who certainly lives because of God's power but who wastes that life by willfully doing evil.

And then, even the way to God is different. Nowhere in this world is there a heavenly mountain *(Meru)* on which the tree of paradise grows and in whose grottos I can taste heavenly fellowship. Nowhere is there a mystical ladder on which I can climb to Allah's throne and get behind the thousands of shrouds that cut off his light. With all my own efforts and all my searching in the earthly realm, I remain weighed down by the leaden weight of my sins, banned from God's presence because of the enormous guilt sticking to my life as a curse. I can only enter the heavenly realm when I am reconciled by him who bore the sins of the world and by whose Spirit I am renewed in his image.

This is the way in which the gospel of Christ penetrates the world of Asia. The form of Jesus Christ is already now beginning to assume a position in Asia. The more compellingly that attention is drawn to him as the Word and the Son of God, the more effectively will all thoughts and assumptions of people in Asia gradually begin to change. They will begin to see — by means of his light — the world, humanity, and their own means of survival differently. They will do so because they now see God differently and because they now more deeply fear, implore, and love him.

All of this is work that takes a long time. We cannot define ahead of time the lines along which specifically Asian thought about Christ will develop. Many factors exist that will determine that process. A great deal of hard thinking still needs to be devoted to it before people will be able to draw the clear, broad lines running from the gospel to all areas of life and spirituality. But of one thing we are certain, that Christ will increasingly receive and maintain a position of triumph in the world of Asia. We believe that not because the times are so propitious, but because he is the Conqueror who will not falter but will bind the heart of Asia to the truth of God.

At the moment, many factors resist the spread of the gospel in Asia. The example of western Christianity offers Asian people very little that would cause them to hold in high esteem the dominant religion in the West. The force of nationalism sweeping across Asia like a storm automatically hampers an Asian person from recognizing a westerner as an expert on the sensitive subject of religion. Our alarming shortage of truly prophetic faith and our lack of fervent love for the cause of God's kingdom are other factors. The rampantly increasing worldliness of the secularization also squeezing Asia is another. Numerous forces inhibit the gospel, but his kingdom will nevertheless arrive and his name will be glorified in the hearts of all those peoples who have sought and reflected about God for so many centuries.

When a living, blossoming church will certainly arise in the world of Asia, Christ will accomplish amazing things there. Asia has gifts and abilities that will then render its people exceedingly suited to understanding the meaning of the gospel. From childhood, they are more strongly convinced than we of the all-encompassing religious nature of everything pertaining to daily life, so they will then be well positioned to see the hand of Christ in all of life. They are not as far removed from the miraculous as we are, and for that reason Christ will do amazing things among them. They also listen better than we do, and they are capable of waiting more quietly for the voice of God and depending on God more submissively. Above all, they are less attached to externals like money and material things, like honor and making a name for themselves. They know better than we that the things of this age are fleeting. The gospel of Christ will thus also enable them to see more fully that we may not despise this world, since it is God's handiwork and is the context in which he will realize his eternal counsel. The same gospel will also guide them to look upward and to expect the everlasting kingdom that will one day appear and for whose coming we all yearn with great longing.

Thus, we can expect great things with regard to the faith. We stand at a point of terrible crisis, of struggle and confusion. Our modern world bears guilt of every kind; no one can tell where all of this will lead.

But blessed is the person who believes, waits, and knows that in Christ Jesus the power to accomplish great things in this amazing world has come. May we simply learn to expect those great things from him.

Proper Name Index

Subject Index

414

Scripture Index

Made in the USA
Middletown, DE
15 July 2024

57308751R10255